Jewish Scholarship and Culture in Nineteenth-Century Germany

Studies in German Jewish Cultural History and Literature

PAUL MENDES-FLOHR, SERIES EDITOR

Jewish Scholarship
and Culture in
Nineteenth-Century Germany

Between History and Faith

Nils H. Roemer

THE UNIVERSITY OF WISCONSIN PRESS

This book was made possible with the support of
the George L. Mosse/Laurence A. Weinstein Center for Jewish Studies
at the University of Wisconsin–Madison.
In memory of Laurence A. Weinstein.

The University of Wisconsin Press
1930 Monroe Street
Madison, Wisconsin 53711

www.wisc.edu/wisconsinpress/

3 Henrietta Street
London WC2E 8LU, England

Library of Congress Cataloging-in-Publication Data
Roemer, Nils H.
Jewish scholarship and culture in nineteenth-century Germany:
between history and faith / Nils H. Roemer.
p.   cm. — (Studies in German Jewish cultural history and literature)
Includes bibliographical references and index.
ISBN 0-299-21170-3 (hardcover: alk. paper)
1. Jews — Germany — Intellectual life — 19th century.
2. Jews — Germany — Identity.   3. Jews — Germany — Historiography.
4. Jewish learning and scholarship — Germany — History — 19th century.
5. Judaism — Germany — History — 19th century.   I. Title.   II. Series.
DS135.G33R54   2005
907′.2′023924043 — dc22   2005001337

To Jennifer and Jonas

Contents

viii   *Contents*

Acknowledgments

This book would have been impossible without the instruction, assistance, and encouragement that friends, colleagues, and teachers offered me throughout my years of studying, researching, and writing. Among the many teachers I had the privilege to study with, I must single out Professor Yosef Hayim Yerushalmi, who supported me throughout my graduate training and early on directed my interest in the history of German Jewish historiography. Without his advice, recommendations, and support, this work would not have been possible. I feel equally fortunate to have studied and worked with Professor Michael Stanislawski, who furthered my critical historical thinking. I owe a great debt to Professors Yerushalmi and Stanislawski, as well as to my other teachers at Columbia University, including Professors Elliot Wolfson and Aryeh Goren. Moreover, I am glad to have had the opportunity to study with Professor Andreas Huyssen in the field of modern German cultural history. I owe thanks to the helpful criticism and comments by Professors Volker Berghahn and Mark Anderson.

I am particularly fortunate to have friends and colleagues like Olga Litvak, Avi Matalon, and Jonathan Karp, whom I thank for their unlimited and invaluable support. They helped with their encouragement, patience, and critical observations, as well as with style and language. I am also grateful for the remarks on various parts of the manuscript by Elisheva Baumgarten, Stephen Burnett, Allison Coudert, David Cesarani, Willi Goetschel, Kenneth Koltun-Fromm, Tony Kushner, Michael Meyer, David Myers, and Gideon Reuveni. Special thanks also go to Michael Brenner for his pointed inquiries and gracious support. Additionally, I would like to thank my friends and colleagues at Columbia University, Michael Miller and David Wachtel, who were with me throughout my graduate training. While researching this book, I received helpful advice from Andreas Brämer, Andreas Gotzmann, and

Marion Kaplan. Finally, I want to thank my graduate student, Hannah Villette-Dalby, for her help in preparing the manuscript.

My research would not have been possible without the assistance of librarians and archivists. I thank in particular Diane Spielmann and Frank Mecklenburg of the Leo Baeck Institute (New York); Jerry Schwarzbart of the Rare Book Room of the Jewish Theological Seminary (New York); Judith Leifert of the Center for Advanced Judaic Studies at the University of Pennsylvania (Philadelphia), as well as the librarians and staff at Columbia University, the Jewish Division of the New York Public Library, and the Central Archives for the History of the Jewish People (Jerusalem).

It is also my pleasure to express my gratitude to several institutions for their generosity and support of my research. The David Baumgarten Memorial Fellowship from the Leo Baeck Institute (New York) enabled me to carry out extensive research at the LBI's archive and library. The fellowship from the Stiftung Dialogik: Mary und Hermann Levin Goldschmidt-Bollag (Zurich) was indispensable to my work. I would also like to thank the Memorial Foundation for Jewish Culture (New York) and the National Memorial Foundation for Jewish Culture (New York) for their generous support. I am additionally very grateful for the invitation from the University of Pennsylvania's Center for Advanced Judaic Studies to participate in the "Hebraica Veritas? Christian Hebraists, Jews, and the Study of Judaism in Early Modern Europe" research group during 1999–2000. I am particularly indebted to the director of the center, Professor David Ruderman, for his support and encouragement and to the other fellows and guests of the Center for their suggestions and stimulating discussions.

I'm most grateful for my family's unremitting support: my parents, Karin and Klaus, and my in-laws, Heidi and Don. Finally, thank you to my beloved wife, Jennifer, as well as my young son, Jonas, who makes new discoveries every day and continues to remind me of the existence of a world beyond my research. I could not have done it without them.

Jewish Scholarship and Culture in Nineteenth-Century Germany

Introduction

Nineteenth-century German Jewish historical scholarship, known as *Wissenschaft des Judentums* (science of Judaism), has long been recognized as one of the major spiritual and intellectual responses to the crisis of modernity and as an instrument in the struggle for emancipation. But to what extent did the achievements of Wissenschaft scholars find a broader audience and shape the formation of a distinct diaspora culture during the nineteenth century? The existing intellectual histories of scholarly luminaries, movements, and institutions have largely neglected to explore Wissenschaft's popularization in nineteenth-century Germany. This book addresses the chiefly ignored central role German Jewish scholarship played in the formation of those cultures during this period. Challenging the assumption of German Jewry's unmitigated assimilation and secularization during the nineteenth century, it stresses the importance of historical memory as a cultural and religious factor in the formation of German Jewish postemancipation identities.

The book is based on the study of modern Jewish historiography and its reception during the nineteenth century. It was during this period that Jewish historiography metamorphosed into a major agent of cultural self-assertion. Situating the development of modern Jewish historiography within the struggle for emancipation, debates about religious cultural reform and the fight against anti-Semitism, the book traces the development of Jewish Wissenschaft during the nineteenth century. In doing so, it reveals a hitherto largely unnoticed dynamic character and Jewish historians' constant engagement with political, social, and economic factors. To follow along the path of the reception of German Jewish historiography adds a previously ignored dimension to the history of Wissenschaft and its evolution. Such an approach reveals that a mutual interdependence existed between the scholarly interpretation of the past and the popular German Jewish culture.[1] German Jewish historiography thus evolved from a discipline that redefined Judaism to a program of public education that promoted historical memory and fostered modern Jewish identities.

The aim of this study is, therefore, not a detailed history of Wissenschaft but of its evolution and reception to comprehend the role the historicizing of Judaism played in the creation of modern Jewish culture in nineteenth-century Germany. By historicizing I mean the conception of Judaism as a historically evolving entity. Time and place became crucial signifiers and altered the status of previously sacred texts and traditions, as historians combined their examination of sources with their quest for a Jewish essence. I evaluate the impact historical studies had on the formation of Jewish identities by analyzing historical works in respect to their understandings of Jewish history and the changing functions ascribed to historical studies, as well as to their reception. For the purposes of this study, reception is broadly understood as a process of intertextuality in which new works are derived from others insofar as they refer, incorporate, and displace them. Moreover, within this spectrum of scholarly and popular reception, this study describes the popularization of Jewish historiographical works as a process of dissemination of "text" and its constant reconfiguration, manifesting itself not only in reading but also in the foundation of historical societies, public lectures, the process of canonization, and marketing strategies that publishers employed.[2]

Twentieth-century historians portray *Wissenschaft des Judentums* as the intellectual force that powered the transformation of German Jewry. According to some scholars, Wissenschaft appears as an irrevocable fissure in Jewish life that wrought havoc on all elements of Jewish culture. In their view, the historians of Wissenschaft eliminated Judaism's particularistic and national elements in order to bring it into accord with modern rationalism, the meaning of citizenship, and concepts of enlightened religiosity. One proponent of this view, Gershom Scholem, attacked this purported self-defeating apologetic approach to the Jewish past and insisted that German Jewish historians had at best an antiquarian interest in Jewish history.[3] Conversely, other scholars stress Wissenschaft's innovative impact upon the development of German Jewry.[4] Ismar Schorsch, for example, believed Wissenschaft was the supreme form of Jewish self-expression.[5] More recently, Susannah Heschel provided an important corrective to Scholem's damning assessment of German Jewish historiography by arguing that scholars like Abraham Geiger forged a polemical counterhistory of Christianity.[6] Moving beyond these intellectual studies, Amos Funkenstein, Michael Meyer, and Shulamit Volkov claim that the Jewish historian played as prominent a role in the establishment of modern Jewish culture as German historians played in the creation of a German national culture.[7]

These various historians view German Jewish historiography as an extension of the ideological position that favored social, cultural, and religious reform. By presenting Wissenschaft in this way, nineteenth-century German Jewish historians are portrayed as the all-powerful agents of reform and cultural reassertion. Instead, I argue that these historians responded to political, social, and economic factors they themselves neither determined nor controlled. In contrast to German Protestant scholars of Christianity and historians like Leopold von Ranke and others who, to a large extent, dictated, shaped, and controlled the image of their religion and national past, the process of redefining Jewish history and identities was a much more contentious and fractious affair.

When, during the 1820s, the members of the *Verein für Cultur und Wissenschaft der Juden* (Society for culture and science of the Jews) outlined the program for the historical study of Judaism, they did not map out unexplored territory. Rather, they joined a debate that had already been shaped by Enlightenment historians and the rising philosophies of history. In their effort to insert Wissenschaft into the canon of the modern German curriculum, Jewish historians were denied entry. German theologians and historians challenged Wissenschaft's attempts to place Judaism at the center of Western civilization. By the categorical exclusion of Wissenschaft from the German universities, German Jewish historiography became institutionalized within rabbinical seminaries.

Equally decisive were the changing fortunes of Jewish civic emancipation, social integration, and the splintering of the Jewish communities into different denominations that shaped the conceptions of Jewish history and the self-understanding of the historians' craft. Writing from the perspective of the present and therefore always embedded in particular experiences and expectations, Jewish historians created different images of the Jewish past over the span of the nineteenth century and fundamentally redefined their role within the Jewish community.

Furthermore, the dissemination of historiographical works was not simply a process of reception, but the German Jewish reading public, popular institutions, and associations actively took part in the formation of Wissenschaft. Far from duplicating its ideological agendas, this was a realm in its own right, governed by distinct ideas and programs. These popular societies and institutions not only disseminated reading material but acted as organizers and initiators of Jewish culture.[8] Conversely, the reception of German Jewish historiography fundamentally redefined the contours of the culture that had emerged out of the prolonged struggle over emancipation and centered originally on *Bildung* and bourgeois respectability.

Often excluded from German societies, Jews in Germany (beginning in the 1820s) formed their own parallel associations outside the framework of the religious community.[9] In the second half of the nineteenth century, when Jews were more readily granted entrance into German associational life, Jewish organizations not only continued to exist but actually flourished. Nevertheless, German and German Jewish cultures and identities remained fluid and overlapped, and boundaries remained permeable.[10] As Fritz Stern has pointedly noted, the uncertainty of the answer to the question "What is Jewish?" mirrored a similar hesitation in regard to the question "What is German?"[11] Both of these cultures remained internally heterogeneous and mutually implicated and, as Steven Aschheim has recently argued, coconstitutive.[12] Thus Abraham Geiger's polemical engagement with German Protestant scholarship has to be balanced with his concurrent German nationalism, which led him to extol—in an exchange with the French Jewish scholar Joseph Derenbourg—the virtues of the German war against France leading up to Germany's unification.[13] Even the increasing importance of the Jewish heritage production in the second half of the nineteenth century remained framed by the larger German background. Popularizing the Jewish past did not efface the previous emphasis on *Bildung*, bourgeois respectability, and Jews' participation in German life. These two sides were not diametrically opposed but rather facilitated each other.

Confronted with German liberalism that was built around a duality of tolerance and intolerance and particularism and universalism, German Jewish culture displayed similar tensions.[14] Renegotiating the contours of German and Jewish culture, historians, teachers, and rabbis attempted from the 1850s on to place the Jewish past at the center of a newly emerging Jewish culture in which aspects of traditional Jewish religious thought, practice, and institutions continued to play a central role, often fusing the secular and sacral.[15] Within the parameters of this emerging German Jewish culture, the secular heritage of the Enlightenment as well as modern liberalism were tacitly overcome in favor of a program of cultural revival that stayed decisively religious in nature. Yet this German Jewish culture, far from being homogeneous, was a highly diversified realm of production and consumption, placed at the crossroads of both external and internal debates. It was no less diversified, contested, gendered, and ordered around inclusion and exclusion than the German culture.[16] The structuring principles of German Jewish culture were the opposition to and adaptation of the German *Kultur* as well as the tensions with traditional religious Jewish heritage, institutions, culture, denominational foes, and contentious struggles that involved Jewish scholars, educators, rabbis and the public at large. Hence, the German Jewish subculture marked a spectrum of elite and popular cultures and was at the same time defined by the continuing influence, tension, and antagonism of the dominant German culture.

Interacting with these various factors, Wissenschaft's reformulation of the Jewish tradition is best understood as a production that was never completed and remained in flux.[17] Clearly distinct periods existed in the evolution of German Jewish historiography, each of which were informed by common challenges, responses, and concerns. In describing these changes, my approach is consciously chronological to better convey the developments of an intricate web of factors that shaped the scholarly discipline and the popularization of Jewish history. The study thus traces Jewish historians' reformulation of the Jewish traditions along with the emergence and evolution of the popularizing tendency within Wissenschaft des Judentums. At the same time, interlaced with the development of historical writings, the contours of the German Jewish culture equally shaped the dissemination of the products of Wissenschaft. The changing nature of the public's opposition to and interest in Wissenschaft, the community's cohesiveness, division, religiosity, and secularization, the degree of Jews' integration and difference, and Germans' tolerance and hostility, determined failures and success as well as the nature that the popularization of Jewish history acquired.

Jewish historical scholarship surfaced as a critical response to the Enlightenment. Utilizing the works of Christian Hebraists, eighteenth-century German historians subscribed to the providential view of

Jewish history that encompassed past, present, and future. Yet as German scholarship rapidly transformed itself, Judaism was viewed as a passing stage in the development of humanity that had degenerated from the Second Temple period on. In a typical Enlightenment fashion, this process was viewed as the result of continuous legal restriction and persecution. Thus the history of Judaism in the Diaspora appeared as an aberration that could be reversed to its original pristine Mosaic stage by the politics of the tutelary state. It was in response to these multifaceted and ambiguous historical perspectives propounded by German scholars that Wissenschaft emerged.

Within the debates over emancipation and internal reform, Wissenschaft promised to function as the neutral arbiter that would replace prejudicial representations of the Jews in the public domain with an accurate and unbiased rendition. At the same time, Jewish scholarship became a means to hasten the already ongoing process of social, economic, cultural, and religious change, which heightened historians' estrangement from the traditional communities. Influenced by the debates on Jewish civic improvement and cultural integration, historians reconceptualized the Jewish tradition. Transforming the status of previously sacred texts and traditions, these historians ushered in the turn from "text to context," that is, from a self-understanding that revolved around exegesis to a comprehension of Judaism as a historical entity.[18] Wissenschaft historians explained Jewish religious concepts, customs, and institutions within their historical context. While overtly turning against the Enlightenment, Jewish historians nevertheless succumbed to the ideal of a pristine Mosaic religion and the lachrymose understanding of postbiblical history.[19] By basing their arguments on historical research, they attempted to reverse the course of history and restore Judaism to its stipulated original and immaculate state. Beginning in the 1830s, however, Jewish historians began more forcefully to reject this view of their heritage and portrayed the history of the Diaspora as one of a culturally vibrant era.

Notwithstanding these important changes, the Jewish past continued to be a contested field of divergent interpretations. Denied a place at German universities, Jewish historiography became linked to the development of the various denominations within German Jewry with the establishment of the rabbinical seminaries between the 1850s and 1870s. In light of this, every major scholarly Jewish publication during these decades with its conflicting interpretations was instantly embroiled in fiery public debates about the nature of Judaism, its past, present, and future.

The internal fragmentation of both scholarship and the Jewish communities produced a consistent discourse about utilizing Jewish history to re-create a new unifying vision of modern Jewry in continuity with the past. Instead of questions of historical methodology, Jewish historians reflected more intensely on the role of their scholarship. Wary of the unraveling of Jewish culture and uncertain about the future development of Jewish history, the historians' quest for the *Wesen des Judentums* (essence of Judaism) became increasingly complicated in light of the forces Jewish scholarship had unleashed. In response to these challenges and obstacles, Abraham Geiger and Heinrich Graetz reversed the more radical historicization of the 1820s and framed their accounts of Jewish history in theological rhetoric. Concurrently, new associations like Jewish book clubs emerged that partly overcame the divisiveness by adopting policies of neutrality. With the intention of marketing works on Jewish history and literature to a broad audience, these book clubs shaped the development of Jewish historiography through a process of selection and exclusion as well as by the monopolization of the book market.

From the 1850s to 1870s, the production of Jewish historiography was marred by denominational differences. These frictions had already been partly overcome on the level of reception. In the aftermath of Germany's unification, Jewish intellectuals and historians started to reevaluate their original enthusiastic embrace of liberalism. While they continued to subscribe to the ideals of tolerance of equality, they denounced liberal politics of cultural homogeneity and asserted the right of cultural and religious differences for themselves. This tacit change became even more pronounced in the face of the revitalized anti-Semitic movement and resulted in a joint effort of Reform, Conservative, and even neo-Orthodox leaders to popularize Jewish history from the 1880s on.

Pressure from German scholars intensified these constant confrontations and resulted in the refashioning of the historians' craft. As Jewish scholarship was sharply attacked on numerous fronts and drawn into public trials about the Talmud, Jewish historians shifted to an internal literary, religious, and cultural perspective in their studies on the Jewish past. This shift in focus augmented the history of suffering and learning *(Leidens- und Gelehrtengeschichte)* with descriptions of religious practices and customs, and coincided with a major reevaluation of the task of Jewish historiography. Initially less troubled by the question of their scholarly objectivity, Jewish historians, when faced with challenges from outside as well as internal divisions, engaged in an elaborate and fierce debate over their subjectivity. In the course of these wide ranging discussions, Jewish scholarship underwent a fundamental reconfiguration.[20] Instead of furthering the religious and cultural reform of Judaism and the Jews, Jewish scholarship, according to Heinrich Graetz, acquired the task to "reconcile the hearts of the parents with the hearts of the children in unity."[21]

During this period, Jewish history was employed to fend off anti-Semitic attacks and to strengthen and refashion Jewish identities. Several nationwide organizations such as the German Israelite Community Organization and Masonic lodges launched initiatives to weave historical knowledge into the fabric of the German Jewish culture. This trend coincided with a reassessment of the scholar's persona in the public eye and helped turn the image of the founding father of modern Jewish scholarship, Leopold Zunz, into a religious leader.

The last decade of the nineteenth century witnessed the merging of these different developments. During this time, popular historical associations propagated a retheologized version of Jewish history in the realm of public education. Building on the politics of the first Jewish book clubs of the 1850s, the popular associations similarly adopted a neutral position in political and religious matters. Accordingly, the German Jewish subculture was characterized by a fairly pluralistic popularization of Jewish history. Jewish historians replaced the redemptive narrative of emancipation and the belief in the progress of humanity as the propelling force in Jewish history with the notion of providence that elevated Judaism above the realm of profane history.

At a time when the Union of the Associations for Jewish History and Literature had become one of the largest Jewish organizations in Germany, Jewish history was a means to strengthen a decisively religious Jewish identity, not a secular one. In the effort to utilize Jewish history to refashion the contours of the German Jewish culture, less emphasis was placed on the changing nature of Judaism in the course of its history than on single moments, movements, and luminaries. These popularizing accounts were predicated on a static portrayal of paradigmatic plots in which the history of persecution was singled out in light of its purported edifying power. Historical narratives that switched between past and present functioned as conduits for the revitalization of historical memory. Popular coffee-table histories like Adoph Kohut's *Geschichte der deutschen Juden* (History of the German Jews) nostalgically presented Jewish history and invited the readers to join in the journeys to the past.

By the end of the nineteenth century, works by Jewish historians were widely read, public lectures organized, new libraries erected, and historical documents preserved. As the professionalization of Jewish scholarship continued, Graetz's *Geschichte der Juden,* along with several textbook histories, became canonized not so much for its scholarly merits but because it imparted solace and pride in its readers. These works were printed in affordable editions that could be purchased in installments as well as more lavishly crafted ones marketed as ideal presents for religious occasions.

Jewish history became pervasively popularized with the reconfiguration within Wissenschaft and popular German Jewish culture. Together, these two realms interacted in numerous ways that ultimately transformed each other. Jewish historiography propelled the unraveling of premodern Jewish identities, fostered denominational fissures, and aimed finally to re-create a new unity based on a common past. At the same time, renegotiating a path between its Jewish and German heritage, German Jewish popular culture refashioned itself from a hallmark of Enlightenment culture and religiosity to one marked by a particular veneration for Jewish history. While the popularization of Jewish history ushered in a marked change in the fabric of German Jewish culture, it did not represent a fundamental break from the previous dominance of German *Bildung*. Rather, the rediscovery of Jewish heritage provided the backdrop for the continuing process of cultural integration. This duality was likewise maintained among the early German Zionists, who involved themselves in the already existing framework of associations, libraries and publication organs.

PART I

HISTORICIZING JUDAISM

1

Between Theology and History

In the second half of the eighteenth century, a new consciousness of discontinuity in German life emerged that manifested itself in terms such as "change" and "progress." German *Aufklärer* transformed the political and social vocabulary, and embedded key concepts in historical time. These conceptual ideas were implicated in the formulation of a new vision of German society. Words from the Enlightenment political vocabulary such as *Bürger* (citizen), *Bildung* (self-formation), and *Aufklärung* (Enlightenment) did not reflect contemporary conditions of German society and culture but rather the expectations and hopes of what German society ought to become.[1] In respect to Jewish history, these new visions transformed the providential view of the Jewish past that both Jews and Christians, albeit for different reasons, had shared. German historians, philosophers, and publicists of the Enlightenment replaced the Christian hope of Jews' conversion with the anticipation of their social and cultural integration.[2] With the study of the Jewish past becoming increasingly attached to debates over Jews' social and legal status, members of the Jewish Enlightenment believed that historical investigations would aid their efforts to rejuvenate Jewish religion and culture. The contemporary relevance of the study of Jewish history rendered the nascent scholarship a divisive cultural force. This cast a long shadow on the virulent and contentious nature of Jewish historiography, which continued to obstruct efforts to popularize the Jewish history up until the second half of the nineteenth century. Thus, far from representing only the prehistory to Jewish historiography, eighteenth- and early nineteenth-century debates over Jewish history shaped the evolution of *Wissenschaft des Judentums*.

Until the end of the eighteenth century for Christians and Jews alike, Jewish history was the realm of God's action. Based on the Augustinian heritage, the degraded but protected status of the Jews validated for Christians the superiority of the new Gospel. Jews, on the other hand, understood life in exile as God's punishment (Deuteronomy 28) that was, however, only temporary since the Covenant with God is eternal. In line with this providential view of Jewish history, Jews in the early modern period continued to deem their history an essential record of the particular relationship between God and his people. Accordingly, medieval and early modern Jewish chroniclers did not understand history as the outcome of a historical development, but rather saw themselves in continuity with ancient Jewry and expected the future at the end of days to be an eruption of transcendence.[3]

Within medieval and early modern Jewish culture, historical writings were exceptional and had to be legitimized as an appropriate intellectual occupation.[4] In the aftermath of the Spanish expulsion, an unprecedented outburst of historiographical productivity occurred, and several Sephardic Jewish historians attempted to discern signs of redemption in the recent calamitous events.[5] Against this trend, Azariah de Rossi critically examined Jewish chronology in his *Me'or 'Einayim* (Light for the eyes), printed in Mantua between 1574 and 1575, and diminished messianic speculations, which he contended were based on faulty chronology.[6] Solomon ibn Verga likewise refrained in his *Shevet Yehuda* (The staff of Yehuda) from messianic speculation and utilized natural causes to explain the Spanish expulsion without, however, replacing the providential view of Jewish history.[7]

Within the Ashkenazic world, only one major new historiographical work appeared during the sixteenth century that distanced itself critically from Azariah de Rossi. David Gans in his *Zemach David* (The offspring of David), whose study of Jewish and world history was likewise an exegesis in the divine plan for redemption, upbraided de Rossi for his critical approach to Jewish sources.[8] Both *Zemach David* and ibn Verga's *Shevet Yehuda* achieved certain popularity in Ashkenaz that was rivaled only by the tenth-century *Sefer Yosippon* (Book of Yosippon), which detailed the events leading up to the destruction of the Second

Temple. In the Ashkenazic cultural orbit, these chronicles functioned as a reminder of the heroic steadfastness of Jews in the past and offered a divinely ordained history of suffering.[9] They were reprinted several times and translated into Yiddish up until the end of the eighteenth century, while the rabbinic luminary Jacob Emden regarded Jewish chronicles like *Zemach David* as "true holy books."[10]

The first comprehensive history of the Jews, by the French Huguenot Jacques Basnage titled *Histoire du people Juif depuis Jésus Christ jusqu' a present* (History of the Jews from Jesus Christ to the present, 1706-11), played a less prominent role in Germany if compared to his place in the French and English historiographical traditions. Probably uneasy with Basnage's messianic undertones, his tacit sympathies with the fate of the Jews, and his inclusion of radical anti-Christian and antireligious clandestine literature, Christian Hebraists dominated the field of scholarly inquiry in Germany.[11] While German Protestant Hebraists like Johann Eisenmenger and Johann Jakob Schudt at the beginning of the eighteenth century had attempted to strip Judaism of its exceptional sacred status, the providential view of Jewish history received renewed imminence in the second half of the eighteenth century.[12] Johann Gottfried von Herder, for example, poignantly summarized this view in his *Briefe, das Studium der Theologie betreffend* (Letters concerning the study of theology), when he contended that the history of the Jews and their survival in exile confirmed the miracles and divine interventions narrated in the Bible: "History validates Scripture and Scripture validates history."[13]

More traditional in their outlook than their French counterparts, German historians like Siegmund Baumgarten in Halle noted the existing chaos in chronological studies but continued to construct ancient history by relying on biblical chronology. In 1744 in the *Algemeine Welthistorie* (Universal history), Baumgarten presented history as a supplement to theology that provided countless examples of God's providence.[14] When Johann Semler continued Baumgarten's *Algemeine Welthistorie,* the survival of Jews in exile led him to conclude that God not only watched over Israel but ensured that Jews were spared and protected for a particular divine purpose.[15] This providential view of Jewish history was also expressed in Ludvig Holberg's comprehensive history of the Jews that appeared in a German translation in 1747 from the Danish. Whereas in general, Holberg understood history in an anthropocentric secular fashion as the history of mankind, he explained the perseverance of the Jews as the result of God's providence.[16]

Without a comprehensive vision of humanity's development, no secular model existed that subsumed Judaism into the flow of history. As German historians and philosophers began to unravel the theological nature of world history, they aimed to subsume Judaism into a new secular model of succession. Influenced by Montesquieu's 1748 *De l'esprit des lois* (Spirit of the laws), Johann David Michaelis, a professor of Oriental languages at Göttingen, asserted that Mosaic Law distinguished the Israelites from the surrounding Egyptian culture of antiquity without fully displacing older laws of nomadic origin. This duality led to inconsistencies and contradictions characteristic of the stage Michaelis called the "childhood of the nations" *(Kindheit der Völker)*.[17] Emphasizing the cultural context of Mosaic Law, Michaelis placed Judaism into the stream of history by presenting it as a derivative of Egyptian culture, relegating it to a distant past and geographic realm.[18]

This detailed study of Mosaic Law was part of the larger attempt to decenter Judaism's elevated role in world history. Under the increasing influence of Voltaire's critical new history, Johann Christoph Gatterer, an eminent historian in Göttingen, mockingly dismissed the *Welthistorie* as a "historical archive."[19] August Ludwig Schlözer, Gatterer's colleague, reviewed the multi-volume history in the *Göttinger Gelehrte Anzeigen* and regarded it as a mere collection of national histories. Schlözer insisted that singular facts and events must form a coherent whole.[20] In contrast to the *Welthistorie*'s eclectic arrangement, Gatterer and Schlözer proposed a linear view of humanity's evolution, which relegated Jewish history to the biblical period.[21]

Following this line of inquiry, Gotthold Ephraim Lessing tried his hand at a philosophical construction of world history in his *Erziehung des Menschengeschlechts* (Education of the human race) in 1780. He appreciated Judaism as the "childhood of mankind" and contended that Jewish postbiblical literature was a corruption of Mosaic Law. With the ascent of Christianity, Lessing opined that Judaism had stepped down from the stage of history. Although he envisioned humanity's final state as a condition of "absolute enlightenment," he remained ambivalent regarding the status of Judaism when, in passing, he called the Jews "the future educators of the human race" who had "the special ability to carry out divine purposes." While Lessing overtly regarded Judaism as outdated, he continued to accord it a special status in the unknown future.[22]

Without such ambiguities Anton Büsching followed Michaelis's efforts to grant Judaism a new, yet outdated, position in world history with the publication of his *Geschichte der jüdischen Religion* (History of the

Jewish religion) in 1779. In this small-scale study of the Jewish religion, Büsching outlined Judaism's development from the biblical period up until his own time. He focused on the Talmud and compared so-called distortions and absurdities of rabbinic interpretations to those of the "enlightened" Karaites, who denied the validity of the Talmudic-rabbinic tradition. Unstinting in his praise for Moses, he regarded Mosaic legislation as the most advanced constitution in its time. The same, however, could not be said about contemporary Jews, whom Büsching regarded as the continuation of rabbinical Judaism. Whereas Jews prided themselves on their divine election, Büsching regarded them as treacherous.[23]

His derogatory and dismissive treatment of Jewish history triggered critical responses in the major German Enlightenment periodicals. In Friedrich Nicolai's *Allgemeine deutsche Bibliothek*, the reviewer denounced Büsching's criticism of Judaism that negated the Enlightenment ideal of "tolerance and love."[24] Moreover, Büsching's *History of the Jewish Religion* encapsulated a profound disjuncture between his views of ancient and postbiblical Judaism. Loosely organized by the notion of regression and corruption, Büsching, similar to Lessing, failed to delineate a causal development. Describing Judaism simply as anachronistic and immoral did not suffice to explain the Jews' current status.

None of the German enlighteners had provided a pragmatic history of the Jews that unearthed historical causes and effects, and placed historical developments within a system of active and interactive relationships.[25] It was this situation that Christian Wilhelm Dohm addressed with the publication of *Ueber die bürglicher Verbesserung der Juden* (On the civic improvement of the Jews) in 1781, when he combined the past and present of the Jews in a comprehensive historical conception. In this seminal work, which drew widespread attention and numerous responses, Dohm explored what caused the "degeneration" of the Jews; Dohm, a councilor in the Prussian War Ministry, originally envisioned writing a history of the Jews.[26] In placing the question within a historical perspective, Dohm, who was familiar with the works of Michaelis and Büsching, appealed to the ideal of enlightened pragmatic histories. He maintained that Christian persecution and intolerance of Jews were responsible for their current status. Ultimately, postbiblical Jewish history emerged as a regression from "the religious laws and their original goodness and utility." Dohm's work accorded to Judaism a place within humanity's history by casting Jewish history as an extension of Christian European policy and not as an internal history actively shaped by its constituents.[27]

After Dohm, Immanuel Kant took up the issue of Judaism's providential role in history in his *Religion innerhalb der Grenzen der bloßen Vernunft* (Religion within the limits of reason alone) in 1793. He argued against the idea of Judaism as a set of divinely revealed moral laws and postulated a radical disjunction between Christianity and Judaism. Moreover, Kant invalidated the elevated status of Judaism by attacking supernatural explanations for Jewish perseverance. Similar to Spinoza and Voltaire, Kant explained the existence of the Jewish people in light of the Mosaic Laws as well as by the fact that Jews could reconnect with their heritage wherever they lived because the Old Testament had become part of Christianity and Islam.

Kant dismissed both the Jewish and Christian providential views of Jewish history and stated that it would be hazardous to base edifying observations upon this preservation of the Jewish people.[28] Together with Dohm, he ushered in a secular understanding of Jewish history that German scholars subsequently pursued in their studies of local Jewish communities.[29] Yet the eminent Jewish philosopher Moses Mendelssohn disregarded the new historical argumentation and staunchly opposed the idea of progress as well as any substantive distinction between past and present in his well-known criticism of Lessing's *Die Erziehung des Menschengeschlechts*.[30] His familiarity with historical studies notwithstanding, Mendelssohn did not adopt a historical perspective in his own work. His 1783 *Jerusalem, oder über die religiöse Macht des Judentums* (Jerusalem, or on religious power of Judaism) lacked a historically differentiated notion and portrayed Judaism above the vicissitudes of history.[31] Likewise, he did not accord a special status to his contemporary time as a new period in Jewish history but referred only to "now," "our better days," "once," and "the old Judaism."[32]

In spite of the lack of historical perspective, Mendelssohn's life and the politics of the Enlightenment inaugurated a new period in Jewish history that ultimately fostered a more secular understanding of the Jewish past. Guided by the new Zeitgeist, Jewish cultural and political ambitions in Germany revolved around key terms like *self-formation* and *Enlightenment*. Under the spell of these new visions and the dynamic understanding of history, the *maskil* (an exponent of the Jewish Enlightenment) Naphtali Herz Wessely viewed his own time on the cusp of a new period marked by external events such as religious tolerance. Wessely ultimately set contemporary time within a divine plan and, thereby, subscribed to the providential view of Jewish history. Yet at the same time, Wessely echoed Dohm's ideal of the enlightened pragmatic view of Jewish history. In his inquiry into the causes for the debased Jewish culture and the shortcomings of Jewish education, Wessely presented a succinct historical explanation. Jews had in the course of history abandoned *torat ha-'adam* (teachings of men), that is, good custom, morals, character, and civility, because the nations among which they lived "have afflicted us, bound our bodies to the dust and oppressed the spirit within us."[33]

While Wessely provided a summary of Dohm's pragmatic account of Jewish history in the Diaspora, the *maskilim* lacked a comprehensive vision of Jewish history and produced very few historical studies, even though they accorded an educational function to history.[34] In line with a more traditional and moderate Enlightenment conception of history, the maskilim pursued history largely for moralistic and didactic ends. Thus the Hebrew periodical *Ha-me'assef* (The collector) included biographies of famous scholars, merchants, and intercessors worthy of emulation, and it operated on the premise of historical similarity, rather than a sense of distance and historical particularity.[35]

This limited and still fairly traditional approach to Jewish history was soon refashioned in response to the heightened expectations following the French Revolution. Viewing their own time at a crossroads, the maskilim attempted to hasten the ongoing process of political, social, and cultural development. To this end, the latter-day Jewish Enlighteners utilized historical arguments in their quest for civic amelioration and internal reform, and relied on the few existing histories of Judaism as well as Enlightenment historiography. The republication of Azariah de Rossi's series of critical essays on Jewish history in 1794 titled *Me'or 'Enayim* (Light for the eyes), published originally between 1574 and 1575, testified to the increasing importance of history.[36]

Despite the scarcity of historical works, the second-generation maskilim were not troubled in defining within a historical purview the nature of Judaism; they simply assumed the existence of an eternal core of Judaism. For them, the *Wesen des Judentums* (essence of Judaism) was located in biblical Judaism, which, as a result of persecution, had undergone a process of degeneration soon to be reversed by the efforts of the maskilim themselves.[37] Postulating the existence of a timeless essence, these Jewish enlighteners explored along the lines of Dohm the historical process that led to Judaism's deviation from its essence. In 1793 Lazarus Bendavid, for example, set out to cleanse contemporary Judaism of accidental aberrations. Endless persecutions had forced Jews into cultural seclusion, while Jewish ceremonial laws still reflected the spirit of the slave and, therefore, ought to be abandoned, Bendavid argued.[38]

For the maskilim, the record of Jewish history pointed toward internal reforms to restore the original core of Judaism that would make Jews worthy of civic improvement. The application of these pragmatic accounts of the Jewish past remained contested even among the proponents of the Jewish Enlightenment. Shalom Cohen reproached later maskilim for their readiness to disavow the Jewish tradition. Cohen lamented that what time and persecution had not destroyed would now be abandoned by the later generation. Cohen, who had edited a more moderate version of *Ha-Me'assef* and worked as a teacher at the Jewish Free School in Berlin, saw Enlightenment disdain for traditional Judaism leading to the disregard for worthy remnants of the Jewish past, such as Hebrew poetry.[39]

This opposition notwithstanding, the ongoing civic improvement of the Jews during these decades continued to fuel the maskilic aspiration and radicalize their historical perception. Since the beginning of the nineteenth century, several principalities had extended new rights to the Jews as part of the ongoing transformation from ancient regimes to modern citizen states. Jews in the grand Duchy of Baden received full citizenship between 1807 and 1809; Bavaria followed suit in 1813. Prussia granted Jews the status of natives and citizens in 1812.[40] Certain restrictions remained in place, but by and large this partial achievement of civic integration intensified expectations and the quest for internal reform.

In response to the apparently rapidly progressing civic improvement, a more radical application of historical inquiry on behalf of a program of internal religious reform and genuine *Bildung* among Jews manifested itself in the newly founded periodical *Sulamith*. An ostensible continuation of the *Me'assef*, the journal set out to increase respect for Judaism among Jews and non-Jews alike and intended to show that the true teachings of Judaism were fully compatible with civic society. The periodical called for a return of the Jewish religion to its original pristine state *(Urbildung)*, untainted by superstitious additions.[41] Yet as in the earlier maskilic journal, most historical contributions concentrated on the lives and works of famous Jews of the past and present for didactic purposes.[42] With the exception of the more radical Galician historian, Peter Beer, whose article promoted a more dynamic and less normative historical understanding of Judaism by emphasizing the existence of various sectarian movements within Judaism, overall, the actual historical contributions to *Sulamith* provided little more than glimpses into Jewish history.[43]

Nevertheless, the periodical represented a remarkable advance in the historical view that brought the past, present, and future of Judaism together. The present seemed no longer static but dynamic, set within the scope of an all-encompassing historical process. David Fraenkel, one of the journal's editors, identified Maimonides' interpretation of the messianic age as a natural political event within the ongoing process of civic and cultural improvement.[44] Moses Mendelssohn's disciple, David Friedländer, greeted the Prussian edict of 1812 with a pamphlet in which he outlined a plan for educational and religious reforms. The work, which succinctly narrates the history of religious services from the Tabernacle to the present, displays an acute historical sensibility. Friedländer regarded the ascent of Frederick the Great as a turning point that ushered in a new period of tolerance and the absence of persecution, contemporaneous with internal awakening heralded by Moses Mendelssohn.[45]

Friedländer's pamphlet had brimmed with expectation and enthusiasm. Yet the reactionary political climate in Prussia from 1812 on became increasingly unfavorable for the realization of universal Jewish emancipation, particularly when German intellectuals quickly abandoned the heritage of the Enlightenment and embraced Romanticism. In 1815, the eminent University of Berlin historian Friedrich Rühs declared that he had abandoned Enlightenment ideals after studying the history of the Jews during the Middle Ages. Challenging Dohm's paradigmatic understanding of Jewish history, Rühs, who was joined by the philosopher Jacob Friedrich Fries, maintained that the debasement of the Jewish character did not result from persecution but rather from the religious and political Jewish law that distinguished the Jews from the people among whom they lived. In order to buttress this last point, Rühs referred to Spanish and Polish Jewish history. Despite generous protective legislation, the Jews of Spain and Poland had not abandoned commerce, peddling, and finance, and accordingly never became part of the general population, as he contended.[46]

In response to Rühs, the teacher of the Frankfurt Jewish maskilic Philanthropin, Michael Hess, reiterated Dohm's basic contention that persecutions were the primary reason for the current status of the Jews.[47] Together with Josef Wolf and Gotthold Salomon, these Jewish enlighteners derided Rühs and emphasized that he was insufficiently trained to write on Judaism and, therefore, relied excessively on Christian Hebraist and Enlightenment historiography. They marshaled numerous examples of persecution to vindicate Dohm's original insight that Judaism's alleged degradation did not reflect an innate Jewish character but was the result of oppression and persecution.[48]

With these public exchanges, the study of Jewish history received increasing importance and became fully intertwined with the debates over emancipation and internal religious, cultural, political, and economic reforms. Even a moderate maskil like Shalom Cohen provided a historical study as a guide for religious reform. Basing his arguments on primary sources and Christian Hebraists, his work was intended to show "what is essential and was is not essential, what is Mosaic and what is rabbinical."[49] Likewise, Isaac Jost, encouraged by David Friedländer and Lazarus Bendavid, began his work on a comprehensive history of the Jews in 1815,[50] while Leopold Zunz arrived in Berlin to study at the university and became associated with the increasingly radicalizing Reform movement. Zunz initially shared the maskilic criticism of rabbinical Judaism and participated in the debates over emancipation.[51] However, lack of standards in the quest for religious reform, reigning anarchy in the field, and disregard for and hostility toward Judaism that he encountered at the university dismayed Zunz.

The publication of his programmatic essay *Etwas ueber rabbinische Literatur* (Regarding rabbinical literature) in 1818 transformed the internal discussion of the Jews' status and their religious reform. Zunz challenged the ideology of the Jewish maskilim and reformers. He attacked the readiness with which certain aspects of Judaism were abandoned as the quid pro quo for emancipation and warned that "every unconsidered so-called amelioration *(Verbesserung)* is avenged by its crooked outcome."[52] The term "amelioration" that came into use following Dohm's *Ueber die bürgerliche Verbesserung der Juden* (1782) clearly served to identify Zunz's target. In contrast to Dohm and the maskilim, Zunz sketched out a comprehensive research project for the future historians of Judaism and thereby redefined Jewish enlightened perceptions of Judaism.

With this epoch-making treatise, Zunz affirmed the importance of a radically new approach to Jewish history. He turned against the traditional providential view of Jewish history and distanced himself from the more radical enlightened concept of the Jewish past as a process of degeneration. Wissenschaft thus emerged in opposition to the models of historical comprehension that had hitherto dominated the debates. Instead of theological expositions and enlightened historical criticism,

Zunz demanded detailed philological reconstruction of the Jewish heritage, since neither providence nor persecution could be viewed as the sole factors shaping Jewish history. Focusing on Judaism's religious and cultural history, Zunz constructed a history that was fashioned by its members and not a product of divine providence, legal restrictions, and persecution. In addition, Zunz already started to replace the goal of the restoration of a pristine state of Judaism with a comprehensive program of recovering the Jewish past. Yet the tension between these two poles continued to shape Jewish historiography for the next decades. Moreover, both the providential view of Jewish history and the elevation of persecution resurfaced in the second half of the nineteenth century in German Jewish historiography and eventually formed a central component in the popular culture.

2

Returning Judaism to History

The legacy of the Enlightenment and the failure to universalize Jewish emancipation at the Vienna conference in 1815—and the renewed antagonism toward the Jews—became defining experiences for the second generation of maskilim and a few university-trained intellectuals. In contrast to the ambiguities of Enlightenment conceptions of Jewish history, this generation faced a German historical school that reduced Judaism to a single idea and disregarded the existence of a postbiblical history. Friedrich A. Wolf, who had become famous with his studies on Homer, excluded Judaism from classical studies since only the Greeks and Romans among the ancient people had created genuine cultures.[1] For the theologian and preacher Friedrich Schleiermacher, Judaism was deemed an "imperishable mummy."[2] By depicting Judaism as not only superseded by Christianity but also as oriental, Georg Wilhelm Friedrich Hegel and others effectively erased Judaism from world history.[3] Together, these various disciplines disregarded and relegated Judaism to the stage of world history that had long since passed. In light of these new challenges, the emerging Wissenschaft confronted a formidable task during the next decades when it comprehended Judaism from a historical perspective and asserted the vital role Judaism played in world history. Yet their prolific endeavor encountered a disinterested, if not hostile, German academia and an equally unenthusiastic Jewish public. Thus far from presenting a seamless evolution, the beginning of Jewish scholarship displays discontinuous developments with only

Isaac Jost and Leopold Zunz forging ahead once the *Verein für Cultur und Wissenschaft der Juden* (Society for culture and science of the Jews) had folded.

Several young Jewish intellectuals, including Eduard Gans, Moses Moser, Immanuel Wolf, Heinrich Heine, Isaac Jost, and Leopold Zunz, together with representatives of the second generation Berlin *Haskalah* (Jewish Enlightenment) such as Lazarus Bendavid and David Friedländer, formed the *Verein für Cultur und Wissenschaft der Juden*. According to its statutes, the Verein devoted itself to scientific and educational efforts in order to augment *Bildung* and *Wissenschaft* among the Jews. The final version of the statutes included plans to create a scientific institute, organize an archive, publish a periodical, and erect a Jewish free school. The Verein thus combined classical maskilic activities such as youth education, enlightening, and training Jews in crafts, agriculture, and practical sciences with the more novel program of *Wissenschaft des Judentums*.[4] The Verein, therefore, also did not simply come into being in response to the anti-Jewish riots in 1819 as has previously been claimed.[5] The goals that the Verein set out to accomplish reflect rather a broader social-political situation.

The members of the Verein belonged to a generation that had personally experienced the emancipation during the French occupation, when civic equality was introduced in all German territories ruled directly or indirectly by Napoleon.[6] Zunz recalled in his autobiographical account from the early 1840s that he saw the approaching French armies as a sign of imminent salvation. The writer Heine exclaimed in a letter that he too understood himself as belonging to the generation that was "hit by the blow of the revoked edict."[7] While the removal of emancipation was a profound disappointment, it did not translate itself into disillusionment but rather gave rise to clear expectations regarding the future. The revocation and delay of universal emancipation gave renewed impetus to all those activities that would hasten its onset.

Nine years to the day after Prussia's emancipation edict of March 11, 1812, Eduard Gans assumed the presidency of the Verein and delivered a programmatic speech. He believed the Verein's task was "to hasten the time that [emancipation and cultural renewal] would occur otherwise, with all the required power and effort: this is the task, gentlemen, that you set before yourselves with this society."[8] The other members of the Verein also believed that only an objective treatment of Jewish culture would remove the existing prejudicial representation and function as a guide for the internal reform of Jewish society and Judaism.[9]

Gans, the student prodigy of Hegel, posited that history progresses according to a clearly charted path mapped out by a specific idea. Accordingly, it was the task of the historian to elucidate this idea and to delineate its progressive fulfillment. In a subtle turn against Hegel, Gans postulated that to trace the historical place and nature of this idea one would have to clarify "what is the present Europe" and "who are we Jews."[10] In contrast to Hegel, Gans replaced the German Reich as the fourth empire along the lines of the prophecies contained in the book of Daniel with Europe as an organic entity into which the "spirit" was unfolding.[11]

In the quest to hasten the ongoing process toward emancipation, elements of Jewish messianism merged with the eschatological hopes of many German intellectuals who had begun to identify Prussia as the most progressive state. The members of the society, therefore, turned to Wissenschaft with impatience, or to use a formulation by Immanuel Kant, with "chiliastic urgency," and believed that Wissenschaft would influence the future unfolding of Jewish history.[12] Zunz regarded the year 1820 as another fundamental turning point in Jewish history: "Israel has eight epochs, each of 450 years past totaling 3600 years. These are marked by Deborah, Elisha, Nehemiah, the *Mishna*, the *Gemara*, and the years 1370 and 1820."[13] A few years later, he observed that with the inauguration of cultural and social changes among the Jews promoted by Wissenschaft, "the Messiah will not remain absent."[14] To be sure, this messianic belief was modern and not particularistic and anticipated a general political process, rather than divine intervention.[15] Thus both Zunz and Heine distanced themselves from more traditional messianic contemplations entertained by Eliezer Kirschbaum, a Verein member, who gave a speech titled "Hilkhot yemot ha-mashiah" (Laws for the days of the Messiah).[16] According to Kirschbaum, Mordecai Noah's plan to create a Jewish state in America was an unmistakable sign for the arrival of the Messiah.[17]

Despite the conglomeration of opposing tendencies, the Verein at its core represented a turn away from the *Haskalah*. Whereas according to Horst Blanke, the Enlightenment was an important stepping stone in the development of German historical studies, the Verein represented "a drastic leap into a new kind of thinking" that clearly separated it from the maskilim, as Yosef Yerushalmi has pointedly noted.[18] Eduard Gans was not the only Verein member who attacked the Jewish Enlightenment as having displayed only scorn and disdain for Jewish tradition without providing new content. No return to "intimacy"

(Innigkeit) occurred, and no new relationships to Judaism had been forged.[19] While Zunz still shared the Enlightenment's bias against the Ashkenazic tradition and its elevation of Sephardic Jewry, he nevertheless went against the enlightened usage of history and devoted a study to the medieval rabbinic Ashkenazic luminary Rashi. In this work, Zunz lashed out against the maskilim biographers who "carve out figures of bygone times according to the model of their cultured friends." Without apologetics, Zunz frankly declared that Rashi was dominated by the Talmud, intolerant, not particularly learned outside the Jewish tradition, and "an ignoramus in history."[20]

To overcome the impact of the Enlightenment, the Verein, with its emphasis on historical studies, represented the wish to fundamentally redefine Judaism.[21] Zunz viewed historical investigation as a yardstick with which one could "recognize and distinguish among the old and useful, the obsolete and harmful, the new and desirable."[22] The young historians investigated the Jewish past in the hope of finding Judaism's core *(Wesen)*, which would guide them to reconfigure contemporary Jewish culture and religion. Joel Liszt argued that it was only this core or essence that could become the new unifying force among Jews.[23] In his programmatic essay, Wolf postulated that the scholarly investigation seeks to analyze Judaism's essence.[24] Yet the question of how to identify an essence within a historical approach was fraught with difficulties. Was the essence in the origin, development, evolution, or contemporary forms of Judaism? The methodological problems were intensified by the ambiguity of the central category: *Das Wesen des Judentums*. Were Jewish historians attempting to define the essence of the Jewish people or the essence of Judaism? The German word *Judentum* captures both meanings, denoting a people and a religion.

For all the difficulties in elucidating the essence of Judaism, this project loomed large in the minds of nineteenth-century scholars who understood their scholarship as a major guide in the intended transformation of Jewish life and culture. Wolf's description of the essence wanted to identify the core of Judaism in its philosophical tradition. Accordingly, he started his description not with rabbinic Judaism but rather created a trajectory that has its origin in the Sadducees, Hellenistic Jewish philosophy, and the Kabbalah and culminates in Spinoza.[25]

In contrast to Wolf, Zunz increasingly strove for a comprehensive all-encompassing understanding of Judaism. He imagined Jewish history in a spatial metaphor like a palace. Upon entering the palace, one would be in awe of the way in which each moment from within and

outside the essence of Judaism was shaped.[26] Accordingly, Zunz outlined a research program that included cultural productions ranging
from mathematics, science, and the arts to Jewish poetry and liturgy.
All of these were components of the single canon of Jewish creativity.
By listing all kinds of texts under the rubric of historical sources, Zunz
altered the canon of Jewish texts and diminished existing hierarchies.
Mathematical and medical treatises appeared alongside philosophical
texts and exegetical and halakhic literature.

By uniting all texts under the single description of historical sources,
Jewish scholars fundamentally altered their status and obliterated the
demarcation between the sacred and profane. No text could maintain a
meaning that elevated it above the time and place out of which it
emerged. At the heart of this approach resided the examination and
evaluation of the sources.[27] Zunz emphasized that only those documents that had undergone a careful scrutiny could become part of world
culture: "In this fashion every historical datum that diligence has discovered, astuteness deciphered, philosophy utilized and taste put in its
proper place becomes a contribution to the knowledge of man, which is
the most worthy goal of all research."[28]

Leopold Zunz's former schoolmate, Isaac Jost, confronted other
vexing problems in his evaluations of the sources. Trained in Göttingen
by the eminent biblical scholar and historian Johann Gottfried Eich-
horn, he was mostly interested in the external history of the Jews and
the shifting relations between Jews and the government. For Jost, the
focus on the legal, political, and social history was a preparatory step
toward a cultural history. Therefore, the question of historical criticism
emphasized the issue of non-Jewish sources to which he attributed an
equal, if not higher, status than sources of Jewish origin. In theory then,
Jost diminished those hierarchies that had still dominated early modern
Jewish historiography. He discussed the composition and canonization
of the Bible and devoted considerable attention to the Talmud as a historical source, thereby introducing new methods into the study of the
sacred tradition. He swiftly reevaluated the notion of orality in order to
comprehend the creation of the Mishna. Whereas traditionally the content of the Mishna was seen as part of the oral Torah that was revealed
together with the written Torah at Sinai, Jost understood the orality in
a radically different manner. For him, the Mishna was a collection of
oral traditions and customs that did not date back beyond the times of
Herodotus.[29]

The "historical operation" entailed not only source criticism but also situating ideas, texts, individuals, and communities in a historical context.[30] In order to assign each document its proper place in time, Jewish historians divided the past into several periods. These periods functioned as reference points that in turn bestowed a new meaning into the text. Both Jost and Zunz continued in the footsteps of Spinoza and Mendelssohn, and regarded the destruction of the First Temple as the turning point in Jewish history. According to this view, the Jews who returned from the Babylonian exile no longer formed a political body and the year 586 B.C.E. marked, therefore, the end of the political character of the Jews.[31] This periodization entailed the denigration of Jewish culture in the Second Temple period as rapidly fossilized, culminating in a stifled rabbinic Judaism. For Jost, writing in a spirit of the radical *Haskalah*, Jewish history was in decline thanks to the development of rabbinic Judaism. He succumbed to the distinctly Christian view of Jewish history, according to which postbiblical literature reflected the spiritual and political decline of Judaism. In his *Geschichte der Israeliten* (History of the Israelites) he therefore located the beginnings of this decline in the Pharisees, whom he depicted as teachers offering their goods without creating anything genuine. Finally, Jost charged the Pharisees with the death of Jesus.[32] In contrast to Jost, Zunz distanced himself from this view by positing that only the period after the Reformation was one of decline, dominated by a degraded version of rabbinic Judaism.[33]

While both Zunz and Jost still lacked a comprehensive philosophy of Jewish history, Immanuel Wolf not only proposed a program of empirical Jewish studies but also delineated a religious idea that powered Jewish history, by presenting the major components for future counterhistories against the reigning Christian-centered account of Jewish history. For Wolf, this idea was one of "unlimited unity in the all" or put differently, the recognition of divine presence. Taking his cue from Exodus 19:6 ("You shall be unto Me a kingdom of priests"), Wolf regarded Jews as a "nation of priests in the sense of guardians of the idea of God." He asserted Judaism's continued importance for world history by viewing Christianity as a vehicle for disseminating monotheism, and he insisted on Judaism's crucial role as a cultural transmitter in medieval Spain and elevated Spinoza to the supreme expression of Judaism's religious idea.[34]

Heinrich Heine, who joined the Verein, was particularly attuned to the way historicization reshaped Judaism. He highlighted the multifaceted function German idealism fulfilled in the creation of Jewish historiography. While it denied Judaism an independent history, this idealism provided the members of the Verein with the tools to historicize Judaism. In one of his nightmarish fantasies that he confided to his friend Moses Moser in May 1823, a mob of children taunted him. Running into the arms of Moser to be comforted, Heine was told that "Heine" was only an idea. Once Moser started to point out a rather confusing part of Hegel's logic, Heine became enraged and screamed: "I am not an idea and know nothing about any idea, and never even had an idea."[35] Heine's reference to the notion of ideas echoes both the Hegelian philosophy of history as well as the influential *Ideenlehre* of the statesman and philosopher of art, language, and history, Wilhelm von Humboldt. In a small essay titled "On the Historian's Task" (1821), Humboldt defined the task of the historian as detecting the ideas that govern and dominate all other forces in world history.[36] The application of this approach to Judaism entailed reducing it to the idea of rational ethical monotheism. In this jesterlike staging, Heine was not only at odds with the reigning German school of philosophy of history but also criticized the historicization carried out by the Verein itself. Not only had David Friedländer and Eduard Gans become ideas, but Zunz too was on the verge of being turned into one, according to Heine.[37]

In their quest, however, the young university-trained scholars found only a limited reception in the Jewish communities, and the Verein folded in 1824. The members' sense of elitism may have been responsible for antagonizing possible allies. Gans expressed this self-elevation openly when he declared that Verein members were "summoned here by virtue of greater intelligence."[38] Isaac Jost, who left the Verein in 1822, was irritated by the arrogance with which the Verein made its claim to leadership.[39] While the association had 81 members, those who were part of the Hamburg branch hardly subscribed to the scholarly agenda of the Verein and instead were more concerned with the goals of the Reform movement.[40]

The Verein's periodical, the *Zeitschrift für die Wissenschaft des Judentums,* had a print run of 500 in 1822, yet Samuel Meyer Ehrenberg, Zunz's former high school teacher, was hard-pressed to find subscribers.[41] When Ehrenberg expressed his difficulties, Zunz's response once more revealed a note of arrogance. For Zunz "the periodical is not a Jewish periodical and is also not intended to educate the Jews in Braunschweig." Instead, Zunz believed that the *Zeitschrift* appealed to the "better forces in Israel."[42] Heine, on the other hand, regarded the academic German of the *Zeitschrift* as simply "unpalatable."[43] Put differently, whereas the Verein directed its education efforts at a wider Jewish audience, the academic branch appealed to the select few.

Similarly, Isaac Jost lacked sufficient subscribers to his history of the Jews. In the end, his *Geschichte der Israeliten* (1820–28) had subscribers for 251 copies. More than half of these individuals lived in Berlin.[44] The difficulties in finding more readers for his history of the Jews, however, may have been only partially due to a lack of interest in Jewish history. David Ottensosser, who also was a member of the Verein, elicited 412 subscribers mostly from Bavaria for his *Die Geschichte der Jehudim* (The history of the Jews), published in 1821, a work in which he utilized Ludvig Holberg's history of the Jews.[45] The book of a latter-day maskil, *Die Geschichte der Jehudim* was written in German with Hebrew characters and marks a vast difference from the works that emanated from the other Verein members. For Ottensossor to query the traditional chronology of the creation of the world would have been tantamount to destroying the foundation of the Jewish religion. Going against Azariah de Rossi's critical investigation of biblical chronology, Ottensosser sided with David Gans and asserted the validity of the biblical and Talmudic sources. Closer in spirit to the work of moderate German enlighteners than the radical maskilim and the other members of the Verein, his work had a completely different geographic distribution in comparison to Jost's comprehensive history of the Jews.[46] Although Jost found only eight subscribers in Frankfurt and Fürth, these cities made up more than one-third of Ottensosser's subscription lists.[47] The greater familiarity with the Hebrew script as well as a preference for a more moderate didactic account of the Jewish past may have been responsible for this discrepancy. Moreover, the dissemination of Jost's works highlights the Verein's dependence on the centers of the emerging Reform movement. The differences between Jost and Ottensosser, and their respective receptions, illustrate the Verein's novelty and comparative isolation as well as the ongoing importance of other modes of historical comprehension.

The Verein was short-lived and had failed to significantly penetrate the wider Jewish culture. Yet Moses Moser grasped its intellectual significance when he compared the introduction of Jewish historiography to the contemporaneous liberation movement in Spain and Portugal. The Verein reinscribed Judaism as an acting subject into the pages of world history. After the periods of exile had been dominated by passivity in the expectation of divine redemption, Judaism's return to history brought on by the Verein inaugurated a new period.[48] While, in the words of Moser, the Verein was "created on the fly," Jost and Zunz pursued the historical studies and functioned as mentors to younger university-trained scholars like Abraham Geiger, Zacharias Frankel, Michael Sachs, and Moritz Steinschneider during the 1830s and 1840s, mainly through elaborate correspondences. Jost noted that he composed about 500 letters annually, and Zunz was no less productive as a writer of letters.[49] Although the Verein represented at its core a fairly homogenous program, Jewish historiography would soon become embroiled in religious debates that would shatter the cohesion. Competing with dogmatic and philosophical expositions of Judaism's core, the remaining active members of the former Verein, together with the next generation of historians, had moreover to establish the centrality of their historical approach.

3

Recovering Jewish History
in the Age of Emancipation
and Reform

Aside from Jost's *Geschichte der Israeliten,* Jewish historians had produced few valuable essays that reflected the formulation of an ambitious program. With the exception of Jost and Zunz, only a small number of former Verein members continued along the path of Wissenschaft. Its association with religious reform and the battle over emancipation further contributed to its importance and energy. Yet the very quality that allowed Jewish historiography to blossom made it increasingly divisive and hindered efforts to find an institutional home for it outside of the German universities. Moreover, its conflicting nature obstructed attempts to garner a wide-ranging readership. Far from presenting the dominant discourse during this period, the study of the Jewish past still had to vindicate its primary role within the intellectual culture of German Jewry. Yet with Wissenschaft's ascendancy, it confronted criticism for its lack of impact upon the wider Jewish society. Despite this nascent condemnation and the emerging ideological differences, Jewish historians continued to regard Wissenschaft as a tool in the hands of the intellectual elite and not an educational force. In this respect, it functioned as *"historische Aufklärung"* (enlightenment through history) with the purpose of elucidating Judaism's true essence and countering its biased representation in the German public. It was only during the late 1830s and 1840s that the first efforts to popularize Jewish history were made in the form of textbook histories. Simultaneously, Heinrich Heine and Ludwig and Phöbus Philippson had been dismayed by the lack of impact the scholarly representation of Jewish history had had on Jewish education and proposed poetic treatments instead.

For most of the historians, historical scholarship continued to be seen as the supreme instrument in the fight for emancipation and internal reform. As Zunz stated in 1832, "the neglect of Jewish science is intricately bound up with the Jews' civic degradation." The linkage of emancipation and reform also formed the cornerstones of his first comprehensive analysis of Jewish liturgy. The study was sandwiched between a call for emancipation in the first chapter, which was censored out of the first edition, and an appeal for internal reform in the last chapter.[1] In line with this self-understanding, Zunz and Jost engaged in elaborate public defenses of the Jews in the face of Luigi Chiarini's slandering of the Talmud.[2] When the Prussian government attempted to ban Jews from acquiring non-Jewish names, the Berlin community commissioned Zunz to write a treatise that would counter this prohibition in exchange for 100 thaler.[3] Zunz's *Die Namen der Juden* (The names of the Jews) amply illustrated that Jews in the past had had names like Jason, Abu-Hassan, Fischlin, and Esperanza.[4] Similarly, in 1840, the community leaders of Berlin asked Zunz to write about the notorious blood-libel accusation in Damascus, which quickly became an issue that was debated in the European press.[5]

Strung together, emancipation and internal reform nevertheless produced the opposing dynamics of discontinuity and development. In respect to the debate over emancipation, Jewish participants pointed to advances and discontinuities between premodern and contemporary Jewry.[6] Jost made this point clear when in defense of emancipation he wrote, "all of us who were still in our childhood thirty years ago are witnesses to unbelievable transformations. . . . We have wandered, or better, flown through a thousand-year history!"[7] If Jost understood the last few decades as the equivalent of a thousand years, he simply underscored the advancements and discontinuity in light of the accelerated process of social, cultural, and religious transformation. From the 1840s on, however, Jewish historians more strongly grounded current Judaism in the past. Whereas Jost's scholarship presented a program to overcome elements of the Jewish past that were mainly associated with the dark ages of Ashkenazic Jewry and to return Jewish society to its biblical state, other Jewish historians increasingly reintegrated the premodern period into their conceptions of Judaism's development. Instead of discontinuity, they emphasized change and progress and highlighted the particularistic aspects of Judaism.

Zunz's study presented an elaborate attempt to come to terms with the question of development and continuity and to legitimize the modern sermon in the vernacular. In his magnum opus, Zunz portrayed postbiblical Judaism as a thriving culture and stressed that during those times when there was no Jewish state, cultural creativity nevertheless flourished.[8] Positing an organic development, Zunz bridged the disjuncture between the Israelite religion and rabbinic Judaism. For him, halakhah and haggadah represented the continuation of biblical law and the freedom of prophecy.[9]

In contrast, Jost's 1832 *Allgemeine Geschichte des israelitischen Volkes* (General history of the Jewish people) failed to provide a basic developmental scheme and to differentiate between the various historical epochs. By mostly neglecting Jewish cultural and religious history, Jost did not accord historical agency to the Jews.[10] In a review of Jost's history that appeared in Gabriel Riesser's *Der Jude,* the critic expressed the hope that a history of the Jews would be written that combined political with religious history.[11] A few years later, Abraham Geiger upbraided Jost's history when he declared that the external history of the Jews does not offer a reasonable principle of development. In the external history of the Diaspora, Geiger maintained, "the smell of mustiness of the field of corpses approaches one."[12]

Jost had daringly begun with two attempts at writing a comprehensive history of the Jews. However, more research was needed to bring the development of Judaism into clearer perspective. New studies appeared that charted the Second Temple period, the history of Spanish Jewry, as well as the neglected field of Jewish law. Levi Herzfeld brought the Second Temple period into focus as one of profound religious transformation in which monotheism only slowly took hold.[13] Michael Sachs, a rabbi and preacher in Berlin, published *Die religiöse Poesie der Juden in Spanien* (The religious poetry of the Jews in Spain) in 1845, which brought together a collection of medieval religious poetry in translation and represented to a large extent the German Jewish enchantment with the Golden Age of Spanish Jewry.[14] Concurrently, Zacharias Frankel delved into the realm of Jewish law, and Abraham Geiger described the language of the Mishna.[15]

With this blossoming scholarship, the Jewish public sphere developed. When, in the aftermath of the Napoleonic defeat, many societies excluded Jews from membership, German Jews founded their own societies. In particular, Jewish reading societies emerged within smaller communities during the 1830s, a time when the overwhelming majority of Jews in Germanic lands still lived in small and middle-sized towns.[16] While up until the 1830s most of these reading societies devoted themselves to general education, they slowly took up education in the field of Jewish history. The first such clubs appeared in communities like Baiersdorf in 1837 and Jebenhausen in 1838.[17] In 1842 Abraham Geiger founded in Breslau the Learning and Reading Association *(Jüdischen Lehr- und Leseverein,* later *Israelitischer Lehr- und Leseverein).* The society, which in 1846 had 110 members, provided them with the opportunity to familiarize themselves with publications on Judaism. To this end, a library was established, and public talks were organized. Geiger gave numerous lectures here during the 1840s that covered almost all periods of Jewish history.[18]

The exact number of these reading clubs and societies is unclear, but their existence increasingly expanded the readership of Jewish periodicals. In 1836 Ludwig Philippson started the *Allgemeine Zeitung des Judenthums.* From its inception, it reviewed scholarly publications and even introduced a special rubric for Jewish history in 1838.[19] Jost edited the *Israelitische Annalen* (1839–41), which was dedicated to Jewish history, culture, and literature of all times and countries. In addition to these periodicals, Julius Fürst published the *Orient* (1840–51), which included a separate literary insert dedicated to scholarship.[20] Abraham Geiger edited the first major scholarly journal, the *Wissenschaftliche Zeitschrift für jüdische Theologie* (1835–47), after he completed his studies at the university in Bonn. Jost claimed in one of his letters to Philipp Ehrenberg that one copy of the *Israelitische Annalen* reached about 50 readers because Jewish reading societies had ordered them. Jost went on to say that the *Orient* had only 115 subscribers in 1841. The total circulation of the *Allgemeine* and the *Orient* was about 700 copies by 1850.[21] Yet despite these advances, with the exception of the *Allgemeine,* none of these journals lasted beyond a few years.

This situation also dominated the reception of the works by Wissenschaft scholars. Zunz bemoaned the lack of an audience for scholarly works in a letter to Meyer Isler in December 1830 when he wrote, "it is a real misfortune to write for Jews! The rich Jews do not pay attention, the Jewish scholars cannot read it, and the fools review it."[22]

Zunz's *Gottesdienstliche Vorträge* immediately found 300 subscribers in 1832 from Cracow, Brody, Lemberg, Tarnopol, Odessa, Vienna, Triest, Padua, Copenhagen, Stuttgart, Pest, and Leyden.[23] In view of the wide geographic distribution, the readership was fairly limited. Moreover, only 200 additional copies were sold during the next eight years. It was only at the beginning of the 1850s that the first edition of 750 copies was finally out of print. Twenty years after their initial publication, the 950 sets of Jost's history were still not sold out, and his *Allgemeine Geschichte des israelitischen Volkes* "lay like lead," as he remarked in 1841.[24] A similar fate met the publication of more than one thousand copies of Zunz's *Die Namen der Juden*.[25] Only Ludwig Philippson during this period was more successful in reaching a wider audience, including Christians, when he delivered several public lectures between 1846–47.[26]

Efforts during the 1840s to create a publishing society for the promotion of works on Jewish history and literature similiarly failed. While Gabriel Riesser, Albert Cohn, and other rabbis and teachers lent their support to this cause, only two hundred members signed up.[27] In 1841, Leopold Zunz revitalized the Verein of the 1820s to "support all Jewry" through the nursing of science and art.[28] While over nine hundred copies of the society's statutes were distributed, the response from Jewish communities and individuals remained limited. The society offered the substantial sum of two hundred thaler to the author of the best monograph that answered the question "What was, is, and should the rabbi be?" When after two years no manuscripts were received, the society amended the question to a study of the rabbinate since 1782. Yet no historian responded, and the prize was never awarded. Among the few scholarly projects supported by the society was the publication of Judah Halevi's *Kusari* by David Cassel. Next to these activities the society had a small library for its members, which was hardly ever used.[29] Zunz's lectures during the 1840s about Jewish history and literature equally attracted only a small number of attendees[30] Consequently, the society folded in 1847.[31]

It was this situation that Ludwig Philippson and others addressed with the creation of historical novels. For many Reform-oriented pedagogues, rabbis, and writers, the scholarly treatment of Judaism was, as one observer put it, not successful in overcoming the lack of "Jewish *Bildung*," since they were for the most part simply not accessible nor particularly effective as teaching tools. Instead, pedagogues demanded the creation of religious folk and youth literature.[32] Historical novels, like Berthold Auerbach's *Spinoza: Ein Denkerleben* (Spinoza: the life of a thinker), Phöbus Philippson's *Die Marranen* (The Marranos), followed by Heinrich Heine's *Der Rabbi von Bacharach* (The rabbi of Bacharach), depicting mostly the history of Spanish Jewry, filled this gap.

While Philippson and others attempted to educate German Jews about their history in the form of historical novels, Jewish history became a subject of instruction in several Jewish and general schools. When, at the end of the 1830s, Moses Elkan and Ephraim Willstätter published the first textbooks, they relied heavily on Jost's *Allgemeine Geschichte*. Yet they nevertheless wanted to educate and further the formation of the heart and the spirit, while pupils had to memorize the material.[33] In contrast to Jost, Willstätter struck a very different tone when he emphasized the importance of historical memory for the Jews to maintain their identity and to remain faithful believers before their God. Illustrating his work with historical examples, he pleaded in his introduction for unity among the Jews based on the common remembrance of Israel's past. To familiarize pupils with Israel's past would further German Jews' integration and maintain their distinctiveness.[34]

In line with Willstätter's understanding of the moral and religious function of historical memory, the reviews clearly indicate that Jewish history was not to be taught as a secular subject. In the eyes of pedagogues, Jewish history instructed students in God's providence, the religious-moral vocation, and the veracity of Judaism. With respect to these educational goals, numerous reviews attacked these early textbooks. The criticisms echoed the early reproach Jost had faced. In these textbooks, Jewish history "appears as a sad and desolate field of human humiliation."[35] Elkan was reprimanded for having slavishly followed Jost and therefore lacked the "warmth with which the Jewish youth could excite themselves for their religion and co-religionists." In particular, the adaptation of Jost's portrayal of Jesus from the perspective of enlightened rationalism was seen as "peculiar objectivity in a textbook for 'Israelite schools.'"[36]

Offered at an affordable price, Elkan's textbook, despite its criticism, had several editions.[37] The readership of this work must, however, have remained fairly limited since only a few Jewish schools offered postbiblical history as a formal field of instruction.[38] Nevertheless, these textbooks and their reception point to a distinct historical tradition that only slowly regained its voice during the 1840s and began to impact more forcefully on the evolution of Jewish historiography in the second half of the nineteenth century. The authors of the textbook histories subscribed to a morally instructive concept of history that was closer in spirit to the moderate German Enlightenment and the first generation maskilim than the critical works that disseminated from the nascent Wissenschaft school.

In contrast to the attribution of the moral and religious significance of the Jewish past, Jewish historians remained critical of any popularizing tendencies of Wissenschaft. They understood the inception of Jewish historiography as the dialectical summation of the previous decades of enlightenment and reform and the telos of their ambitions. In Zunz's study of synagogal sermons, a new epoch in Jewish history began in the 1750s. Taking his cue from Gans's speech, he posited the recent history as a development that progressed from the Enlightenment to the age of education and reform. Zunz understood the fourth period as the outcome of the liberating Wissenschaft.[39] This movement was to raise the comprehension of Judaism to a new level and was not an educational program. Jost, for example, in his 1832 *Allgemeine Geschichte,* addressed not the general Jewish reading public but, as the subtitle indicates, "politicians, lawyers, theologians and scientifically educated readers."[40] Along these lines, Geiger opposed the popular treatment of Jewish history in the pages of the *Allgemeine Zeitung des Judenthums* as long as the inner connection of the entirety of Jewish history was not fully understood.[41]

Notwithstanding its self-avowed reluctance to educate a broader public, Wissenschaft during the 1840s became a contentious affair and increasingly mirrored the polarization of the Jewish communities in light of the revitalized debates over reform that led to three rabbinical conferences of the 1840s.[42] In the course of the conferences' deliberations, the traditional messianic hope was reshaped in the form of the mission theory that became a cornerstone of Jewish historiography. As Ludwig Philippson declared at the conference, "Every people has its mission in history. The Jews too have their mission: they are the people of religion."[43]

Despite the wish to utilize the conferences to build a unified program for religious reforms, they became the rallying point for divergent voices. Zacharias Frankel walked out of the rabbinical conference over the issue of Hebrew in the services and went on to found the short-lived journal *Zeitschrift für die religiösen Interessen des Judenthums,* which was filled with criticism of the Reform movement. For Frankel, the readiness with which Reform Judaism handed over some of the tenets of Judaism in the expectation of emancipation defiled the memory of those Jews who in the past had gladly sacrificed their lives for them.[44] Frankel was not alone in his discontent with Reform Judaism and its scholarship.

Michael Sachs equally attacked it because of its alleged thoroughly negative approach toward Judaism. Like Heinrich Heine, Sachs also deplored the reduction of Judaism to a single idea. In a letter to his friend Moritz Veit in Berlin, Sachs wrote: "They study history as an isolated [object], authors and book titles they investigate with the same fear like the mixture of meat with milk products. They call this meticulous. Sheer foolishness! If there is a Judaism—I only ask that it is not watered down into *Shema Yisrael* and called essence—step into the path that you see and form it further with its own power!"[45]

The divergence intensified when the radical laity in Frankfurt questioned the necessity of circumcision, and members of the Rothschild banking family in Frankfurt commissioned Zunz to write a defense of this institution.[46] In an article Zunz published in 1844, he defended the tradition and challenged the Reformers' readiness to discard elements of the Jewish religion.[47] To jettison the belief in the messiah or the Talmud was, in the eyes of Zunz, a repudiation of the Jewish past. Zunz, therefore, turned down an invitation to participate in the rabbinical conference in Breslau.[48] In 1845, in his *Zur Geschichte und Literatur* (On history and literature), a work that elucidated the history of legal, liturgical, exegetical, and ethical literature of Ashkenazic Jewry, Zunz attacked Reform-oriented scholarship as tendentious and selective. Against these scholars, Zunz argued Jewish history should be studied as an end in itself and not in anticipation of political and social advantages to be gained.[49]

In light of these religious controversies, Jewish scholarship developed more sharply along the lines of denominational differences. Heated debates occurred in Breslau in which the right for free scholarly inquiry was upheld by Abraham Geiger's followers against their traditionalist opponents led by Salomon Tiktin.[50] Concurrent with these controversies, Jewish theologians and philosophers promoted dogmatic theological and philosophical expositions of Judaism and challenged the importance of historical research in an attempt to regain a clearly delineated notion of the essence of Judaism. Philosophical expositions of Judaism by Salomon Formstecher, Samuel Hirsch, and Salomon Ludwig Steinheim appeared for which stages in the divine education, not the contingencies of history, were the only things that mattered.[51] Jost captured the sense of disintegration quite pointedly when he wrote, "Among twenty scholars, and there are barely more who can claim this title, everyone has nineteen pursuers, if not even mockers."[52] Jost may have slightly overstated his point, yet he nevertheless vividly expressed the sense of disunity among Jewish scholars.

As Wissenschaft became more fractured and contested, several Jewish historians became wary of a radical reformulation of Judaism. Reform-minded scholars like the Hungarian Moses Brück pulverized the status of previously sacred texts and rituals and posited the return to the Mosaic level of Jewish law.[53] In contrast, the Reform scholar Abraham Geiger aimed to reassert the importance of historical continuity and wondered how historical studies could "set the course for us to follow."[54] He therefore became increasingly interested in showing how contemporary Judaism was the product of a long development that was still ongoing. Geiger hoped that the historical understanding would not only relativize previously normative texts but construct an image of continuity.[55]

Similar to Geiger, Heinrich Graetz, the new champion of the emerging positive-historical school, reaffirmed the centrality of the historical approach against theological and philosophical expositions of Judaism's core. Graetz, who had established himself as a scholar in his own right with his dissertation from the University of Jena on Jewish gnosticism, published a lengthy pamphlet in Frankel's periodical titled "Die Construction der jüdischen Geschichte" (The construction of Jewish history), in which he outlined a program for a history of the Jews. In these reflections on Jewish history, Graetz turned against Samuel Hirsch and Salomon Steinheim when he unequivocally exclaimed "the totality of Judaism is only discernible in its history."[56] With unparalleled sophistication, Graetz combined external and internal aspects of Jewish history, whereby different elements of a multifaceted essence shaped the various epochs in Jewish history. For Graetz, the contingent historical progression represented even in its remote aspects a continuously developing unity.

Unlike the members of the Verein, Graetz utilized the concept of the idea of Judaism in a new fashion. History became the "reflex of the idea," the realm in which the core of Judaism and its manifestations were validated.[57] In their quest for a new historical understanding, Geiger and Graetz regarded the fact that *Judentum* denoted a religion and a people as a major advantage. The historical individuality of the Jewish people testified to the veracity of Judaism's universal teachings. These historians justified Jewish particularism in terms of its universal mission to humanity. Accordingly, Graetz quite confidently concluded his essay by writing that from a historical perspective, Judaism had in contrast to Christianity a "winning game" *(ein gewonnenes Spiel).*[58]

Turning against Christian scholarship, Graetz, like Zunz, asserted that Judaism continued to have an active history beyond the times in which it formed a state.[59] Therefore, Graetz insisted that it was not the destruction of the Second Temple but rather the end of the First Temple period that represented the beginning of a new historical epoch in Jewish history.[60] While Graetz had restructured the flow of Jewish history in order to avoid a Christian reading, he was clearly aware of the far-reaching implications of his approach. It became obvious that the recognition of Jewish history would not only do justice to it but disturb the construction of world history that still had Christianity as its backbone.[61]

This resurgence of expressing Judaism's irreducible role and its particular historical vocation was not restricted to the followers of the emerging positive-historical school. Heine, Geiger and Philippson insisted on the existence of a rich and vibrant post-biblical Jewish culture and directly assaulted Christian scholarship for its biased treatment of Second Temple Judaism in particular and its overall disregard of Jewish scholarship. Their ambition was not exhausted by a reevaluation of Jewish history. In the shadow of the Jewish past, a continuous historical vocation of Judaism in the present and future emerged.

In his dissertation *Was hat Mohammed aus dem Judentume aufgenommen?* (What did Mohammed adopt from Judaism?) in 1833, Geiger argued that Islam did not develop from sectarian Christian movements in Arabia. Rather, Islam came from rabbinic Judaism, which helped to emphasize Judaism's postbiblical historical impact.[62] Similarly, Heine reclaimed Judaism's irreducible role when he revised the commonly assumed direction in the process of the integration of German Jews into European societies: "But it is not Germany alone that possesses the features of Palestine. The rest of Europe too raises itself to the level of the Jews. I say raises itself—for even in the beginning, the Jews bore within them the modern principles which only now are visibly unfolding among the nations of Europe."[63] Judaism thus encapsulated already all the elements of modernity, while Europe still had to follow suit. Ludwig Philippson powerfully expressed a similar notion in 1847. For Philippson, Judaism not only represented a rich past but also provided the blueprint for the ideal modern state and the solution to the social question. Jewish history was also seen as a central element of world history beyond the biblical period.[64]

Despite these advances in the scholarly elucidation of the Jewish past, German universities did not endorse the idea of chairs for Jewish studies. In 1836 Abraham Geiger tried to rally support behind a Jewish faculty at a German university.[65] Calling on both the Christian and Jewish public, Geiger proposed that the resources could be gathered from a soon-to-be-founded society in commemoration of Maimonides' 700th birthday. Geiger posited that Jewish theology could maintain its rank as a scholarly discipline solely in independent institutions dedicated to the free pursuit of knowledge.[66] In 1842 Julius Fürst's initiative followed, which envisioned the establishment of a chair for Jewish studies at the University of Leipzig where he taught Oriental studies.[67] In 1848 Zunz's attempt to secure a faculty chair for Jewish studies at the University of Berlin failed when the commission turned down his request. In a possibly intentional misreading of Zunz's proposal, the commission rejected the plan by claiming the university was not the place to educate rabbis and strengthen Jewish parochialism. Since Jews ceased having a state, their history would be taught across the established disciplines such as theology, classical studies, and cultural studies.[68]

In contrast to these initiatives, Ludwig Philippson launched in 1837 a public campaign for the establishment of a Jewish theological seminary. He envisioned an institution devoted to scholarly studies in combination with a seminary for the education of rabbis and teachers. Not affiliated with a German university, this faculty was to be financed by an endowment of 100,000 thaler.[69] According to Philippson's report, the appeal evoked an immediate response among Christians as well as in Jewish circles. He was pleased to see that the influential Paris daily, *Journal des Débats,* the Protestant newspapers *Universal-Kirchen Zeitung* of Frankfurt am Main and the *Hamburger Correspondent* carried favorable articles. Moreover, Abraham Geiger joined the fray with a second publication, *Ueber die Errichtung einer jüdisch-theologischen Facultät* (On the establishment of a Jewish theological faculty), and enlisted noted Reform rabbis like Samuel Holdheim, Salomon Herxheimer, Meyer Isler, and Immanuel Wolf in this campaign.[70] Despite the initial success, during which more than 1,700 donors made their pledges, only 13,000 thaler were raised. Most of the Jewish communities remained indifferent to this project or may have rescinded their participation because they were fearful of governmental disapproval.[71] With the exception of Heinrich Heine's uncle, Salomon Heine, who contributed one thousand thaler, other Jewish bankers like the Frankfurt Rothschilds gave nothing. Because it lacked the financial backing of wealthy Jewish families and the larger communities like Berlin, Hamburg, and Frankfurt, the project was doomed.

Efforts to institutionalize Jewish historiography were thus frustrated by the increasing fragmentation of Jewish scholarship and communities, as well as the disregard displayed by German academia. With most of the newly founded periodicals having folded, Jewish historians operated in a highly charged, divisive and, ultimately, fairly limited Jewish public sphere. These historians had not acquired the position of the unchallenged arbiters in debates over religious and cultural renewal. For Jewish historians to gain a lasting foothold in the emerging German Jewish culture, they would have to find an institutional home and establish Jewish historical studies also as an educational force. Despite these shortcomings, Jewish historians like Geiger and Graetz had not only defended the centrality of the historical approach against competing disciplines but also underscored Judaism's particularism. They had overcome Dohm's legacy that portrayed Jewish history in the Diaspora as an aberration and instead emphasized development and change over break and discontinuity.

Whereas Jewish scholarship remained embroiled in public disputes, Jewish historians during the next decades appealed to a broader reading public. Established within rabbinical seminaries, historians moreover softened the radical historicizing of Judaism. Lacking a substantial academic readership and wary of the internal disintegration of the communities, Wissenschaft's scholars turned to history as an educational tool to reshape modern Jewish identities and to create a new unity among the conflicting denominations. As we shall see, while the divisions between the historians reached a high point and were intensified by bitter debates with Christian scholars, the creation of Jewish book clubs facilitated during the next decades a lasting and fairly diversified reception of Jewish scholarship.

PART 2

FISSURES AND UNITY

4

Jewish Historiography at the Center of Debate

The revolution of 1848–49 failed to carry out the legislative emancipation of the Jews in the German lands. Overall, Jews had to wait until the 1860s and even the 1870s before their legal emancipation was fully completed. Nevertheless, the post-1848 era marks some important innovations in German Jewish history. Concurrent with German Jews' prominent participation in the Frankfurt Parliament, Jewish political activism manifested itself in calls for democratic community structures. The unequivocal emancipation the Frankfurt Parliament had promised also threatened to unravel the existing state framework for religious life by replacing compulsory membership in the communities with voluntary alliances. In an editorial in the *Allgemeine*, Ludwig Philippson regarded the complete suspension of all state influences on communal affairs and unconditional independence of communities and individuals as a "dangerous gift," should they be used to destroy communal bonds.[1]

Responding to this potential danger, Philippson suggested in 1848 to form a synod to unify German Jewry. Such a body seemed necessary to counter the increasing religious indifference among German Jews. For Philippson, a synod was desperately needed when considering the "empty houses of worship" and the "communities falling apart." Yet his plan failed to curry sufficient support from community leaders and met the opposition of several Jewish liberals, who regarded a synod as a

49

potential threat to their religious liberties.[2] Nevertheless, Philippson's call to create a representative body of German Jewry was followed by the proposal of the Jewish community of Berlin, which urged the establishment of a central authority for Prussian Jewry.[3] However, Jewish communities' increasing ideological divisions were not conducive to these plans. Fearful of central authority, Jewish historians and religious reformers like Leopold Zunz and Abraham Geiger categorically opposed centralization lest it impinge on the freedom of the individual communities.[4]

The failure to universalize Jewish emancipation and to unite under a new umbrella organization, together with the internal political fragmentation and religious division of the communities, intensified the growing uncertainty. While hopes of finding a home for Jewish scholarship at German universities did not materialize, attempts at erecting Jewish seminaries finally came to fruition. Mirroring the increasing polarization, Jewish scholarship in Germany became institutionalized along denominational lines that ultimately accentuated the already existing friction. In 1854 the *Jüdisch-Theologische Seminar* opened in Breslau, followed in 1872 by the *Hochschule für die Wissenschaft des Judentums* and the *Rabbiner Seminar für das Orthodoxe Judentum* in Berlin in 1873. None of these institutions devoted themselves solely to scholarship; they also provided modern education for rabbis and teachers. Together with the Jewish press, these seminaries presented the different parties with powerful platforms for religious debates, public discussions, and scholarly polemics that intensified the fragmentation of Jewish scholarship.

Notwithstanding the sometimes highly charged exchanges, several Jewish historians abandoned their previous elitist self-understanding and aimed to educate a broad readership about the Jewish past. These new efforts at fostering modern Jewish identities by popularizing works about the Jewish past were reflective of the larger process of renewal, indicative of the post-revolution period. While during the revolution German Jews often emphatically expressed their patriotism, the years after this event witnessed a conscious surge in the formation of a new German Jewish culture.[5] In line with this cultural reorientation, Jewish book clubs emerged that created a fairly diversified audience at a time when differences among scholars became even more cemented with the foundation of the rabbinical seminars.

In Breslau, in accordance with the will of the wealthy merchant and philanthropist Jonas Fraenkel, a seminary for the education of rabbis and teachers was founded, which furthered the connection between

Jewish historiography and the modern rabbinate.[6] When the modern rabbinical seminary in Breslau opened in 1854, it had secured some of the most outspoken representatives of the positive-historical approach, including the director Zacharias Frankel, Heinrich Graetz, and the renowned philologist and classicist Jacob Bernays. By 1879 the seminary had instructed a total of 272 students and succeeded in placing its graduates as teachers, preachers, and rabbis in some of the most important Jewish communities throughout Europe.[7]

Closely associated with Breslau was the prestigious journal *Monatsschrift für Geschichte und Wissenschaft des Judenthums* founded by Frankel in 1851. In his introduction to the first volume, Frankel emphasized the need for a new scholarly journal in light of the preceding decade's domination by religious-political journals in which "weapons" were raised. In contrast, Frankel understood Wissenschaft as a means to unite and transform the debate and to revitalize an interest in Judaism.[8] Accordingly, the *Monatsschrift* contained a more popular section titled "History" for the lay audience that included biographical essays chiefly about early rabbinic sages in addition to its scholarly content. Frankel realized that without a lay audience, the journal would have had barely one hundred subscribers.[9] In addition to the *Monatsschrift,* the Conservative camp founded the weekly newspaper *Israelitische Wochenschrift* (1870–94) to represent the party of the middle and forge a new united modern Jewry.[10]

Despite the widespread desire to overcome existing differences, the polarization of German Jewry and scholarship was furthered by the convention of a synod on June 29, 1869, in Leipzig, where 83 rabbis, religious leaders, and scholars came together under the chairmanship of Moritz Lazarus with the goal to overcome religious disunity. They had sought to reconcile the oppositional voices and to unite modern Jewry in their shared religious beliefs as well as in their common past. Yet aligned with the Reform movement, the synod resulted in no concerted action and failed to create a permanent central institution that would represent German Jewry.[11]

The proposal to establish a Jewish seminary with an alternative religious-ideological program only contributed to the existing religious conflicts. Ludwig Philippson once more utilized his resources and supported this effort. In a series of articles, he called upon the pride of the Berlin Jewish community, which could not see itself bereft of an institution of higher education when other German communities were establishing such seminaries.[12] When the Hochschule finally opened as an autonomous body, its instructors were required to abide only by the interests of scholarship and to preserve, develop, and disseminate *Wissenschaft des Judentums*.[13]

The *Hochschule für die Wissenschaft des Judenthums* nevertheless became largely associated with the Reform movement, especially after Abraham Geiger took up his post as a professor. In order to increase its public impact, the Hochschule organized lectures for the laity. In the *Jüdische Zeitschrift für Wissenschaft und Leben,* edited by Geiger beginning in 1866, Reform-oriented scholars had their own publication in addition to the *Allgemeine,* which continued to align itself with the cause of the Reform movement.

In addition to these institutions, another modern rabbinical seminary was founded in 1873 in Berlin under the leadership of Esriel Hildesheimer, whose faculty included David Zvi Hoffmann, Abraham Berliner, and Jacob Barth. Like the other institutions, this seminary set out to advance modern historical research as well as religious life.[14] While the seminary was neo-Orthodox in outlook, Hildesheimer insisted that the students be acquainted with the scientific method.[15] In propagating the neo-Orthodox platform, he relied on the *Jüdische Presse,* founded in 1870, which had a monthly literature supplement and, later, a popular scientific one, the *Israelitische Monatsschrift.* Moreover, neo-Orthodox scholars also published their articles in periodicals like the *Magazin für jüdische Geschichte und Literatur,* which also contained the Hebrew supplement *Ozar Tov* (Good treasure).[16]

Despite their differences, all three institutions aligned themselves with Wissenschaft, which had finally become the arena in which discussion and polemics were carried out. In respect to the Breslau seminary, Philippson remained mostly silent and did not use the *Allgemeine* to support or attack the institution. If he reported at all on the seminary, his articles were usually short and fairly muted.[17] Nevertheless, the institutions also became objects of conflicting debates. Prior to the opening, published inquiries from a member of the neo-Orthodox community demanded an explanation about the seminary's theological tendencies. The fact that Breslau was not only a scholarly institution but a place for the education of rabbis and teachers greatly antagonized the neo-Orthodox camp. The mixing of scholarship and religion was understood as impinging upon both scholarship and the Jewish religion.[18] Furthermore, rumors circulated in the press indicating that the Breslau professors had *yein nesekh* (nonkosher wine) served to them by Christians during the initial examination of potential students.[19] Equally, the Hochschule in Berlin brought out scornful neo-Orthodox

criticism.[20] For the proponents of neo-Orthodoxy, there was no significant difference between the Breslau seminary and the Hochschule.[21]
Esriel Hildesheimer considered the Hochschule an institution of destruction. In an 1873 circular eliciting support for the foundation of a
rabbinical seminary, he cited Psalm 137:7 in reference to the Hochschule: "Raze it, raze it to its very foundation."[22]

The Breslau seminary became furthermore the object of traditionalist opposition led by Samson Raphael Hirsch, who condemned modern
Jewish scholarship and responded to the *Monatsschrift* and the Breslau
seminary with the periodical *Jeschurun* (1854–70). Hirsch's severe opposition did not entail a total neglect of Jewish history on the part of neo-
Orthodoxy. For Hirsch, as he explained in his prospectus to *Jeschurun*,
the periodical was devoted to those publications that regarded the rabbinical traditions as the only legitimate basis of Judaism. Continuing in
the didactic Enlightenment model of historical writing, he advocated
the discussion of institutions of Judaism and great figures from the past
as the real form of Wissenschaft.[23] Toward this end, the neo-Orthodox
camp led by Hirsch founded, in 1860, a more successful periodical in the
Israelit, edited by Marcus Lehmann. Lehmann felt the need to include
"small, appealing stories and descriptions about the Jewish past and
present."[24] The *Israelit* regarded Jewish history as the realm in which
God's providence manifested itself and was, therefore, an important educational tool. It was for this reason that neo-Orthodox scholars complained about the absence of a properly written history of the Jews in
the spirit of their tradition.[25]

The neo-Orthodox opposition against Jewish scholars was, therefore, not directed at the field of Jewish history per se, but more often at
the religious affiliation of the historians and their denial of the divine
revelation of the written and oral traditions. Hirsch in particular looked
askance at Jewish historians because they subordinated Jewish customs
to the critical tools of Wissenschaft without contributing to the preservation of them. Understanding himself as the sole defender of the Jewish tradition, Hirsch mockingly imitated the modern historians in a
sermon on Tisha be-Av in 1855: "We let the old Jews fast and pray *Seli-
hot* and cry *Kinot* on Tisha be-Av. We, however, know much better than
they do in which centuries these 'poets' blossomed. . . . We carry such
an admiration for this Jewish antiquity in our hearts so much that we
raise all the dust in the libraries and collections in order to spot the
dates of birth and death of these authors and to register correctly the
inscription on their tombstones. We take care that now, as the old

Judaism is carried to its grave, at least its memory is kept alive in histories of literature."[26]

Thus for Hirsch, modern scholarship only weakened Jewish identities and replaced religious practice and devotion with flimsy historical knowledge. Yet even among the most prominent Jewish scholars, the openings of the seminary in Breslau and the Hochschule in Berlin were not enthusiastically embraced. The Breslau graduate Adolf Kohut published a vitriolic satirical account of the seminary in which he mocked the institution as a Jesuit college. He ridiculed the alleged self-elevation of Frankel and mocked Graetz as a falsifier of Jewish history.[27] Moritz Steinschneider maintained that scientific research within the confines of rabbinical institutions was limiting and, therefore, the only proper place for Jewish historians was the university.[28] Against the theological premise of many Jewish scholars, he founded his own periodical, the *Hebräische Bibliographie* (1858–82), which ostensibly devoted itself exclusively to scholarship.[29] Zunz also failed to support the institutions and even purposely stayed away from the opening ceremony of the Hochschule.[30]

With these divisions in place, every major scholarly publication during these decades became immediately embroiled in public debates. In 1857 Abraham Geiger published his *Urschrift und Uebersetzung der Bibel* (The original writing and translation of the Bible) in which he set out to show how the biblical text developed and changed over time in response to political and religious challenges. In a highly innovative fashion, Geiger linked political and religious history of the Second Temple period. For him, the history of this time was powered by the antagonism of two religious parties: the priestly aristocratic Sadducees and the middle class Pharisees. Based on this assumption, Geiger suggested that the Bible was formed by the struggle between these two entities. Accordingly, he regarded the Bible as a living text whose content was shaped and reconfigured in the course of its history.[31]

While several Christian scholars favorably reviewed Geiger's *Urschrift*, Leopold Zunz remained indecisive.[32] Leopold Löw criticized the central thesis but nevertheless regarded the book as a major scholarly achievement.[33] The prestigious *Monatsschrift*, however, did not even bother to review Geiger's book at the time of its publication. It was not until 1871 that Heinrich Graetz attacked it in an anonymous review. Graetz's review was so harsh that even the editors distanced themselves from the style of the review, if not from its content. For Zacharias Frankel the *Urschrift* was simply a "book of shame" *(Schandbuch)*.[34] Viewing

Geiger's *Urschrift* as tantamount to a denial of the divine origins of the Bible, Hildesheimer cited from scripture: "Because thou has joined thyself with Ahazyahu, the Lord will destroy what thou has done."[35]

Similarly, Geiger's *Das Judenthum und seine Geschichte* (Judaism and its history) became the target of severe controversy.[36] When Geiger published his lectures, Christian scholars, rather than Jewish historians, fiercely attacked him. In his review of *Das Judenthum und seine Geschichte*, Heinrich Julius Holtzmann, a Heidelberg professor, characterized the book as a mixture of Jewish polemics and apologetics, although he was surprised to find a book from the "mouth of a rabbi" so clearly written. Holtzmann was most outraged by Geiger's attempt to discredit the originality of the Christian faith.[37] Heinrich Ewald also rejected Geiger's claims and disregarded the book, as did the liberal theologian Ludwig Diestel, who was horrified by Geiger's alleged glorification of Judaism.[38] In the *Allgemeine Kirchenzeitung*, Geiger's understanding of Jesus' Jewish background was attacked as excising the flesh of Christ "with Shylockian exactitude."[39]

Throughout this time, Zacharias Frankel continued his work on the history of Halakhah. With the publication of *Darkhe ha-Mishnah* (The ways of the Mishnah), he too provoked a major controversy. Utilizing both Jewish and non-Jewish sources, Frankel contended that the Mishnah was the result of an almost seven-hundred-year development stretching from Ezra in the fifth century C.E. to Judah Ha-Nasi, the redactor of the Mishnah, in the third century C.E. Frankel conceptualized the growth of Halakhah as resulting from newly emerging circumstances. He regarded those laws that were neither related to the Bible nor to logical inference — traditionally referred to as *halakhah le-moshe mi-sinai* (law given to Moses at Sinai) — as later creations.[40]

While Geiger considered Frankel's *Darkhe ha-Mishnah* the work of a highly ambivalent scholar, Samson Raphael Hirsch engaged in an embittered assault on Frankel.[41] In the eyes of Hirsch, Frankel had denied the divine origin of the Oral Law by turning it into the work of men and the product of changing circumstances. For Esriel Hildesheimer, *Darkhe ha-Mishnah* was the work of a *meshumad* (apostate); he exclaimed that it would be a religious duty to burn the book had it not contained God's name.[42] Even when pressed by Hirsch, Frankel refused to deliver the dogmatic confession of the divine origin of all Jewish law, and stated only that his work was filled with love and loyalty and that he had demonstrated the antiquity of the halakhic system in a critical and scientific way.[43] In the ensuing dispute, Hermann Cohen, then a young student at the Breslau seminary, expressed his support for Frankel in a private letter, while others rallied behind the director of the Breslau seminary in the Jewish press.[44] Frankel received further backing from the Austrian rabbi and scholar Solomon Judah Rapoport. Despite these interventions, Hirsch could not be silenced. [45]

Similarly, the work of Heinrich Graetz became the object of criticism and scornful reviews. When in 1856 Graetz published the third volume of his history of the Jews, covering the period up until the destruction of the Second Temple, the publishers persuaded him to omit the chapter about the origins of Christianity.[46] His former teacher, Samson Raphael Hirsch, was furious about Graetz's attempt to explain the development of Jewish law from the biographies of rabbis.[47] If Hirsch attacked him for his historical approach, more Reform-minded scholars criticized Graetz's adulation of the Talmudic period.[48] Other reviewers like Abraham Geiger, Moritz Steinschneider, and Meir Wiener accused Graetz of alleged self-aggrandizement, plagiarism, and disrespectful treatment of scholars like Leopold Zunz.[49] Moreover, Geiger stepped in and declared that Graetz's narrative lacked a unifying thrust and that Graetz's history was not a product of "real historical research or historical writing" but rather loosely connected stories *(Geschichten)*.[50]

When in 1863 Graetz vividly expressed his concept of constant Jewish rejuvenation he became the target of a lawsuit. In his article, Graetz argued that the return from the Babylonian exile was evidence of the Jews' perseverance. Graetz viewed this period, which Christian scholars regarded as one of decline and fossilization of Judaism, rather as a time of cultural creativity. He believed that the frequently cited expression "suffering servant of the Lord" in Deutero-Isaiah buttressed his reading. Assuming that an unknown postexilic author had written Second Isaiah, Graetz interpreted Isaiah 53 in line with many traditional Jewish commentators as referring not to an individual messiah but to the people of Israel. Moreover, he pointed to the prophesies of Isaiah to underscore that the suffering of the Jewish people was instrumental in their salvation.[51]

Upon the publication of this essay, an attack appeared in the anti-Semitic *Wiener Kirchenzeitung*. Consequently, the Viennese public prosecutor charged the editor of the yearbook *Jahrbuch für Israeliten*, Leopold Kompert, with contradicting the teachings of Judaism and violating Catholic sensibilities. Graetz purportedly had offended Judaism, an officially recognized religion, by denying one of its fundamental principles. In addition, Graetz was accused of having offended Christianity when he posited that the Christian interpretation of the "suffering servant of the Lord" as referring to a single person reduced biblical prophesies to a caricature.

During the trial deliberations, the question was raised as to whether a schism or sect existed within Judaism and if, therefore, Graetz had or had not slandered a state-protected religion. The two expert witnesses, Isaac Noah Mannheimer and Lazar Horowitz, strongly denied claims of a schism and explained that the differences within modern Jewry were insignificant. Rather, Mannheimer and Horowitz argued, a slight gradation existed between lenient and strictly observant Jews. In addition to these witnesses, the defense had collected written testimonies from Solomon Rapoport, Zacharias Frankel, and Heinrich Graetz. However, their statements were not utilized; Kompert was acquitted on the first count of slandering an officially recognized religion and convicted for the lack of oversight in the publication of his yearbook.[52]

The conflicting testimonies and contributions highlight the extent to which religious polarizations threatened to unravel Jewish self-understanding. In their defense of Kompert, Mannheimer and Horowitz had, in effect, muddled the definition of a Jew. In a wide-ranging public debate, neo-Orthodox leaders not only took offense at Graetz's assertion of a postexilic Isaiah but also emphasized that there was only one definition of Judaism that encapsulated the written and oral laws and, thereby, also the messianic hope.[53] Esriel Hildesheimer immediately enlisted the support of more than one hundred rabbis, who exclaimed that whoever denied a fundamental principle of Judaism rejected the whole Sinaitic revelation.[54] Similarly, Samson Raphael Hirsch agitated against the diluted definition of Judaism and asserted that the acceptance of the written and oral traditions defined Judaism. Hirsch maintained that whoever denied a fundamental principle had essentially left Judaism.[55]

The debate illustrates that the results of Jewish scholarship were not simply of antiquarian interest but touched the very core of the self-understanding of the various Jewish groups. While *Der Israelit,* unlike *Jeschurun,* refrained from viewing Reform and Conservative Judaism as independent sects, both periodicals nevertheless clearly posited that a schism existed within Judaism.[56] By contrast, Ludwig Philippson was in full agreement with Graetz's interpretation of Isaiah 53 and refused to understand Reform Judaism as an independent sect.[57]

It is not coincidental that this public debate arose in response to the messianic belief and the interpretation of Isaiah. Biblical criticism, the denial of the binding nature of Oral Law, and the reinterpretation of messianic hopes merged in Graetz's historical interpretation. Periodicals like *Der Israelit* and *Jeschurun* restated the traditional belief in the personal messiah.[58] It is against the background of these discussions that Graetz once more published an article in Kompert's yearbook that surveyed the historical evolution of Jewish messianism.[59]

With the publication of Graetz's eleventh volume covering the modern period starting with Mendelssohn, the Reform-oriented scholars rallied against him. Denouncing Reform Judaism, Graetz used Heine's terminology and called David Friedländer, the disciple of Mendelssohn, a *"Hühneraugenoperateur"* (corn remover), whose only function was to remove blemishes and superficial accretions from Judaism. Turning Steinheim, Börne, and Heine into the heroes of modern Jewish history provided Graetz with an opportunity to highlight the ongoing historical vocation of Judaism even in the modern period. Thus Graetz quoted a frequently cited passage from Heine in which the poet introduced the idea of the affinity between Germans and Jews: "Striking, indeed, is the deep affinity which prevails between these two ethical nations, Jews and Germans. . . . Fundamentally, the two peoples are alike, —so much alike, that one might regard the Palestine of the past as an oriental Germany, just as one may regard the Germany of today as the home of the Holy Word, the mother-soil of prophecy, the citadel of pure spirituality." In line with Heine, Graetz argued that it was upon Europe to raise itself to the level of Judaism. Graetz believed that Börne and Heine were the key messengers of Judaism's mission and that they exemplified its ability to be a "light unto the nations."[60]

Even before the *Berliner Antisemitismusstreit* (Berlin anti-Semitic debate), Graetz's version of modern Jewish history antagonized both Jews and non-Jews alike. Geiger declared that those who devoted a chapter to the life of Heine in a history of Judaism were not true historians of Judaism.[61] Ludwig Philippson assailed Graetz for his partisan portrayal of Reform Judaism and consequently rejected volume eleven for publication by the Institute for the Promotion of Jewish Literature, which had previously published several volumes of Graetz's history.[62] Moreover, prior to the Berlin debate, scholars of German literature at Breslau University attacked Graetz in the German press for his disrespectful depiction of German cultural icons like Johann Wolfgang Goethe, Johann Gottlieb Fichte, and Friedrich Schleiermacher.[63]

As these debates took shape, they aggravated not only the various scholarly camps but also the Jewish communities at large. The internal disunity together with the delayed emancipation triggered a sense of uncertainty about the future of Jewish life that increasingly marred the delineation of Judaism's essence in a purely historical fashion. In response to these challenges and obstacles, Jewish historians like Geiger and Graetz balanced the application of the historical method in their understanding of Judaism and embedded their narratives in theological rhetoric. Especially Graetz and Geiger emphasized the particularistic aspect of Judaism, and, unlike the members of the Verein, wrote works that provided guidance for a Jewish audience, thereby imparting pride about the common heritage and Judaism's historical vocation.

5

"Bringing Forth Their Past Glories"

In the late 1840s and early 1850s, Jewish historians were fairly optimistic about the internal cultural transformation of German Jewry. During this time, Isaac Jost used the term *Neuzeit* to describe the period after 1750, a time he considered a "sunrise" within the historical process. Jost believed in the imminence of emancipation and cultural renewal.[1] Similarly, Heinrich Graetz in his 1846 work *Die Construktion der jüdischen Geschichte* (The construction of Jewish history) revealed his anticipation when, in a Hegelian maneuver, he divided Jewish history into three periods, each made up of three cycles. Graetz split the past into ancient, medieval, and modern Jewish history, and established a dialectical relation of succession between them. For him, Mendelssohn's era, of which Graetz was a part, formed the last cycle in the third period. The completion of the historical formation of Judaism's idea was, therefore, close at hand.[2]

In 1856, when Graetz set out to write a full-length history of the Jews, he cautiously reconceptualized Jewish history by parsing it into four epochs. In this new arrangement, the modern times formed an independent period in which the era beginning with Mendelssohn formed the first cycle. Upon the completion of his *Geschichte der Juden* in the 1870s, Graetz had described Jewish history until 1848. Yet Jewish history had not advanced from the first cycle of the fourth period.[3]

The same transformation can also be observed in the work of Leo-pold Zunz, who had originally welcomed the new age with almost mes-sianic expectation. Zunz's messianic rhetoric was significantly altered in the second half of the nineteenth century. During the 1848 revolution, Zunz still fervently believed in the progress of the democratic cause, and his letters once again contained references to the messianic age. His hopes were, however, dashed after the Prussian-Austrian war of 1866, during which the German liberals lost ground.[4] After the war, Zunz no longer saw current history as heralding the messianic age but hoped in-stead that the messianic age would put an end to the horrifying devel-opments of the nineteenth century.[5] At this point, Zunz's messianic ref-erences contain what Nahum Glatzer has rightly called an "outright apocalyptic pessimism."[6]

The growing apprehension intensified in light of the delayed eman-cipation, the cultural and religious changes and the internal fragmen-tation. Zacharias Frankel captured the rapid transformation when he referred to the "stormy movements of the present" in 1852.[7] The experi-ence of the internal disintegration of the Jewish communities led Abra-ham Geiger to regard the present as a time of decomposition.[8] This ap-prehension intensified during the next decades and profoundly shaped the writing and popularization of Jewish history.

After the failure to achieve universal emancipation in 1848, Jewish periodicals featured reviews of the past years. While up until 1848 con-temporary time progressed on a clearly charted and feverishly antici-pated course, it soon became a source of confusion and frustration. The return to a policy of gradual emancipation provided only equivocal signs of progress. As late as the 1860s, the majority of Jews were still subject to some legal restrictions in the Germanic lands. Whereas Prussian reac-tionaries had blocked attempts at full legal emancipation, the city-state of Hamburg granted Jews full citizenship in 1860. These contradictory developments made it increasingly difficult to attribute prognostic functions to the past and present. As one reader of the *Allgemeine* quoted from *Hamlet* in 1852, "time is out of joint."[9]

An article published in the *Allgemeine* in the 1850s titled "Das vorige und das gegenwärtige Jahrhundert" (The previous and the current cen-turies) reveals that the eighteenth century functioned as the space of ex-perience, whereas the nineteenth century marked the horizon of expec-tation. The article notes that "the previous century was the century of promise, and the current century is the century of fulfillment." This hopeful comparison, however, was dimmed when the author discovered that these promises were wrecked because cultural development in Germany was at a standstill, Judaism was internally fragmented, and religiosity was on the decline.[10] In another leading *Allgemeine* article "Unser Jahrhundert" (Our century), which appeared in 1870, the eighteenth century is seen as having had "one thought, one ambition, one act," whereas the nineteenth century is still in a process of creative fermentation.[11] Moreover, many new compound nouns highlighting the obsession with the present time came into use in the second half of the nineteenth century, including *"Zeitlage"* (condition of time), *"Zeitfrage"* (question of time), *"Zeitbetrachtung"* (observation of time), *"Jetztzeit"* (present time), and *"Zeitschäden"* (damages of time).[12]

When Isaac Jost set out in the 1850s to write his *Geschichte des Judentums und seiner Secten* (History of Judaism and its sects), the question of the Jewish essence, therefore, had already markedly changed. True, Jost once more attempted to comprehend the essence of Judaism and to understand its transformation "in light of the sad destinies of its believers, inner growth, and influences through the general progress of mankind." Yet the delineation of this essence was already obstructed by an uncertain future. Jost, in contrast to his earlier histories, was unable to narrate Jewish history "up to the present." In this book, however, he observed that the historical development was still active and could, therefore, not be summarized.[13] Similarly, Graetz ended his description with the year 1848 when he completed the eleventh volume in 1870.[14] Thus a widening gap between narrated history and present time emerged.

The growing uncertainty about the essence of Judaism not only fundamentally impacted the way Jewish historians looked at their contemporary time but also the function they ascribed to Jewish scholarship. Whereas Jewish scholarship was originally meant to reveal the true nature of Judaism, from the 1850s on various scholars augmented this agenda by focusing on the popularization of Jewish history in order to counter the impact of religious decline and internal fragmentation. Historical novels appeared in greater numbers after Ludwig Philippson's brother, Phöbus Philippson, serialized *Die Marranen* in the *Allgemeine* in 1837. Unlike other writers of historical novels, Ludwig Philippson clearly differentiated between literature and scholarship and asserted the right of poetic representation of the Jewish past. In his introduction to a collection of novels entitled *Saron* (1843), he put forth that the literary treatment of Jewish history was meant to "refine" and "rejuvenate" both Jews and Judaism.[15] Most likely in response to the success of Ludwig Philippson's historical novels, the neo-Orthodox writer Marcus Lehmann turned to the same genre to combat Reform Judaism.[16]

Equally, within Jewish scholarship there was a conscious effort to recover Jewish history in order to reshape Jewish identities. Alongside the fiery debates about their scholarship, these historians nevertheless aimed at the same time to create a basis for a new self-understanding of German Jews. Jewish scholarship thus became marked by its partisanship and the desire to bridge the apparent disunity. Whereas the Haskalah aimed to overcome the Ashkenazic heritage, the past now became the object of recovery. After the publication of Jost's history of the Jews, Heinrich Graetz's *Geschichte der Juden* represented an artfully crafted balance between source-oriented research and philosophical constructions. Graetz's *Geschichte* was a break from stable conceptions of essence. The potentially atomizing tendency of a comprehensive historical understanding of Judaism was kept in check by a subtle dialectical construction and dramatic representation of Jewish history. For Graetz, the Jews had emerged from the night of the grave ruins *(Grabesnacht)*, "rubbing their eyes, . . . searching to restore their memory and bringing forth their past glories."[17] In this sense, Graetz believed Jewish scholarship was instrumental in the recovery of the past that would lead to a new self-consciousness. For Graetz, Jewish scholarship thus had become primarily a work of recollection and memory construction, which at least rhetorically veiled the novelty of the scholarly inquiry.[18]

Suffering was not understood traditionally as God's punishment. Nor was it viewed as pointless chains of sorrow providing only an explanation for a process of perceived cultural degradation. For these Jewish historians, the history of suffering was imminently important because it vindicated the Jews and illustrated their moral victory in moments of defeat.[19] Zunz's introduction to his 1855 *Die synagogale Poesie des Mittelalters* (The poetry of the synagogue in the Middle Ages), titled "Leiden" (Suffering), spanned from the triumph of Christianity to the Reformation and summarized the experience of the Jews during these centuries: "If there is a ladder of suffering, then Israel has reached the top. If the span of pain and the patience with which it is borne ennoble [the sufferer], then Jews surely are a match for the nobility of any land."[20] Heinrich Graetz summed up the essence of Jewish history in a similar fashion in his introduction to the fourth volume of his *Geschichte* (1853): "To study and wander, to think and endure, to learn and suffer, these are the hallmarks for this long era."[21] While he gave the "lachrymose conception of Jewish history" its formulation in his well-known broad strokes, he provided more than a simple account of endless persecutions. Graetz unequivocally stated that Jews had to endure martyrdom for the sake of their mission.[22] Similarly, for Abraham Geiger, the history of Jewish suffering served to demonstrate the marvelous endurance of Judaism in comparison to other nations that had perished, such as the Greeks and Romans.[23]

If in particular Zunz and Graetz bestowed this new importance on the history of suffering as an integral part of Jewish history, Graetz at the same time turned to those aspects that he regarded as deviations from the core of Judaism. Whereas in his earlier *Die Construktion der jüdischen Geschichte* he comprehended the disparate historical material as part of the unfolding of one idea of Judaism, in the 1850s Graetz confronted manifestations of Judaism that contradicted his eloquent descriptions.

In order to locate the origins of deviations within Judaism, Graetz turned to the Second Temple period. He believed that Christianity emerged from the Essenes, a Jewish sectarian group.[24] While this had been a given in Christian scholarship, Graetz put this interpretation to a radical new use for Jewish history. The scholarly consensus of the nineteenth century was that Essene mysticism originated in Egypt and India. Graetz believed that Jewish mysticism also came out of this context. In this sense, both Christianity and Jewish mysticism distanced themselves from mainstream Pharisaic Judaism. Consequently, Graetz outlined a continuous mystical tradition from the Alexandrian Essenes to the medieval Kabbalists and early modern Hasidim.[25] From this vantage point, Sabbatai Zevi was just another example of the ancient mystical tradition as was Spinoza, who Graetz contended was influenced by the Kabbalah.[26] Moreover, Graetz previously had suggested in his dissertation, *Gnosticismus und Judenthum* (Gnosticism and Judaism), that Reform Judaism was a variation on this theme insofar as it represented a form of "modern pantheism."[27]

Mainstream Pharisaic Judaism, therefore, appeared untainted by mysticism and what Graetz regarded as allegorical quibbling and superstition.[28] While Christianity originated from Judaism, it adopted "foreign elements" and became antagonistic toward its source.[29] Unmarred by these "foreign elements," only the "authentic" Judaism embodied in the modern conservative movement remained faithful to its original content and continued its mission.

Coming to terms with these alleged aberrations from mainstream Judaism, Graetz once again was able to capture Judaism's uninterrupted historical development from antiquity to the present. He, therefore, also rejected the traditional Christian understanding of the destruction of the Second Temple as the termination of Jewish history and emphasized not only the existence of postbiblical history but presented all of Jewish history as a miraculous event. Echoing remarks by German

Enlightenment historians, Graetz underscored the miraculous quality of Jewish history when he wrote of other nations perishing while Judaism always revitalized itself: "Even those who don't believe in miracles must acknowledge the miraculous element in the course of Israel's history. It offers not only the pattern of growth, flowering and decay like the histories of other nations, but also the extraordinary phenomenon that decay is followed by a new process of greening and blossoming and that this rise and decline has occurred three times."[30]

Graetz's reassertion of the divine quality of Jewish history is less idiosyncratic if we remember that also the German historian Leopold von Ranke believed that God's providence was discernible in the unfolding of world history.[31] By presenting Jewish history until his own time as one of exceptional miraculous development, Graetz framed the history of learning and suffering with the notion of God's providence and thereby balanced the novelty of the historical approach with traditional concepts.[32] Moreover, the fact that Graetz stressed the miraculous aspect of Jewish history in his introduction served as a guide to the reader. This feature of Judaism not only provided his *Geschichte* with pervasive appeal but also went to the core of his understanding of the Jewish people as able to rejuvenate themselves.

Whereas Abraham Geiger hesitated during the 1840s to prematurely present the results of Jewish scholarship to a wider readership, he too intentionally addressed "a larger educated audience" in his *Das Judenthum und seine Geschichte*. No longer could the results of Jewish scholarship be held back in "spiritually stirred up times," as he had asserted. In his attempt to reshape modern Jewish identity, Geiger appealed to memory in his lectures on Jewish history. For Geiger, the process of recollection was mediated by the spirit *(Geist)* that sifted through existing memories and selected those elements from the Jewish past that served current needs. In light of this assertion he did not attempt to write a comprehensive history, but selected only those moments from Jewish history that were "great world-historical phenomena."[33]

In his *Das Judenthum und seine Geschichte*, a work originally delivered as a series of lectures in Frankfurt and Berlin between 1863 and 1871, Geiger provided his audience with a historical narrative that stretched from biblical times to the present. In a lengthy discussion of the differences between "talent" and "genius," Geiger posited that an original and genuine creation inaugurated by revelation could not be explained by the cultural context in which it emerged because it is "an elemental force *[Urkraft]* that creates out of itself, without an external impetus." With the Jews' return from exile, this original creative power of revelation was incrementally replaced by tradition.[34] The origin of Judaism is thus clouded by the concept of an original *ex nihilo* beginning, untainted by historical explanation.

Basing his arguments on his findings in his *Urschrift*, Geiger used the conflict between the Pharisees and the Sadducees as a paradigmatic typology on which he also relied to explain the later history of Judaism. Accordingly, Geiger's account of the postbiblical history does not provide a developmental understanding of the content of the essence of Judaism, as Steinschneider rightly pointed out, but an exposition of internal struggles.[35] For Geiger, the essence resided in the biblical prophetic religion. Thus modern Judaism was not the outcome of a long historical process that began in Sinai, but rather one that had already achieved its utmost rational expression at the end of the Second Temple period. Geiger's history chronicled, therefore, the extent to which the biblical revelation was expressed throughout the ages. He was not interested in delineating the historical circumstances that brought biblical revelation into being or its historical transformation. In his lectures, he pointed to Judaism's essence in its historical forms of expression and to the status of this essence among the Jews and throughout the world. In this respect, the sociological perspective helped Geiger offset the otherwise radical historization of Judaism. What changed in the course of history was not the idea but its expression. Moreover, Geiger placed Jesus within the tradition of the Pharisees and thereby undermined the originality of the founder of Christianity. Not unlike Graetz, he posited that Christianity succumbed to paganism under Paul and betrayed its Jewish origin. Asserting Judaism's irreducible role in the modern world, Geiger charged that modernity was not Christian and Christianity not modern.[36]

Jewish historians' effort to reconceptualize their own craft and to appeal to a wider audience was augmented when Emanuel Hecht published in 1855 a textbook titled *Israels Geschichte von der Zeit des Bibel-Abschlusses bis zur Gegenwart* (Israel's history from the time of the completion of the Bible to the present). In fast-paced narratives, the textbook relates the history of the Jews from the end of the Second Temple period up to the present and includes short excerpts from sources. Hecht quoted Jewish historians verbatim and brought together "that which according to time does not belong together" in order to highlight the larger historical development. Accordingly, he placed a chapter on "Famous Scholars" out of sequence between the Middle Ages and the modern period. The chapter features Jewish luminaries from the

Iberian peninsula immediately next to Rashi and concludes with the false messiah Sabbatai Zevi and the apostates Baruch Spinoza and Uriel Acosta.[37]

Hecht created a "sublime image of our ancestors" to endear the Jewish heritage to its youth. Following the missionary theory, Hecht considered the destruction of the Second Temple not as a calamity but as a circumstance that enabled the Jews to carry out their vocation as evidenced by Judaism's role in the emergence of Islam. With the Christianization of the Roman Empire however, the end of the Jewish civil *(bürgerliche)* happiness had been reached. Following this assumption, Hecht viewed the Middle Ages in a lachrymose fashion. For him, the historical sources of this period read like the "diary of a hangman." The emergence of Mendelssohn inaugurated a period of rejuvenation that led to the work of Reform Judaism. For Hecht, the annals of history testified to God's providence and leadership.[38]

These initial efforts were quickly augmented, when writers like Leopold Kompert and Aron Bernstein nostalgically recalled the Ghetto, and Jewish scholars began to scrutinize popular Jewish culture.[39] The new attention paid to folk culture represented a highly innovative approach that may be seen in part as a response to the difficulties in describing the elusive essence of Judaism. Moritz Steinschneider, who was critical of meshing theology with history, defined the distinctiveness of Judaism with respect to its national literature. This literature included not only exegetical and philosophical treatises but folk literature as well, which formed the "spirit of the nation."[40]

Following along similar lines, Abraham Berliner chronicled daily culture. Berliner recovered a rapidly disappearing past and was, like Geiger, Philippson, and Graetz, concerned with the preservation of historical memory. Berliner strongly maintained an internal perspective on Judaism that led him to publish *Aus dem inneren Leben der deutschen Juden im Mittelalter* (From the internal life of the Jews in the Middle Ages) in 1871. His contribution was praised not only in the *Israelitische Wochenschrift* but also in the *Allgemeine*, which lauded the work's innovative approach and regarded it as highly educational and entertaining.[41]

For neo-Orthodox scholars, Berliner's study of Jewish medieval daily culture, including education, the celebration of the Sabbath, card and board games, and popular songs, provided a way to describe the uniqueness of Judaism by leaving the lofty question of its essence untouched. Originally delivered as lectures to the neo-Orthodox society *Sephat Emet* (Words of truth), Berliner's work aimed to present medieval

Jewish history in a scholarly yet nostalgic fashion. For Berliner, the customs he described were part of a culture that had already passed yet deserved to be saved from oblivion. His study was thus an attempt to turn back to the past to "eavesdrop on our ancestors in their art of life." Moreover, this approach provided Berliner with the "particular pleasure to be able to point in this work to the happier sides of Jewish life during the Middle Ages," a time typically depicted as brutal and violent. His analysis of daily life enshrined a culture that was only sustained by its belief in God. Berliner's own study, therefore, aimed to recover a traditional deep-rootedness that he called the "real science of Judaism" (ächtjüdische Wissenschaft).[42]

Moreover, Jewish historians employed new genres to bring their works to larger audiences. Beginning in the 1850s, the traditional Luah (calendar) was transformed into yearbooks that not only included information regarding the holidays but also articles devoted to Jewish history. These yearbooks were regarded as the "channels through which Bildung and knowledge are directed unto the lowest classes of the people";[43] some yearbooks even included timetables of Jewish history.[44] Leopold Zunz used the Gregorian calendar as an instrument for the creation of a Jewish collective memory when he summarized the last two millennia of the Jewish past in his Die Monatstage des Kalenderjahres (The days of the month of the calendar year). Beginning with the month of January and arranged according to the days of the Gregorian calendar, the Monatstage contained the yahrzeit of some eight hundred people, including non-Jewish heroes like Columbus, Zunz's teacher Wilhelm de Wette, Alexander Humboldt, and Benjamin Franklin.[45]

When in 1845 Zunz published his Zur Geschichte und Literatur, he dedicated approximately 150 pages to a historical analysis of the ways in which Jews commemorated their righteous dead. In the chapter "The Remembrance of the Righteous," Zunz elaborated on the history of tombstones and epitaphs and pointed out the historical value of these sources. Citing his own translation of Job 19:25 ("there is a living advocate for them, and he will be the last to arise from the dust"), Zunz invoked an understanding of history in which the Jewish historian is called upon to be the "advocate" of the Jewish dead.[46] Accordingly, he urged his contemporaries to preserve the memory of Jewish heroes destroyed by the ravages of time and persecution.

Zunz's plea to the communities was indicative of the renewed interest in local communities' histories, which saw—with Moses Mannheimer's small history of the Jews of Worms during the 1840s—the publication of the first history of a Jewish community.[47] A few years later, in June 1853, the *Allgemeine Zeitung des Judenthums* enjoined "all of Israel" to preserve the tombstones of the Jewish cemetery in Worms and to publish books of epitaphs. Ludwig Lewysohn and Moses Mannheimer, who were behind this declaration, formed a committee to pursue this aim. Their declaration emphasized that Worms still had a chapel that dated back to Rashi, as well as a tombstone of martyrs from the First Crusade.[48] Three years later, Lewysohn published *Nafshot Zadikim* (Souls of the righteous), which contained sixty inscriptions on tombstones in the Worms cemetery. He explicitly referred to Zunz's call in *Zur Geschichte und Literatur* to preserve the cemeteries. Among the inscriptions was the tombstone of the twelve community leaders widely believed to have been slaughtered in 1096.[49] The significance of these martyrs was highlighted in Lewysohn's concluding remarks: "Soon 800 years will pass since these horrifying events took place. The memory of these immortal martyrs will be kept alive by their descendants. The simple stone is a more beautiful memorial than the blood-colored trophies of those who add another page to the history of mankind, a page marked by the stigma of disgrace."[50] In Lewysohn's eyes, keeping alive the memory of those who sanctified God's name was imperative for his contemporaries: "This painful and extensive, anguished and glorious past may teach Israel the task for the present and its obligation for the future: to live and to die for God, the only one, and to remain dignified for the ancestors, to whom we thankfully say: Your memory will be preserved forever!"[51]

Following upon the histories of the Jewish community of Worms, Ludwig Geiger composed a history of communal life in Berlin at the request of local leaders on the occasion of the two-hundredth anniversary of the Berlin Jewish community. During the celebration, his *Geschichte der Juden in Berlin* (History of the Jews in Berlin) was given to every member of the community, and special services were held in the city's synagogues. On September 10, 1871, Abraham Geiger, Joseph Aub, and Esriel Hildesheimer delivered sermons to mark the occasion. Whereas Abraham Geiger reveled in the history of the persecution the Jews in Berlin had experienced, his son Ludwig took up a much more conciliatory approach that eventually dominated this genre.[52] In these community histories, the Jewish past was inscribed into the annals of urban centers often in cooperation with local German historical societies. Geiger's book was indicative of other community studies that appeared during the years leading up to Germany's unification. The plethora of local community studies aimed to demonstrate that Jews' roots in Germany reached far back in history.[53]

Wissenschaft's scholarship during this period defined the uniqueness of the Jewish tradition, inscribed Jews into German historical traditions, and countered the impact of religious decline and internal fragmentation. Not in the least for these goals did Jewish scholarship remain an embattled field. Yet the concurrent creation of Jewish book clubs that acted as powerful agents of cultural and religious education ensured the dissemination of Wissenschaft's scholarship and ameliorated the existing tension between the various camps in the realm of reception.

6

Finding Common Ground in the Creation of a German Jewish Reading Public

The decades after the failed revolution exhibited contradictory features. At a time when Jewish scholarship mirrored internal division of the Jewish communities, historians aimed to create a new foundation for an inclusive German Jewish culture, while their scholarship further accentuated the existing frictions. Yet paradoxically, it was the recognition of the internal fragmentation of the German Jewish public that fueled the consistent debate about unity. While the various newspapers, journals, and seminaries cemented the division, a new and powerful agent of cultural production and distribution emerged that fostered a more inclusive German Jewish readership.

Whereas Jewish historians and publicists believed that writing about Jewish history could reshape modern Jewish identities, they realized their readership remained limited. The internal divisiveness of Jewish scholarship threatened to split the potential readership into Jewish denominational constituencies. Forced by necessity to forge a united readership, publishers, educators, and scholars created new institutions facilitating the reception of Jewish literature and scholarship. By ordering works by Geiger, Jost, Graetz, and others, readers from various denominational backgrounds established a common ground in the popular realm. Moreover, the Jewish book clubs became more than distributors; they became active shapers of the reception process, which in turn exerted a constant pressure on Jewish historians to adjust their writings to the demands of these book clubs. This established interdependence between the scholarly interpretation of the past and public culture that ultimately refashioned both.

The popularizing of Jewish historiography involved a partial overcoming of differences in the way books were disseminated. The widening of the readership also entailed a form of internal censorship. In order to engage the interest of the lay audience in the *Monatsschrift für Wissenschaft und Geschichte des Judenthums,* Frankel repeatedly criticized manuscripts and felt compelled to rework some of them intensively. As he reminded Steinschneider in a letter, without the lay reader, the *Monatsschrift* would barely have had one hundred readers.[1] At the same time, the situation forced authors to seek new methods to finance the publication of their works. When Zunz wanted to publish his *Literaturgeschichte der synagogalen Poesie* (Literary history of synagogue poetry) in 1865, he had to employ a new strategy to secure financial backing for the book. Following Moritz Lazarus's advice, Zunz had thirty copies of the work printed on vellum and sold them for 20 thaler each.[2] This early marketing effort notwithstanding, in 1862 Moritz Steinschneider complained that scientific literature could prosper only if the benefactors would also be the buyers of the books.[3]

This situation slowly started to change with the rise of Jewish reading societies and borrowing libraries. German publishing and book selling *Lesevereine* (reading societies) founded at the end of the eighteenth and beginning of the nineteenth centuries formed a crucial element of the middle-class readership that comprised also Protestant and Catholic reading associations.[4] Beginning in 1840 with associations like the Learning and Reading Association *(Jüdischen Lehr- und Leseverein,* later *Israelitischer Lehr- und Leseverein)* in Breslau, Jewish reading clubs appeared rapidly into the 1850s.[5] These societies acquired books about Jewish history and religion, and, unlike their Enlightenment forerunners, their gatherings did not take place in private houses but often in rooms owned by the institutions in which the library was located. For example, the Breslau reading society succeeded in establishing a significant collection that eventually became the library of the Jewish community in 1861. Slowly and steadily, other Jewish communities built up their own libraries.[6]

Even though access to the salons at the end of eighteenth century was restricted to a select few, this new form of institutionalization contributed to an expanded Jewish readership. Members had borrowing privileges that usually included permission to take out a limited number of books for a specified period of time. Besides newspapers, periodicals, scholarly works, and literature, a library usually contained several key reference works and a collection of rare books.[7] These resources facilitated the scheduling of public lectures, a popular offering of reading societies even in the smallest cities.[8]

There is no way to establish precisely the number and size of these Jewish reading associations and borrowing libraries. Reading societies and lending libraries represented a significant portion of the total book consumption in the German publishing market. Publishers during the 1860s estimated that about 90 percent of their copies would be sold to reading associations and lending libraries.[9] With the emergence of similar Jewish organizations, it is safe to assume that they too made up a significant percentage of potential book buyers, even though no documentation presently exists that establishes the number of books bought by these Jewish reading associations. The few existing data suggest that their membership was quite substantial. The Jewish Reading and Learning Society in Breslau numbered 110 members in 1846, while the reading society in Laupheim had anywhere from 120 to 130 members.[10] The reading association in Laupheim encompassed almost the entire Jewish community, whereas the one in Bad Homburg had only 18 members.[11]

Despite these initial advances, Jewish reading associations and borrowing libraries lost ground during the 1850s and 1860s while German *Leihbibliotheken* experienced their own crisis.[12] Confronting this situation, Ludwig Philippson, together with Adolf Jellinek and Isaac Jost in 1855, called upon reading societies, lending libraries, pedagogues, rabbis, community leaders, and German-reading Jews to support the foundation of a Jewish book club.[13] After Geiger's unsuccessful attempt in the 1850s to found an institute for the promotion of Jewish literature, Ludwig Philippson created a new Jewish reading public.[14] Countering market trends that destined books on Judaism to very limited editions, the *Institut zur Förderung der israelitischen Literatur* (Institute for the promotion of Jewish literature) employed rabbis, preachers, cantors, teachers, and book dealers as agents of the Institute to handle distribution and advertise its activities.[15]

In a tireless effort, Philippson fully utilized the potential of the *Allgemeine Zeitung des Judenthums* as well as his *Jüdische Volksblatt* to promote and sustain the Jewish book club. The initial call to found a publication society was reprinted in the *Allgemeine* and the *Jüdische Volksblatt,* and 10,000 copies were distributed separately.[16] Almost every week, the *Allgemeine* informed its readership about upcoming publications as well as the number of subscribers and book dealers who had ordered the books.[17]

Out of this effort, Ludwig Philippson, who was joined as the director of the Institute by Isaac Jost and later Levi Herzfeld, created a German Jewish reading public out of scattered readers, societies, and educational institutions. While previous attempts during the 1840s to gather 500 subscribers for a publishing society had failed, the Institute easily enlisted 2,500 subscribers during its first year. During its second and third years, membership exceeded 3,400 and 3,600 individuals, respectively. While the almost exclusively male dominated membership fluctuated very slightly, the Institute's subscribers numbered roughly 2,500 over the next several years.[18]

The membership entailed a substantial number of international readers. About one-third of members resided outside of the Germanic lands, thereby securing German Jewish scholarship an elevated status abroad. Out of 3,000 subscribers in 1865, about 2,100 came from the Germanic lands; 547 from Austria, and another 533 from Russia, England, America, Denmark, Sweden, Switzerland, France, Belgium, and Italy combined.[19] In 1855, for example, the Institute distributed it publication through literary agents in Baltimore, Chicago, and New York. Fifty-four American Jews were officially inscribed as members of the Institute in 1867.[20] Works of the Institute were published in American Jewish newspapers and in separate editions.[21] It is probably partly due to the success of Institute that several works by Jewish historians started to appear in English and Hebrew translations. In particular, Heinrich Graetz's *Geschichte der Juden* appeared during the 1860s and 1870s in English, French, and Hebrew translations.[22]

During its eighteen years of operation until 1873, the Institute published some 87 titles, an average of nearly five books a year. This meant that during its operation it succeeded in putting over 200,000 volumes into the hands of its readers excluding those books that it offered to its subscribers at reduced cost that had not been published by the Institute.[23] The list of published books included works of poetry, fiction, travel, and theology, as well as a number of historical works like Graetz's *Geschichte der Juden* and Jost's *Geschichte des Judenthums und seiner Secten*.[24] The Institute also subsidized works like Michael Sachs's *Die religioese Poesie des Juden in Spanien* (Religious poetry of the Jews in Spain) and Zacharias Frankel's *Der gerichtliche Beweis* (The judicial evidence).[25] Moreover, the Institute offered at reduced prices texts like Salomon Munk's edition of Maimonides' *Guide of the Perplexed*, Leopold Zunz's *Die synagogale Poesie des Mittelalters* and *Zur Literaturgeschichte*, and those volumes of Graetz's *Geschichte der Juden* that had appeared prior to the existence of the Institute.[26]

Its lasting impact is evident in light of the fact that many of the works published by Philippson enjoyed second editions. In 1865 he reported that out of the 55 volumes published, 10 were republished and another 16 were subsequently reprinted outside the Institute.[27] Moreover, the new system of publication and distribution increased the number of books on Jewish history that were privately owned and transformed books of scholarship into commodities for individual consumption. The well-run distribution system ensured that large numbers of readers almost instantaneously received their books within weeks. Jost, for example, reports that his *History of Judaism and its Sects* reached about 4,000 German and international subscribers within two to three weeks.[28]

Because the Institute published these books, they were offered at an affordable price. For the annual fee of two thaler, members received one copy of all publications. Yet according to Ludwig Philippson, the Institute not only provided affordable works but helped create a reading public.[29] The policy of neutrality adopted by the Institute seems to have been at least partially successful. Thus the readership was not limited to the followers of the Reform movement but also included readers from Conservative and even neo-Orthodox backgrounds. The Conservative *Israelitische Wochenschrift* and *Der Israelit* reviewed works published by the Institute. While the reviews in the *Israelitische Wochenschrift* were at times critical, the newspaper nevertheless saw merit in the Institute and defended it against attacks.[30]

Creating a reading public for works of Jewish scholarship and historical novels and acting as a powerful agent of cultural production also triggered criticism from authors and book manufacturers, all of whom attacked the Institute for monopolizing the Jewish book market. Steinschneider criticized the Institute for its undemocratic character and charged the Institute with catering to the lowest denominator while disregarding purely scientific works for publication.[31]

To a large extent, the Institute began controlling the German Jewish book market. Authors whose works had been rejected by the Institute found it even more difficult to find a publisher, as one columnist noted.[32] Philippson even suggested at times the types of books needed and thereby attempted to regulate and control the production of Jewish books.[33] He persuaded Graetz to omit the chapter about the origins of Christianity from his *Geschichte* and rejected volume eleven of Graetz's *Geschichte der Juden* for publication.[34] Aside from these particular cases, the Institute influenced Wissenschaft's reception by publishing works that strengthened the attachment to "the Jewish religion and its spiritual life," while works that were deemed purely scientific were at best subsidized.[35] In light of this, the Institute's directors were criticized for promoting their own scholarship, while they deemed Geiger's *Urschrift* as too scientific in nature for publication.[36] Unrivaled, the Institute thus accomplished much more than simply putting books at an affordable price into the hands of readers. The Institute's formidable success turned the simple book club into an important cultural force that encouraged the publication of more popular books, while it destined those that had been rejected for publication to a less prominent place within the German Jewish book market.

The accomplishment of the Institute is further corroborated by its wide geographic distribution. Whereas initially, for example, almost 50 percent of the subscribers to Jost's *Geschichte der Israeliten seit der Zeit der Maccabäer bis auf unsre Tage nach den Quellen bearbeitet* (1820–28) had come from Berlin, the Institute relied on members coming mainly from smaller communities, while the larger urban centers were notably underrepresented. While Philippson insinuated that Moritz Steinschneider's opposition was responsible for the disproportionately low number of 100 subscribers from Berlin in 1863, the geographic distribution of the subscribers points to an overall lack of support from the larger Jewish communities. Prussia and the other Germanic lands made up 2,153 of the 3,400 subscribers in 1865, but the cities of Berlin, Breslau, Mainz, Posen, Frankfurt a. M., Hamburg, and Königsberg together contributed only 387 members during the same year.[37]

When the Institute folded in 1873, Philippson claimed its demise was the result of an increase in book-production costs. Membership had decreased to 1,400 in 1873 due to the Austro-Prussian and German-French wars. Also, new censorship regulations resulted in the loss of the 500 Austrian members, which dealt Philippson's club another severe blow. This was not the first time that Philippson had come into conflict with Austrian regulations. In 1855 the Austrian government prohibited its citizens from joining the society, and in 1868 Philippson had been expelled from Austrian territory when he was on a tour in Milan. In light of these ongoing difficulties for the Institute with its international membership, it is rather astonishing that it had managed to exist for some eighteen years.[38]

After the folding of the Institute, a similar book club, the *Israelitischer Literatur-Verein* (Israelite literary society) was founded in Magdeburg under the leadership of Moritz Rahmer in 1875. Much like Philippson's club, this society was established to provide "educating and entertaining works on Jews and Judaism."[39] For an annual fee of eight marks, members received a copy of every book published by the book club. The organization numbered nearly 2,000 members and published works by Josephus Flavius, Graetz, Moritz Güdemann, as well as several historical novels. The society also offered the *Populär-wissenschaftliche Monatsblätter* edited by Adolf Bruell at a reduced price to its members. After two years of existence, however, this book club also folded.[40]

Despite the book clubs' demise, these associations nevertheless helped to create a reading public for works on Jewish history as other Jewish societies started to popularize Jewish history. Societies of the Jewish Enlightenment that had focused on the productivization of the Jews began to metamorphose. The *Studentenbeförderungsverein* (Society for the promotion of students), founded in Berlin in 1845, was originally devoted to traditional charitable activities and financially supporting pupils and students. In 1851, however, it added public lectures about Jewish literature by scholars like Leopold Zunz to these activities.[41] In the town of Krefeld, the charitable *Hevra Shevet Yehuda* (Society of the staff of Judah) for the promotion of craftsmen, teachers, and farmers, offered lectures on Jewish literature.[42] Professional societies, such as the *Handlungsdienerinstitut* (Institute for commercial employees), also organized lectures by Abraham Geiger.[43] In 1862 the *Verein zur Verbreitung der Wissenschaft des Judenthums* (Society for the dissemination of the science of Judaism) was founded in Breslau and numbered 260 members.[44] A series of weekly lectures opened with one by Geiger on Wissenschaft. This was followed by talks by Joel, Güdemann, Finkenstein, and Perles.[45] Similarly, *Sephat Emet* under the leadership of Hildesheimer organized an entire series of lectures in 1870.[46]

Ultimately, the book clubs could not sustain themselves for long, yet they nevertheless transformed the nature of the German Jewish reading public. Works on Jewish history that were initially unpopular, slowly became consumer products. Although Zunz's *Die gottesdienstlichen Vorträge* (1832) had not sold all the 760 copies of its original print run roughly twenty years after it was published, he was asked by the Institute to prepare a new edition during the 1860s.[47] In 1877 the Jewish book publisher Kaufmann also turned to Zunz for permission to republish *Die gottesdienstlichen Vorträge*.[48] Similarly, the first volumes of Heinrich Graetz's *Geschichte* barely sold out; it was only when the Institute published his work that it reached a larger audience. In 1877 Graetz happily conveyed after lecturing in several Jewish communities that his *Geschichte* had finally "sparked."[49]

This remarkable success was predicated on institutions like reading societies and book clubs created out of new networks of communication and Jewish bourgeois sociability. Therefore, Jost, Geiger, and Graetz essentially had the same readership, which displayed a variety of denominational backgrounds. Within the new reading public, the reception of Jewish scholarship remained separate from religious institutions. While local communities, individual rabbis, and teachers appeared on the subscription lists, religious institutions sponsored only the establishment of the Jewish Theological Seminary, the Hochschule, as well as the Rabbinical Seminary, but not the popular reception of Jewish historiography. Once the Jewish book clubs collapsed, new networks of dissemination had to be created for the popularization of Jewish scholarship. During the next decades, the institutions of Jewish bourgeois sociability merged with religious institutions to further the popularization of Jewish historiography.

PART 3

CHALLENGES AND
RESPONSES

7

Wissenschaft on Trial

The unification of Germany in 1871 finally universalized Jewish emancipation and promised the possibility of unity without homogeny by bringing diverse regional and religious cultures together into one nation. This diversity provided ample justification for Jewish self-assertion as a distinct ethnic group and renewed attempts at overcoming internal Jewish disunity. The existing French Jewish consistorial system and the *Alliance Israélite Universelle,* the Board of Deputies of British Jewry, and the Board of Delegates of American Israelites served as the models for constant appeals to unite German Jewry.[1] To this end, a few Jewish communities had already formed the *Deutsch-Israelitische Gemeindebund* (German Israelite community organization) on June 29, 1869. This voluntary association aimed to represent the communities before the state authorities in matters regarding social welfare and communal administration and subsidized Jewish education and community religious instruction. When in April 1872 the Gemeindebund had enlisted one hundred communities, it finally became a permanent association and established its place in Leipzig before moving to Berlin in 1882. Nevertheless, during its early years of existence, the Gemeindebund confronted formidable resistance from the communities, which struggled to uphold their age-old autonomy. It was only during the 1880s and 1890s that it finally succeeded in enlisting the support of the majority of German Jewry.[2]

In respect to Jewish scholarship, the political unification of Germany intensified anticipation for a constructive cooperation and reconciliation. In its response to Germany's unification, the Conservative *Israelitische Wochenschrift* expressed the hope that Jewish historiography would overcome its partisan character and unite the Jewish denominations.[3] Yet in 1880, the same periodical remarked "that it seems hardly thinkable that any kind of unity can be achieved in view of the existing gaping contradictions."[4]

The continuing friction notwithstanding, German Jews joined forces when faced with revitalized anti-Semitism during the *Kaiserreich*. The virulence of these new challenges and rebuffs created, however, a profound dilemma for German Jewry that resulted in self-questioning and a fundamental reevaluation of liberalism. In order to face the new contestations, German Jews relied on liberal ideals of tolerance and equality that had emerged in the Enlightenment. From a political point of view, civic equality could only be defended in alliance with the liberal camp. From a cultural perspective, however, German Jews became fearful of the secular and homogenizing principles of the Enlightenment that threatened to unravel German Jewish communities.[5] German Jews, therefore, had to defend their civic equality with liberal arguments and reassert their distinctiveness by tacitly reformulating their relationship to the cultural politics of liberalism.

These opposing tendencies manifested themselves in the refashioning of modern Jewish scholarship during this period. As Jewish historians were sharply attacked on numerous fronts and drawn into public trials about the Talmud, the inherent tension between Wissenschaft as a science and as an agent of Jewish self-definition resurfaced in public debates. Instead of furthering political emancipation and the religious and cultural reform of the Jews, Wissenschaft acquired the task of reconciling German Jews with their heritage without, however, abandoning the ideal of scholarly objectivity. These debates, together with the popularization of Jewish history, profoundly refashioned Jewish scholarship and revitalized a sense of a collective past for German Jews.

In the years preceding the unification and increasingly with the onset of the Great Depression in 1873, anti-Semites had targeted German Jews. While the *Kulturkampf* of the early 1870s accentuated the differences between Protestants and Catholics, the German chancellor Bismarck jettisoned his liberal alliances in 1878–79 in exchange for those of the conservative Catholics of the Center Party. This precarious political and economic climate contributed to the revitalization of an

anti-Semitic movement led by the court preacher Adolf Stöcker and his
Christian Social Party. In 1881 the anti-Semitic movement presented
the German government with a petition bearing some 250,000 signa-
tures that demanded the revocation of Jewish emancipation.[6] Renewed
attacks on Jews and Judaism fueled these campaigns.

Jewish scholars not only refuted the claims of notorious anti-
Semitic compilations like August Rohling's 1871 *Der Talmudjude* (The
Talmud Jew), but also participated in an array of public debates and
trials that received in-depth coverage in the German-Jewish press.[7] In
the Tiszaeszlar blood libel, the notorious Rohling, professor of Hebrew
literature at Charles University in Prague, volunteered to testify under
oath that Jewish religious sources contained the prescription for the ritual murder of Christians. Joseph Bloch, a rabbi, publicist, and politician,
challenged Rohling's competence as a scholar and accused him of per-
jury. He offered Rohling 3,000 florins if he could translate a random
page from the Talmud. In the end, Rohling withdrew his accusation before the trial opened in 1885.[8]

Concurrently, the anti-Semitic platform had gained influence in
Hessen under the leadership of Otto Böckel, who had published his in-
famous anti-Semitic book *Die Juden, die Könige unserer Zeit* (The Jews,
the kings of our time) in 1885 that was most likely inspired by the French
author Alphonse Toussenel.[9] Within an increasingly charged atmosphere, Jewish children were mocked in the local school. Leo Munk, the
Marburg rabbi, spoke out against this and cited a campaign speech by the
local teacher and anti-Semitic propagandist Ferdinand Fenner. Fenner,
Munk claimed, had incited the children's taunting. Consequently, the
Marburg state attorney tried Fenner for slandering a state-protected religion. In an ensuing trial in Kassel, Paul de Lagarde served as the expert
witness for the defense, while Hermann Cohen testified for the plaintiff.

On the day of the trial in 1888 the courtroom was crowded with
journalists, who covered the trial in the press.[10] Lagarde used this public platform to exclaim that everything worthy in the world was the
creation of non-Jews and denied any valuable Jewish contribution to
world culture.[11] In his testimony for the defense, Lagarde based his ar-
gument primarily on Rohling's anti-Semitic *Der Talmudjude*. He testified that criticism of the Talmud did not constitute a slandering of the
Jewish religion, since a defamation of Luther's table-speeches would
not mock Protestantism. Hermann Cohen in turn emphasized the centrality of the Talmud for religious Jews and dismissed Lagarde's statement as unscientific.[12]

These anti-Semitic attacks were only the most prominent examples of a new and powerful trend that had also manifested itself in the so-called *Berliner Antisemitismusstreit* (Berlin anti-Semitic debate). In an attempt to enshrine German heroes of the past, Heinrich von Treitschke, one of Germany's foremost historians of this period, wrote his *Deutsche Geschichte im neunzehnten Jahrhundert* (German history in the nineteenth century), which appeared in the 1870s and 1880s. He presented Germany's recent history as culminating in the foundation of the Kaiserreich under the auspices of Prussia. While Treitschke had the reputation of a liberal who rejected the theological and racial attacks upon the Jews, he constructed the image of an "international Judaism" that obstructed the ideal of German unity. This "international Jewry" was for Treitschke represented by Heinrich Heine, whose alleged inability to assimilate was traced back to his "inborn oriental character." Only Jews like Moses Mendelssohn, David Friedländer, and Gabriel Riesser, as well as the followers of the Reform movement, received a more positive evaluation.[13] For Treitschke, it appeared that these men were ready to abandon their Jewish identity and become wholly German. During his lecture in 1879 at the Berlin university, he was publicly criticized for his anti-Jewish stance by some of his Jewish listeners.[14]

When Wilhelm Marr's widely read *Der Sieg des Judenthums ueber das Germanenthum vom nicht confessionalen Standpunkt* (The triumph of Judaism over Germany from a non-confessional point of view) appeared, and the initial meeting of the Anti-Semitic League convened in Berlin in September 1879, Treitschke, as the editor of the *Preussische Jahrbücher,* devoted the final portion of the current events summary to the anti-Semitic movement. Shortly after the publication of the November issue, a wide-ranging public controversy arose that was also extensively discussed outside of Germany. When Treitschke exclaimed, "the Jews are our misfortune," he gave anti-Semitic agitators like Adolf Stöcker additional respectability.[15] Countering these charges, various Jewish scholars including Harry Breslau, Manuel Joel, Hermann Cohen, Moritz Lazarus, along with Jewish politicians like Ludwig Bamberger, entered the debate.[16]

The German Jewish press extensively covered the ensuing dispute. Joël's pamphlet *Offener Brief an Herrn Professor Heinrich von Treitschke* (An open letter to Professor Heinrich von Treitschke) in 1879 quickly went through at least eight editions and sold 20,000 copies, and Heinrich Graetz's initial response sold out three hours after its appearance in Breslau. In addition, special sermons were delivered in various synagogues on the anti-Semitism confrontation.[17]

Part of Treitschke's indictment of German Jewry centered on Heinrich Graetz, who openly responded to the attacks, which culminated in a fierce exchange of words. Because Treitschke considered Graetz's work an influential text on Jewish history, he attacked the Jewish historian for his denunciation of German heroes and for his hatred of Christianity: "What a fanatical fury against the 'arch enemy' Christianity, what deadly hatred of the purest and most powerful exponents of German character, from Luther to Goethe and Fichte!"[18] In his eleventh volume, Graetz indeed had chastised and reproached German intellectual luminaries. In a letter to Moses Hess in 1868, he expressed his intentions quite clearly: "But the Germans! What an overconfident and arrogant people! . . . I am excited to whip them and their geniuses like Schleiermacher, Fichte, and the whole ordinary Romantic school."[19]

In the ensuing debate, those affiliated with the Reform movement were hostile toward Graetz and disassociated themselves from his work. The German liberal Jewish politician Ludwig Bamberger even called Graetz the "Stöcker of the synagogue." Graetz's former student Hermann Cohen saw in Graetz's writing a "frightful perversity of emotional judgment,"[20] and Ludwig Philippson reminded the public that several years before, the Institute for the Promotion of Jewish Literature had turned down Graetz's eleventh volume for publication, thereby denying any responsibility.[21]

While the initial Jewish responses were overwhelmingly critical of Graetz, the Jewish press did not unequivocally share these strong outbursts. Hermann Cohen's intervention against Graetz was unanimously upbraided, and although Harry Breslau's pamphlet *Zur Judenfrage* (On the Jewish question) was welcomed, his criticism of Graetz went unmentioned in *Der Israelit* and was rejected in *Das jüdische Literaturblatt*.[22] More importantly, members of the Conservative movement came to Graetz's defense, led by the Breslau seminary graduate Moritz Güdemann. Güdemann attacked the willingness with which Graetz was sacrificed in the Reform-oriented Jewish press.[23] Siding with Graetz, the Conservative press justified his engaged style of writing and his portrayal of the history of Jewish suffering and persecution.[24] Graetz's former student Glück, a rabbi in Oldenburg, came to his aid and exclaimed: "History is not permitted to withhold these images of misery [from Jewish history], but rather has to present them. Not to press a thorn into the chest of the grandchildren of the hounded sacrificial offerings to waken the spirit of revenge, but rather to illustrate Israel's greatness of suffering."[25]

Glück was not alone in his defense of Graetz and the memory of Jewish suffering. In a sermon delivered in Erfurt, Jecheskel Caro emphasized that Jewish history was indeed a *Leidens- und Gelehrtengeschichte*.[26] The neo-Orthodox *Israelit* attacked Philippson for his readiness to dissociate himself from Graetz in the face of Treitschke's charges and called upon Ludwig Bamberger to read Graetz himself rather than rely on Treitschke's paraphrases.[27] Similarly, the neo-Orthodox *Jüdische Presse* identified itself with Graetz's portrayal of the Jewish history of suffering: "Who would not be seized with wailing and be filled with bitterness . . . when he passes through the great Jewish history of suffering?"[28]

In 1880 the Anti-Semitic debate finally came to an end. Critical reviews of Treitschke's work, however, continued to appear in the German Jewish press. Concurrently, the criticism of Graetz's eleventh volume among Reform scholars did not subside.[29] Moreover, the virulence of German anti-Semitism did not go unnoticed abroad, as Jewish and non-Jewish papers extensively covered the attacks. While these often passionate responses from abroad provided solace to Graetz and others, they nevertheless further intensified German Jews' experiences of anti-Semitism and made their precarious situation even more apparent to them.[30]

Reflecting on this developing situation, American Jews expressed their concerns in several articles titled "An American Voice," published in the *Allgemeine Zeitung des Judenthums*.[31] On December 28, 1880, a letter from the United States appeared in the newspaper that called for the formation of an emigration society for Jews in Germany, and particularly in Prussia. Jews from Germany would be able to leave for the United States, France, Italy, or England. The published response of the *Allgemeine*'s editor, however, rejected the necessity of forming such a society and emphasized the negative ramifications public announcements by such a society would have on the Jews in Germany.[32] A year later, an article from *American Correspondent* was published in the *Allgemeine* that discussed the possibility of the United States intervening in Germany on behalf of the German Jews.[33]

Similar communications were carried out between German Jews and the Anglo-Jewish Association. Various local branches of the association discussed the situation in Germany and inserted reports about the anti-Semitic movement into the English and Anglo-Jewish press.[34] Eventually, local branches urged the executive committee to take action. Yet based on the advice of Jews from Germany, the association refrained from mounting pressure on Germany. Here, too, German Jews had suggested that "any interference on the part of the non-Germans would be totally opposed to the wishes of the German Jews" and would make their situation only more precarious.[35]

Most of the attention in the pubic debate had been devoted to the vociferous attacks. Equally troubling was the defense of German Jewry put forward by some German liberals. Less noticed at the time, these voices indicate even more clearly German Jews' predicament as well as the ensuing reevaluation of their relationship to German liberalism. Treitschke, with his obsessive abhorrence about cultural confluences, viewed diversity as threat to the integrity of Germany's national and religious identity.[36] Yet Theodor Mommsen, the German classical historian, member of the German and Prussian governments, and powerful critic of the anti-Semitic movement, equally could not contend with Jewish particularism when he joined the debate with a separate publication.

Mommsen dismissed the racial vision of the postulated "purity" of the German nation and said that the citizens of Prussia represented a conglomerate of people of various origins. Jews had, therefore, become as much Germans as the descendants of French emigrants.[37] Yet in comparison to other regional or religious minorities, the "peculiarities of the Jews" are felt more vividly, Mommsen explained. Adopting the lachrymose conception that Dohm had earlier utilized, Mommsen regarded these "peculiarities" as outgrowths of Jews' persecution. Ultimately, Mommsen contended that the formation of a nation coincides with the overcoming of these peculiarities. This was, he postulated, a necessary prerequisite, and Jews functioned in Roman as well as in contemporary times as an "element of decomposition" *(Element der Decomposition)* in this process. Mommsen was actually appreciative of Jews' role in the emergence of modern nation-states insofar as they greatly contributed to the overcoming of differences and promoting homogeneity. As he explained it, admission to the German nation came with the price of Jews' conversion to Christianity in order to propel their integration into German society. Religious prejudices and separate Jewish associations had, however, more often prevented this from happening. Mommsen's liberal progressive politics were predicated on the vision of a newly forged German unity based around vague concepts of a reformulated Christianity that still "defines the entire internal civilization of our day." [38]

Unconvinced by this argumentation, Graetz sensed that Jewish particularism represented an anathema to Mommsen and was not alone in his caution regarding Mommsen's underlying conception of a homogenous German nation.[39] Berthold Auerbach dismissively noted that Mommsen had erected in his contribution to the debate a "baptismal font" for German Jews.[40] The *Allgemeine* as well as the Conservative and neo-Orthodox periodicals critically noted the uncanny resemblance between Treitschke and Mommsen in their unwillingness to deal with cultural diversity.[41]

Mommsen's contention stood also in sharp contrast to Moritz Lazarus, who along with others, engaged in an elaboration on the nature of nations. For Lazarus, *Volk* was not an ethnic homogenous entity but an intellectual and cultural construction based on a common language. Judaism, therefore, did not pose an obstacle to Jews' integration into the German society any more than Kant's Scottish ancestry disqualified him as a German.[42] By renegotiating the conception of nationhood, these German Jews put forward a vision of the German society that radically differed from the view held by many German liberals insofar as it promoted cultural diversity. Despite Lazarus's association with the Hochschule in Berlin, the Jewish press across the denominations unanimously praised his defense.[43] In contrast, only very few German liberals, like the novelist Paul Heyse, wholeheartedly endorsed this pluralistic position.[44]

The debates aptly illustrate that German Jews could defend themselves politically with liberal ideals, but had to distance themselves from the German nationalist liberal cultural politics. In the eyes of many German Jews, the Berliner Antisemitismusstreit was only the most obvious case for the revitalized anti-Semitism in Germany, which, therefore, also left a fundamental imprint on the Jewish communities at large. Moreover, the debates in the German Jewish press highlighted once again the internal division of Jewish scholarship and the public. Yet it was not only the Conservative school that rallied to Graetz's defense; even the neo-Orthodox press upbraided the fastidiousness of those who dissociated themselves from Graetz.[45] Nevertheless, the Berliner Antisemitismusstreit and its charged political atmosphere severely curtailed Graetz's reception. No new editions of his *Geschichte der Juden* appeared between 1879 and 1888.[46]

In the aftermath of these challenges, German Jews started to once again renegotiate a path between their Jewish and German heritage. At issue was not only the question of Graetz's portrayal of German cultural icons but the lachrymose conception of Jewish history. This *Leidensgeschichte* had acquired an edifying power that "seized" the reader, and neither Conservative nor neo-Orthodox commentators were ready to abandon it. Couched often in religious terms as a sacrificial offering, the annals of persecution validated Israel's mission. On the other hand, the public debate with Treitschke punctuated the difficulties of a historical narrative that reveled in the persecution of the Jews and the Jewish mission. The notable Reform follower and Dresden representative Emil Lehmann addressed this in an 1883 article titled "The Tasks of the Germans of Jewish Ancestry." Echoing Mommsen's proposal, Lehmann pushed for a dual integration of Germans and Jews. Comparable to a marriage, both partners would have to relinquish parts of their heritage. According to Lehmann, Germans should abandon the notion that their forebearers were crusading knights, and German Jews should cease to commemorate the martyrs of 1096.[47]

While these attempts at integration were by and large unsuccessful, they nevertheless reverberated in scholarly narratives and debates. The shift from a history of persecution to internal cultural studies of Jewish history represented a central response to the difficulties the Berliner Antisemitismusstreit had brought to the fore. These works, unlike Graetz's *Geschichte,* accentuated the existing contact between Christian and Jewish cultures. In 1873 Moritz Güdemann had already published his first study on Jewish education in Spain titled *Das jüdische Unterrichtswesen während der spanisch-arabischen Periode* (The Jewish education system during the Spanish-Arabic period). Three successive volumes followed this work between 1880 and 1888 under the general title *Geschichte des Erziehungswesen und der Cultur der Juden* (History of the education system and culture of the Jews), in which Güdemann elaborated on the internal life of Franco-German and Italian Jewry from the ninth to the mid-fifteenth century. Güdemann nostalgically noted it was the task of his study "to enter the *Judengasse*" in order to capture a picture Jewish medieval life.[48]

Following an overall chronological approach, Güdemann examined Jewish educational institutions, literature, languages, mystical movements, dress, moral standards, and interactions with the outside world. Because the first volume, devoted to the Jews in France and Germany, included a description of anti-Jewish remarks by the clergy, Güdemann was worried that this would give ammunition to the ongoing anti-Semitic campaign. The motto, "the behavior of the Jews follows in most of the places the behavior of the Christians," taken from the medieval *Sefer Hasidim* (The book of the pious), was meant to fend off such hostile readings.[49] Along these lines, Güdemann challenged the understanding of Jewish history as an endless *Leidensgeschichte*. He pointed to amicable Jewish-Christian relations before 1096, and his studies of Yiddish illustrated the extent to which Franco-German Jews knew the language of their environment to underscore the existence of a shared culture beyond religious differences.[50] In contrast to Graetz, Güdemann's Middle Ages were dominated by stability, harmony, and mutual influence, rather than endless persecution and harassment.[51]

Despite Güdemann's apologetic candor, Ludwig Geiger criticized his work. For Geiger, Güdemann's *History* was an erudite yet thoroughly tendentious work. Geiger opined that Güdemann had not only made a case for the intimate social and cultural contact between Jews and Germans during the fourteenth and fifteenth centuries, but he had also suggested that the Jews had excelled morally over their Christian neighbors.[52]

Güdemann responded at length and denounced the charges. Yet he asserted that for Christian historians, the work of Jewish scholars must appear apologetic insofar as it was their task to challenge and correct Christian misconceptions.[53] In order to buttress this point, Güdemann quoted Abraham Geiger, the father of his critic, and even went so far as to claim that a true scholar of Judaism must be Jewish.[54]

As the title "How Ludwig Geiger attacks Graetz's disciples for his sins" in the *Israelitische Wochenschrift* indicates, this exchange was conceived of as the internal continuation of the Berliner Antisemitismusstreit.[55] In his comments in the *Allgemeine*, Ludwig Philippson walked a thin line between demanding historical objectivity and claiming that the historian should "immerse himself lovingly" in his topic. For Philippson, "cold objectivity" would not yield a profound understanding of Judaism but only a superficial comprehension. While Jewish historians should not become apologists, Philippson argued that it was impossible to demand total detachment in light of the endless persecution Jews had endured.[56]

In the following weeks, an anonymous correspondent, introduced as a "proven historian," challenged Philippson by reasserting explicitly an idealized notion of the Rankean tradition of detachment and objectivity. According to this view, historical understanding rested on the ability to place oneself into the times in order to comprehend the subject in its essence from its own perspective. Only then was the historian entitled to pass his judgment.[57] This "noble dream" of objectivity, as Peter Novick has called it, presents the historian as a disinterested judge, who does not ally himself with advocacy and propaganda. The historian's detached position is guarded by the insulation of the historical profession from social and political pressures.[58] This idea notwithstanding, virtually all nineteenth-century German historians were politically active and understood the political function of their scholarship.[59]

The anonymous correspondent charged the neo-Prussian German historical school—represented by Treitschke and Heinrich von Sybel—with having abandoned the ideal of historical objectivity. He thus retraced the way in which German historians like Droysen, Treitschke, and Sybel had, since the 1850s, critically distanced themselves from Ranke for his alleged lack of political involvement, his characterless objectivity, and his absence of an ethical perspective.[60] In his response, Philippson thus joined a debate that had also taken place in the German historical arena. At the outset, Philippson declared that he was in agreement with the correspondent but nevertheless differentiated between "cold" and "true objectivity." Philippson maintained that minutely detailed studies with material culled from archives provided only a political history. These works, with their "cold objectivity" and their impartial treatment of history, were inevitably partial to their subject *("Unpartheilichkeit, partheiisch werdende Geschichtsschreibung")* and failed to yield a real understanding of the contours of Judaism and world history.[61] In other words, Philippson insisted that empathy with Jewish suffering was a sign of impartiality simply because the historian followed a genuine moral impulse to identify himself with those who were persecuted. Conversely, any attempt that obfuscated this universal human dimension was fraudulent because it negated scholarship's moral dimension.

Constrained and enabled by the Berliner Antisemitismusstreit, Jewish historiography had to balance contradictory impulses and square the hermeneutic circle of scholarly objectivity and subjectivity, detachment and engagement. This tension continued to exert itself in Jewish historiography and its popularization, where, despite the criticism that was leveled against Graetz's lachrymose conception of Jewish history, it nevertheless continued to inform both scholarship and popular reception. Güdemann's history of daily culture is a case in point. While he apparently wanted to go beyond the presentation of the Jewish Middle Ages as a period of relentless persecution, those passages chronicling persecution were paraphrased at length and singled out for praise.[62]

8

History as a Shield
of Judaism

In the midst of the debates and trials, Judaism's defenders deemed its
history as an instrument against renewed anti-Semitic challenges. The
defense initiatives and the renewed quest for Jewish unity based on a
common past signaled a departure from an era in which German Jews
had fully identified themselves with the cause of liberalism. The resurgence of anti-Semitism played a central role in this process, but it was
by no means the only factor that contributed to the emerging tension
between German and Jewish liberalism. As early as 1872, the *Allgemeine*
sharply criticized the egalitarian tendencies of German liberalism,
which it contemptuously described as French rationalism. Liberalism,
the *Allgemeine* contended, represented a "leveling without freedom"
(Gleichmacherei ohne Freiheit), once it had allied itself with the state.
This stood in sharp contrast with what was conceived of as English and
American classical liberalism that left room for the self-determination
of particular religious and social groups.[1]

The *Allgemeine,* as well as Heinrich Graetz, maintained that anti-
Semitism and the decline of religiosity had wrecked the promises offered by the modern era.[2] The *Allgemeine* condemned the secular influence, which allegedly threatened the foundation of modern society as
well as Jewish particularism.[3] Jewish writers regarded the modern ideal
of egalitarianism with its secular disdain for all religious communities

and the materialist liberalism of the *Kulturkampf* as a major challenge to Judaism. Materialism, couched in the language of natural sciences of Charles Darwin, had, during the 1870s, become a major anticlerical weapon in liberalism's crusade against what was perceived as Catholic obscurantism, as evidenced by the liberal responses to the apparition in Marpingen in 1876.

German Jews became particularly suspicious of liberalist enchantment with Darwinism. Darwinism represented a challenge not only because it undermined the biblical narrative of creation; it also displaced the divine providence with a new model of human descent. Viewed as a form of materialistic philosophy, Darwinism was deemed hostile to all religion. Survival of the fittest and a model of human descent threatened to replace spiritual refinement and progress. It was for this reason that members of the Center Party taunted Rudolf Virchow with cries of "get on to the apes" in the Prussian Parliament, when he exclaimed that if evolution were to be proved a correct theory, the Catholic church would have to succumb to what science dictates.[4]

The importance of Darwinism, which became particularly popular with the German translation of Darwin's complete works in 1875, cannot be underestimated. For the liberal discourse of science and progress, Darwinism had became paramount. Even in the midst of the *Berliner Antisemitismusstreit,* Seligmann Meyer, the editor of the neo-Orthodox periodical *Jüdische Presse,* challenged not only Treitschke, but noted in the same pamphlet how materialism promoted through the writing of Darwin, Ernst Haeckel, and David Friedrich Strauss led to blaming the Jews for the ills of modern society.[5] Other Jewish commentators in Germany subsequently reasserted the centrality of God's governance and the preeminence of the spiritual development in opposition to the natural forces.[6]

These now more clearly emerging tensions and the ensuing distancing from German liberalism coincided with an overall reevaluation of the modern period and culture. Graetz, in particular, increasingly regarded modern culture as a morally corrupt outgrowth of paganism.[7] In his fictional *Briefwechsel einer englischen Dame ueber Judenthum und Semitismus* (Correspondence with an English lady on Judaism and Semitism, 1883), he buttressed this contention by referring to statistics on the spread of syphilis, the increase in prostitution, and the growing number of illegitimate children. These manifestations of depravity and carnal lust, concluded Graetz, are the "successes" of European culture and the outcome of unresolved vestiges of paganism in Greek culture and Christianity. Only ethical monotheism that demands sexual chastity could safeguard against this abyss. In response to this portrayal, the English lady asked Graetz whether one could "de-Europeanize us?"[8]

This repositioning of Jews and Judaism in opposition to modern European cultures led to the fundamental refashioning of German Jewish scholarship and popular culture.[9] New efforts to popularize Jewish history were made, as several nationwide organizations, such as the 1872 Gemeindebund and Masonic lodges, launched initiatives to weave historical knowledge into the fabric of the German Jewish culture. These attempts were not limited to an apologetic defense but promoted Jewish particularism in terms of its history and universal mission.

The ensuing unprecedented popularization of Jewish history, however, was at first predicated in part on congregation leaders overcoming religious divisiveness. Even in the midst of the Marburg trial, Esriel Hildesheimer expressed his admiration for Hermann Cohen's courageous defense in the trial, and the neo-Orthodox *Die jüdische Presse* asserted that Cohen argued his case with "pious love and courageous truthfulness."[10] Similarly, the Gemeindebund, founded in 1872 and dominated by followers of the Reform movement, gained new support, but it was only after 1882 that the alliance's membership grew, no doubt in part due to the support of the neo-Orthodox Hildesheimer family.[11] Some of the new emerging intellectual and scholarly leaders transcended the denominational boundaries. Gustav Karpeles, for example, a graduate of the Breslau Seminary, became the editor of the *Allgemeine* in 1890. Similarly, Siegmund Maybaum originally studied at the Hildesheimer Yeshiva in Eisenstadt and the rabbinical seminary in Berlin before he became a professor at the Hochschule in 1888.

In light of the external pressure, the Gemeindebund dedicated significant resources to the popularization of Jewish history. One of the initial responses by the organization toward the anti-Semitic movement of December 1880, "How the Jew Should Conduct Himself Toward the Anti-Semitic Movement," entailed not only the timid mixture of self-criticism and moral pleas but also plans to cultivate the scholarly study of the Jewish past.[12] Only two years later, David Honigmann, one of the organization's founders, unequivocally proclaimed its objectives at its 1882 convention in Berlin: "What is most important for me is not the promotion of scholarship for its own sake, but rather the promotion of scholarship as a means for spreading correct opinions about Judaism in Jewish and non-Jewish circles. In this regard I believe that all the attacks and persecutions of the last years essentially have their roots in the ignorance about the actual conditions, fundamentals, and achievements [of Judaism]."[13] Honigmann redirected the function of scholarship. It was not to be pursued for its own sake but to fend off external challenges and thus enlighten Jews about their past. Similarly, Ludwig Philippson opined that Jewish history was the "palladium of Judaism and its believers."[14] Thus, while partly directed at the German public at large, the various Jewish organizations also targeted the Jewish public.

In pursuit of this two-fold goal, the organization invested considerable resources into the dissemination of a sympathetic article titled "The Significance of the Jews for the Preservation and Revival of Science in the Middle Ages" (1877) by the Christian botanist Matthias Jakob Schleiden. Schleiden's work was not original but derivative. Yet the fact that a Christian author sympathetically described Jews' involvement in the sciences promised to authenticate the already existing work carried out by Zunz, Steinschneider, and Graetz.[15] A year later, the Gemeindebund had sold 1,500 copies. Upon Heinrich Graetz's suggestion, Schleiden's second article, "The Romance of Martyrdom Among the Jews in the Middle Ages" (1878), was reprinted with the financial assistance of the Gemeindebund.[16] Graetz even recommended the translation of the second essay by Schleiden to the *Alliance Israélite Universelle* and tried to curry support for the establishment of a Schleiden foundation.[17]

In 1885 the Gemeindebund launched another initiative to alter the public's perception of Judaism. Under its auspices, the *Historische Commission* was established, consisting of three Jewish and three Christian medievalists. From its inauguration, the commission aimed to promote a new research agenda by sidelining the established Jewish historians and centers of scholarly investigations. In the commission's announcement, Harry Breslau explained that previous historians had failed to make further progress since the publication of Otto Stobbe's 1866 *Die Juden in Deutschland während der Mittelalters in politischer, sozialer und rechtlicher Beziehung* (The Jews in Germany during the Middle Ages in political, social and legal matters). Necessary sources had not been utilized, claimed Breslau, and most historians lacked the ability to understand German Jewish history as an integral part of German history. Moreover, Breslau contended that the theological training of many Jewish historians was an obstacle to the objective treatment of Jewish history.[18]

From its inception, the commission failed to secure sufficient support from the Jewish communities. Several community leaders questioned the exclusion of reputable Jewish scholars like Heinrich Graetz, David Cassel, and Abraham Berliner. Yet for Harry Breslau, Heinrich

Graetz was unacceptable. Harkening back to the Berliner Antisemitis-musstreit, Breslau asserted that Graetz's method of judging great non-Jews on the basis of their attitude toward Judaism was apologetic and tendentious. Breslau maintained that Graetz had "created a lot of bad blood" and was responsible for a few reputable German historians join-ing the ranks of the anti-Semites.[19]

The Jewish communities' reluctance and criticism continued to shake the establishment of the historical commission. When the Ge-meindebund sent out its circular to the Jewish communities soliciting financial support, several of them insisted on clarification regarding the omission of Graetz. After long deliberations the Jewish community of Berlin, for example, declined to support the commission, emphasizing they were puzzled by the absence of the some of the more renowned Jewish scholars.[20] For this reason, the followers of the Jewish Theologi-cal Seminary opposed the historical commission, which initially found support in Hirsch from Halberstadt and members of the Hildesheimer circle in Berlin. The neo-Orthodox historian Abraham Berliner solic-ited contributions during the course of a public lecture in Hamburg to more than six hundred listeners.[21] Several neo-Orthodox scholars sub-mitted articles to the commission's *Zeitschrift für die Geschichte der Juden in Deutschland* (Journal for the history of the Jews in Germany); they later withdrew their support once Ludwig Geiger's Reform-oriented editing emerged. In the end, the neo-Orthodox press also criticized the work of the commission.[22]

While the commission did not secure the active participation of Moritz Steinschneider, he nevertheless wrote a review of existing sources on its behalf.[23] Consequently, the organization followed the model of *Monumenta Germaniae Historica* and published several valuable sources during its few years of existence, including medieval chronicles from the First Crusade.[24] The collection and publication especially of Hebrew sources would make this history also accessible to the nonspecialist and illustrate above all, the deep-rootedness of German Jewry in the Ger-manic lands.[25] None of these publications, however, found a wide recep-tion. The journal had roughly seventy subscribers, and the number of subscribers to the monographic publication was even smaller.[26] At the end of 1892, Breslau announced that the commission would disband be-cause of declining financial support from the Jewish communities.[27]

The failure of the Commission to sustain its novel research program underscores the existence of a reading public with goals diametrically op-posed to the commission. Despite the initial hostile debates over Graetz and the status of the lachrymose conception of Jewish history, the Jewish reading public, represented in this case by the individual communities, had become accustomed to viewing Graetz and others as the historians of their heritage. The folding of the commission, therefore, highlights the advances that had been made in the popularizing of Jewish history. Moreover, the withdrawal of the neo-Orthodox scholars from the journal pointed to the need for any successful attempt to popularize Jewish history to be inclusive of the various strands of German Jewry.

Next to these initiatives, the Gemeindebund engaged in public education efforts that represented a response to what was perceived as the decline in Jewish religiosity. In 1879, on the occasion of Moses Mendelssohn's 150th birthday, the Gemeindebund called for the establishment of new Mendelssohn societies. While the Mendelssohn societies of the 1840s in Dresden, Dessau, and Berlin focused on charitable activities, the newly founded *Mendelssohn-Vereine* of the 1880s had decidedly different objectives.[28] They organized not only the yearly commemorative celebrations of Mendelssohn but also popularized Jewish history. As the call to erect Mendelssohn societies by the Gemeindebund stated, these organizations wanted "through public lectures on religious-historical, religious-scientific and other related fields to awaken and maintain an interest for Judaism and its noble ideas, and a feeling of unity and community . . . among our younger generation."[29] For example, the Mendelssohn society in Frankfurt, founded in 1879, organized public lectures and started the publication in 1881 of the *Populärwissenschaftliche Monatsblätter* under the editorship of Adolf Bruell. The journal's aim was the "dissemination of correct and unspoiled knowledge of Jewish Wissenschaft and literature through word and print."[30]

In 1884 the Rabbinical Conference in Berlin similarly acknowledged the importance of popularizing Jewish historiography. The conference stressed its neutral position in religious matters and thereby hoped to appeal to a broader Jewish audience. The proposed initiatives of the meeting provided a minimal program to be augmented by the individual communities. In the course of the deliberations, the delegates called upon Jewish communities and organizations to build special libraries and create literature for the Jewish youth.[31] The inclusion of textbooks for the Jewish youth signaled an important departure from previous practice in the realm of education that hitherto had received only scant attention. Contrary to Wissenschaft scholars' goals to familiarize the wider public with the Jewish traditions, Conservative and neo-Orthodox educators had remained reluctant and even opposed, at times, to the introduction of postbiblical Jewish history as a field of instruction in schools. Therefore, only a few textbook histories existed until the 1870s.[32] This situation started to change when Rhineland and Westfalia introduced Jewish history into their curricula in 1867; other communities in Bavaria introduced this subject in 1885.[33]

With the renewed importance bestowed upon textbook histories by the Rabbinical Conference in Berlin in 1884, several new ones appeared that addressed not only schoolchildren but, because of the declining numbers of Jewish pupils in Jewish schools, often the whole family. Works of particular popularity included David Cassel's 1868 *Leitfaden für die jüdische Geschichte und Literatur* (Guide for Jewish history and literature), which by 1895 was in its ninth edition. This highly condensed work conveyed the history of suffering and learning from the creation of the world to the present. In addition to this short textbook, Cassel also published a more detailed *Lehrbuch der jüdischen Geschichte und Literatur* (Textbook for Jewish history and literature) in 1879 that was intended to fill the gap between shorter textbooks and Graetz's multivolume work.[34] Besides Cassel's works, Emanuel Hecht's *Handbuch der Israelitischen Geschichte* (Handbook of Israelite history), edited by Moritz Kayserling, was published in 1900 for the seventh time. This textbook covered the period from the Second Temple period and included a timetable of Jewish history.[35]

In line with the Rabbinical Conference, these texts were instruments of religious instruction. As one reviewer of the *Leitfaden* emphasized, "the history of Judaism is one of the most important tools to awaken enthusiasm and love for the Jewish religion."[36] In addition, the conference suggested that in the interest of adult education, references to exceptional Jews and important events in Jewish history be made in sermons. For public lectures on Jewish history outside the synagogue, a subcommission suggested lecture topics, which were reprinted in the German Jewish press. The catalogue included lectures on Judaism and its contribution to world history; the development of oral tradition; sectarian movements within Judaism; Jewish mysticism; anti-Semitism; and on Jewish luminaries like Rabbi Akiva, Saadia Gaon, Moses Mendelssohn, and Zacharias Frankel.[37]

Next to the Gemeindebund and the Rabbinical Conference, the B'nai B'rith similarly devoted itself to public education. In the fall of 1880, several Jewish merchants in Berlin gathered to create an organization to strengthen Jewish self-consciousness in response to the exclusion of Jews from Masonic lodges.[38] While several B'nai B'rith lodges had existed for years in the United States, a chapter was finally established in 1882 in Berlin. By 1897 there were 33 German B'nai B'rith lodges with upwards of 3,000 members.[39] The importance of these chapters extended beyond their numerical strength. Adopting a policy of neutrality, B'nai B'rith enlisted several notable public figures. The lodge gained a great following among neo-Orthodox Jews once Hirsch Hildesheimer, a member of the Berlin secessionist "Adass Jisroel" congregation and editor of the influential *Jüdische Presse,* joined the Montefiore lodge. Hildesheimer was instrumental in the foundation of the Berend-Lehmann lodge in the neo-Orthodox community of Halberstadt. Together with this chapter, Hildesheimer succeeded in establishing one in Frankfurt in 1888 that set the stage for other local branches in neo-Orthodox communities in the west and south of Germany.[40]

In 1887 the president of the lodge called upon the local branches to organize public lectures about Jewish history.[41] As one of the leading figures of the B'nai B'rith, Maximilian Stein stressed it was the goal of the Masonic lodge to overcome the loss of the power of religion *(Glaubenskraft)* that had occurred during the nineteenth century. B'nai B'rith aimed to regain ground by reintroducing contemporary Jews to their religion as well as to their shared ancestry, culture, and history.[42] This revitalization, Stein contended, was not aimed at a return to the past but rather "out of a sincere reverence for the old, we seek to disseminate knowledge about the history and literature of Judaism, [in order] to transform its ancient treasures into a timely possession."[43]

In addition to these societies, newly founded Jewish student organizations utilized Jewish history to strengthen Jewish identity in an increasingly hostile university environment. Founded at the Berlin university in 1883, the *Akademische Verein für jüdische Geschichte und Literatur* (Academic association for Jewish history and literature) saw its membership climb from 9 to 98 members in 1893.[44] Regular members, as well as honorees of the society like Gustav Karpeles, Immanuel Ritter, Adolf Rosenzweig, and Martin Philippson, delivered many of the lectures. Eventually, the student association organized courses in Jewish history and established a Jewish library.[45] Several Jewish nationalist student groups that likewise promoted knowledge about the Jewish past soon followed this student organization. These groups included the *Jung Israel–National-jüdischer Verein* (Young Israel–Jewish national association), created in 1892 by Heinrich Loewe.[46]

While some of the initiatives, like the *Historische Commission,* failed to sustain themselves, they nevertheless represented an important acknowledgment of the use of history for edifying and apologetic ends. Moreover, some of the initiatives saw a merging of the denominational gaps. Thus Esriel Hildesheimer, for example, supported the circulation of speeches by the Reform-oriented scholar Moritz Lazarus for the *Comiteé zur Abwehr judenfeindlicher Angriffe* (Committee for the defense against anti-Jewish attacks).[47] In 1884, the neo-Orthodox scholars David Hoffmann and Jacob Barth joined the *Verein zur Förderung der jüdischen Geschichte und Literatur* (Society for the promotion of Jewish history and literature), a group that emerged from the Reform Hochschule.

These first cooperative steps, while tentative and at times severely criticized, nevertheless inaugurated the beginnings of fundamental changes.[48] While (in the aftermath of the Berliner Antisemitismus-streit) no new editions of Graetz's history appeared between 1879 and 1888, the discovery of Jewish history as a shield revitalized Graetz's reception.[49] Moritz Rahmer, the editor of the *Israelitische Wochenschrift,* founded the *Graetz Verein für jüdische Geschichte und Literatur* (Graetz association for Jewish history and literature) in the 1890s in Magdeburg.[50] Both the *Allgemeine Zeitung des Judenthums* and the neo-Orthodox popular periodical *Die Laubhütte* recommended his *Volkstümliche Geschichte der Juden* (Popular history of the Jews) in the late 1880s. At the end of the nineteenth century, Graetz's *History* appeared in its third edition. Thus, despite the severe internal and external criticism Graetz's work received, it slowly became the most widely read account of the Jewish past.

These attempts at popularizing Jewish history were quite provisional, and, in the case of the Jewish student organization in Berlin, exceptional. Nevertheless, the renewed importance that was attributed to Jewish history exerted an increasing pressure on Jewish scholars to meet the popular demand for works about the Jewish past. These demands in turn transformed Jewish scholarship and refashioned Jewish historians into religious leaders of their people.

9

Reconciling the Hearts of the Parents with the Hearts of the Children

During the last quarter of the nineteenth century, an era of Jewish historiography slowly came to an end. At a time when the major Jewish historians stopped writing, like Leopold Zunz, or died, like Abraham Geiger (1874), Zacharias Frankel (1875), and Heinrich Graetz (1891), Jewish historiography confronted new challenges. Jewish historians no longer employed scholarship in the fight for universal emancipation or as a guide for internal religious reform. The changed political climate of the 1880s, along with the internal debates about scholarly objectivity, offered new perspectives for Jewish historians. During a period when several Jewish associations and societies set out to popularize Jewish history, various commentators from the Reform to neo-Orthodox camps bemoaned the failure of Jewish historiography to impact the Jewish public.[1] In response to these new demands, Jewish historians more forcefully attempted to educate the Jewish public at large. Insofar as these historians and publicists aimed to further not a secular modern identity but to revitalize an attachment to the Jewish religion, they engaged in a process that Olaf Blaschke has recently called a "second confessional era" in respect to Catholic and Protestant renewal during this period. Whether one can go so far as Blaschke remains disputed. Yet it is true that religious traditions continued to shape culture, society, and politics throughout the Second German Empire.[2] Jewish scholarship adopted a new religious function without abandoning its earlier devotion to the ideal of scholarly objectivity and detachment. These overtly opposing tendencies clearly framed the public perceptions and commemorations of Leopold Zunz and Heinrich Graetz.

In the 1870s Abraham Geiger charged that Wissenschaft had dissociated itself from the traditional teachings and institutions of Judaism.[3] Steinschneider contended that Wissenschaft had labored for emancipation and internal religious reform too long. For Steinschneider it was the obligation of the state to facilitate education of religious teachers, while Jewish historiography was to more strongly define itself as a secular scientific endeavor.[4] Ludwig Philippson posited that Jewish historiography had become wrapped up in superficial rationalism, which led to religious indifference. Instead of comprehending Judaism's spirit in the past, present, and future as an organic development, claimed Philippson, Jewish historiography occupied itself with historical facts and dates and thereby yielded only "microscopic history" *(Geschichtsmikroskopie)*. This type of historiography, he contended, only interested scholars.[5] Yet Philippson never challenged the centrality of the historical approach. He believed that Jewish historiography remained the most central innovation within Jewish culture and, during the 1880s, repeatedly asserted Jewish history's importance and defended the historical science against the rise of new scientific paradigms like ethnographic and racial studies.[6] To this end, Philippson maintained Jewish history was "the shield of Judaism and its believers. It not only legitimizes and honors its existence and martyrdom and validates its world historical mission, but the history of Judaism is also an essential fundament of its religious teachings *[Glaubenslehre]*."[7]

Philippson not only put forward the centrality of history as a shield *(Palladium)*, but also attributed a religious significance to the 3,000 years of Jewish history. Next to the teachings in biblical Judaism, instruction in postbiblical history was key, Philippson believed, because this history was a central "pillar" on which a Jewish identity rested. Whereas the former provided a religious belief in accordance with reason and the heart, the latter offered the concrete particularistic form and historicity. Similarly, during the Rabbinical Conference in 1884 in Berlin, Jewish history was justified as an element of religious instruction, and not as a secular subject.[8]

In the face of this new understanding of Jewish history as an instrument of religious education, the public perception of Jewish scholars was refashioned. After decades of fiery debates and external challenges, Jewish historiography began reasserting itself by focusing on the ideal of detached scholarship. For this new generation of scholars, Leopold Zunz and Moritz Steinschneider embodied this ideal, while Heinrich Graetz functioned as the antipode. In the chapters on Wissenschaft in the histories of the Jews written by Marcus Brann, David Cassel, and Adolf Kohut, Graetz is hardly mentioned, whereas Leopold Zunz is celebrated as the father of the modern study of Judaism.[9]

In the realm of public education, the ideal of detached scholarship was replaced by identifying the historian as prophet. Graetz had done this early on, likening himself to Elijah in his *Volkstümliche Geschichte der Juden* (Popular history of the Jews). At the end of the *Volkstümliche Geschichte,* Graetz anticipated a new development within Jewish scholarship when he expressed the hope that the future Wissenschaft would help to "reconcile the hearts of the parents with the hearts of the children in unity."[10] In comparing Jewish scholars with Elijah, Graetz gave their craft a new meaning. By expressing the hope that Wissenschaft would forge continuity among the generations, Graetz turned to Malachi (Malachi 4:6), the last classical prophet from the postexilic period, who faced the challenges of the people and priests and reproached the Jews. According to Malachi, God would send Elijah to reconcile parents with their children, which would then set the stage for the arrival of the messianic age.

Graetz's portrayal of himself as both historian and prophet was not at all idiosyncratic. During the 1880s, the image of the Jewish historian underwent a fundamental transformation in the course of public celebrations and events. Whereas a handful of young university-trained intellectuals, who used tools of scholarship to challenge the authority of the rabbinic elites, initiated Jewish historiography in the 1820s, public celebrations in the 1880s reinscribed these figures as religious leaders and fighters for emancipation. These celebrations asserted the centrality of the historians and their craft for the creation of modern Jewish culture.

While the press reported Isaac Jost's and Abraham Geiger's deaths and Zacharias Frankel's birthday, Zunz's birthday celebration evolved from small scholarly gatherings to major public festivities. Similar events for Heinrich Graetz were restricted to a particular audience, but nevertheless represented a more appreciative attitude toward his work. In 1879, the year of the Berliner Antisemitismusstreit, the Jewish Theological Seminary in Breslau celebrated Graetz on the occasion of his twenty-fifth teaching anniversary. The Vienna *Beith Midrash,* the *Alliance Israélite Universelle,* the *Deutsch-Israelitische Gemeindebund,* and several Jewish communities sent him congratulatory addresses.[11] A few years later, on the occasion of his seventieth birthday, Graetz was even more widely acknowledged. During these years, biographies of Graetz appeared that were also included in the first edition of his popular history, while a laudatory poem was published in the Conservative press that described him as a prophet.[12] Graetz gained additional recognition when, in 1888, he was made an honorary member of the Royal Academy of History in Madrid.[13]

At the time of his death in 1891, antagonism toward him waned even further. The historian David Kaufmann, while still noting clearly his criticism of Graetz, nevertheless concluded that if the twelve tribes of Israel still existed, representatives of each tribe would have had to carry a volume of Graetz's *Geschichte* during his funeral procession.[14] The neo-Orthodox popular press carried articles that noted his contribution to a greater understanding of Jewish history and the Reform-oriented *Allgemeine* cited his accomplishments.[15] In light of this renewed appreciation, the neo-Orthodox popular periodical *Die Laubhütte* and the *Allgemeine Zeitung des Judenthums* recommended Graetz's *Volkstümliche Geschichte* in lengthy reviews.[16]

But Leopold Zunz, deemed the founding father of *Wissenschaft des Judentums,* received much broader public acclaim than Graetz because his work crossed denominational boundaries. In contrast to Geiger and Graetz, Zunz's multilayered life and works provided the public with a array of biographical elements: the founder of Wissenschaft, a fighter for emancipation, a supporter of reform, and a defender of the Jewish tradition. Thus, the Reform, Conservative, and neo-Orthodox press all easily found aspects of Zunz's life to celebrate.

On the occasion of Zunz's seventieth birthday in 1864, the Zunz Foundation was established in support of Wissenschaft.[17] Zunz proudly noted in his correspondence that he received over ninety letters and telegrams, five Hebrew poems, and proclamations from more than fifty different locations. Many printed works were dedicated to him as well, several copies of which were delivered to him at home.[18] Ten years later, the Zunz Foundation published his collected works followed by a Festschrift in 1884 that originally was to have comprised articles by scholars from all fields, religions, and national backgrounds.[19] All major Jewish newspapers, as well as the German liberal press and even some Conservative newspapers, carried articles about Zunz's life and work and the celebrations in his honor.[20] The internal religious crisis coupled with revitalized anti-Semitism augmented the significance of Zunz's work and cast it in a new light. Not only was his scholarship a source of true religiosity but also a shield against hatred.[21]

The Academic Association for Jewish History and Literature organized a party during the course of which David Cassel delivered a speech on Zunz's accomplishments. In his lecture, Cassel emphasized Zunz's character and the tremendous work Zunz had carried out in bringing order to the previously chaotic historical material.[22] Several deputations made their way to Zunz's house. The Berlin rabbinate and the *Gesellschaft der Freunde* (Society of Friends) handed over specially crafted proclamations that praised Zunz. Frankl, who spoke for the Berlin rabbinate, introduced the address by comparing Zunz to Moses, noting that the historian be referred to as "our rabbi."[23] In another example of the Jewish communities' indebtedness to Zunz, Moritz Lazarus submitted an address on behalf of the *Deutsch-Israelitische Gemeindebund*. In it, Lazarus expressed the Gemeindebund's intention to establish another Zunz foundation that would award an annual prize to a scholarly publication on Zunz's birthday.[24] In addition to the numerous letters and congratulatory messages from Jewish societies, organizations, and communities, Zunz received special addresses from the London rabbinate and the Berlin *Beith Midrash* and Reform community. Lastly, the already aged Joseph Derenbourg came from Paris to present Zunz with an honorary membership to the *Société des Études Juives*.[25]

While all groups claimed Zunz as their own, they nevertheless emphasized different points in his life and work. For the neo-Orthodox press, he was foremost a renowned scholar, a fighter for emancipation, and a defender of the Jewish tradition, who early on had distanced himself from the Reform movement.[26] In contrast, the speaker for the Hochschule emphasized that Zunz was the founding father of modern Jewish scholarship.[27]

Zunz's death in 1886 brought on another deluge of reviews of his life and accomplishments together with several poems that appeared in the German Jewish and the general press.[28] Already in the year preceding his death, *Die Laubhütte* reprinted a photograph of Leopold Zunz followed by a sketch of Sinai. In the subsequent pages, the periodical explained this juxtaposition by underscoring that Zunz had contributed a great deal to the preservation of the Sinaitic revelation.[29]

In Zunz's memorial services, this religious imagery continued. On March 18, 1886, in the new Berlin synagogue, Sigmund Maybaum, a professor at the Berlin Hochschule, cited his altered translation of Isaiah 42:1, "Behold my servant, whom I uphold: my elect, in whom my soul delights: I have put my spirit upon him: he declares the right of the nations." Maybaum portrayed Zunz not as a leader who "brings forth judgment to the nations," as the Hebrew reads, but as fighter for the underprivileged people in the world. The Breslau rabbi Manuel Joel's sermon followed that of Maybaum's. Joel invoked the famous parable of the Pardes, the paradise of Gnostic speculation, from Talmud Hagigah 14b. According to this parable of the four rabbis, only Akivah returned unharmed, much like Zunz, who had "entered and left the sciences in peace." By contrast, the three remaining scholars lost their faith and peacefulness during the course of their research. Upon completion of the memorial service, the coffin was brought out and "followed by a big crowd" to the old cemetery in Schönhauser Allee, as noted in an obituary.[30]

At the beginning of the summer semester, Joel Müller conducted another memorial service in the Hochschule in Berlin. Müller built his eulogy around "the Torah of the wise is a fountain of life" (Proverbs 13:14), and thereby presented Zunz's scholarship as a wellspring that rejuvenated Jewish culture and would once again inspire contemporary Jews. In keeping with the already well-established Jewish rhetoric in eulogizing Zunz, Müller called Zunz's scholarship a Torah that "has issued out of the sanctuary" (Ezekiel 47:12).[31]

While one may argue that likening Zunz to a religious leader occurred only during religious services, the memorial sermons exhibited a conscious and virtuous employment of religious texts. When, on the occasion of Zunz's 100th birthday, articles appeared in the press that reviewed his accomplishments and provided biographical information, the various authors used the already familiar religious rhetoric.[32] Once again, all sides claimed Zunz as their own.[33] On August 11, 1886, memorial services were conducted in various communities and at the cemetery.[34] In Gustav Karpeles's speech to the Association for Jewish History and Literature in Berlin, the work of providence had sent Leopold Zunz to the communities to lead them.[35] Adolf Rosenzweig, the rabbi of the Berlin Jewish community, compared Zunz's mission to Jochanan ben Zakkai's role in securing a new basis for Judaism after the destruction of the temple in Javneh. Again citing Isaiah 42:1, Rosenzweig commemorated Zunz as a divinely elected prophet of Israel. In an allusion to the previously mentioned verse from Malachi, Rosenzweig expressed the hope that Zunz's work would raise the "hearts of the children" when they realize how glorious Israel's past and future are.[36]

As the German Jewish press elaborately celebrated Zunz's life, the image of him as a divinely elected leader became part of his public persona that continued to intrigue. Anecdotes and first-hand accounts appeared in the press, along with numerous photographs and lithographs that illustrated Zunz's elevated status among the Jewish historians.[37] When the publication of a letter by Empress Augusta in 1890 endangered Zunz's reputation, the German Jewish press immediately refuted anything that could possible tarnish his image as a religious leader. The empress's correspondence contained not only the frequently cited indictment of modern anti-Semitism but also allegations that Zunz had contemplated conversion. According to these passages, Zunz regarded Judaism as a "silly notion" *(Grille).*[38] While the authenticity of the letters was challenged early on, such accusations threatened to taint Zunz's emerging public image. After the *Jewish Chronicle* consulted with the *Allgemeine,* a detailed refutation appeared in the press that also circulated as separate offprints. In his defense of Zunz, Salomon Neumann rightly pointed out that the formulation "silly notion" was culled from Heine's *Ludwig Marcus: Denkworte* (Ludwig Marcus: words of commemoration) and was, therefore, most likely fabricated by the editors of the empress's letters.[39]

The swift and forceful rebuttal of these allegations underscores Zunz's newly acquired importance in the public imagination. What was at stake here was an attempt to provide an image of continuity in a period of radical change. The celebrations strove to bring the public perceptions of these historians in line with the German Jewish culture, in which Jewish history was popularized as a form of religious instruction. Yet going beyond the religious rhetoric, the portrayals of Graetz as a prophet and Zunz as a divinely elected religious leader clearly accentuate the fundamental transformation of the perception of the Jewish historian's craft and persona. Moreover, the overtly contradictory impulses of viewing Zunz as a model for objective scholarship and as a religious leader echoed the debate between Güdemann, Geiger, and Philippson about historical objectivity and engagement.

While these opposing ideals framed the commemorations of Leopold Zunz, Heinrich Graetz's position was more ambiguous. Zunz's and Graetz's receptions displayed the intensified tension between Wissenschaft as a science and agent of Jewish self-definition in the aftermath of the Antisemitismusstreit. Although Graetz had written the canonical historical accounts and trained a new generation of historians, he remained almost insignificant when compared to Zunz on the scale of public celebrations. Put differently, while Zunz's and Graetz's legacies continued to inform Jewish scholarship, only Graetz's histories of the Jews became popular.

During the 1890s, these various trends converged into a wide-ranging popularization of Jewish history. Under the aegis of a new popular umbrella organization, *Verband der Vereine für jüdische Geschichte und Literatur* (Union of associations for Jewish history and literature), Jewish history reshaped popular German Jewish culture. Institutions like Jewish libraries secured the centrality and lasting impact of Jewish scholarship in the public realm, while local societies preserved historical landmarks. At a time when Jewish educators, religious leaders, and historians increasingly questioned the promises of the modern era, Jewish history became a source of consolation and pride.

PART 4

READING
JEWISH HISTORY IN
THE FIN DE SIÈCLE

10

Past, Present, and
Future of Jewish History:
Between Hope and Despair

In 1898, Adolf Kohut published an elaborately illustrated and beauti-
fully decorated coffee-table history of German Jewry. The frontispiece
features the Prague Jewish cemetery and depicts a walking path curving
into the distance under a canopy of trees with tombstones on either
side. Placed at the beginning of the book, the sketch captures the en-
counter with Jewish history. The reader of Kohut's *Geschichte der deutschen Juden* (History of the German Jews) must follow the path along
the tombstones into a far and distant past.[1] Whereas almost thirty years
earlier, Abraham Berliner's cultural history was criticized for having
portrayed Ashkenazic customs in the past perfect, in Kohut's time, the
daily life and customs he described belonged to a distant and self-
enclosed past to which the reader had to travel.[2]

Kohut's history of German Jewry was part of an unprecedented popularization of Jewish history. With the support of nationwide groups
like the German Israelite Community Organization and the B'nai B'rith
lodges, a whole array of new historical associations and Jewish libraries
emerged. While these initiatives strove to restore the memory of the
past, archives and Jewish museums collected and preserved the physical
remnants of Jewish history. Born by the crisis and transformation of

liberalism and the experience of modern anti-Semitism, these activities became central to the existing defense work in addition to the Zionist aspiration for a cultural renewal. What Martin Buber coined in 1901 as the Jewish Renaissance reflected a larger German Jewish cultural movement and not simply the Zionist quest for renewal.[3]

During the Kaiserreich, Germany, almost despite itself, had evolved into a more pluralistic nation, and several minority cultures existed along with the German Jewish culture. At the same time, the Kaiserreich brought with it a new intensity in the popularization of German history and literature. The federal state and the communities supported the universities and research institutions, built art academies, museums, and monuments, and preserved historical sites. As part of the process of nation-building, the German state sponsored and popularized a particular version of German history, with the help of historians, educators, and architects, which originated with Herman the Cheruscan and culminated in the foundation of the German Reich under the leadership of Prussia. These efforts were augmented by a new wave of popular German associations that arose during the last decade of the nineteenth century. While local city councils and private initiatives worked feverishly to preserve historical landmarks, German classics found an unprecedented mass consumption in the form of affordable penny editions.

The success of the popularization of German history was part of what George Mosse labeled the "nationalization of the masses" and a response to the acceleration of modernization in Germany. For many Germans, modernization coincided with the experience of the disintegration of local social relations and dislocation that led to expressions of contempt for the modern and urban landscape. Genuine German *Kultur* became pitted against the alleged devastating impact of *Zivilisation*. The recording, gathering, and preserving of historical sites and artifacts were, therefore, motivated by discontent with the pervasive powers of the modernizing process. From this perspective, what Richard Terdiman has called the obsession with the past—museums, libraries, exhibitions, and the preservation of historical sites—aimed to ground identities in a rapidly changing world.[4]

Yet the educated German middle-class critics of modernity were highly selective in practice and cherished the fruits of technology when it suited them.[5] German culture was not solely dominated by antiurban and antimodern trends that manifested themselves in a pervasive malaise of the fin de siècle. For example, the readers of the German periodical *Berliner Illustrirte* looked proudly back at the cultural, political, and technological achievements of the nineteenth century: they voted for Johann Wolfgang Goethe as the greatest poet, considered Wolfgang Menzel the greatest thinker, and agreed that Richard Wagner was the most accomplished composer.[6] In this sampling of German opinion, readers considered the nineteenth century above all to be an era of invention and German unification.[7] Similarly, national guidebooks of Germany prominently featured not only historical monuments and museums but also many industrial and commercial sites.[8]

For most of the Jews in Germany, the situation was very different. By the end of the nineteenth century, the majority of Jews lived in urban centers and participated in the developments of a bourgeois society. German Jews belonged disproportionately to the propertied and educated middle class and tended to an unusual degree to identify themselves with the currents of modernity and progress. What Germans may have experienced at times as social disintegration was, in the case of German Jews, woven into the fabric of their almost unmitigated social advance. Not discontent for the modern world but the crisis of the liberal ideal of relentless political, social, and moral progress increasingly shaped a new attitude toward Jewish history.

In his important analysis of the emergence of the new landscape of Jewish associations during this period, Jacob Borut has rightly pointed out the reassertion of other regional and religious cultures as well as the importance of anti-Semitism as the causes behind German Jews' pervasive reorientation.[9] Yet the factors that contributed to the unprecedented popularization of Jewish history reflect also Jews' tacit reevaluation of liberalism, concerns about the decline in Jewish religiosity, and the ongoing transformation of *Wissenschaft des Judentums* itself. The popularization of Jewish history did not present a break in German Jews' self-understanding as culturally integrated members of German society. Assimilation and self-assertion were part of the constant renegotiation of the Jewish and German heritages in the formation of German-Jewish identities.

In the fin de siècle, many German Jewish liberals regarded the rationalistic critique of religion as trivial, leaving it bereft of its unique spiritual quality.[10] In the quest to reverse the impact of secularization and the weakening of Jewish religiosity, rabbis, historians, and pedagogues turned increasingly to Jewish history, which provided ample examples to enhance the appeal of religion. As the century closed, these tendencies came powerfully to the fore, and German Jews became frustrated and dismayed over the course modern Jewish history had taken.[11]

Anti-Semitic outbursts and propaganda still punctuated the early nineties. In 1892 a new ritual murder accusation in Xanten seized the attention of the Jewish public, while the Conservative Party adopted an anti-Semitic clause in its Tivoli program and gained sixteen seats in the national election a year later.[12] In response to these ongoing challenges, in 1893 German Jews established a formidable defense organization known as the *Centralverein deutscher Staatsbürger jüdischen Glaubens* (Central association of German citizens of the Jewish faith).[13] Moreover, the growing discontent with the unfolding of the most recent history intensified and found an outlet in the many articles that reviewed the passing century. These reflections on the turn of the century placed German Jews in a symbolic fashion at the crossroads between the past and future. During the last decades of the 1900s, a growing sense existed that time's arrow did not always fly straight. Time was no longer conceived of as progressing in a linear movement but as moving in "spirals."[14]

Already the reviews of the decades written during the 1880s emphasized the decline in religiosity, the inner fragmentation of German Jewry, and revitalized anti-Semitism as the outstanding characteristics of the nineteenth century.[15] The fin de siècle intensified this perception, and contemporaries were more often struck by profound feelings of closure, uncertainty, and pessimism. One article in the *AZJ* noted: "Also the past century was not free of faults, and its biggest failure was that it did not keep its promise in old age that it had made in its youth; it destroyed in its old age that which it had erected in its youth."[16]

An array of articles reviewing the passing century emphasized the quasi-medieval character of modern times.[17] In the neo-Orthodox periodical *Der Israelit,* an article titled "Unzeitgemäße Betrachtungen zur Jahrhundertwende" (Untimely considerations toward the turn of the century) appeared that was influenced by Nietzsche's work *Unzeitgemäße Betrachtungen* (Untimely considerations) on historical thinking. Historical time no longer appeared as a progressive force but rather as an entity that threatened to swallow up its children: "The ancient Greek legend depicted time as the god Kronos, who cannibalized his own children. The legend expresses the profound truth that the children of time, the children of the world whose entire hopes and endeavors aim to please time . . . actually are destroyed by it. He who passes along with time will be passed over by time *(Wer mit der Zeit geht, vergeht mit der Zeit)*."[18]

These reviews indicate that past, present, and future were not united in a dynamic and progressive concept of history but rather appeared as distinct entities. Once the cumulative developmental understanding of

Jewish history was endangered, the question of continuity achieved utmost importance, as the philosopher and follower of Wissenschaft, Ludwig Stein, observed.[19] In light of these difficulties, Jewish scholars grounded their perceptions of Jewish history in a qualitative, essential concept of Judaism that focused on Judaism's eternal task. Thus the future was imagined only in the form of theologically inspired reviews of the past, present, and future of Judaism.[20] These scholars distanced themselves from Graetz's national history of the Jews when they based their studies on a temporal theological interpretation of Jewish history. This altered understanding of the Jewish past illustrates the increasing difficulties within the Kaiserreich in negotiating the balance between the promotion of a national concept of Jewish history and German Jewish integration, as Jacques Ehrenfreund has highlighted in his book on historical memory among the Jews of Berlin during this period.[21] Moritz Lazarus, the Jewish philosopher and professor at the Hochschule, eloquently argued this point when he gave a keynote lecture in front of the *Verein für jüdische Geschichte und Literatur* (Association for Jewish history and literature). Taking his cue from Friedrich Schiller's "Was heißt und zu welchem Ende studiert man Universalgeschichte?" (What is and to what end does one study universal history?) given at Jena in 1789, Lazarus elaborated on the purpose of studying Jewish history. He underscored that one cannot study the history of the world without knowing the history of Judaism. While this assertive opening centralized Jewish history, Lazarus declared that Jewish history had started with the patriarchs and had ended with the fall of Betar, the last stronghold of Bar Kokhba in the war against Rome: "We now no longer experience Jewish history. We experience Prussian, German and French History." For Lazarus, there was no history of the Jews but only a history of Judaism.[22]

Lazarus thus contended that there was no secular political or cultural Jewish history, but only a *religious* history of Judaism. In other words, the religious history defined for Lazarus the uniqueness of the Jewish people. Along these lines, Jewish history was defined as a sacred history to which the usual categories of historical understanding were not applicable.[23] Karpeles recited in a public lecture the same verse from scripture that Abraham Geiger had already used: "Put off thy shoes, for the place is holy ground" (Ex. 3:5) to remind those who study Jewish history that they enter a sacred and miraculous space.[24] Studying Jewish history had therefore a religious function, as Lazarus stated in a programmatic fashion: "We Jews devote ourselves to the history of Judaism for no other reason than to be good Jews."[25]

When the eminent Church historian Adolf von Harnack questioned the originality of Judaism's religious core, Jewish publicists feverishly defended its uniqueness. In the winter of 1899–1900, Harnack delivered a series of lectures titled "Das Wesen des Christenthums" (The essence of Christianity) at the university in Berlin. In front of a captivated audience, he created a sensation. Harnack devoted himself in his lectures to a critical exposition of the unfolding of the Christian spirit. Maintaining the essence of Christianity lay in its origin, he postulated that Jesus' teachings represented an original innovation that set Christianity apart from what Harnack regarded as the fossilized pharisaic Judaism. Not only was Judaism portrayed in a highly negative light, but almost more importantly, Judaism was represented as a passing stage in world history, superseded by Christianity.[26]

In numerous monographs, articles, and public lectures, Jewish scholars criticized Harnack and elaborated on the question of a Jewish essence. Leo Baeck described Judaism without differentiating between epochs and emphasized that its essence resided in a timeless Jewish piety based on ethical monotheism.[27] Other Jewish scholars turned culture into a defining element of the essence of Judaism, encompassing not only high literary productions but also folkloristic customs that grounded the core of Judaism in the historical reality of the Jewish people.[28] This assigned centrality to Jewish culture echoed the increasing numbers of publications devoted to daily culture that described the Jewish essence not as a dogmatic system but as a culture permeated by Jewish values.

During the 1870s, Moritz Steinschneider and David Kaufmann propagated such studies, while Abraham Berliner and Moritz Güdemann published material on Jewish daily culture.[29] With Max Grunwald's foundation of the *Gesellschaft für jüdische Volkskunde* (Society for Jewish folklore) in 1897 in Hamburg, these first initiatives and studies proliferated. The *Gesellschaft* aimed to further "the knowledge about the internal life of the Jews" by publishing a journal, establishing a library, and exhibiting artifacts of Jewish daily life.[30] The society quickly gained a substantial, geographically dispersed and culturally, religiously, and politically diverse membership, numbering almost 300 in 1899. Grunwald enlisted the support of eminent figures like Moses Gaster and Elkan Ader from London; Jewish historians like Moritz Steinschneider, David Kaufmann, and Markus Brann; the Hamburg banking family Warburg; the Zionist Max Bodenheimer and various Jewish associations and Masonic lodges.[31] Moreover, the Jewish public at large helped in the collection of the fleeting remnants of Jewish customs. In October 1896, the Henry Jones lodge called upon the public to collect Jewish folktales, songs, and customs.[32] This call was echoed by the German Jewish periodical *Ost und West,* which virtually deemed every reader a practitioner in researching Jewish daily culture.[33]

Focusing on everyday culture led to a recovery of aspects of the Jewish past that earlier historians had criticized with rationalistic zeal as superstitious. For Grunwald, the study of Jewish folklore promised the elucidation of the particularistic aspect of the Jewish heritage, as he related in a programmatic lecture at the Hamburg Association for Jewish History and Literature on Jewish folkloristic studies. Intended to diffuse racial classification of Jews as an important element in the pervasive *Abwehrkampf* (defense work), Grunwald cited Güdemann in order to buttress his contention that these studies would illustrate a daily culture shared by Jews and non-Jews. Despite this goal, Grünwald, however, also believed that folkloristic studies would reveal once again the true essence of Judaism. Whereas other fields of scholarly inquiry elucidated rather universal aspects of truth, beauty, and morality, the study of daily Jewish culture promised to bring into focus the particularistic aspect of Judaism: "Nowhere else do we recognize our nationality, our ethnic belonging more clearly than in the mirror of ancestral traditions *(Väterbrauch)* and fatherly customs *(Vätersitte),* the old traditions of our people."[34]

Studying daily culture was advantageous insofar as this focus was less confrontational. It also augmented Graetz's historical narrative that reveled in persecution and martyrdom and denounced the Church, Christian leaders, and German cultural heroes. In contrast to Graetz, Kohut, in his cultural history of German Jewry, stated that historical understanding provided a way to forgive past persecutions.[35] In his elegantly styled book with paragraphs set apart by colored display initials, Kohut fashioned the design to convey a sentimentalized past to which he invited his readers to travel. Praised in a review for its "pleasant warmth,"[36] the *Geschichte der deutschen Juden* contains accounts of famous Jewish sages, scholars, poets, as well as the martyrs. Kohut's narrative, marked by switches between past and present tense, functioned as a conduit to the Jewish past. Kohut enjoined the "gentle reader" to "follow us to the ghetto" and the many places about which he narrated.[37] More than his narrative, the accompanying photos and illustrations of sites of Jewish history served to territorialize Jewish history and firmly ground it in Germany's landscape. Intended for the family, the

book urged readers to familiarize themselves with their Jewish ancestors' days of sorrow and happiness, customs, dress, celebrations, games,
and contributions to mankind.

Kohut ostensibly stayed away from theological introspection on the
essence of Judaism and its development. Undisturbed by despotism and
persecution, the Jews portrayed in Kohut's work lived in a culture permeated by the Jewish religion. Daily life, like the houses in the Judengasse, centered on the synagogue that shaped "all thinking and emo-
tions, all ambitions and wishes of the German Jews. The entire Jewish
community was like a large united family, and all community members
participated lively in the happiness and sorrows of their neighbors."[38]

The portrayal of an all-encompassing religious life did not capture
the essence of Judaism but the way Jewish teachings and values shaped
daily culture. By placing Jewish culture at the center of Jewish history,
Kohut strove to reinvigorate contemporary Jewish life. Popularizing
Jewish history, therefore, became desirous to counteracting the purported amnesia that the modern transformation of German Jewry had
created. For too long, Gustav Karpeles noted, German Jews neglected
their history in the expectation of a better future.[39] Knowing about the
continuous mission of the Jewish people and their glorious history was
imperative in order to make a "certain modern martyrdom plausible."[40]
Moreover, not only was Jewish history recalled for the comprehension
of the present but to provide solace, courage, and pride, as one observer
noted: "The sufferings of the past have to console for the manifold pain
and tribulations of the present."[41] Similarly, Kohut reassured his readers
by applying Exodus 3:2 — "The bush burned with fire, and the bush was
not consumed" — to German Jewry.[42]

In light of the imminent importance bestowed upon the past by
Jewish historians and educators, collecting and preserving documents
became a quasi-sacred duty. With the expulsion of Jews from most of
the urban centers by the end of the Middle Ages, many physical remnants of Ashkenazic history were destroyed.[43] Moreover, when the
German states mandated that German become the official language of
legal documents from the late eighteenth century on, those that were
still written in Yiddish or Hebrew lost their value. Finally, negligence of
and contempt for documents that reminded Jews of a dark past were responsible for even fewer written materials surviving.[44]

This was Ezechiel Zivier's assessment when he traveled through
southern Germany in 1904 to survey the situation after he had already

proposed the plan for a central archive in 1903 to the members of the B'nai B'rith Lessing lodge in Breslau. According to his report, relatively few recently founded community archives existed in Worms, Darmstadt, and Frankfurt am Main. In light of this, Zivier exclaimed it was a "holy duty" to preserve whatever had remained.[45] Along similar lines, Gustav Karpeles asserted the immediate need to gather and collect and thereby preserve the slowly disappearing traces of German Jewish history. In a lead article in the *Allgemeine*, Karpeles posited that his generation had "the obligation . . . to rescue what can be saved before it is too late."[46] Subsequently, Eugen Täubler founded the *Gesamtarchiv der deutschen Juden* (Central archive of the German Jews) in October 1905 with the support of the Gemeindebund, the B'nai B'rith, and the financial assistance of several larger Jewish communities like Berlin, Frankfurt a. M., Breslau, and Hamburg. By 1907 material from 88 communities had reached the central archive.[47] Influenced by his training under Theodor Mommsen and his experience at the Prussian *Geheimes Staatsarchiv*, Täubler hoped that the work of the Gesamtarchiv would propel the use of archival resources in the study of the Jews.

Guided in his work by the wish to bridge the gap between general history and the study of Jewish history, Täubler postulated at the inauguration of the Gesamtarchiv that the history of the Jews in Germany would be studied as a historical experience, shaped and influenced by German and Jewish history. Existing concepts for historical studies, like state, nation, or church, did not apply to the case of the Jews in Germany. Instead, Täubler suggested analyzing the Jewish past in Germany around the concepts of settlement, assimilation, and particularity.[48] After the demise of the *Historische Commission* and its journal, Täubler combined the task of preservation with a novel research proposal in the hope that the work of the Gesamtarchiv would familiarize German Jews with their distinct heritage. Yet if Täubler aimed to establish through the work of the Gesamtarchiv links with general German as well as general Jewish history, he faced formidable opposition from individual communities that strove to integrate their past into the annals of local and regional histories. Less acknowledged in current scholarship on the Gesamtarchiv, tensions between local communities and the Berlin institution rendered the actual work of moving archival collections from the individual communities to the central archive far more difficult.

The journal of the archive proudly reported on the growing collection, which, however, mainly comprised documents from smaller

communities that had ceased to exist. For some regions, the Gesamtarchiv relied on the work of trusted people like the Rabbi Aron Hepp-
ner, who managed the transfer of several collections from smaller Jewish communities in the Prussian provinces of Posen. Yet as the Jewish
historian Martin Philippson observed, many other communities refused to hand over their archives out of an "unjustified particularism and
local self-consciousness" *(unberechtigten Partikularismus und lokalen
Selbstbewusstsein)*. Local patriotism must have indeed posed a serious
obstacle. To counter this opposition, the Gesamtarchiv stipulated that
the individual communities would remain the legal owners of the materials. Along with others, Zivier and Täubler engaged in large-scale efforts to promote the idea of a central Jewish archive to the communities.

Philippson was not alone in referring to local patriotism in his
speech at the opening celebration of the Gesamtarchiv in 1910 at its new
location in the Oranienburgerstrasse in Berlin. On the same occasion,
Täubler branded the opposition to the Gesamtarchiv as motivated by a
"poorly thought out local patriotism." He admitted that the idea of uniting all Jewish archives would not only worry the local patriots but also
professional archivists since "documents are part of the foundation upon
which they grew." As Täubler went on to explain, such a practice seemed
in direct opposition to common theories about archival work. Removing
documents from their original place appeared problematic from scholarly and cultural points of view insofar as the connection between the
past and present of individual communities would be destroyed. Yet he
contended that the publication of the periodical *Mitteilung des Gesamtarchivs der deutschen Juden* would reinsert the past into the present and
future by stimulating and furthering the work of local historians.

The tension between the reassertion of localism and the impetus for
centralization indicates that the work of archives involved more than a
simple collection of otherwise neglected material. In centralizing the
various local collections, the Gesamtarchiv aimed to illustrate the close
historical ties between the Jews and the Germans. By ridiculing the
local patriotism of individual Jewish communities and their lack of sufficient expertise, the Gesamtarchiv reasserted its own particular vision
of German Jewish history by physically taking possession of its remnants. In line with this orientation, the organizers of the central archive
also declined the Frankfurt Jewish community's offer of housing the
archive. Without any qualms, Philippson exclaimed that the central
Jewish archive had to be located in the German capital and the Berlin
Jewish community.[49]

In light of these tensions between the center and the periphery, research on individual communities and local initiatives continued to play a great role in the preservation movement at a time when the safeguarding of German historical sites became a major objective in the creation of a national past.[50] In Frankfurt, the director of the Düsseldorf art museum, Heinrich Frauberger, established the *Gesellschaft zur Erforschung jüdischer Kunstmäler* (Society for research on Jewish monuments) that mapped out the topography of Jewish cultural history. Frauberger urged his contemporaries to gather the artifacts of a vanishing Jewish past that in light "of the extraordinary technical and industrial development of our time" were rapidly disappearing.[51]

To stave off the ongoing erasure of Jewish landmarks, Ludwig Levysohn transcribed parts of the Jewish tombstone inscriptions of the Worms cemetery in 1853. David Kaufmann continued this work in 1893, which he completed at the beginning of the twentieth century. With the foundation in 1879 of the *Altertumsverein* (Antiquarian society), to which several Worms Jews belonged, Jewish history in the city received wide attention. In 1883, at the conference of the *Gesamtverein der deutschen Geschichts- und Altertumsvereine* (Union of the German historical and antiquarian societies), the archivist August Weckerling lamented the devastated status of Worms's famous *Mikve* (ritual bath), which until the end of the nineteenth century had been used as a cesspool. In response to Weckerling's call, the Jewish community reestablished the *Mikve* in 1895 and began to display cultural and religious artifacts in the Rashi Chapel. This renewed interest in Worms's Jewish history also led to the naming of a newly erected gate as the *Raschi-Tor* (Rashi Gate) in 1907. Moreover, while only briefly noted in travel guides like Baedeker's, local tourist guides, which apparently had Jewish visitors in mind, extensively described Jewish sites.[52]

The attention devoted to the Worms cemetery was not exceptional. In many other communities, local rabbis and scholars engaged in the preservation of cemeteries, which were viewed as sanctified and historical sites often representing the only physical remnant of a community's history.[53] At a time when travel guides and newspaper articles described Jewish cemeteries in detail, these sites became a central component in the narratives about the Jewish past.[54] In 1883, the director of the Philantropin, Hermann Baerwald, published tombstone transcriptions with the financial support of the Jewish community.[55] This initiative was followed in 1904 by the *Comité zur Erhaltung und Wiederherstellung der Grabdenkmäler auf dem alten israelitischen Friedhof am Börneplatz*

(Committee for the preservation and restoration of tombstone monuments of the old Israelite cemetery at the Börneplatz), which engaged in large-scale restoration projects.[56]

Yet not every historical landmark was treated with undivided reverence. When in 1869 several older Frankfurt houses fell into ruin, the local press and German Jewish newspapers carried longer articles on the history of the Judengasse.[57] When the Judengasse vanished, its topography was renamed. Although the façade of the Rothschild house in Frankfurt was restored following large-scale city alterations "with piety according to the old one," the Judengasse disappeared.[58] Even the street names changed; the Judenbrücken, for example, became Einhorngasse and Judengasse became Börneplatz.[59] At first the members of the local historical association welcomed the passing of the Judengasse because it contradicted the self-understanding of a progressive and tolerant city.[60] Similarly, the *Allgemeine* called the Judengasse a "monument of disgrace," and the *Jüdische Presse* welcomed its dissolution and posited that the memory of prejudicial barriers had finally passed.[61] Yet the *Allgemeine* quickly pointed out that Goethe, Heine, and Börne, as well as George Eliot's novel *Daniel Deronda*, which had become very popular in Germany, would preserve the Judengasse's memory.[62]

More comfortable with literature as the location of memory instead of the actual site, the remembrance of the Judengasse reveals the interdependence of amnesia and nostalgia. Along these lines, picture postcards depicted not only Worms's Jewish historical landmarks but other paintings and photographs commemorated the Judengasse.[63] Daniel Moritz Oppenheimer's *Bilder aus dem Altjüdischen Leben* (Images from the old Jewish life) with its claim of presenting traditional Jewish family life in Frankfurt and originally published in the 1860s, was printed in great numbers. Whereas originally these paintings were marketed in forms that made them affordable only for fairly affluent consumers, Kauffmann offered single paintings at reasonable prices.[64] Oppenheimer's paintings were used on pewter plates and Sabbath porcelain trays. His works appeared on picture postcards and replicas of traditional Frankfurt religious objects, like the famous Frankfurt Zobel Torah finials *(Rimmonim),* which were also mass-produced.[65]

Historical sites provided contemporaries with a rich historical landscape from which images were conjured that no longer questioned Jews' position in German society.[66] Fearing the fading away not only of the physical remnants but memories of the past, popular historical associations developed far-reaching programs of public education. Weary about the weakening of Jewish identities and dismayed about the modern age, leaders, scholars, and pedagogues placed Jewish history at the center of German Jewish culture. They promoted the program outlined by Heinrich Graetz at the end of the 1880s to restore the memory of past glories and to reconcile the hearts of the parents with the hearts of the children.

11

The Jewish Past at
the Center of Popular Culture

In the 1890s the popularization of Jewish history reached a new level. An article in the *Israelitische Wochenschrift* from 1892 called the trend toward establishing historical associations "a powerful movement."[1] The *Allgemeine Zeitung des Judenthums* proclaimed in 1893 that a *Verein für jüdische Geschichte und Literatur* (Association for Jewish history and literature) was founded almost on a weekly basis.[2] Approximately 48 local associations existed before the nationwide umbrella organization, the *Verband* (Union), was formally constituted in Hannover in 1893. By 1900 it had become one of the largest Jewish organizations in Germany, with 12,149 members in 131 local societies.[3] Concentrated in the eastern provinces of Prussia, Westphalia, the Rhineland, and Hessen-Nassau, the individual societies together offered at least 2,615 public lectures from 1895 to 1900. In 1900 alone, the Union reported that 1,000 lectures had been given in 150 communities.[4] In addition to organizing public talks, some associations offered Hebrew classes, discussion groups, and evening courses in Jewish history.[5]

The public lectures and discussion groups organized by the associations were well attended.[6] Lecturers were in demand and asked for up to 300 marks for their talks, which placed a great financial strain on smaller associations in particular.[7] In respect to a lecture by the anthropologist Felix von Luschan, Gustav Karpeles made certain that the lecture hall could hold between 600 to 800 guests.[8] An article written on the occasion of the foundation of the fiftieth historical association in 1895 claimed that 500 men and women attended the lectures and 200 participated in the discussion evenings.[9]

The fact that the article specifically mentions women indicates that these new associations tried to become more inclusive. In contrast, the B'nai B'rith, for example, had decided in 1891—unlike its counterparts in the United Kingdom and the United States—not to accept women. Initially, women were not only banned from joining some of the new associations but also blamed for the alleged religious indifference of modern German Jews.[10] Realizing this "indifference" could be overcome only by allowing women to participate in the traditionally male-dominated lecture series, the associations for Jewish history and literature slowly invited women to join in the evening discussions. That this victory was achieved against substantial opposition from within the ranks of the associations illustrates the novelty of this step.[11]

Reflecting these debates, the Henry-Jones Lodge in Hamburg initiated in 1893 the establishment of the *Israelitisch-humanitärer Frauenverein* (Israelite humanitarian women's association). This charitable organization that chiefly represented married Jewish women belonging to the middle and upper middle classes and the Hamburg Reform community, organized public lectures in cooperation with the local Zionist group and the local association for Jewish history and literature in an effort to educate women about the Jewish historical heritage.[12] A few years later, in 1904, Sidonie Werner and Bertha Pappenheim transformed the role of Jewish women in the public sphere when they founded the *Jüdischer Frauenbund* (Jewish women's union). The foundation of the Frauenbund reflected the growing concern on behalf of rabbis, educators, and journalists about the hitherto exclusion of Jewish women from the educational endeavors of the various German Jewish associations. In addition to the traditional social work of women, the Frauenbund offered resistance to anti-Semitism and aimed to bring its educational work into Jewish homes.[13]

Alongside the more inclusive politics of these fin-de-siècle associations, the Union and individual associations broadened their impact by functioning as publication societies for lectures and the successful periodical, the *Jahrbuch für jüdische Geschichte und Literatur* (Yearbook for Jewish history and literature).[14] The Yearbook, which consisted of reviews of events concerning Jews and Judaism during the past year, literature, and scholarly treatments of the Jewish past, had a print run of

5,300 in 1903 and 6,000 in 1904.[15] Larger associations even managed to frequently give away copies of their publications to their members.[16]

Similar to the Institute for the Promotion of Jewish Literature, the history and literature associations declared their neutrality in Jewish religious and political questions and therefore appealed to a broad and diversified audience.[17] With the exception of the *Austrittsorthodoxie* (Secessionist orthodoxy) in central and southern Germany, all other major religious and political groups rallied behind the Union's attempt to place the Jewish past at the center of the Jewish community.[18] For this reason, the neo-Orthodox press suggested that the associations become "a central point" for all factions of the German Jewish communities to combat religious indifference and nihilism.[19] In light of this new spirit, Gustav Karpeles worked together with the prominent neo-Orthodox leader and son of Esriel Hildesheimer, Hirsch Hildesheimer, as well as with the Zionist Max Bodenheimer, both of whom were on the board of the Union. Occasionally, neo-Orthodox rabbis founded local chapters of the historical association. In contrast to the statutes of the federation, these branches emphasized that their purpose was to disseminate knowledge about Jewish history and literature on the basis of traditional Judaism.[20]

Likewise, the leadership of the Union as well as local branches comprised Zionists. The ideological differences between national and religious definitions of Jewry notwithstanding, these early Zionists and other German Jews could easily cooperate. The leading German Zionist Willy Bambus served on the board of the Union, while Max Bodenheimer participated in the formation of a local Jewish historical association in Cologne in 1892. Moreover, when Bodenheimer created the *National-Jüdische Vereinigung* (National Jewish association) in 1894 in Cologne, its program aimed at revitalizing Jewish self-confidence through the promotion of knowledge about Jewish history and literature.[21]

Ostensibly taking up neutral political and religious positions, the Union nevertheless employed a religious rhetoric by fashioning itself as the sole bearer and defender of Judaism. Bestowing a religious significance to the study of the Jews' past represented another step in the ongoing transformation of *Wissenschaft des Judentums* that had commenced in the previous decade. Whereas historical studies had started out at the beginning of the nineteenth century as a critical tool to evaluate the Jewish heritage, they evolved into a supplementary field of Jewish education for religious learning. In response to recent anti-Semitic attacks, the *Allgemeine* exclaimed with Jeremiah 51:5 "lo 'alman

Israel" (Israel has not been widowed).[22] In another article, the *Allge-meine* called the associations "the bet ha-midrash of the future." Once the teachings and the history of Israel were disseminated, German Jews could again exclaim with their forefathers, "This is the Torah, this is the word / That God has given us / That we will preserve forth and forth / And will carry it through life."[23]

Nevertheless, criticism emerged from neo-Orthodox participants. The *Israelit* opposed at times not only the attempt to utilize history and literature as a "Torah substitute" but questioned outright the purpose of history for Jewish education.[24] It is probably for this reason that several neo-Orthodox associations remained outside the Union's fold. These associations combined traditional Jewish learning with an effort to popularize Jewish history. The *Mekor Hayyim* (Fountain of life), founded in 1862 by the neo-Orthodox chief rabbi in Hamburg, Amschel Stern, metamorphosed at the beginning of the 1880s from a traditional society devoted to Torah and Talmud study to an organization that housed public lectures on Jewish history. In front of a male audience, teachers from the Hamburg Talmud Torah school and major neo-Orthodox scholars like Abraham Berliner and Hirsch Hildesheimer delivered their lectures.[25] In the same way, the Frankfurt *Mekor Hayyim*, founded in 1874, arranged lectures about "the glorious history and literature of our people" in 1898 upon the suggestion of several of its members.[26] Following Abraham Berliner's creation of a Montefiore Society in Berlin in 1884, Jacob Horowitz, the rabbi of the nonsecessionist neo-Orthodox synagogue, founded a Montefiore Society in Frankfurt, which furthered "the ideal interest of the Jewish youth" through lectures on Jewish history and the establishment of a library. During its first year of existence in 1897, the society numbered 500 members and over 1,200 in 1907.[27] The *Verein zur Pflege jüdischen Wissens "Tiferes Bachurim"* (Society for the care of Jewish knowledge, "splendor of young men"), founded the same year in Frankfurt, dedicated itself to lectures on Jewish history and literature as well as the establishment of a library for its members.[28]

Similarly, the neo-Orthodox *Jüdisch-Literarische Gesellschaft* (Jewish-literary association), established in 1902 in Frankfurt a. M., had members in Hamburg, Ansbach, Halberstadt, and Mainz. From 1902 to 1903, the association had approximately 450 members; by 1907, there were over 1,200.[29] Not satisfied with the task of popularizing the Jewish past, the Verein subsidized neo-Orthodox scholarship and published its own yearbook, the *Jahrbuch der jüdisch-literarischen Gesellschaft* (Yearbook of the Jewish literary society), to promote and disseminate Jewish scholarship.[30] In addition to these societies, the associations, founded during the 1880s, continued to thrive outside the Union. In 1897, the local branches of the B'nai B'rith, which entailed a large neo-Orthodox following, reported they had held over 1,000 public lectures, while the *Akademische Verein für jüdische Geschichte und Literatur* (Academic association for Jewish history and literature) claimed it organized 186 public lectures during its first decade of existence.[31]

While some associations remained outside the Union, a cooperative atmosphere nevertheless was maintained. The Union streamlined many activities by providing lists of available speakers and their topics and financially assisting smaller associations.[32] The speakers, as well as the themes of the lectures, reflected the neutral position of the Union in all religious and political matters. Scholars, teachers, rabbis, and preachers from all denominations and parties lectured not only on the Bible, Mendelssohn, Heine, and Jewish literature but also on Sabbatianism, Frankism, Hassidism, and Zionism. Speeches about Lessing, Goethe, Humboldt, and Rembrandt illustrated the existence of tolerant non-Jews.[33] Other lectures and commemorative services in synagogues were occasioned by the anniversaries of famous Jews and non-Jews. Gustav Karpeles, for example, lectured on Maimonides, Benno Jacob on Heinrich Graetz, Moritz Lazarus on Ludwig Stein, Abraham Berliner on Rashi, and Hirsch Hildesheimer on Josephus Flavius.[34] Special attention was also directed to the founding father of Jewish historiography, Leopold Zunz.[35]

Yet while these lectures concentrated on singular events, people, and movements, they did not so much as provide a historical understanding of the long *durée* of Judaism as they did an exemplary representation of Jewish history. By focusing on ethical monotheism, cultural accomplishments, persecution, and tolerant Gentiles, the lectures presented constant paradigmatic patterns that were not subject to historical change or development.[36] Geared toward personal identification with the Jewish ancestors, these lectures diminished the historical difference and blended past and present. Gustav Karpeles tried to address this lacuna with his cycle of six lectures that he gave on several occasions. Promoted by the Union, Karpeles offered his still unpublished manuscript to other speakers.[37] But even this lecture series did not provide a historical understanding of the Jewish past but rather retheologized Jewish history. The miraculous endurance of the Jewish people was comprehensible only as a sacred history chronicling Judaism's mission to unite all religions in the acceptance of one God, as Karpeles made clear.[38]

Jewish luminaries received wide attention in public lectures and articles in the Jewish press, yet no monuments commemorated them. In 1902 Karl Emil Franzos searched in vain for monuments to Jews in addition to Moses Mendelssohn's in Dessau. He soon realized that with few exceptions, none existed.[39] When the Mendelssohn monument was unveiled in 1890, it was rather exceptional since its erection was carried out by the city and not by Jewish organizations.[40] The plan to construct a monument to honor the "Pioneer of the days of the blossoming of German spiritual life" was originally supported in 1885 by the *Allgemeine*.[41] The *Allgemeine* and the *Israelitische Wochenschrift* would later reverse their positions and side with the *Jüdische Presse* insisting that a monument was against Jewish law and custom.[42] While German Jews may have financially contributed to the monument and participated in its public unveiling, members of Jewish organizations were largely absent from the event.[43]

The example of the Mendelssohn statue reveals the reluctance and opposition met by attempts to erect monuments to Jewish figures. Yet the continuous emphasis on singular events, individuals, and movements found another outlet to commemorate outstanding Jews. In one of his lesser known works, *Deutsche Briefe* (German letters) of 1871, Leopold Zunz noted "that the educated *(Gebildeten)* in their education *(Bildung)* turn everything into images *(Bilder)*."[44] Zunz pinpointed one of the central principles by which Jewish history was popularized. Removed from the flow of history, photos, lithographs, and picture postcards created a very different mode of representing history.

During the last decades of the nineteenth century, several surveys of paintings appeared that depicted scenes from the past.[45] Adolph Kohut's *Geschichte der deutschen Juden* and his anthology of famous Jews contained many illustrations and functioned as a storehouse of images from which Jewish periodicals culled their material.[46] Several Jewish publishers in Germany carried, in addition to their books, a variety of broadsides and lithographs in part due to technical innovations that made low-cost illustrations more affordable. "Selection of twelve leaves in a fine linen folder with embossing" featured portraits of Moses Mendelssohn, Michael Sachs, Salomon Eiger, Moritz Veit, Moses Montefiore, and Leopold Zunz. The publisher Poppelauer offered a portrait of Zunz with the historian's facsimile signature.[47] Moreover, Poppelauer carried miniature portraits of rabbinic sages from the Middle Ages, maskilim, bankers, composers, representatives of Reform, Conservative, and neo-Orthodox Judaism, and Jewish historians like Jost and Zunz.[48]

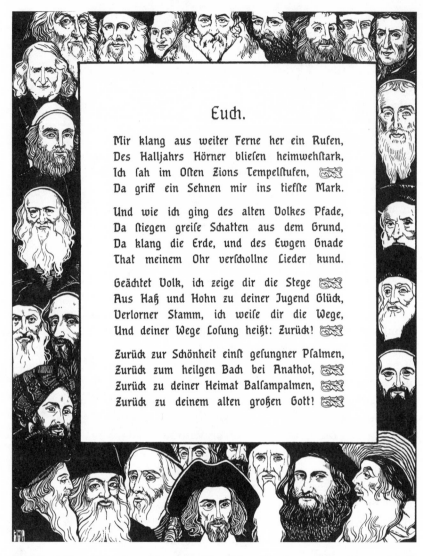

Ephraim Lilien illustration of the poem "Euch" from Börries von Münchhausen's *Juda* (1900). (Courtesy of the Center for Advanced Judaic Studies Library, University of Pennsylvania)

In addition, publishers used picture galleries and collages to depict Jewish financiers, religious leaders, and philosophers alongside political activists and heads of Jewish organizations. Poppelauer's catalog advertised a picture gallery of rabbinic figures from the seventeenth to the nineteenth centuries along with a collection of 23 portraits titled "Gallery of Famous and Virtuous Men of Israel of the Present Century" that featured among others, Samson Raphael Hirsch, Isaac Adolphe Cremieux, and Abraham Geiger.[49] Other collages like "Learned and Distinguished Individuals of Our Time" positioned portraits of Jews from Europe and Palestine adjacent to famous rabbis, members of the Rothschild family, political notables, and literary figures.[50] The renowned Jewish artist Ephraim Lilien also employed the collage format. In his illustrations to Börries von Münchhausen's cycle of poems, he created a collage around a poem that placed Ashkenazic and Sephardic rabbinic scions next to Leopold Zunz.[51]

The emotional and nostalgic appeal of these pictures and collages was enhanced by the decontextualization of history. These "museums without walls"[52] obliterated historical specificity and differences. Place and time no longer mattered; these objects conveyed an eternal association between figures of the past and present. This is even true for Kohut's illustrated history of German Jewry. Scattered throughout the book, the illustrations often appear out of context, thereby undermining the historical specificity of the events described in the narrative.

While historical artifacts were preserved and collected, and the Jewish past was placed at the center of German Jewish culture, the library became the main repository that furthered the popularization of Jewish historiography. By the end of the nineteenth century, Jewish historiography was surveyed in an attempt to create lists of canonical works. In these still largely unexplored libraries, the antagonism of the 1850s and 1860s had waned, as friends and foes were cataloged and shelved next to each other.

12

Libraries with and without Walls

In the last decades of the nineteenth century, local associations preserved historical landmarks, scholars and educators popularized Jewish history in lectures and public celebrations, and libraries furthered the dissemination and preservation of the common heritage. Earlier, in 1861, Abraham Geiger noted that "the most eloquent witness for the respect of the spiritual work is the foundation and maintenance of a library. A library provides not only nutrition for the spirit, but is also a monument to the spirit where our ancestors are gathered. . . . A library pictorially represents for us the ties of times, where gray antiquity is intertwined with the bright present." By the end of the nineteenth century, these words were again cited in the report of the Jewish community library in Berlin.[1] A library represented not only continuity with the past but was a site of memory that testified to the increasing dissemination and canonization of works by Wissenschaft's scholars. During the 1890s, community leaders and members of the Association for Jewish History and Literature propagated the establishment of Jewish libraries to secure knowledge about a fleeting Jewish past.[2]

With the creation of the so-called *Lesehallen* (reading halls), the number of Jewish libraries steadily increased.[3] The *Deutsch-Israelitische Gemeindebund*, Masonic lodges, Jewish communities, and other Jewish societies subsidized the Lesehallen, which were primarily located in urban centers like Breslau, Berlin, Frankfurt a. M., and Hamburg.[4] In addition, efforts were made to bring these libraries to the rural areas. The Frankfurt a. M. lodge, for example, had a travel library from the beginning of the twentieth century.[5] There, Jewish book collections were open to the public in the Lesehalle, the Frankfurt lodge, the Montefiore Society, the *Verein zur Abwehr des Antisemitismus* (Association for the defense against anti-Semitism), and other Jewish educational institutions.[6] In Berlin, readers had access to the community and *Bet Midrash* libraries, the *Jüdische Lesehalle und Bibliothek* (Jewish reading hall and library), the library of the *Deutsch-Israelitischer Gemeindebund*, the library of the Masonic lodges, as well as those of smaller societies like the Academic Society for Jewish History and Literature.[7]

Borrowing privileges were often restricted to paying members, while nonmembers usually read books in the reading room.[8] In the case of the library of the Jewish Community Council in Berlin, the young Gershom Scholem only needed to provide a note from his mother before he could use the collection.[9] Although the opening hours of some community libraries were fairly restricted, the library of the Henry-Jones Lodge and the reading hall in Berlin were open during the week and on the weekends, and were especially popular on Saturdays.[10] By and large these libraries were extensively used; in 1899, approximately 50 users frequented the Berlin reading hall daily, while about 200 patrons borrowed books from the library throughout the year.[11] From 1906 to 1910, more than 300 readers used the library yearly and checked out close to half of the collection, while the reading room had over 20,000 visitors per year.[12] In 1907, the considerably smaller reading hall in Frankfurt a. M., which possessed only 1,232 volumes, had 144 users check out books 1,496 times, while 5,704 readers used the library.[13] The collections of the various libraries usually contained a significant number of scholarly and popular histories of the Jews, and next to literature and popular-scientific works, these books were frequently taken out.[14]

The libraries aimed at gathering all relevant Jewish texts. Berlin's Jewish school library, for example, had amassed by the end of the 1880s "one hundred volumes in which all of the stories of the Jewish past and present, biographical accounts of famous men of Judaism, descriptions of Jewish travelers . . . in short everything, that could arouse the children's feelings."[15] While this rhetoric appealed to an image of completeness, the question of which books to regard as essential in light of the rapidly expanding production of newspapers, periodicals, and historical works became increasingly difficult if not impossible to answer.

Often donations, rather than planned acquisitions, made up libraries' holdings.[16] Moreover, funding restrictions affected the sizes of their collections. Whereas the Jewish reading hall boasted a collection of 7,200 volumes in 1910, association libraries in Danzig and Bochum contained 600 volumes, while Dortmund's numbered 300.[17]

In light of these difficulties, a discussion regarding the essential Jewish library took shape at the turn of the century and continued well into the 1900s.[18] To remedy the situation, historians, teachers, and publishers analyzed the available books and ranked them to distill an essential collection to be found in every Jewish library. Various institutions, associations, and periodicals participated in this debate and drew up lists of suggested book titles. One of the first contributions, published in the *Allgemeine,* provided "a list of books for a small Jewish library, as it is necessary for literature associations." The history category featured, for example, Heinrich Graetz's complete and popular history, next to works by Moritz Güdemann, Leo Herzfeld, Isaac Jost, Abraham Geiger, and Abraham Berliner.[19] The history of literature category listed books by David Cassel, Gustav Karpeles, Moritz Kayserling, Moritz Steinschneider, Michael Sachs, Abraham Sulzbach, and Leopold Zunz. The Union promoted this essential library and updated it with works such as Adolf Kohut's cultural history of German Jewry. By 1903, this "library without walls" featured 152 scholarly works and 203 titles of belles lettres.[20]

Not all books on these lists were equally popular. The inclusion of Jost, Geiger, and Zunz in the essential library was foremost a form of recognition and reverence but not necessarily an indication of their works' popular character or wide dissemination. Their studies were still widely available despite the fact that they had originally been published in small editions decades earlier. Heinrich Graetz's *Geschichte* on the other hand, which had originally met with vituperative responses, nevertheless became widely read. With the exception of the volumes covering the period up to the death of Judah Maccabee and the modern age starting with Moses Mendelssohn, Graetz's *Geschichte* underwent at least three editions, while single chapters were reprinted in the German Jewish press. Similarly, his *Volkstümliche Geschichte* was widely disseminated and saw its fifth edition in 1914.[21]

While new histories of Jewish literature, philosophy, and single communities appeared, the *Jüdischer Verlag* (Jewish publishing house) founded by Martin Buber in 1902 began to create an entirely different library. This publishing house represented the democratic faction within the Zionist movement that had staged a dramatic walkout of the

Fifth Zionist Congress in December 1901.[22] Clashing with the major representatives of political-diplomatic Zionism like Theodor Herzl and some of the religious Zionists, Martin Buber, Berthold Feiwel, and Ephraim Lilien put forward the importance of a Jewish cultural education as an instrument of the Zionist rebellion. Yet the publishing house aimed to function not just as a center for the nascent Zionist cultural movement in Germany but intended to become the central agency for the promotion of Jewish literature, art, and scholarship. During the next decades, the *Jüdischer Verlag* published a fairly diversified library that encompassed not only translations of Hebrew and Yiddish literature, but also German Jewish literature and scholarship.[23] Already the physical appearance of these books was intended to convey an educational effect. Book design as a marketing and branding device achieved here a new importance.

Together with other members of the democratic fraction, Buber also promoted the plan for the establishment of a Jewish university library in Jerusalem.[24] The Jewish national library that originated in 1892 with the assistance of the B'nai B'rith resonated strongly with the concurrent blossoming of Jewish libraries in Germany. The idea of a national library symbolized the richness of Jewish cultural heritage and expressed the far-reaching spiritual and cultural aspirations of the newly emerging Jewish community in Palestine. The issue of a national library mirrored similar efforts on the part of the Zionists to mold existing Jewish libraries. The selection process in particular was to be left to the devices of experts, who would ensure the presence of indispensable books on Zionism within the libraries.[25]

These initiatives testify above all to the shared cultural practices during this period. Heinrich Loewe, for example, promoted the establishment of Jewish libraries in Germany in the pages of the *Allgemeine Zeitung des Judenthums* at the beginning of the 1890s.[26] A few years later, he emerged as a major publicist of the German Zionist movement. He was appointed a delegate to the first Zionist Congress, became a trainee at the university library in Berlin, and edited several Zionist periodicals. At the beginning of the twentieth century, Loewe attempted to curry support for the transformation of the existing Josef Chasanowicz Library in Jerusalem into the Jewish national library.[27] Jerusalem, Loewe posited, was the only possible location for a national Jewish library; not only because "romantic sentiments" were associated with this place but organizers could sidestep the issue of a national Jewish library becoming a German Jewish, Russian Jewish, or American Jewish library. Influenced by the central educational function ascribed to Jewish libraries in Germany, Loewe argued that the national library in Jerusalem was to become a scholarly, public, and popular institution.[28]

At the same time, separate attempts were made to assemble an essential list of recommended readings for the Jewish youth. Influenced by similar developments among German pedagogues, the discussion intensified around the turn of the century. Earlier initiatives during the 1850s had recommended only a few historical novels but no historical works for the Jewish youth bookshelf. Once the discussion recommenced in the late 1880s, historical works gained prominence on the Jewish youth booklist. Already the general list for a Jewish library contained textbooks by Samuel Bäck, Marcus Brann, and David Cassel.[29]

The first more comprehensive list of Jewish youth literature appeared in the *Allgemeine* in 1889 and listed Bäck's textbook history along with several works by Abraham Berliner.[30] A few weeks later, a reader demanded the inclusion of the textbook histories by Hecht-Kayserling, the one-volume history by Herzfeld, and several volumes of Graetz's *Geschichte der Juden*. In response, the *Allgemeine*'s editor added Karpeles's *Geschichte der jüdischen Literatur* and Kayserling's biography of Moses Mendelssohn.[31] These single voices formed a new effort when, in 1903, the *Verband jüdischer Lehrervereine im Deutschen Reich* (Union of the Jewish teachers associations in the German Reich) published the *Blätter für Erziehung und Unterricht* (Periodical for education and teaching) as a supplement to the *Israelitischen Familienblatt* (Israelite family periodical). Moreover, in 1905, the *Jugendschriften-Kommission* (Commission for youth literature), to which Karpeles and Ismar Elbogen belonged, published the *Wegweiser für die Jugendliteratur* (Guide to the Jewish youth literature).[32] This guide contained a detailed list that differentiated between various categories and assigned asterisks to highly recommended books. Among the history books singled out were once again the popular textbooks by Bäck, Brann, Cassel, and Kayserling. Geiger's *Das Judenthum und seine Geschichte* received no star, while Graetz's popular history had the distinction of being the only recommended history book with two asterisks.[33] The canonization of these works resulted in their constant republication, and they could be found in many Jewish libraries.[34]

The shift to a specific youth literature brought with it also a discussion of the goals of instruction in Jewish history. Historical education was meant to familiarize Jewish youth with the faithfulness of their forefathers, the perseverance of the Jewish people, Judaism's mission, and God's providence. In addition to publicists and educators, Jewish mothers were to ensure the transmission of proper Jewish education to their children at home. The guide for Jewish youth literature called upon Jewish women to involve themselves in the selection of proper reading material for their children. Jointly with their daughters and sons, Jewish mothers were asked to read with their children at the family table.[35]

Within this comprehensive educational program, particular attention was devoted to the history of persecution. Commentators singled out the Jewish martyrdom in the Rhineland and the expulsion from Spain for their edifying powers.[36] In addition to the *Leidensgeschichte,* the spiritual development of Judaism became another focal point. Educators emphasized the Jews' premodern social and legal status and their subsequent struggle for emancipation. As one commentator put it, Jewish history was intended to be taught as a "family history" *(Familienge-schichte),* which signaled a difference from the way world history was taught.[37] This idea implied a static pedagogical goal that diminished historical differences. Jewish history "must be comprehended everywhere and represented as a family history that is closer to our hearts because it is the history of our ancestors and forefathers, our own family. Victory and defeat, happiness and sorrow, as they appear in this richly moving history, must be represented to the youth as its own fate and as if they personally are part of it."[38]

Teaching Jewish history was thus not an idle occupation but intended to forge and strengthen a strong emotional attachment to Judaism and the Jewish people.[39] Accordingly, the textbook histories were written in order to "adhere to the fatherly religion," as noted by Marcus Brann.[40] The reviews of these books reinforced these educational goals. The German Jewish press lauded Bäck's book, for example, because it was affordable, concise, and the subject matter clearly presented. More importantly, Bäck also had complied with the reviewer's belief that history is a means to "awaken in the hearts of the upcoming generation respect for our past that commands reverence, interest in our future, and participation in our holiest affairs."[41] Books that did not fully comply with these goals were criticized for their lack of empathy.[42]

Associations and book dealers responded to the ongoing establishment of libraries and the concurrent canonization of Jewish historiographical works by adopting new marketing strategies that shed additional light on the books' receptions. Various associations published lectures within series advertised as a "home library" *(Hausbibliothek).*[43]

The publisher Wilhelm Jacobsohn printed a guide to Jewish literature for individuals who wanted to found a "community, public, society, or youth library, especially for rabbis, teachers, community leaders and librarians."[44] In another example, Kaufmann's catalogs listed "recognized and excellent textbooks" and ideal presents for holidays and Bar Mitzvahs from the essential bookshelf.[45] Similarly, the guide for Jewish youth literature promoted to Jewish parents historical works by Graetz, Brann, Samuel Bäck, and Kohut as presents for religious occasions. The guide included a special section of books suitable as gifts.[46] The young Zionist Gershom Scholem may therefore not have been the only Jewish child in Germany who received Graetz's popular history as a Bar Mitzvah present.[47]

For these occasions, publishers created special editions *(Prachtbände)* of historical works such as Samuel Bäck's textbook history. The production of these high quality books testifies to a mostly middle- and upper middle-class audience. The publisher of Graetz's *Geschichte der Juden* offered an edition in "linen with goldleaf." [48] The well-known publisher of books on the occult, mythology, and folklore, Eugen Diedrichs, offered Georg Liebe's 1903 *Das Judentum in der deutschen Vergangenheit* (The Jews in the German past) as a limited edition of one hundred copies on handmade paper.[49] At the same time, however, these books continued to appear in simple editions. The major publisher *Deutsche Verlag* also offered Adolph Kohut's *Geschichte der deutschen Juden* in installments to enable the "less affluent" to acquire it, as one reviewer noted in the *Allgemeine*.[50]

These marketing efforts point to a fairly diversified distribution. This impression is further corroborated by the social makeup of the library users. They too came from the middle and upper middle classes and consisted chiefly of merchants, lawyers, professors, writers, teachers, rabbis, cantors, book dealers, and publishers, in addition to workers, artisans, and technicians. Despite the variation of professions, clear clusters existed with merchants, pupils, and students representing two-thirds of the members of the Berlin community library and the Frankfurt reading hall.[51] Yet despite this diversified consumption, the periodical *Ost und West,* which pictured in 1905 a mostly middle-class audience wearing bowlers and attending the Berlin reading hall, presented Jewish libraries as an integral component of German Jewish middle-class culture. Moreover, while the photo captures a mainly male audience, a single woman is placed at the center of the group ascending the staircase to the library.[52]

Entrance to the Jewish Reading Hall in Berlin from *Ost und West* (1905). (Courtesy of the Center for Advanced Judaic Studies Library, University of Pennsylvania)

The central location of the woman in this photo of the group of readers entering a Jewish library may very well reflect an effort to market the libraries to women. When, a few years later, *Ost und West* carried another article on the Jewish reading hall, it once again placed photos alongside the text that elevated the place of women in these newly emerging centers of reading.[53] Whereas the images of the library display almost exclusively men sitting around tables reading newspapers and books, a woman is captured only as she checks out a volume at the circulation desk. It might very well be that this portrayal is not accidental but reflects the different prescribed gender roles within the newly

Circulation desk of the Jewish Reading Hall in Berlin from *Ost und West* (1908). (Courtesy of the Center for Advanced Judaic Studies Library, University of Pennsylvania)

established libraries. According to such a reading, men utilized these new associations also to socialize among themselves, whereas women tended to frequent libraries primarily to take out books to read at home.

Whereas the field of Jewish scholarship continued to be male dominated, the more inclusive politics of some of the associations as well as novel marketing efforts suggest a softening of the gender gap among the readers. The evidence here, however, is not conclusive, especially since the actual use of these libraries was not restricted to their members. The statistics provided by some of the libraries in their yearly reports do not, in most cases, indicate the sex of their users. The report of the Jewish community library of Berlin, for example, lists a total of 145 users for 1902–3 and 176 for 1904–5. The list is categorized according to professions and mentions 24 male and female teachers for 1902–3 and 45 male and female students in the same year. While the specific gender divide is uncertain, a separate entry lists 32 "ladies" (for 1902 and 34 for 1903, with no mention of their occupation).[54] In contrast, the Jewish reading hall in Frankfurt counted only 7 women among its 143 members in 1905.[55] The available information does point to the continued male dominance, which illustrates an important limitation of the otherwise unprecedented popularization of Jewish history. Not only were women excluded from some of the neo-Orthodox associations, but they could only participate, for example, in the Association for the Promotion of Jewish Literature in Breslau as "special members."[56]

Despite these limitations, the canonization of certain works by Wissenschaft scholars reveals their lasting impact and, in the case of Graetz, his elevated status among historians. In their canonization, books were not simply evaluated according to their scholarly merits but whether they imparted solace and pride to their readers. Popularizing the Jewish past emphasized continuity and perserverence and obliterated historical differences. Thus particular moments of Jewish history were singled out, and narratives about the historical development were replaced with images of the Jewish past.

Conclusion

In his seminal work on historical writing, Michel de Certeau observed that "before we can understand what history says about a society, we have to analyze how history functions within it."[1] This study has been concerned with analyzing constructions of the Jewish past in the scholarly discipline and the popular culture that shaped the identities of German Jewry in the nineteenth century. For a period that has been commonly seen as the century of history, this intellectual and cultural exploration of Wissenschaft has elucidated the importance of the Jewish past for the self-understanding of German Jewry.

At the end of the nineteenth century, Jewish history had become a storehouse from which German Jews invoked images that reassured them of their continuity with the past even as they embraced German culture. In a period of rapid social, cultural, and technological change, Jewish historians recalled the past as a stable and constant realm and invited their readers to travel to the Judengasse. Because of this edifying purpose, the popularization of Jewish history during the last decades of the nineteenth century was predicated on establishing similarities between the past and present. These forged correspondences functioned as conduits that "transported" the past to the present within the historical narratives. While singling out particular moments and events from the annals of the Jewish past, educators and historians did not aim to promote an understanding of the development of Judaism over time but rather presented exemplary paradigmatic moments lifted from all periods of Jewish history.

In this fashion, the recollection of Jewish history was consoling without, however, infringing on German Jews' self-understanding as culturally integrated members of German society. Assimilation and self-assertion were part of the constant renegotiation of the Jewish and German heritages in the formation of German Jewish identities.[2] The *Centralverein deutscher Staatsbürger jüdischen Glaubens* (Central association of German citizens of the Jewish faith), which promoted an assimilatory platform while defending Jewish rights, paralleled in size the associations for Jewish history and literature.[3] In particular, the increasing importance of German Jewish history as a field of scholarly inquiry ensured the compatibility of these two realms insofar as the study of local communities, the collection of archival documents, and the preservation of historical artifacts fused Jewish pride with German patriotism.

German Jews' dual aspirations to integrate into the surrounding society and retain their Jewish identity were, however, not uncontested, as evidenced by the Berliner Antisemitismusstreit. The German Jewish culture was carefully observed by outside forces that suspected Jews of nonconformity, if not disloyalty. German theologians and historians challenged Wissenschaft's attempt to promote the recollection of the Jewish past as an instrument in the formation of Jewish identities. Even Jewish schoolbooks during the 1890s were subjected to state inquiries and public debates.[4]

The constant ambiguity of exclusion and integration, and tolerance and rejection, created the overtly contradictory impulses of self-assertion and assimilation, which manifested themselves from the end of the eighteenth century on. Self-assertion and promotion of a commitment to the past became particularly prevalent with the emergence of a Jewish reading public. Early on, the Institute for the Promotion of Jewish Literature was a significant power. Those works that had not been published by this Jewish book club hardly ever became subsequently important. In comparison, efforts to establish similar book clubs in the United States during this time failed. In the United States, a Jewish Publication Society existed from 1845 to 1851, which had, however, only 450 members.[5] A similar society emerged in 1871 with the largely New York–based American Jewish Publication Society. While the membership boasted at one time 800 readers, the society folded in 1875.[6] Compared with these efforts, the German Jewish book club was a formidable success. With its readership reaching beyond the Germanic world, the institute imprinted the work of German Jewish scholarship onto the fabric of modern Jewish cultures.

With their need to attract readers, the first German Jewish book clubs adopted an overt position of neutrality in religious and political matters and thereby selectively promoted works of Wissenschaft. The institutes thus sponsored the work of authors of various religious orientations. The clubs, with a largely middle-class membership, for example, considered Heinrich Graetz's *Geschichte der Juden* not a bulky product of scholarship but educational and entertaining. Its postulated neutrality notwithstanding, the Institute for the Promotion of Jewish Literature marketed only those books that met these conditions and even occasionally censored its authors' works. Preempting potential criticism from German scholars, the book club forced Graetz to omit chapters on Christianity and then refused to publish the eleventh volume of his *Geschichte der Juden*.

The imagined Jewish community of readers, members of societies, and visitors of libraries became crucial components and active participants in Wissenschaft's refashioning of the collective memory not just in Germany. The Jewish public, as constituted by these societies and communities, halted the professionalization of Jewish historiography when it withdrew its support for the Historical Commission during the 1880s. Moreover, during the last third of the nineteenth century, popular Jewish historical societies and institutions participated in the transformation of Wissenschaft from a scholarly discipline to an institution of public education. This transformation was aided by Wissenschaft's institutionalization within rabbinical seminaries. The exclusion from German universities and the confinement of Jewish historical studies to rabbinical seminaries curtailed the role of scholars like Leopold Zunz and Moritz Steinschneider, who vigorously opted for disengaged scholarship. Consequently, Jewish historians, whether serving as rabbis, preachers, public speakers, or advisors to libraries, became central elements of the German Jewish culture.

Together these political, social, and cultural factors functioned as "social frames," to use Maurice Halbwachs's formulation, which shaped the varying historical conceptions and forms of the popularization of Jewish history in the course of the nineteenth century.[7] German Jewish historiography defined its boundaries for the academic study of the Jewish past against the Enlightenment legacy and the premodern visions of the providential view of Jewish history. Jewish historians reconfigured a divinely governed history with an eternal tradition at its core into a developmental conception of the Jewish past. Within the framework of the evolutionary understanding of this past, Wissenschaft scholars from the middle of the nineteenth century on engaged in a large-scale recollection of the Jewish past as part of scientific and educational agendas.

The original and more limited conception of the essence of Judaism as ethical monotheism gave way to a more comprehensive understanding that encompassed the history of suffering and learning and daily Jewish culture. This widening of the elements for the definition of the essence of Judaism dignified additional historical sources and moments worthy of recollection and remembrance. Jewish daily culture, customs and proverbs, dress and folksongs, and tales and legends, became objects of both scholarly investigation and popular recollection.

Despite the fundamental changes within Wissenschaft during the course of the nineteenth century, the recollection and popularization of the Jewish past displayed continuity and change. On Yom Kippur in 1836, Heinrich Graetz ran away from his family home in order to escape the custom of *kaparot*, whereby the day before the Day of Atonement is marked by swinging a cock or a hen around the head three times to transfer symbolically one's sins to a fowl. His father threatened to destroy his library if he did not return. In the end, Graetz opted for his library.[8] This confrontation seems to encapsulate the clash between old and new, religious practice and scholarly inquiry, and religion and science. Without debating the fundamental novelty of the scientific inquiry of the Jewish past as it took shape during the nineteenth century in Germany, this shift was ultimately not as radical as it has previously appeared.

Even the inception of Jewish historiography was not a radical departure but continued to succumb to the lachrymose conception of Jewish history that had already achieved renewed prominence in eighteenth-century writings on Jewish history. Similarly, Jewish historians and the popular historical associations at the end of the nineteenth century did not promote a secular self-understanding but a new attachment to the Jewish religion that remained a critical factor in the self-definition of German Jews. Graetz described the advent of Wissenschaft, therefore, not as rupture but as an awakening of the Jews, who emerged from the night of the grave *(Grabesnacht)* "rubbing their eyes . . . searching to restore their memory and bringing forth their past glories."[9]

This process of recollection and popularization cannot simply be seen as an answer to anti-Semitism. Rather, the popularizing tendency within the Jewish historical writings as well as the spread of Jewish historical associations emerged also in response to the threat of secularization ushered in by the growing importance of the natural sciences and anti-Semitism displayed by Protestant scholars. Gustav Karpeles perceptively observed that Jewish scholarship had to face up to world views "that deconstruct all religions and . . . denigrate Judaism to the level of a national cult."[10]

Jewish historical associations, therefore, were not simply defense organizations but also aimed to revitalize an interest in Jewish history and strengthen the attachment to Judaism. Hence, contemporaries viewed the pervasive proliferation of Jewish history as a process of "re-judaization" *(Rejudaisierung)*.[11] They regarded the newly emerging associational landscape as one of the central unifying forces that led to an affirmation of Jewish heritage and brought together the various denominational and political groups.[12]

The popularization of the Jewish past constantly negotiated a balance between continuity and change and German culture and Jewish history. Nineteenth-century constructions of a usable Jewish past were often riddled with paradoxes and fraught with tension as a result of attempts to undermine particularistic aspects of Judaism and efforts to promote pride in the common heritage, as Jacques Ehrenfreund has also argued.[13] Yet nationalism not only curtailed new expressions of Jewish identity, it also enabled them. When German Jews popularized Jewish history as a means to ally their contemporaries to the organization and ideals of a distinct group, they consciously and subconsciously adopted the language of nationalism. To be sure, their nationalism defined modern Jews as a culture in light of a common past and not as a political body. Both the *Allgemeine* and *Ost und West* cited Ernest Renan's famous essay on nationalism to capture their own attempts at formulating a Jewish identity based on the Jewish past: "A nation is a soul, a spiritual principle. Two things, which are really only one, go to make up this soul or spiritual principle. The one is the past, the other is the present. The one is the common possession of a rich heritage of memories, and the other is actual agreement, the desire to live together, and the will to continue to make the most of the joint inheritance that was received undiminished."[14]

Renan's elevation of suffering and sacrifice in the past mirrors the meaning the lachrymose conception of Jewish history had achieved when he wrote, "Among national memories, times of sorrow have greater value than victories, for they impose duties and demand common effort."[15] Whereas originally the lachrymose conception created a dichotomy between the pre-modern and modern periods by contrasting the dark ages of persecution with the modern age of freedom, the history of suffering acquired a new function. In the second half of the nineteenth century, Jewish historians cited, for example, the martyrdom of the Jews in the Rhineland during the First Crusade to engender the reader's compassion and to impose the duty to remember the Jewish past.[16]

The pervasiveness of this trend to bind contemporary German Jews to the memory of the past did not go uncriticized. Hermann Cohen dismissed, for example, the idea of placing the memory of Jewish martyrdom at the center of public education.[17] Zionists like Max Nordau attempted to liberate contemporary culture from the purported overbearing influence of history. Reflecting on the acceleration of time, he questioned the edifying power of history in general. For Nordau, historiography constantly replaced past memories with new ones. Accordingly, he compared historical writings to novels that follow seasonal fashions and have therefore no lasting cognitive value.[18] Nordau's observation made outside of his Zionist writings could be taken as a fundamental rejection of the ideal of historical education. Yet neither Nordau nor the cultural Zionists in Germany adopted this perspective in their cultural program that also strove toward the rejuvenation of Jewish identities during this period.[19]

Zionists and non-Zionists differed indeed sharply in their understanding of Judaism and clashed in particular over national and cultural-religious definitions of modern Jewry and its history.[20] The responses to the first Zionist conference clearly demarcated these differences. The so-called *Protestrabbiner* challenged Herzl's original intention of Munich as the place of the Congress on political, religious and cultural grounds. They believed that Zionism presented a threat to their political loyalty to the German state. Moreover, they contended that to create a Jewish state in Palestine contradicted the basic premises of Jewish messianic expectations.[21]

Debates about national and cultural-religious definitions of Jews continued to divide the camps. Yet this conflict was less pronounced within Germany where the Zionists in Cologne, for example, underscored in their declaration that Jewish patriotism and political loyalty to the German state were not at odds.[22] They intentionally downplayed the political aspect of their nationalist aspirations in favor of their cultural educational activities.[23] The definition of Jewish nationalism adopted by the Zionists in Cologne echoed to some extent the understanding of nineteenth-century German Jewish historians, when they stated that Jews are united by common descent and history.[24]

The existing ideological differences remained less pronounced until the Zionist conference in Posen in 1912 and the ascendancy of a more radical generation of German Zionists.[25] Yet no matter how sharply the different camps clashed over the national interpretation of the Jews, they shared the goal to propagate the study of the Jewish past. Already in the course of the first Zionist Congress in Basel in 1897 Max Bodenheimer declared that studying Jewish history would persuade especially the Jews of Western Europe that Jews had maintained a national unity despite assimilation and emancipation throughout the ages.[26] While ostensibly elevating the centrality of the rise of Zionism by inscribing Theodor Herzl and the First Zionist Congress into the annals of modern Jewish history, the Zionist *Jüdische Almanach*'s calendar of historical events essentially listed the same pre-Zionist events and luminaries in Jewish history.[27] Likewise, the renowned Zionist artist Ephraim Lilien illustrated Börries von Münchhausen's poem "Euch" (You), which called upon the Jews to return to the glory of antiquity, not with images of Palestine but with major Jewish intellectual representatives of the Diaspora.[28] Zionists supported the periodical *Ost und West*'s efforts to reeducate the Jewish middle class and intellectuals about their culture and heritage.[29]

German Zionists went to the Jewish libraries, attended lectures, and actively participated in the Associations for Jewish History and Literature. At the third congress of the German Zionists in Frankfurt a. M., the *Zionistische Vereinigung für Deutschland* (Zionist union of Germany) adopted not only a program in support of Jewish settlement in Palestine but also the popularization of Jewish history and literature. They aimed to promote the Jewish heritage by partly aligning themselves with "already existing organizations," apparently referring to the Association for Jewish History and Literature.[30] The associational landscape that had emerged with many local historical associations even provided at times the framework for like-minded Zionists to meet. Max Bodenheimer, for example, became acquainted with David Wolfssohn at a meeting of the Cologne Association for Jewish History and Literature.[31]

Several Zionists even saw nineteenth-century Jewish scholarship as a source of confirmation for the nationalistic understanding of the Jews.[32] More conscious of the ideological gap that separated Zionists from nineteenth-century German Jewish scholars, the Hebrew writer, journalist and Zionist activist, Nahum Sokolov, emphasized during the fifth Zionist Congress the importance of the national perspective in the study of the Jewish past. Despite this new orientation, Sokolov continued, however, to revere the accomplishments of German Jewish historians like Heinrich Graetz. In an attempt to embrace this legacy, Sokolov put forward a new interpretation of their work by asserting that these historians had often "unconsciously" already expressed the national unity of the Jewish people.[33]

Likewise, the opposition toward Zionism within the *Central-Verein* was at first fairly limited. Emphasizing its neutrality in political and religious matters, representatives of the *Central-Verein* like Eugen Fuchs downplayed as late as 1912 the differences between themselves and the Zionists.[34] Differences, however, still persisted. The local branch of the B'nai B'rith, for example, had protested forcefully against Munich as the place of the first Zionist congress.[35] This original opposition even led the national body of B'nai B'rith in 1897 to issue a general declaration against Zionist aspirations. The opposition further manifested itself when the highest committee of B'nai B'rith in Germany ordered all of its local branches to prohibit discussions about Zionism within their local branches.[36] Yet many of these branches did not unanimously follow this policy. In Hamburg, for example, a Zionist program was carried out in the rooms of the Henry-Jones Lodge once the Zionist association folded after 1887.[37]

Notwithstanding the existing differences, non-Zionists shared with their opponents the goal for unity. The popularization of Jewish history was the result of a joint effort by various groups and associations. It was fairly pluralistic and eclectic in its content, and new elements could easily be added on without rattling the foundations of this German Jewish popular culture. Speakers lectured on topics such as Jewish luminaries and famous non-Jews, local communities, mysticism, ethical monotheism, and Zionism. Even consciously Zionist periodicals like *Der Jude*, originally conceived in 1903 by Martin Buber but realized only in 1916, allowed many voices to express themselves within the pages of the journal.[38] Likewise, the twice-monthly *Neue Jüdische Monatshefte*, which appeared for the first time in October 1916, aimed for the formation of a united German Jewish community. For this reason, its editors included the Reform-oriented philosopher Hermann Cohen, the chairman of the *Central-Verein*, Eugen Fuchs, and the Zionists Adolf Friedman and Franz Oppenheimer. These initiatives thus reflected the ambition and politics of the Association for Jewish History and Literature that equally had aimed to overcome the cultural and religious disunity. Moreover, these cultural ambitions likewise expressed themselves in the concurrent attempts to forge a new unity between Western and Eastern European Jews as evidenced by periodicals like *Ost und West*, which began appearing in 1901 and the more short-lived journal *Die Freistatt*, which Mordechai Kaufmann published from 1913 until 1915.[39] The aloof goal to unite German Jewry into a new sense of community was also the hallmark of German-Jewish cultural politics during the Weimar Republic, as Michael Brenner persuasively has argued.[40]

Like their ideological opponents, several Zionists criticized contemporary Jewish historiography mainly for its failure to reinvigorate Jewish culture and its mistaken orientation toward scholarly objectivity.[41] This continuous criticism reflected the ongoing debates about the nature of Jewish scholarship that had emerged in the aftermath of the Berliner Antisemitismusstreit. These different critics demanded the adaptation of a more broadly conceived approach to Jewish history and culture covering all aspects of Jewish life in an effort to revitalize contemporary Jewish culture.[42] It was against this pervasive criticism that the *Gesellschaft zur Förderung der Wissenschaft des Judentums* (Society for the promotion of science of Judaism) was founded in 1902. The initial circular letter coupled the ideal of scholarly objectivity with the language of resistance and defense and aimed to bolster ethnic pride. In the words of the widely disseminated call to establish this society, the study of Judaism was deemed "the holiest duty towards our religion" and "a duty towards science."[43] The founding of this society thus testifies to the lasting tension between Wissenschaft as a science and as an agent of Jewish self-definition that continued well into the Weimar Republic.

These continuous conflicts were not unique to Germany. The newly emerging centers of research outside of Germany tended to display the same dynamics between Wissenschaft as a scholarly discipline and as a formal educational tool. In the East, a new generation of Russian Jewish historians applied themselves to the study of Eastern European Jewry that had been only dismissively treated in the West. The new studies came to augment and partly supplant the existing maskilic historical studies as well as the translated works by German Jewish scholars.[44] More clearly than in the West, these Eastern European historians came to delineate a nationalistic core of the Jewish past that they located in political history as well as in daily Jewish culture. During the early 1890s, Simon Dubnow propagated the plan to establish a Jewish historical society, which came to fruition with the foundation of the Jewish Historical Ethnographical Committee of the Society for the Promotion of Culture among the Jews of Russia in 1892.[45]

In England, France, and the United States, Jewish scholars fused their scholarly investigation of the Jewish past with passionate patriotism for their respective countries as they charted new pathways between universal and local conceptions of Jewish history.[46] This more often implied that the new centers consciously saw themselves in contrast to the German Jewish scholarly community. When in 1879 Zadok Kahn founded the *Societé des Études Juives*, French scholars embraced the notion of Wissenschaft: "We are not in the business of making religious propaganda, nor are we aiming at edification." In the same fashion, Kahn affirmed that the society would apply itself to all aspects of the Jewish past. Despite this open enchantment with the lore of Wissenschaft, Kahn stressed that the society would pursue "patriotic interests" in its attempt to create a "French library of Jewish science and literature." While historical objectivity and French patriotism may seem to contradict each other, both statements were directed at German Jewish scholars insofar as Kahn pursued the goal to "relieve France of its inferior position" in comparison to German Jewish scholarship.[47]

Concurrently, the opening of the Anglo-Jewish exhibition in 1887 at London's Royal Albert Hall signaled the beginning of new scholarly agenda emerging in England. The exhibition aimed to collect material to "facilitate the compilation of a history of the Jews in England" and also to promote "a knowledge of Anglo-Jewish history" and a "deeper interest in its records and relics."[48] While Heinrich Graetz opened this exhibition with an elaborate lecture in which he marveled at the prospect of a Jewish academy that would engage in a critical study of Jewish religion, philosophy, and history, Anglo-Jews were much more concerned with a narrowly defined research agenda, which operated in various ways in opposition to Graetz and the German Jewish community of scholars. Graetz indeed had no interest in encouraging the study of Anglo-Jewish history but rather hoped for a revival of Talmudic and biblical studies in England.[49]

The exhibition thus served as a vehicle for the Anglo-Jewish community to take control of the public discourses about Jews in England as well as the representation of Anglo-Jewish history by German Jewish scholars. Consequently, the Anglo-Jewish historians inscribed into their scholarly agenda English patriotism when they reminded their readers that scholars "on English soil to whom England is their home" conducted the new research.[50] Israel Abrahams accentuated the importance of Englishness as an instrumental element in the construction of an Anglo-Jewish past when he asserted that historical truth was only attainable if scholars shared not only "our general Jewish sentiments" but also our "local patriotism."[51] On the popular level, the German Jewish Union of Associations for Jewish History and Culture found its mirror image in the Union of Jewish Literary Societies in England.[52]

Inspired by the Anglo-Jewish Exhibition as well as by the approaching celebration of the 400th anniversary of the discovery of America, the Historical Society's main objective in its formative years was to highlight the significance of the Jewish presence in the United States from the colonial period on.[53] This was a practical imperative given the wave of anti-Semitism that beset the American Jewish community in the 1890s. Urged by Reform rabbi Bernhard Felsenthal in Chicago, Cyrus Adler took the initiative in directing the Historical Society into the scholarly realm. In 1892 Oscar Straus, the president of the Jewish Historical Society, stressed that its objective was "to throw an additional ray of light upon the discovery, colonization, and history of our country."[54] Seeking to defend the Jewish status in the United States, the society countered the claim that Jews arrived in America too late to contribute to the creation of the Republic.

The slippery slope between Jewish and local patriotism and scientific and educational ideals framed also the early reception of Heinrich Graetz in these countries. Israel Abrahams rebuked Heinrich Graetz's work as unscientific in his presidential address "The Science of Judaism" and stated that Graetz's work was not the starting point of a school, but rather an end of one. At the same time though, he praised Graetz as an exponent of Jewish "world view."[55] Similarly, the French Jewish chief rabbi Zadoc Kahn noted in his afterword to the French edition of Graetz's history that from a scholarly perspective, this multivolume work did not represent the latest status of Jewish scholarship. Kahn promoted the translation nevertheless, when he expressed the hope that Graetz's *Histoire* would reach the reader in the Jewish families since there was nothing that bound Jews as much to their religion as their common past.[56]

While the Jewish Publication Society of America published Heinrich Graetz's *Geschichte*, several members of the organization questioned the value of publishing "foreign" works that attributed only a footnote to the history of the Jews in America.[57] Among the most pronounced critics was Emanuel Schreiber, who had already contributed in Germany to a lengthy and highly critical pamphlet that dealt mainly with the notorious eleventh volume of Graetz's *Geschichte der Juden*.[58] Despite this criticism, the Jewish Publication Society of America advertised Graetz's *History of the Jews* with the slogan "Should be in Every Jewish Home," as it was deemed the ideal gift for a "confirmation, Bar Mitzwah, graduation or birthday."[59]

Amid these new political and cultural debates, the study and popularization of the Jewish past continued to be marked by continuity and change. Despite the emergence of new centers of Jewish research and Zionist challenge, Wissenschaft's creation of a usable Jewish past remained a significant component of the complex historical formation of German Jewish and modern Jewish identities and cultures in the twentieth century. Translated into various languages, Heinrich Graetz's history of the Jews in particular enjoyed continued success.[60] Moreover, Wissenschaft's reception, transition and transformation was clearly manifested in the publication of the first *Jewish Encyclopedia*. Even during the 1840s, Moritz Steinschneider had conceived of the plan for a comprehensive guide to Jewish history and culture, which, however, did not materialize.[61] During the early 1890s, Isidore Singer once again promoted this idea and negotiated the publication of the encyclopedia in Germany with the Brockhaus publishing house. Although advertised, the encyclopedia did not come to fruition.[62] Isidore Singer relocated to the United States, where the *Encyclopedia* ultimately was published in cooperation with Jewish scholars from various countries and political and religious orientations, who, however, based themselves largely on the results of German Jewish scholars, as Wilhelm Bacher noted in the *Allgemeine*.[63] The dissemination of German Jewish scholarship in the form of translations, critical reworkings, and compilations, therefore, also ensured in this form its lasting impact not just on German Jewry but also on the formation of modern Jewish cultures in general.

Notes

Abbreviations

AZJ	*Allgemeine Zeitung des Judenthums*
BLBI	*Bulletin des Leo Baeck Instituts*
HUCA	*Hebrew Union College Annual*
JjlG	*Jahrbuch der jüdisch literarischen Gesellschaft*
JjGL	*Jahrbuch für jüdische Geschichte und Literatur*
JQR	*Jewish Quarterly Review*
JZWL	*Jüdische Zeitschrift für Wissenschaft und Leben*
LBIYB	*Leo Baeck Institute Yearbook*
MGDJ	*Mitteilungen des Gesamtarchivs der deutschen Juden*
MGjV	*Mittheilungen der Gesellschaft für jüdische Volkskunde*
MGWJ	*Monatsschrift für Geschichte und Wissenschaft des Judentums*
PAJHS	*Publications of the American-Jewish Historical Society*
TJHSE	*Jewish Historical Society of England—Transactions*
WZjT	*Wissenschaftliche Zeitschrift für jüdische Theologie*
ZGJD	*Zeitschrift für die Geschichte der Juden in Deutschland*
ZrIJ	*Zeitschrift für die religiösen Interessen des Judentums*
ZWJ	*Zeitschrift für die Wissenschaft des Judentums*

Introduction

1. For a recent discussion of the interplay between the history of effects *(Wirkungs-geschichte)* and the history of reception *(Rezeptionsgeschichte)*, see Martyn P. Thompson, "Reception History and the Interpretation of Historical Meaning," *History and Theory* 32 (1993): 248–72.

2. Michel de Certeau, *The Practice of Everyday Life* (Berkeley: University of California Press, 1984), xi–xxiv; and Roger Chartier, *The Order of Books: Readers, Authors, and Libraries in Europe Between the Fourteenth and the Eighteenth Centuries* (Stanford: Stanford University Press, 1994), 1–23. For a survey of the various theories of reception, see Robert C. Holub, *Reception Theory: A Critical Introduction* (London: Routledge, 1989).

3. Gershom Scholem, "Mi-tokh hirhurim 'al hokhmat yisra'el," [1944] *Devarim be-go: Pirke morashah u-tehiyah*, 2 vols. (Tel Aviv: 'Am 'oved, 1982), 2: 385–403; and his "Wissenschaft vom Judentum einst und jetzt," *Judaica* (Frankfurt a. M.: Suhrkamp, 1963), 1: 147–64.

4. Gerson D. Cohen, "German Jewry as a Mirror to Modernity," *LBIYB* 20 (1975): ix–xxi, here xv; and Jonathan Frankel, "Assimilation and the Jews in Nineteenth-Century Europe: Toward a New Historiography?" *Assimilation and Community: The Jews in Nineteenth-Century Europe*, ed. Steven J. Zipperstein and Jonathan Frankel (Cambridge: Cambridge University Press, 1992), 1–37, here 25–26.

5. Ismar Schorsch, *From Text to Context: The Turn to History in Modern Judaism* (Hanover: University Press of New England, 1994), 1–6.

6. Susannah Heschel, *Abraham Geiger and the Jewish Jesus* (Chicago: University of Chicago, 1998); see also Christian Wiese, *Wissenschaft des Judentums und Protestantische Theologie im Wilhelminischen Deutschland: Ein Schrei ins Leere?* (Tübingen: J. C. B. Mohr, 1999).

7. Amos Funkenstein, *Perceptions of Jewish History* (Berkeley: University of California Press, 1993), esp. 1–21, here 19; Michael A. Meyer, "The Emergence of Jewish Historiography: Motives and Motifs," *History and Theory* 27 (1988): 160–75, here 175; Michael A. Meyer, "Jewish Scholarship and Jewish Identity: Their Historical Relationship in Modern Germany," *Studies in Contemporary Jewry* 8 (1992): 181–93; and Shulamit Volkov, "Die Erfindung einer Tradition: Zur Entstehung des modernen Judentums in Deutschland," *HZ* 253 (1991): 603–28.

8. For a criticism of subsuming the production of historical memory solely to politics and ideology, see Alon Confino, "Collective Memory and Cultural History: Problems and Methods," *AHR* 102 (1997): 1386–1403.

9. David Sorkin, *The Transformation of German Jewry, 1780–1840* (Oxford: Oxford University Press, 1987), 113–23; and David Sorkin, "The Impact of Emancipation on German Jewry. A Reconsideration," *Assimilation and Community*, ed. Fraenkel and Zipperstein, 177–98.

10. Jacob Borut, "'Verjudung des Judentums': Was there a Zionist Subculture in Weimar Germany?" *In Search of Jewish Community: Jewish Identities in Germany and Austria, 1918–1933*, ed. Michael Brenner and Derek J. Penslar (Bloomington: Indiana University Press, 1998), 92–114.

11. Fritz Stern, *Gold and Iron: Bismarck, Bleichröder, and the Building of the German Empire* (New York: Knopf, 1977), 471.

12. Steven E. Aschheim, "German History and German Jewry: Boundaries, Junctions and Interdependence," *LBIYB* 43 (1998): 315–22. See also Samuel Moyn, "German Jewry and the Question of Identity: Historiography and Theory," *LBIYB* 41 (1996): 291–308; and Till van Rahden, "Mingling, Marrying, and Distancing Jewish Integration in Wilhelminian Breslau and its Erosion in Early Weimar Germany," *Jüdisches Leben in der Weimarer Republik*, ed. Wolfgang Benz, Arnold Paucker, and Peter Pulzer (Tübingen: J. C. B. Mohr, 1998), 197–222.

13. Ludwig Geiger, *Abraham Geiger: Leben und Lebenswerk* (Berlin: G. Reimer, 1910), 212–14.

14. On German liberalism's growing hostility toward Jewish enfranchisement, see Dagmar Herzog, *Intimacy and Exclusion: Religious Politics in Pre-Revolutionary Baden* (Princeton: Princeton University Press, 1996), 52–84.

15. On this, see the very informative articles by Andreas Gotzmann and Olaf Blaschke. Andreas Gotzmann, "Zwischen Nation und Religion: Die deutschen Juden auf der Suche nach einer bürgerlichen Konfessionalität," *Juden, Bürger, Deutsche: Zur Geschichte von Vielfalt und Differenz, 1800–1933,* ed. Andreas Gotzmann, Rainer Liedtke, and Till van Rahden (Tübingen: J. C. B. Mohr, 2001), 241–61; Olaf Blaschke, "Bügertum und Bürglichkeit im Spannungsfeld des neuen Konfessionalismus von den 1830er bis zu den 1930er Jahren," Gotzmann, Liedtke, and van Rahden, eds. *Juden, Bürger, Deutsche,* 33–66.

16. See, for example, Marion A. Kaplan, "Women and the Shaping of Modern Jewish Identities in Imperial Germany," *Deutsche Juden und die Moderne,* ed. Shulamit Volkov and Elisabeth Müller-Luckner (Munich: Oldenbourg, 1994), 57–74; and Marion A. Kaplan, *The Making of the Jewish Middle Class: Women, Family, and Identity in Imperial Germany* (New York: Oxford University Press 1991).

17. Stuart Hall's observation that identity is understood in this fashion equally applies to formulations of modern German-Jewish self-understanding. See Stuart Hall, "The Question of Cultural Identity," *Modernity and Its Future,* ed. Stuart Hall, David Hell, and Tony McGrew (Cambridge: Open University, 1992), 273–316, here 287.

18. Schorsch, *From Text to Context.*

19. On the lachrymose conception of Jewish history see Salo Baron, "Ghetto and Emancipation: Shall We Revise the Traditional View?" *Menorah Journal* 14 (June 1928): 515–26.

20. On this debate in Jewish historiography in general, see David Myers, "Selbstreflexionen im modernen Erinnerungsdiskurs," and Yosef Hayim Yerushalmi, "Jüdische Historiographie und Postmodernismus: Eine abweichende Meinung," in *Jüdische Geschichtsschreibung heute: Themen, Positionen, Kontroversen,* ed. Michael Brenner and David N. Myers. (Munich: C. H. Beck, 2002), 55–74 and 268–74, and 75–94 and 275–79.

21. Heinrich Graetz, *Volkstümliche Geschichte der Juden,* 3 vols. (Leipzig: O. Leiner, 1888), 3: 749.

1. Between Theology and History

1. See the introduction by Reinhart Koselleck in Otto Brunner et al., eds., *Geschichtliche Grundbegriffe: Historisches Lexikon der politisch-sozialen Sprache in Deutschland* (Stuttgart: E. Klett, 1972), 1: xiii–xviii, here xv–xvii; Koselleck, "'Space of Experience' and 'Horizon of Expectation': Two Historical Categories," *Futures Past, On the Semantics of Historical Time,* trans. by Keith Tribe (Cambridge: MIT Press, 1985) 267–88.

2. Nils Roemer, "Colliding Visions: Jewish Messianism and German Scholarship in the Eighteenth Century," in *Hebraica Veritas? Christian Hebraists and the Study of Judaism in Early Modern Europe,* ed. Allison Coudert and Jeffrey Shoulson (Philadelphia: University of Pennsylvania Press, 2004), 266–85.

3. Salo Wittmayer Baron, "Homilies and Histories," *A Social and Religious History of the Jews*, 18 vols. (New York: Columbia University Press, 1952–83), 6: 152–234; and Yosef Hayim Yerushalmi, *Zakhor: Jewish History and Jewish Memory* (New York: Schocken, 1989), 39–75; Gershom Scholem, "Toward an Understanding of the Messianic Idea in Judaism," *The Messianic Idea in Judaism and Other Essays on Jewish Spirituality* (New York: Schocken, 1995), 1–36, here 10; and Jacob Katz, *Exclusiveness and Tolerance: Jewish-Gentile Relations in Medieval and Modern Times* (Oxford: Behrman House, 1961), 17 and 26.

4. Ibn Verga's contention that writing history was a Christian practice attests to the novelty of these works. See Salomon ibn Verga, *Shevet Yehuda*, ed. A. Shohat with an introduction by Y. Baer (Jerusalem: Mosad Bialik, 1947), 21.

5. See, for example, Samuel Usque, *Consolation for the Tribulation of Israel*, trans. and ed. Martin A. Cohen (Philadelphia: Jewish Publication Society of America, 1965), 204 and 236. On Jewish historiography in the sixteenth century, see Yosef Hayim Yerushalmi, "Clio and the Jews: Reflections on Jewish Historiography in the Sixteenth Century," *Essential Papers on Jewish Culture in Renaissance and Baroque Italy*, ed. David Ruderman (New York: New York University Press, 1992), 191–218; Yosef H. Yerushalmi, "Messianic Impulses in Joseph ha-Kohen," *Jewish Thought in the Sixteenth Century*, ed. Bernard Dov Cooperman (Cambridge: Harvard University Press, 1983), 460–87; and Robert Bonfil, "How Golden was the Age of the Renaissance in Jewish Historiography?" *History and Theory: Beiheft* 27 (1988): 78–102.

6. Lester A. Segal, *Historical Consciousness and Religious Tradition in Azariah de Rossi's Me'or 'Einayim* (Philadelphia: Jewish Publication Society of America, 1989), 31.

7. Yosef Hayim Yerushalmi, *The Lisbon Massacre of 1506 and the Royal Image in the "Shebet Yehuda"* (Cincinnati: Hebrew Union College, 1976); and Marianne Awerbuch, *Zwischen Hoffnung und Vernunft: Geschichtsdeutung der Juden in Spanien vor der Vertreibung am Beispiel Abravanels und Ibn Vergas* (Berlin: Institut Kirche und Judentum, 1985).

8. Ben-Zion Degani, "Ha-mivneh shel historiah ha-'olamut we-ge'ulat yisra'el be-Zemah David le-R. David Gans," *Zion* 45 (1980): 173–200; and M. Breuer, "Modernism and Traditionalism in Sixteenth Century Jewish Historiography," *Jewish Thought in the Sixteenth Century*, ed. Cooperman, 49–88.

9. Mark R. Cohen, *Under Crescent and Cross: The Jews in the Middle Ages* (Princeton: Princeton University Press, 1994), 186–99 and Michael Stanislawski, "The Yiddish Shevet Yehudah: A Study in the 'Ashkenization' of a Spanish-Jewish Classic," *Jewish History and Jewish Memory: Essays in Honor of Yosef Hayim Yerushalmi*, ed. Elisheva Carlebach, John M. Efron, and David N. Myers (Hanover: University Press of New England, 1998), 135–49.

10. For the various editions see Moritz Steinschneider, *Die Geschichtsliteratur der Juden* (Frankfurt a. M.: J. Kaufmann, 1905), no. 19, 90, and 132. See also Jacob Emden, *Sefer Mor u-kezy'ah* (Altona, 1761–68) on Orakh Hayyim 307; and Robert Bonfil, "Jewish Attitudes Towards History and Historical Writing in Pre-Modern Times," *Jewish History* 11 (1997): 7–40.

11. Jonathan M. Elukin, "Jacques Basnage and the 'History of the Jews': Anti-Catholic Polemic and Historical Allegory in the Republic of Letters," *Journal of the History of Ideas* 53 (1992): 603–30; Gerald Cerny, *Theology, Politics and Letters at the Crossroad of European Civilization: Jacques Basnage and the Baylean Huguenot Refugees in the Dutch Republic* (Hague: M. Nijhoff, 1987); and Richard H. Popkin, "Jacques Basnage's *Histoire des Juifs* and the Bibliotheca Sarraziana," *Studia Rosenthaliana* 21 (1987): 154–62.

12. Johann Andreas Eisenmenger, *Entdecktes Judenthum*, 2 vols. (Königsberg, 1700), 2: 515–73; and Johann Jacob Schudt, *Jüdische Merkwürdigkeiten*, 4 vols. (Frankfurt, 1714–18). 1: 5–55 and 311–21.

13. Johann Gottfried Herder, *Briefe, das Studium der Theologie betreffend*, in *Herders Sämtliche Werke*, 33 vols., ed. Bernhard Suphan (Berlin: Weidmann, 1877–1913), 10:140.

14. Siegmund Jacob Baumgarten, *Übersetzung der Algemeinen Welthistorie die in England durch eine Gesellschaft von Gelehrten ausgefertigt worden* (Halle: Gebauer, 1744), 26–32, 240.

15. Johann Jacob Semler, *Uebersetzung der Algemeinen Welthistorie der Neuen Zeiten die in England durch eine Gesellschaft von Gelehrten ausgefertigt worden* (Halle: Gebauer 1765), 308–9.

16. Ludvig Holberg, *Jüdische Geschichte von Erschaffung der Welt bis auf gegenwärtige Zeiten*, trans. by Georg August Detharding (Altona: Korte, 1747), 3: 712 and 719.

17. Johann David Michaelis, *Mosaische Recht*, 6 vols., 2nd edition (Reutlingen: J. Grözinger, 1793), 1: 3 and 8–13.

18. Peter Reill, *The German Enlightenment and the Rise of Historicism* (Berkeley: University of California Press, 1975), 197. Herder for one criticized Michaelis for having presented Mosaic Laws according to eighteenth-century concepts while not fleshing out a historical picture of ancient Judaism. See Herder's review of *Mosaische Recht* that originally appeared in 1772 in the *Frankfurter gelehrter Anzeigen* in *Herders Sämtliche Werke*, ed. Suphan, 5: 423–26.

19. Johann Christoph Gatterer, "Vom historischen Plan, und der darauf sich gründenden Zusammenfügung der Erzählung (1767)," *Theoretiker der deutschen Aufklärungshistorie*, 2 vols., ed. Horst Walter Blanke and Dirk Fischer (Stuttgart-Bad Cannstatt: Frommann-Holzboog, 1990), 2: 621–61, here 637, and 646. On the reception of Voltaire in Germany see Otto Dann, "Voltaire und die Geschichtsschreibung in Deutschland," *Voltaire und Deutschland: Quellen und Untersuchungen zur Rezeption der Französischen Aufklärung*, ed. Peter Brockmeier et al. (Stuttgart: Metzler, 1979), 463–67.

20. August Ludwig Schlözer, "Vorstellung seiner Universal-Historie (1772)," *Theoretiker der deutschen Aufklärungshistorie*, ed. Blanke and Fischer, 2: 663–68, here 687.

21. Gatterer, "Vom historischen Plan," 628 and 637; and Schlözer, "Vorstellung," 687.

22. Gotthold Ephraim Lessing, *Erziehung des Menschengeschlechts*, in *Gotthold Ephraim Lessing. Werke*, ed. Herbert G. Göpfert, 8 vols. (Darmstadt: Wissenschaftliche Buchgesellschaft, 1996) 8: 489–510. See also Michael Graetz, "Die 'Erziehung des Menschengeschlechts' und jüdisches Selbstbewußtsein im 19. Jahrhundert," *Judentum im Zeitalter der Aufklärung: Wolfenbütteler Studien zur Aufklärung* 4 (1977): 273–95.

23. Anton Friedrich Büsching, *Geschichte der jüdischen Religion* (Berlin: J. C. F. Eisfeld 1779), 181–82, 189–92, and 246.

24. Review of Büsching's *Geschichte* in *Allgemeine deutsche Bibliothek* 41 (1780): 576–82, here 580. See also Michaelis's review of Büsching's *Geschichte* in *Orientalische und Exegetische Bibliothek* 15 (1780): 103–26.

25. On the notion of pragmatic history, see Peter Reill, *The German Enlightenment and the Rise of Historicism*, 41–45.

26. Christian Wilhelm Dohm, *Ueber die bürgerliche Verbesserung der Juden*, 2 vols. (Berlin: Nicolai, 1781–83), 1: 1; and Horst Möller, "Aufklärung, Judenemanzipation und Staat: Ursprung und Wirkung von Dohms Schrift *Ueber die bürgerliche Verbesserung der Juden*," *Tel Aviver Jahrbuch des Instituts für deutsche Geschichte: Beiheft 3: Deutsche Aufklärung und Judenemanzipation* (1980): 119–49.

27. Dohm refers several times to these authors. On Michaelis see Dohm, *Ueber die bürgerliche Verbesserung der Juden* 1: 17, 19, 97, and 136–37; and on Büsching see Dohm, *Ueber die bürgerliche Verbesserung der Juden* 2: 358. On post-biblical Judaism, see 50–51 and 143.

28. Immanuel Kant, *Die Religion innerhalb der Grenzen der bloßen Vernunft*, in *Immanuel Kant: Werkausgabe*. 12 vols, ed. Wilhelm Weischedel (Darmstadt: Suhrkamp, 1983), 4: 649–879, here 804. See also Arnold Eisen, *Rethinking Modern Judaism: Ritual, Commandment, Community* (Chicago: Chicago University Press, 1998), 24–30.

29. Arnold Herzig, "Die Anfänge der deutsch-jüdischen Geschichtsschreibung in der Spätaufklärung," *Tel Aviver Jahrbuch für Deutsche Geschichte* 20 (1991): 59–75.

30. Moses Mendelssohn, *Jerusalem oder über religiöse Macht und Judentum*, in *Moses Mendelssohn. Gesammelte Schriften. Jubiläumsausgabe*, ed. Alexander Altmann et al. (Stuttgart-Bad-Canstatt: Frommann-Holzboog, 1983), 8: 93–204, here 162; and Sorkin, *The Transformation of German Jewry, 1780–1840*, 67–73.

31. My reading of Mendelssohn differs slight from Shmuel Feiner, *Haskalah and History: The Emergence of a Modern Jewish Historical Consciousness*, trans. Chaya Naor and Sondra Silverston (Oxford: Littman Library of Jewish Civilization, 2002), 26–28 and 40–43. See also Edward Breuer, "Politics, Tradition, History: Rabbinic Judaism and the Eighteenth-Century Struggle for Civil Equality," *HTR* 85 (1992): 357–83; and Matt Erlin, "Reluctant Modernism: Moses Mendelssohn's Philosophy of History," *Journal of the History of Ideas* 63 (2002): 83–104.

32. Moses Mendelssohn, "Menasseh Ben Israel: Rettung der Juden nebst einer Vorrede," *Moses Mendelssohn*, ed. Altmann et al., 8: 1–71, here 6 and 9; and *Jerusalem oder über religiöse Macht und Judentum*, 157.

33. Naphtali Herz Wessely, *Divre shalom ve-'emet le-kahal 'adat yisra'el ha-garim be-'arazot memshelet ha-kaisar ha-gadol ha-'ohev 'et ha-'adam u-mesameah ha-briyot* (Words of peace and truth) (Berlin, 1782–85), 9, 13–15.

34. Ibid., 1: 15–19 (my pagination) and 4: 51–56v. See also Shmuel Feiner, *Haskalah and History*, 19–24. David Friedländer, who translated this pamphlet, added to Wessely's original text and emphasized that "history is the mirror of mankind" that informs the reader about talents and deeds that are worthy to imitate and would contribute to the

well-being of mankind. See David Friedländer, *Worte der Wahrheit und des Friedens an die ganze jüdische Nation* (Breslau, 1788), 19–20.

35. See also Isaac Euchel, "Toldot gedole yisra'el: davar 'el ha-kore me-to'elet divre ha-hayim ha-kadmonim ve-ha-yedi'ot ha-mehubarot lahem," *Ha-Me'assef* 1 (1784): 7–11 and 21–25, here 8. Reuven Michael, *Ha-ketiva ha-historit ha-yehudit: meha-renesans 'ad ha-'et ha-hadasha* (Jerusalem: Mosad Bialik, 1993), 101–13; and Shmuel Feiner, *Haskalah and History*, 55.

36. "Toldot ha-zeman," *Ha-Me'assef* 5 (1789), 365–67, here 367. See also Lazarus Bendavid, *Etwas zur Charackteristick der Juden* (Leipzig: Stabel, 1793), 32; David Friedländer, *Ueber die durch die neue Organisation der Judenschaften in den Preußischen Staaten notwendig gewordene Umbildung 1. ihres Gottesdienstes in den Synagogen 2. ihrer Unterrichts-Anstalten und deren Lehrgegenstand und 3. ihres Erziehungswesens überhaupt, ein Wort zu seiner Zeit* [1812], ed. Moritz Stern (Berlin: Verlag Hausfreund, 1934), 8; and Shmuel Werses, "Ha-mahapekha ha-tsorfatit be-'aspeklariah shel safrut ha-'ivrit," *Tarbiz* 58 (1989): 483–521. See also Azariah de Rossi, *Me'or 'Enayim* (Berlin, 1794).

37. Friedländer, *Ueber die durch die neue Organisation*, 4–12; G. Salomon, "Ueber das Wesen, den Charakter und die Notwendigkeit der Religion," *Sulamith* 1 (1806): 117–25, 207–14, 314–19, and 441–54; G. Salomon, "Ueber das Charakteristische und das Wesentliche des israelitischen Volkes," *Sulamith* 5 (1812): 27–47; and I. Wolf and G. Salomon, *Der Charakter des Judenthums nebst einer Beleuchtung der unlängst gegen die Juden von Prof. Rühs und Fries erschienenen Schriften* (Leipzig: C. G. Schmidt, 1817), 71.

38. Lazarus Bendavid, *Etwas zur Charackteristick der Juden*, 5, 12, 27, and 65; and Salomon Maimon, *Lebensgeschichte: Von ihm selbst geschrieben*, ed. Karl Philipp Moritz, 2 vols. (Berlin: Vieweg, 1792), 2: 5, 12, 27, 65, and 233–36.

39. Shalom Jacob Cohen, *Morgenländische Pflanzen auf nördlichem Boden, eine Sammlung neuer hebräischer Poesien, nebst deutschen Uebersetzungen* (Rödelheim: Varrentrapp und Wenner, 1807), v–vi.

40. Reinhard Rürup, "The Tortuous and Thorny Path to Legal Equality: 'Jew Law' and Emancipatory Legislation in Germany from the Late Eighteenth Century," *LBIYB* 31 (1986): 3–33.

41. Joseph Wolf, "Inhalt und Zweck und Titel dieser Zeitschrift," *Sulamith* 1 (1806): 1–11, here 9–11.

42. Michael, *Ha-ketiva ha-historit ha-yehudit*, 121–26.

43. Peter Beer, "Ueber einige bei der jüdischen Nation bestandene, und zum Theil noch bestehende jüdische Sekten," *Sulamith* 1 (1806): 263–84 and 352–72. On this see Michael Brenner, "Between Haskalah and Kabbalah: Peter Beer's History of Jewish Sects," *Jewish History and Jewish Memory*, ed. Efron, Myers, and Carlebach, 389–404.

44. David Fraenkel, "Die Lage der Juden alter und neuerer Zeiten: Ein Wort des Trostes und der Vermahnung," *Sulamith* 1 (1807): 353–86, here 385.

45. Friedländer, *Ueber die durch die neue Organisation*, 8–10.

46. Friedrich Rühs, *Über die Ansprüche der Juden an das deutsche Bürgerrecht: Mit einem Anhange über die Geschichte der Juden in Spanien*, 2. verbesserte und erweiterter

Abdruck (Berlin: Realschulbuchhandlung, 1816), 5; and Jacob Friedrich Fries, *Über die Gefährdung des Wohlstandes und Charakters der Deutschen durch die Juden* (Heidelberg: Mohr, 1816).

47. Michael Hess, *Freymüthige Prüfung der Schrift des Herrn Prof. Rühs über die Ansprüche der Juden an das deutsche Bürgerrecht* (Frankfurt a. M.: Hermann, 1816).

48. J. Wolf and G. Salomon, *Der Charakter des Judenthums*, 133, 137, 139, and 151–62.

49. Shalom Jacob Cohen, *Seder Ha-avodah. Historisch-kritische Darstellung des jüdischen Gottesdienstes und dessen Modifikationen, von den ältesten Zeiten an, bis auf unsere Tage* (Leipzig: Rein'sche Buchhandlung, 1819), xi, xii, xvi, and xx.

50. See the footnote in Isaak M. Jost, *Geschichte des Judenthums und seiner Secten*, 3 vols. (Leipzig: Dörfling und Franke, 1857–59), 3: 319.

51. Leopold Zunz and L. L. Hellwitz, *Die Organisation der Israeliten in Deutschland: Ein Versuch* (Magdeburg: Kommission bei Fred. Rubach, 1819). On the background to this pamphlet and the nature of the collaboration see Jacob Toury, "Ein Dokument zur bürgerlichen Einordnung der Juden (Hamm/Westfalen, 1818)," *Michael* 7 (1967): 77–91; and Ludwig Geiger, "Geist der Rabbiner: Ein geplantes Werk von Leopold Zunz," *AZJ* 80 (1916): 413–14, here 413.

52. Leopold Zunz, "Etwas über die rabbinische Literatur," *Gesammelte Schriften*, 3 vols. (Berlin, 1875–76), 1–31, here 5.

2. Returning Judaism to History

1. Friedrich A. Wolf, "Darstellung der Altertums-Wissenschaft nach Begriff, Umfang, Zweck und Werth," *Museum der Alterthums-Wissenschaft* 1 (1807): 10–145, here 15–19 and 30.

2. Friedrich Schleiermacher, *On Religion: Speeches to Its Cultured Despisers*, trans. by John Oman (New York: Harper & Row, 1958), 238.

3. Georg Wilhelm Friedrich Hegel, *Vorlesungen über die Philosophie der Geschichte*, ed. Eva Modenhauer and Karl Markus (Frankfurt a. M.: Suhrkamp, 1992), 241–44 and 388. See also Christhard Hoffmann, *Juden und Judentum im Werk deutscher Althistoriker des 19. Jahrhunderts und 20. Jahrhunderts* (Leiden: E. J. Brill, 1988), 25–27.

4. Sorkin, *The Transformation of German Jewry, 1780–1840*, 134–35.

5. See the letter by Zunz to Adolf Strodtmann in which Zunz explains the origin of the Verein in Ismar Elbogen, "Briefe um Heinrich Heine: Adolf Strodtmanns Anfragen an Leopold Zunz," *ZGJD* 8 (1938): 40–51, here 40. This article was never published but a copy of the galley exists in the Ismar Elbogen Collection, LBI Archives 9006.

6. In 1819, the average age of the members of the Verein was 30.7. See Schorsch, *From Text to Context*, 206.

7. Leopold Zunz, "Mein erster Unterricht in Wolfenbüttel," *JJGL* 30 (1936): 131–40, here 136; and the letter to Wohlwill from April 1, 1823, in *Heinrich Heine. Säkularausgabe. Werke. Briefwechsel. Lebenszeugnisse*, ed. Fritz H. Eisner (Berlin: Akademie-Verlag, 1970), 20:72 (cited hereafter as *HSA*).

8. Salman Rubaschoff, "Erstlinge der Entjudung: Drei Reden von Eduard Gans im Kulturverein" *Der jüdische Wille* 1 (1918): 30–35, 108–21, and 193–203, here 113.

9. Immanuel Wolf, "Ueber den Begriff einer Wissenschaft des Judenthums," *ZWJ* 1 (1823): 1–24, reprinted in Immanuel Wolf, "On the Concept of a Science of Judaism (1822)," trans. by Lionel Kochan *LBIYB* 2 (1957): 194–204, here 204; Siegfried Ucko, "Geistesgeschichtliche Grundlagen für die Wissenschaft des Judentums (Motive des Kulturvereins vom Jahre 1819)," *ZGJD* 5 (1935): 1–34, here 13; Zunz, "Etwas über die rabbinische Literatur," 1–31, here 31; and Isaac Marcus Jost, *Geschichte der Israeliten seit der Zeit der Maccabäer bis auf unsre Tage nach den Quellen bearbeitet,* 9 vols. (Berlin: Schlesinger, 1820–1828), 1: vii–x and 4: iii.

10. Rubaschoff, "Erstlinge der Entjudung," 110–11.

11. Hegel, *Vorlesungen über die Philosophie der Geschichte,* 133–41.

12. See, for example, the letter by Zunz to Ehrenberg on October 13, 1818, in *Leopold and Adelheid Zunz: An Account in Letters 1815–1885,* ed. Nahum N. Glatzer (London: East and West Library, 1958), 42–43. On the chiliasm of historical scholarship, see Immanuel Kant, *Idee zu einer Allgemeinen Geschichte in weltbürgerlicher Absicht,* in *Immanuel Kant: Werkausgabe,* 12 vols., ed. Wilhelm Weischedel (Frankfurt: Suhrkamp, 1977), 11: 33–50, here 45; and Jörn Rüsen, *Zeit und Sinn: Strategien historischen Denkens* (Frankfurt a. M.: Fischer Taschenbuch Verlag, 1990), 35–38.

13. Fritz Bamberger, ed., *Das Buch Zunz: Künftigen ehrlichen Leuten gewidmet: Eine Probe eingeleitet und herausgegeben* (Berlin: Soncino Gesellschaft, 1931), 23; and Alexander Altmann, "Zur Frühgeschichte der jüdischen Predigt in Deutschland," *LBIYB* 6 (1961): 3–59, here 50.

14. See the letter from Leopold Zunz to S. M. Ehrenberg from April 18, 1823, *Leopold Zunz: Jude-Deutscher-Europäer,* ed. Nahum N. Glatzer (Tübingen: J. C. B. Mohr, 1964), 129. See also Eduard Gans's speech in Rubaschoff, "Erstlinge der Entjudung" 42 and Rachel Livneh-Freudenthal, "Ha-'igud le-tarbut u-mada shel yehudim (1819–24) be-hipus' aher musag hadash shel yehudim" (Ph.D. diss., Tel Aviv University, 1996), 72–75.

15. L. Bendavid, "Ueber den Glauben der Juden an einen künftigen Messias (Nach Maimonides und den Kabbalisten)," *ZWJ* 1 (1822): 197–230, here 225.

16. *HSA,* 20: 179. Leopold Zunz, in a letter to Ehrenberg, quotes this passage almost verbatim. See Glatzer, *Leopold Zunz,* 140.

17. Eliezer Kirschbaum, *Hilkhot yemot ha-mashiah* (Berlin, 1822), 18–19.

18. Horst Walter Blanke, *Historiographiegeschichte als Historik* (Stuttgart-Bad Cannstatt: Frommann-Holzboog, 1991), 55; and Yerushalmi, *Zakhor: Jewish History and Jewish Memory,* 83.

19. Rubaschoff, "Erstlinge der Entjudung," 198–99.

20. Leopold Zunz, "Salomon ben Isaac, genannt Raschi," *ZWJ* 1 (1822): 227–384, here 380; and "Ueber die in den hebräisch-jüdischen Schriften vorkommenden hispanischen Ortsnamen," *ZWJ* 1 (1822): 114–76, here 127. On Zunz's turning away from the enlightened position toward a historical perspective, see Maren R. Niehoff, "Zunz's Concept of Haggadah as an Expression of Jewish Spirituality," *LBIYB* 43 (1998): 3–24.

See also Zunz's remark regarding the motifs for his study of Rashi in Leopold Zunz, *Zur Geschichte und Literatur* (Berlin: Veit, 1845), 158.

21. Rubaschoff, "Erstlinge der Entjudung," 113–14; and Michael A. Meyer, *The Origins of the Modern Jew: Jewish Identity and European Culture in Germany, 1749–1824* (Detroit: Wayne State University Press, 1967), 167.

22. Zunz, "Etwas über die rabbinische Literatur," 5.

23. Ucko, "Geistesgeschichtliche Grundlagen," 10.

24. I. Wolf, "On the Concept of a Science of Judaism (1822)," 201.

25. Ibid., 194–204.

26. Zunz, "Etwas über die rabbinische Literatur," 7.

27. Ibid., 7; and Leon Wieseltier, "Etwas über die jüdische Historik: Leopold Zunz and the Inception of Modern Jewish Historiography," *History and Theory* 20 (1981): 135–49.

28. Zunz, "Etwas über die rabbinische Literatur," 27.

29. Jost, *Geschichte der Israeliten*, 3: vii, 4: 105–8; see, for example, Jost's treatment of Titus and Josephus in Jost, *Geschichte der Israeliten*, 8: 168–211 and appendix 2: 55–73 and 101. See also appendix "Zur Erforschung der Zeit, in welcher die biblischen Urkunden verfaßt und gesammelt worden seien" and "Über den Thalmud als historische Quelle," *Geschichte der Israeliten*, ed. Jost, 3: 198–218 and 4: 264–94.

30. Leopold Zunz, "Grundlinien zur einer künftigen Statistik der Juden," *Gesammelte Schriften*, 3 vols. (Berlin: Gerschel, 1875–76) 1: 134–41, here 136; and Zunz, "Ueber die in den hebräisch-jüdischen Schriften vorkommenden hispanischen Ortsnamen," 128.

31. Zunz, "Über die in den hebräisch-jüdischen Schriften," 114; and Jost, *Geschichte der Israeliten*, 1:40. See also Baruch Spinoza, *Theological-Political Treatise*, trans. by Samuel Shirley (Indianapolis: Hackett Publishing Company, 1998), 210; and Mendelssohn, "Jerusalem oder über religiöse Macht und Judentum," 192–98.

32. Jost, *Geschichte der Israeliten*, 1: 297–300.

33. Zunz, "Salomon ben Isaac, genannt Raschi," 380.

34. I. Wolf, "On the Concept of a Science of Judaism (1822)," 194–204; and Schorsch, *From Text to Context*, 223.

35. *HSA*, 20: 86.

36. Wilhelm von Humboldt, "On the Historian's Task," *History and Theory* 6 (1967): 57–71.

37. See the letter to Moses Moser from July 18, 1823, in *HSA*, 20: 97.

38. Schorsch, *From Text to Context*, 213.

39. See Jost's letter to S. M. Ehrenberg from August 16, 1822, *Leopold and Adelheid Zunz*, ed. Glatzer, 34; and I. Jost, "Aktenmäßige Darstellung des kurzen Daseins einer jüdischen Schulkommission der Berliner Gemeinde 1826," *AZJ* 23 (1859): 176–79.

40. Hans G. Reissner, *Eduard Gans: Ein Leben im Vormärz* (Tübingen: J. C. B. Mohr, 1965), 174–85. On the Verein in Hamburg see Albert Friedländer, "The Wohlwill-Moser Correspondence," *LBIYB* 11 (1966): 262–99, here 267.

41. See the letter by S. M. Ehrenberg to Zunz from August 23, 1822, *Leopold and Adelheid Zunz, ed.* Glatzer, 37; and Schorsch, *From Text to Context*, 208.

42. See Zunz's letter to S. M. Ehrenberg from April 18, 1823, *Leopold and Adelheid Zunz*, ed. Glatzer, 43.

43. See the letter by Heinrich Heine to Zunz from June 27, 1823, in *HSA*, 20: 102.

44. Jost, *Geschichte der Israeliten*. The subscription lists are reprinted in volumes 2–3 before the table of contents.

45. He also used Hannah Adams, *History of the Jews from the Destruction of Jerusalem to the Nineteenth Century* (Boston, 1812), which appeared in German translation in Leipzig in 1819.

46. See the introduction in David Ottensosser, *Die Geschichte der Jehudim: Von ihrer Rückkehr aus der babylonischen Gefangenschaft an bis auf unsere Zeiten* (Fürth: I. Zirndorff, 1821).

47. The list of presubscribers is reprinted at the beginning of the second part in Ottensosser, *Die Geschichte der Jehudim*.

48. Ucko, "Geistesgeschichtliche Grundlagen," 24.

49. See Jost's letter to Ehrenberg in 1830 (undated) and November 1841, in the Isaac Jost Collection, LBI-AR 4294; Gotthold Weil, "Das Zunz-Archiv," *BLIB* 2 (1959), 148–61; and Schorsch, *From Text to Context*, 236.

3. Recovering Jewish History in the Age of Emancipation and Reform

1. Leopold Zunz, *Die gottesdienstlichen Vorträge der Juden, historisch entwickelt: Ein Beitrag zur Altertumskunde und biblischen Kritik, zur Literatur- und Religionswissenschaft* (Berlin: Asher, 1832), vii and 479–81.

2. Luigi Chiarini, *Théorie du judaisme appliquée à la reforme des Israélites de tous les pays de l'Europe et servant en même temps d'ouvrage préparatoire à la version du Talmud de Babylone* (Paris: Barbezat, 1830); Leopold Zunz, "Beleuchtung der théorie du Judaïsme Chiarini's (1830)," *Gesammelte Schriften*, 3 vols. (Berlin: Gerschel, 1875–76), 1: 271–98; and Isaac M. Jost, *Was hat Herr Chiarini in Angelegenheiten der europäischen Juden geleistet? Eine freimüthige und unparteiische Beleuchtung des Werkes théorie du Judaïsme* (Berlin: A. W. Hayn, 1830).

3. See Leopold Zunz's letter to Philipp Ehrenberg, November 21, 1836, in *Leopold Zunz*, ed. Glatzer, 189.

4. The *AZJ* favorably reviewed and extensively paraphrased this work. See *AZJ* 2 (1838): 93–95 and 97–98; and *Sulamith* 8:1[1838]: 174–75.

5. Leopold Zunz, "Damaskus, ein Wort zur Abwehr," *Gesammelte Schriften*, 3 vols. (Berlin: Gerschel, 1875–76), 2: 160–71. On the impact of the Damascus affair in general, see Jonathan Frankel, *The Damascus Affair: "Ritual Murder," Politics, and the Jews in 1840* (Cambridge: Cambridge University Press, 1997).

6. Reinhard Rürup, "Jewish Emancipation and Bourgeois Society," *LBIYB* 14 (1969): 67–91.

7. Isaak M. Jost, *Offenes Sendschreiben an Herrn Geh. Ober-Regierungs-Rath K. Streckfuss zur Verständigung über einige Punkte in den Verhältnissen der Juden* (Berlin: Lückritz, 1833), 65.

8. Zunz, *Die gottesdienstlichen Vorträge der Juden,* 2 and 5. This was also singled out as Zunz's accomplishment in the review in *AZJ* 5 (1841): 106–7.

9. See the chapter "Organismus der Haggada," *Die gottesdienstlichen Vorträge der Juden,* ed. Zunz, 304–29. See also Schorsch, *From Text to Context,* 247; and Niehoff, "Zunz's Concept of Haggadah as an Expression of Jewish Spirituality," 3–24.

10. Isaak M. Jost, *Allgemeine Geschichte des israelitischen Volkes, sowohl seines zwei-maligen Staatslebens als auch der zerstreuten Gemeinden und Sekten, bis in die neueste Zeit in gedrängter Uebersicht, zunächst für Staatsmänner, Rechtsgelehrte, Geistliche und wissen-schaftlich gebildete Leser, aus den Quellen bearbeitet,* 2 vols. (Berlin: Amelang, 1832).

11. See the review in *Der Jude* 1 (1832): 94–96.

12. See Abraham Geiger's review of Jost's *Allgemeine Geschichte des israelitischen Volkes* in *WZjT* 1 (1835): 169–82 and *WZjT* 2 (1836): 504–18 and 565, here 180, as well as Jost's rejoinder. Isaak M. Jost, "Beitrag zur jüdischen Geschichte und Bibliographie," *WZjT* 1 (1835): 358–66. See also Heinemann Jolowicz, "Eine neue Ansicht über die Ent-wicklungsgeschichte des Judentums," *Der Israelit des 19. Jahrhunderts* 2 (1841): 177–78, 181–83, 185–87, and 189–90. The neglect of cultural history was also criticized in respect to Isaak M. Jost's *Neuere Geschichte der Israeliten von 1815 bis 1845,* 3 vols. (Breslau: Jacob-sohn, 1846–47). See the review in *Literaturblatt des Orients* 9 (1846): 129–34.

13. The first volume that appeared in 1847 covered only the period from the de-struction of the First Temple up to Esra. Levi Herzfeld, *Geschichte des Volkes Israel von der Zerstörung des ersten Tempels bis zur Einsetzung des Makkabäers Schimon zum Hohen Priester und Fürsten,* 3 vols. (Braunschweig-Nordhausen: Westermann, 1847–57). See also Schorsch, *From Text to Context,* 320–21.

14. The term "Golden Age" stems from Franz Delitzsch, *Zur Geschichte der jüdischen Poesie vom Abschluss der heiligen Schriften des Alten Bundes bis auf die neueste Zeit* (Leipzig: Tauchnitz, 1836), 44, in which he describes the period from 940 to 1040 as the Golden Age of Jewish poetic creation.

15. Zacharias Frankel, *Die Eidesleistung der Juden in theologischer und historischer Beziehung* (Dresden: Arnold, 1840); Zacharias Frankel, *Der gerichtliche Beweis nach mosaisch-talmudischen Rechte. Ein Beitrag zur Kenntniss des mosaisch-talmudischen Criminal-und Civilrechts. Nebst Untersuchungen über die Preussischen Gesetzgebung hin-sichtlich der Zeugnisse der Juden* (Berlin: Veit, 1846); and Abraham Geiger, *Lehr- und Lesebuch zur Sprache der Mischna* (Breslau: Leuckart, 1845).

16. Avraham Barkai, "The German Jews at the Start of the Industrialization: Structural Change and Mobility, 1835–1860," *Revolution and Evolution: 1848 in German-Jewish History,* ed. Werner E. Mosse, Arnold Paucker, and Reinhard Rürup (Tübingen: J. C. B. Mohr, 1981), 123–49; and Steven Lowenstein, "The Rural Community and the Urbanization of German Jewry," *Central European History* 8 (1980): 218–36.

17. "Baiersdorf," *AZJ* 1 (1837): 453–54; and Aron Tänzer, *Die Geschichte der Juden in Jebenhausen und Göppingen: Mit erweiternden Beiträgen über Schicksal und Ende der Göppinger Judengemeinde 1927–1945,* ed. Karl-Heinz Rueß (Weissenhorn: Konrad, 1988), 237.

18. "Breslau," *AZJ* 10 (1846): 52 and 333; "Breslau," 5 (1844): 355–56; and "Breslau," *AZJ* 25 (1861): 223–24. Heinrich Graetz wrote several short articles on the Association. His attitude toward it changed during the course of a year from admiration to sharp criticism. This change of heart was probably partly due to Abraham Geiger's central role in the society. See [Heinrich Graetz], "Breslau," *Orient* 4 (1843): 212, 222–23, and 229–30; and "Breslau," *Orient* 5 (1844): 179–81 and 355–56. See also L. Geiger, *Abraham Geiger*, 129.

19. Ludwig Philippson, "Prospectus," *AZJ* 1 (1837); and "Geschichte: Zur Geschichte der Juden," *AZJ* 2 (1838), 153–55.

20. Isaac M. Jost, "Vorwort," *Israelitische Annalen* 1 (1839): 1–2; and "Ein Wort zur Verständigung über die Tendenz der Annalen vom Herausgeber," *Israelitische Annalen* 1 (1839): 3–6. See Julius Fürst, "Vorwort," *Der Orient* 1 (1840): vi–vii.

21. See the letter to Philipp Ehrenberg from November 1, 1841, in the Isaac Jost Collection, LBI-AR 4294; and Joachim Kirchner, *Das deutsche Zeitschriftenwesen, seine Geschichte und seine Probleme*, 2 vols. (Wiesbaden: Harrassowitz, 1962), 2: 147.

22. Cited after Ludwig Geiger's unpublished manuscript, "Briefe von Leopold Zunz an S. M. Ehrenberg, Philipp Ehrenberg und M. Isler (1916)" in the Leopold Zunz Collection, JNUL 4° 792 V2, 54.

23. See the letter to S. M. Ehrenberg, March 27, 1832, in *Leopold Zunz*, ed. Glatzer, 160.

24. See Jost's letter to Philipp Ehrenberg from November 1, 1841, in the Isaak Jost Collection, LBI-AR 4294; Glatzer, *Leopold Zunz*, 160 and 437; and Schorsch, *From Text to Context*, 236. My reading differs from Schorsch's in respect to Jost. See also Leopold Zunz, *Das Buch Zunz künftigen ehrlichen Leuten gewidmet* in the Leopold Zunz Collection, JNUL 4° 792/C-13, 73d.

25. Ludwig Geiger, "Zunz im Verkehr mit Behörden und Hochgestellten," *MGWJ* 60 (1916): 245–62 and 321–47, here 254–56.

26. See the partial reprint in Ludwig Philippson, "Vorlesungen über Geschichte, Inhalt, Stellung und Beruf des Judenthums," *AZJ* 11 (1847): 1–4, 17–20, 33–37, 49–54, 68–72, 81–86, 97–100, 113–16, and 126–29, which finally appeared as *Die Entwicklung der religiösen Idee im Judenthume, Christenthum und Islam* (Leipzig: Baumgärtner, 1847). See also Kayserling, *Ludwig Philippson: Ein Biographie* (Leipzig: H. Mendelssohn, 1898), 132–34 and 141–45, on the public reception of the lectures and the book that was translated into French and English.

27. "Aufforderung zur Gründung eines israelitischen Literaturvereins," *AZJ* 7 (1843): 334–35; "Der israelitische Kulturverein," *AZJ* 7 (1843): 362–63 and 438; "Der Literaturverein," *AZJ* 7 (1843): 707; and "Aus Württemberg," *AZJ* 8 (1844): 433–34. See also Moritz Kayserling, *Ludwig Philippson: Eine Biographie*, 252.

28. "Der Cultur-Verein zu Berlin," *Israelitische Annalen* 3 (1841): 177–79, here 178, and the documents pertaining to the *Kulturverein* in the Leopold Zunz Collection, JNUL 4° 792/C1.

29. "Der Cultur-Verein zu Berlin," *Israelitische Annalen* 23 (1841): 177–79; "Berlin,"

Der Orient 3 (1842): 139–41; "Berlin," *AZJ* 7 (1843): 579–80; "Berlin," *Der Orient* 4 (1843): 305–6; and "Berlin," *Der Orient* 5 (1844): 252–54 and 259–61.

30. See the letter by Zunz to Bernhard Beer from December 13, 1841, in Glatzer, *Leopold Zunz*, 218. See also Leopold Zunz, *Das Buch Zunz künftigen ehrlichen Leuten gewidmet* in the Leopold Zunz Collection, JNUL 4° 792/C-13, 96.

31. As early as 1844 Zunz wrote to Steinschneider that the association was in crisis. See Alexander Marx, "Zunz's Letters to Steinschneider," *PAAJR* 5 (1933–34): 95–153, here 124. See also "Berlin," *AZJ* 8 (1848): 247; "Berlin," *AZJ* 11 (1847): 299; and "Der Verein zur Unterstützung der jüdischen Lehrer in Preußen," *AZJ* 20 (1856): 31–33.

32. Cohn, "Die Nothwendigkeit religiöeser Volks- und Jugendschriften," *WZjT* 4 (1839): 26–35, here 29–30.

33. Ephraim Willstätter, *Allgemeine Geschichte des Israelitischen Volkes. Von der Entstehung desselben bis auf unsere Zeit. Ein kurzer Abriß nach den vorliegenden Quellen und größern Werken der Geschichte für die ersten Klassen israelitischer Elementarschulen und zum Selbtstudium bearbeitet* (Karlsruhe: Marx, 1836), v, vii, and ix; and Moses Elkan, *Leitfaden beim Unterricht in der Geschichte der Israeliten, nebst einem kurzen Abriß der Geographie Palaestinas für israelitische Schulen* (Minden: F. Essmann, 1839). See also Hermann Baerwald, "Welchen Nutzen gewährt uns das Studium der Geschichte?" (1846) in the Hermann Baerwald Collection, Leo Baeck Institute, New York, AR 744; and *Literaturblatt des Orients* 3 (March 5, 1842): 156–57, here 157.

34. Willstätter, *Allgemeine Geschichte des Israelitischen Volkes*, v–xvii.

35. *Literarisches und homilitisches Beiblatt der AZJ* 3 (1839) 10: 39–40 and 11: 41; *ZrIJ* 2 (1845): 428–29; and *Literaturblatt des Orients* 3 (March 5, 1842): 156–57.

36. *ZrIJ* 2 (1845): 428–29. Jost's *Israelitische Annalen* and the *Orient* reviewed Elkan's textbook more favorably. See *Israelitische Annalen* 1 (1839): 16; and *Literaturblatt des Orients* 3 (1842): 156–57.

37. The book was republished in 1845, 1850, 1855, 1861, and 1870. In 1846 Julius Heinrich Dessauer published a new textbook history. However, he was attacked for plagiarism and the book was reprinted only once in 1870. See Julius Heinrich Dessauer, *Geschichte der Israeliten mit besonderer Berücksichtigung der Kulturgeschichte derselben. Von Alexander dem Großen bis auf gegenwärtige Zeit. Nach den besten vorhandenen Quellen bearbeitet* (Erlangen: Palm, 1846). For the harsh reviews, see *ZrIJ* 3 (1846): 35–40, 72–80, and 156–60 and the rejoinder by Dessauer in *ZrIJ* 3 (1846): 479–84.

38. Wolf Landau, "Wie soll der Religionsunterricht der israelitischen Jugend in unserer Zeit beschaffen sein," *ZrIJ* 1 (1844): 27–36, 73–76, and 129–41, which does not even refer to postbiblical history or any of the already existing textbooks. See the survey of Jewish schools in Franconia "Über das israel. Schulwesen im mittelfränkischen Kreise Baierns," *Israelitische Annalen* 2 (1840): 101–3, which refers only to biblical history. Four years later, several schools in Unterfranken, such as Aschaffenburg, Kissingen, and Niederwerren, introduced postbiblical Jewish history, which, however, was still grouped as "Jewish—especially biblical history." See "Unterfranken," *Der Orient* 5 (1844): 139–40. In contrast, the draft for the *Lehrplan* in Nassau that followed the model of Wiesbaden already included post-biblical history. For instruction in this field, Elkan's textbook is

mentioned as is Zunz's timetable of biblical history. In addition to the weekly instruction in Jewish history, the studies on the Sabbath were also meant to include lectures about Jewish history using Jost's *Allgemeine Geschichte des israelitischen Volkes*. See "Nassau," *Der Orient* 3 (1842): 355–57, here 356, and "Goch," *AZJ* 15 (1851): 46–47, where Elkan's textbook is also used.

39. Zunz, *Die gottesdienstlichen Vorträge der Juden*, 450 and 479.

40. Jost, *Allgemeine Geschichte des israelitischen Volkes*.

41. Abraham Geiger, "Jüdische Zeitschriften," *WZjT* 4 (1839): 286–92, and 459–71; and 5 (1844): 372–90 and 447–77, here 466–67. See also Geiger's response to Cohn's suggestion in *WZjT* 4 (1839): 35–36.

42. Steven M. Lowenstein, "The 1840s and the Creation of the German-Jewish Religious Reform Movement," *Revolution and Evolution*, ed. Mosse, Paucker, and Rürup, 255–97.

43. *Protokolle der ersten Rabbiner-Versammlung, abgehalten zu Braunschweig* (Brunswick: Vieweg, 1844), 61; and *Protokolle und Aktenstücke der zweiten Rabbiner-Versammlung, abgehalten zu Frankfurt am Main* (Frankfurt a. M.: E. Ullmann, 1845), 74.

44. Zacharias Frankel, "Ueber Reformen im Judenthume," *ZrIJ* 1 (1844): 3–27, and "Nachbemerkungen des Herausgebers," *ZrIJ* 1 (1844): 60–73.

45. See the letter by Michael Sachs to Moritz Veit from March 17, 1840, in *Michael Sachs und Moritz Veit: Briefwechsel*, ed. Ludwig Geiger (Frankfurt a. M.: Kauffmann, 1897), 35. See also Michael Sachs's criticism of Abraham Geiger's scholarship in the introduction to Sachs's *Die religiöse Poesie der Juden in Spanien* (Berlin: Veit und Camp, 1845), 160–64 and 195.

46. Leopold Zunz, "Gutachten über die Beschneidung (1844)," *Gesammelte Schriften*, 3 vols. (Berlin: Gerschel, 1875–76), 2:191–203; and Ludwig Geiger's appendix to the unpublished manuscript, "Briefe von Leopold Zunz an S. M. Ehrenberg, Philipp Ehrenberg and M. Isler" (1916) in the Leopold Zunz Collection, JNUL 4° 792 V2, 115–16.

47. Zunz, "Gutachten über die Beschneidung (1844)," *Gesammelte Schriften*, 2:191–203. For the critical responses, see "Zunz, Gutachten über die Beschneidung," *Der Israelit des 19. Jahrhunderts* 5 (1844): 221–25 and 253–55. Zunz's statements were praised on the other hand in the Conservative press. See Cassel, "Gutachten über die Beschneidung von Dr. Zunz," *ZrIJ* 1 (1844): 240–44.

48. Zunz, "Gutachten über die Beschneidung (1844)," 196. See Zunz's otherwise unknown letter from 1846 to Abraham Geiger in Ludwig Geiger's unpublished manuscript, "Briefe von Leopold Zunz" (1916) in the Leopold Zunz Collection, JNUL 4° 792 V2, 119, as well as Abraham Geiger's letter to Zunz Geiger, *Abraham Geiger's nachgelassene Schriften*, 5 vols. (Berlin: L. Gerschel, 1875–78), 5: 180–85.

49. Leopold Zunz, *Zur Geschichte und Literatur* (Berlin: Veit, 1845), 3, 17, 158, and 28. See also Schorsch, *From Text to Context*, 277; and the critical review by Abraham Geiger, "Zur Geschichte und Literatur von Dr. Zunz, Literaturblatt," *Der Israelit des 19. Jahrhunderts* 7 (1846): 2–4, 65–68, 69–72, 78–80, and 81–82.

50. Meyer, *Response to Modernity*, 113.

51. S. Formstecher, *Die Religion des Geistes: Eine wissenschaftliche Darstellung des Judentums nach seinem Charakter, Entwicklungsgängen und Berufen in der Menschheit* (Frankfurt a. M.: Joh. Chr. Hermann'sche Buchhandlung, 1841), esp. 197, 204–10, and 312–15; Samuel Hirsch, *Die Religionsphilosophie der Juden oder das Prinzip der jüdischen Religionsanschauung und sein Verhältnis zum Heidenthum, Christenthum und zur absoluten Philosophie* (Leipzig: Hunger, 1842), xv–xxxii, and 457–528; and L. Steinheim, *Die Offenbarung nach dem Lehrbegriffe der Synagoge*, 4. vols. (Frankfurt a. M., 1835–1865), esp. 1:17–31. See also Meyer, *Response to Modernity*, 67–74; and Aharon Shear-Yashuv, *The Theology of Salmon Ludwig Steinheim* (Leiden: E. J. Brill, 1986).

52. See Jost's letter to S. M. Ehrenberg from 1852 in Nahum N. Glatzer, "Aus unveröffentlichten Briefen von I. M. Jost," *In zwei Welten: Siegfried Moses zum fünfundsiebzigsten Geburtstag*, ed. Hans Tramer (Tel Aviv: Verlag Bitaon, 1962), 400–13, here 405.

53. Moses Brück, *Rabbinische Ceremonialgebräuche in ihrer Entstehung und geschichtlichen Entwicklung* (Breslau: A. Schulz, 1837). See Abraham Geiger's review in *WZjT* 3 (1837): 413–26; Meyer, *Response to Modernity*, 160; and Andreas Gotzmann, *Jüdisches Recht im kulturellen Prozeß: Die Wahrnehmung der Halacha im Deutschland des 19. Jahrhunderts* (Tübingen: J. C. B. Mohr, 1997), 177–83.

54. Ludwig Geiger, "Abraham Geigers Briefe an J. Derenbourg (1833–1842)," *AZJ* 60 (1896): 164–66, here 165; and Michael Meyer, "Abrahams Geiger's Historical Judaism," *New Perspective on Abraham Geiger: An HUC-JIR Symposium*, ed. Jacob J. Petuchowski (Cincinnati: Ktav Pub. House, 1975), 3–16.

55. Abraham Geiger, "Die zwei verschiedenen Betrachtungsweisen: Der Schriftsteller und der Rabbiner," *WZjT* 4 (1839): 321–33; "Jüdische Zeitschriften," *WZjT* 4 (1839): 286–92, 459–71; and 5 (1844): 372–39, here 374–75; and "Einleitung in das Studium der jüdischen Theologie," *Abraham Geiger's nachgelassene Schriften*, 5 vols., ed. Ludwig Geiger (Berlin: L. Gerschel, 1875–1878), 2: 1–31, here 5.

56. Heinrich Graetz, "Die Construktion der jüdischen Geschichte," *ZrIJ* 3 (1846): 81–97, 121–32, 361–81, and 413–21. In the following, the edition by Feuchtwanger is cited. Heinrich Graetz, *Die Konstruktion der jüdischen Geschichte*, ed. Ludwig Feuchtwanger (Berlin: Schocken Verlag, 1936), 8.

57. Ibid., 10; and Geiger, "Einleitung in das Studium der jüdischen Theologie," 4–6.

58. Graetz, *Die Konstruktion der jüdischen Geschichte*, 93.

59. Ibid., 49; and Zunz, *Zur Geschichte und Literatur*, 17–21.

60. Schorsch, *From Text to Context*, 284.

61. Graetz, *Die Konstruktion der jüdischen Geschichte*, 49.

62. Abraham Geiger, *Was hat Mohammed aus dem Judentume aufgenommen? Königl. Preussische Rheinuniversität gekrönte Preisschrift* (Bonn: F. Baaden, 1833); and Heschel, *Abraham Geiger and the Jewish Jesus*, 50–75.

63. Heinrich Heine, "Shakespeares Mädchen und Frauen," *Heinrich Heine: Sämtliche Schriften*, ed. Klaus Briegleb, 7 vols. (München: Deutscher Taschenbuch Verlag, 1997), 4: 171–293, here 258. The English translation is quoted here from *The Poetry and Prose of Heinrich Heine*, ed. Frederic Ewen (New York: Citadel Press, 1948), 678.

64. Ludwig Philippson *Die Entwicklung der religiösen Idee im Judenthume, Christen-thum und Islam.* The book was republished in 1874. See also Ludwig Philippson, "Ge-schichte und Vernunft: Ein Gespräch," *AZJ* 14 (1850): 481–83, 511–14, 602–3, and 630–31, here 631.

65. Abraham Geiger, "Die Gründung einer jüdisch-theologischen Fakultät, ein dringendes Bedürfniss unserer Zeit," *WZjT* 2 (1836): 1–21.

66. Salo Wittmeyer Baron, "Jewish Studies at Universities: An Early Project," *HUCA* 46 (1975): 357–76, here 358–59.

67. Monika Richarz, *Der Eintritt der Juden in die akademischen Berufe: Jüdische Stu-denten und Akademiker in Deutschland, 1678–1848* (Tübingen: J. C. B. Mohr, 1974), 234–37.

68. Ludwig Geiger, "Zunz im Verkehr mit Behörden und Hochgestellten," 338. See also Alfred Jospe, "The Study of Judaism in German Universities before 1933," *LBIYB* 27 (1982): 295–313; and Baron, "Jewish Studies at Universities: An Early Proj-ect," 373.

69. Ludwig Philippson, "Aufforderung an alle Israeliten Deutschlands zu Sub-skriptionen, um eine jüdische Facultät und ein jüdisches Seminar für Deutschland zu begründen," *AZJ* 1 (1837): 349–51.

70. Abraham Geiger, *Ueber die Errichtung einer jüdisch-theologischen Facultät* (Wies-baden: L. Riedel, 1838); and "Die Errichtung einer jüdisch-theologischen Facultät," *WZjT* 4 (1839): 309–12. See also his letter from January 18, 1838, to M. Creizenach in *Abraham Geiger's nachgelassene Schriften,* ed. Geiger, 5: 104; Meyer Isler, "Bemerkungen über die Errichtung einer jüdisch-theologischen Facultät," *AZJ* 2 (1839): 153–55, 157–60, and 162–64. Samuel Holdheim delivered a sermon in support of the plan on Shabbat Ha-nukkah (December 23, 1837). A lengthy excerpt of the sermon appeared in "Die jüdisch-theologische Facultät und das jüdische Seminar für Deutschland," *AZJ* 2 (1838): 58–59.

71. "Liste der Subskribenten zur Begründung einer jüdischen Facultät und eines jüdischen Seminars," *AZJ* 1 (1837): 465–66; 2 (1838): 7–8, 10–11, 19–20, 22–23, 39, 50–51, 71–72, 89–91, 119, 129, 139–40, 167–68, 176, 205–8, 215–16, 222–24, 266–67, 279, 282, 302, 313, 339, 351–53, 372–73, 400–401, 437–38, and 495–96. See Salo W. Baron, "Jewish Stud-ies at Universities: An Early Project," 365.

4. Jewish Historiography at the Center of Debate

1. "Aufforderung an alle israelitischen Gemeinden Preußens," *AZJ* 12 (1848): 741–43, here 742; and Jacob Toury, "Die Revolution von 1848 als innerjüdischer Wende-punkt," *Das Judentum in der Deutschen Umwelt, 1800–1850,* ed. Hans Liebeschütz and Arnold Paucker (Tübingen: J. C. B. Mohr, 1977), 359–76, here 374.

2. "Die Synode," *AZJ* 12 (1848): 469–70, 481–83, and 538–40; and "Aus Baiern," *AZJ* 12 (1848): 564–65.

3. "Central-Behörde in Berlin für jüdische Gemeinden des preußischen Staates," *Orient* 11 (1850): 57–58 and 61–62.

4. [Eugen Täubler], "Zunz und Geiger über eine Zentralbehörde für die jüdische Gemeinden in Preußen, *AZJ* 73 (1909): 413; Kurt Wilhelm, "The Jewish Community in

the Post-Emancipation Period, *LBIYB* 2 (1957): 47–75, here 60–61; Salo W. Baron, "The Jewish Communal Crisis in 1848," *Jewish Social Studies* 14 (1952): 99–144, here 140; and Salo Baron, "The Impact of the Revolution of 1848 on Jewish Emancipation," *Jewish Social Studies* 11 (1949): 195–248.

5. Reinhard Rürup, "The European Revolution of 1848 and Jewish Emancipation," *Revolution and Evolution*, ed. Mosse, Paucker, and Rürup, 1–53, here 50–51.

6. *Statut für das jüdisch-theologische Seminar Fraenkel'scher Stiftung zu Breslau* (Breslau, [1854]), 6 at the CAHJP, TD/979; and Andreas Brämer, *Rabbiner Zacharias Frankel: Wissenschaft des Judentums und konservative Reform im 19. Jahrhundert* (Hildesheim: Georg Olms Verlag, 2000), 318–55.

7. Hugo Weczerka, "Die Herkunft der Studierenden des Jüdisch-Theologischen Seminars zu Breslau, 1854–1938," *Zeitschrift für Ostforschung* 35 (1986): 88–138, here 104–5; and Schorsch, *From Text to Context*, 255–56. A similar motivation lay also behind the foundation of the Jewish Theological Society (Jüdisch-Theologische Verein), founded in 1868, which tried to unite scholars. See "Bonn," *AZJ* 32 (1868): 755; "Der jüdisch-theologische Verein," *Israelitische Wochenschrift* 1 (1870): 157–59; *Vorträge, gehalten im jüdisch-theologischen Verein in Breslau, Ende Juni 1869* (Leipzig, 1869); *Statuten des jüdisch-theologischen Vereins*, CAHJP, TD/805; and Brämer, *Rabbiner Zacharias Frankel*, 395–404.

8. Zacharias Frankel, "Einleitendes," *MGWJ* 1 (1852): 1–6, esp. 2 and 5. For a comprehensive discussion of the *Monatschrift*, see Brämer, *Rabbiner Zacharias Frankel*, 275–96.

9. See the letter from December 26, 1851, to Steinschneider in the Moritz Steinschneider Collection, AR 108 at the Jewish Theological Seminary in New York; and Z. Frankel, "Galerie angesehener für Glauben und Glaubensgenossen wirkender Juden," *MGWJ* 2 (1852): 443–61.

10. A. Treuenfels, "An die Leser," *Israelitische Wochenschrift* 1 (1870): 1–2.

11. M. Lazarus, "Rede zum Schluss der ersten Synode," *Treu und Frei. Gesammelte Reden und Vorträge über Juden und Judentum* (Leipzig: Winter, 1887), 1–17, here 12; and Meyer, *Response to Modernity*, 188–90.

12. "Berlin und die jüdische Facultät," *AZJ* 34 (1870): 1–3, 21–25, 37–41, 57–59, esp. 59; and "Aufforderung an alle nichtdeutschen Israeliten die Gründung einer Hochschule für die Wissenschaft des Judenthums (jüdisch-theologische Facultät) durch Beiträge zu unterstützen," *AZJ* 34 (1870): 141–44.

13. *Erster Bericht der Hochschule für die Wissenschaft des Judenthums in Berlin (die ersten zwei Jahre ihres Bestehens 1872 und 1873 umfassend)* (Berlin: G. Bernstein, 1874), 3–17.

14. *Jahresbericht des Rabbiner-Seminars für das orthodoxe Judentum pro 5634 (1873–1874)* (Berlin: M. Driesner, [1874]), 59.

15. David Ellenson, "Scholarship and Faith: David Hoffman and His Relationship to 'Wissenschaft des Judentums,'" *Modern Judaism* 8 (1988): 27–40, here 27. See also Rabbiner-Seminar zu Berlin: Studienplan, Broadside Collection of the Jewish Theological Seminary in New York.

16. A. Berliner, "Prospectus," *Magazin für jüdische Geschichte und Literatur* 1 (1874): 1. See Mordechai Breuer, *Modernity within Tradition: The Social History of Orthodox*

Jewry in Imperial Germany, trans. by Elizabeth Petuchowski (New York: Columbia University Press, 1992), 184.

17. See, for example, "Die Eröffnung des jüdisch-theologischen Seminars zu Breslau am 10. August 1854," *AZJ* 18 (1854): 424–25.

18. "Offene Anfrage an die Leiter der zu Folge des Programms vom Februar dieses Jahres zu eröffnenden Seminars für Rabbiner und Lehrer," *AZJ* 18 (1854): 243–46. This had previously been published in *Berliner Nationalzeitung* (April 16, 1854). See the Collection Breslau: Jewish Theological Seminary at the Leo Baeck Institute in New York, AR 2044 as well as *Der treue Zioniswächter* 10 (1854): 39–40 and the response to the "Anfrage" by Bernhard Beer, "Dresden," *AZJ* 18 (1854): 282–83.

19. "Magdeburg," *AZJ* 18 (1854): 312–13, here 313.

20. "Wissenschaft und Parteiinteresse," *Israelitische Wochenschrift* 1 (1870): 49–51 and 57–59.

21. H. J. "Die Berliner Facultät und das Breslauer Seminar," *Die jüdische Presse* 3 (1872): 57–58 and 65–66.

22. Max Sinasohn, ed., *Adass Jisroel Berlin: Entstehung, Entfaltung, Entwurzelung, 1869–1939* (Jerusalem: M. Sinasohn, 1969), 17–21, here 18.

23. Samson Raphael Hirsch, "Prospectus," *Jeschurun* 1 (1854): 1–4. See also Kenneth Koltun-Fromm, "Public Religion in Samson Raphael Hirsch and Samuel Hirsch's Interpretation of Religious Symbolism," *Journal of Jewish Thought and Philosophy* 9 (1999): 69–105.

24. Marcus Lehmann, "Prospectus," *Der Israelit* 1 (1860): 1–2.

25. See Marcus Lehmann, "Eine Geschichte der Juden in orthodoxen Sinne und Geiste," *Der Israelit* 1 (1860): 281–83; and S. Lipschütz, "Einiges über das Bedürfnis einer jüdischen Geschichte und deren Darstellung," *Der Israelit* 5 (1864): 371–73 and 383–85.

26. Samson Raphael Hirsch, "Aw: Die Trauer des neunten Aw," *Gesammelte Schriften,* 6 vols., ed. Naphtali Hirsch (Frankfurt a. M.: J. Kauffmann, 1902–12), 1: 123–38, here 131, which appeared originally in 1855 in *Jeschurun.* I follow here with only a slight modification the translation in Paul Mendes-Flohr and Jehuda Reinharz, eds., *The Jew in the Modern World: A Documentary History* (New York: Oxford University Press, 1995), 234–35. See also Samson Raphael Hirsch, "Wie gewinnen wir das Leben für unsere Wissenschaft?" *Jeschurun* 8 (1862): 73–91; and Robert Liberles, "Champion of Orthodoxy: The Emergence of Samson Raphael Hirsch as Religious Leader," *AJS Review* 6 (1981): 43–60.

27. Adoph Kohut, *Memoiren eines jüdischen Seminaristen. Zur Würdigung des Breslauer jüdisch-theologischen Seminars Fränkelscher Stiftung* (Prag: Senders & Brandeis, 1870), 1–12.

28. Alexander Marx, "Steinschneideriana II," *Jewish Studies in Memory of George A. Kohut, 1874–1933,* ed. Salo Baron and Alexander Marx (New York: Alexander Kohut Memorial Foundation, 1935), 492–527, here 521. See also the letter by Steinschneider's old mentor Heinrich L. Fleischer to Steinschneider from July 1, 1875, in the Moritz Steinschneider Collection AR 108, Jewish Theological Seminary in New York.

29. Moritz Steinschneider, "Program," *Hebräische Bibliographie* 1 (1858): 1–3.

30. Leopold Zunz, "Das Buch Zunz," Leopold Zunz Collection, JNUL, 4°792, C13, 73w.

31. Abraham Geiger, *Urschrift und Uebersetzung der Bibel in ihrer Abhängigkeit von der inneren Entwicklung des Judentums* (Breslau: Hainauer, 1857), 72, 101–58, and 170.

32. L. Geiger, *Abraham Geiger,* 152–54; and Zunz's letter to Philipp and Julia Ehrenberg from September 11, 1857, in *Leopold and Adelheid Zunz,* ed. Glatzer, 286.

33. L. Löw, review of *Urschrift* in *Ben-Chananja* 1 (1858): 43–45 and 91–96; and Abraham Geiger's rejoinder, "Kleinigkeiten," *Israelitischer Volkslehrer* 8 (1858): 304–8. More critical reviews appeared years later. See, for example, Eduard Baneth, "Über den Ursprung der Sadokäer und Boëthusäer," *Magazin für die Wissenschaft des Judentums* 9 (1882): 1–37 and 61–95.

34. Heinrich Graetz, "Der Jerusalemer Talmud im Lichte Geigerscher Hypothesen," *MGWJ* 20 (1871): 120–37, here 120. See also the letter by Zacharias Frankel to Meir Wiener, September 20, 1864, in the Zacharias Frankel Collection at the Hebrew Union College in Cincinnati.

35. Max Sinasohn, ed. *Adass Jisroel Berlin,* 18. The quotation is taken from 2 Chronicles 20:37.

36. Abraham Geiger, *Das Judenthum und seine Geschichte bis zur Zerstörung des zweiten Tempels: In zwölf Vorlesungen,* 2nd ed. (Breslau: Schletter, 1865).

37. H. J. Holtzmann, "Jüdische Apologetik und Polemik," *Protestantische Kirchenzeitung für das evangelische Deutschland* 12 (1865): 226–38, here 226; and "Wieder ein Stück jüdischer Apologetik," *Protestantische Kirchenzeitung für das evangelische Deutschland* 13 (1866): 67–75.

38. Heinrich Ewald, review of *Das Judenthum und seine Geschichte* in *Göttingsche gelehrte Anzeigen* 2 (1865): 1330–40. See also Ludwig Diestel, review of *Das Judenthum* in *Jahrbücher für deutsche Theologie* 11 (1866): 145–47 and 12 (1867): 343–44. The liberal nonscholarly press also took issue with Geiger's portrayal of Christianity but was much more sympathetic to Geiger's work. See Moritz Carriere's review of *Das Judenthum* in *Blätter für literarische Unterhaltung* 32 (1865): 507–9 and the review of *Das Judenthum* in *Literarisches Centralblatt* (1865): 395–96, 1243–44, and (1871): 954. See also Heschel, *Abraham Geiger and the Jewish Jesus,* 193, 206–7, and 214.

39. Cited after Heschel, *Abraham Geiger and the Jewish Jesus,* 207.

40. Zacharias Frankel, *Darkhe ha-Mishnah ve-darkhe ha-sefarim ha-nilvim 'elehah Tosefta, Mekhilta, Sifra ve-Sifrey* (Leipzig: H. Hunger, 1859), 2–3, 17, and 20–21.

41. See Abraham Geiger's letter to Steinschneider from April 17, 1861, in the Moritz Steinschneider Collection AR 108, Jewish Theological Seminary in New York. Hirsch included in his journal the translation of a letter by the Hungarian Gottlieb Fischer against Frankel. See Gottlieb Fischer, "Des Oberrabbiners und Seminardirektors Herrn Z. Frankel hodogetisches Werk über die Mischnah: Ein Sendschreiben an alle Freunde der Wahrheit und unserer jüdischen Zukunft," *Jeschurun* 7 (1860): 196–214, 241–52, and 470–91; and "Anmerkungen der Redaktion," *Jeschurun* 7 (1860): 252–69. For a comprehensive discussion of these debates, see Brämer, *Rabbiner Zacharias Frankel,* 365–31.

42. See Esriel Hildesheimer, *Sh'elot u-Tshuvot* (Tel Aviv: H. Gitler, 1976), Yoreh Deah 238; Hildesheimer's letter to W. Feilchenfeld from January 11, 1861, in *Rabbiner Esriel Hildesheimer: Briefe*, ed. Mordechai Eliav (Jerusalem: R. Mass, 1965), 26–27; and David Ellenson, "Rabbi Esriel Hildesheimer and the Quest for Religious Authority: The Earlier Years," *Modern Judaism* 1 (1981): 279–97.

43. See Zacharias Frankel, "Erklärung, die Schrift 'Hodegetik in die Mischna' betreffend," *MGWJ* 10 (1861): 159–60; and Samson Raphael Hirsch, "Herr Dr. Fränkel" *Jeschurun* 7 (1860): 437–44, as well as the defense of Hirsch that was reprinted in the *AZJ* 26 (1862): 289.

44. See Hermann Cohen, *Jüdische Schriften*, 3 vols. (Berlin: C. A. Schwetschke, 1924), 1: 331; and his letter to E. Steinthal in *H. Cohen, Briefe, Ausgewählte*, ed. Bertha Strauss and Bruno Strauss (Berlin: Schocken Verlag, 1939), 11–17. Wolf Landau, who succeeded Frankel in Dresden as the rabbi, defended him against Hirsch and Fischer. See supplement number in *AZJ* 25 (1861). Hirsch responded publicly to Frankel's defense. See *Jeschurun* 7 (1861): 297–98; Leopold Löw, "Die Tradition," *Gesammelte Schriften*, 5 vols., ed. Immanuel Löw (Szegedin: Baba, 1889–1900), 1:241–317; and a positive review by Bernhard Beer in *Zeitschrift der Deutschen morgendländischen Gesellschaft* 14 (1860): 323–33. Beer also defended Frankel in "Aufruf," Beilage zu No. 6 der *AZJ* 25 (1861).

45. Solomon Rapoport, *Divre shalom ve-'emet, 'odot ha-sefer ha-mehulal Darkhe ha-Mishnah ve-divre plugot 'alav* (Prague: D. Ehrmann, 1861), 29–30; and Samson Raphael Hirsch, "Des Herrn Oberrabbiner Rapoport 'Divre shalom ve-'emet,'" *Jeschurun* 7 (1860–1861): 544–60.

46. Ludwig Philippson, "Vom Institut zur Förderung israelitischer Literatur: Eine Erklärung," *AZJ* 20 (1869): 387–89, here 388. This controversial chapter appeared only in Moses Hess's French translation and in his *Rom and Jerusalem*. See Heinrich Graetz, *Sinai et Golgotha ou les Origines du Judaisme et de Christianisme*, trans. by Moses Hess (Paris: M. Lévy, 1867); and Moses Hess, *The Revival of Israel: Rome and Jerusalem, the Last Nationalist, Question*, trans. Meyer Waxman (Lincoln: University of Nebraska Press, 1995), 186–209.

47. The review was originally published in *Jeschurun* in 1856. See Samson Raphael Hirsch, "Geschichte der Juden von Dr. H. Grätz [1856]," *Gesammelte Schriften*, 6 vols., ed. Naphtali Hirsch (Frankfurt a. M.: J. Kauffmann, 1902–1912), 5:318–509, here 320–21.

48. See, for example, the review by Guttmann of the fourth volume in *Israelitischer Volkslehrer* 5 (1855): 35–39.

49. Abraham Geiger, "Berichtigung einiger Behauptungen," *Hebraische Bibliographie* 3 (1860): 1–4; Moritz Steinschneider, "Schriften des Instituts zur Förderung israel. Lit.," *Hebraische Bibliographie* 3 (1860): 103–4; and M. Wiener, "Zur Würdigung des Verfahrens von Graetz bei der Bearbeitung seiner Geschichte," *Ben Chananja* 6 (1863): 373–77 and 391–97. See also the letter by Ludwig Philippson, May 1, 1863, to Meir Wiener in the Ludwig Philippson Collection, Hebrew Union College in Cincinnati.

50. Abraham Geiger, "Aus einem Briefwechsel," *JZWL* 4 (1866): 141–50, here 146.

51. Heinrich Graetz, "Die Verjüngung des jüdischen Stammes," *Jahrbuch für Israeliten 5624* 10 (1863–64): 1–13.

52. "Der Preßprozeß in Wien," *Der Israelit* 5 (1864): 29–32; "Der Kompert-Grätz'sche Preßprozeß," *Jeschurun* 10 (1864): 168–74; "Wien," *AZJ* 28 (1864): 86–87; and "Ein eigenthümlicher Prozess," *AZJ* 28 (1864): 29–36.

53. For further contributions to the trial, see "Die Literatur des Kompert'schen Preßprozesses," *Der Israelit* 5 (1864): 286–88, 305–6, 318–20, 333–35, and 360–61.

54. "Die Erklärung von 121 Rabbinen, die bei dem Kompert'schen Preßprozeß in Wien vorgekommen Auesserungen betreffend," *Der Israelit* 5 (1864): 96–98. This declaration was immediately countered in Leopold Löw's *Ben-Chananja*. See Leopold Löw, "Erklärung zu einer Erklärung," *Ben-Chananja* 7 (1864): 193–96.

55. "Der Kompert-Grätz'sche Preßprozeß," *Jeschurun* 10 (1864): 168–74, here 171 and 174.

56. "Das Rundschreiben des Rabbiner Lazar Horowitz in Wien," *Der Israelit* 5 (1864): 214–16, esp. 216; and J. Guggenheimer, "Zum Kompert'schen Preßprozesse," *Jeschurun* 10 (1864): 189–203, 228–31, and 253–76, esp. 189–203.

57. See "Einige Worte über den Prozess," *AZJ* 28 (1864): 36–37; "Einige Nachwehen des Komptert'schen Prozesses," *AZJ* 28 (1864): 77–78; and also Leopold Löw, "Jüdisch-theologische Fragen vor dem Forum des Landesgerichtes in Wien," *Ben-Chananja* 7 (1864): 241–46.

58. J. Guggenheimer, "Zum Kompert'schen Preßprozesse," *Jeschurun* 10 (1864): 189–203, 228–31, and 253–76, esp. 189–203, here 196–203 and 228–31, and "Die Messiaslehre," *Der Israelit* 5 (1864): 69–71, 83–86, and 98–100.

59. Heinrich Graetz, "Die Entwicklungsstadien des Messiasglaubens," *Jahrbuch für Israeliten 5625* 11 (1864–65): 1–30. See also "Ein eigentümlicher Prozeß," *AZJ* (1864): 29–37. Others republished Graetz's original essay with a footnote in which they hoped that nobody would be offended by this work. See Heinrich Graetz, "Die Verjüngung des jüdischen Stammes," *Volks-Kalender und Jahrbuch für Israeliten auf das Jahr der Welt 5625* (1865): 16–27, here 16.

60. Graetz, *Geschichte der Juden*, here 11: 401, 406, and 412. Here I followed the English translation in *The Poetry and Prose of Heinrich Heine*, ed. Ewen, 678.

61. Abraham Geiger, "Allgemeine Einleitung in die Wissenschaft des Judenthums," *Abraham Geiger's Nachgelassene Schriften*, 2:33–245, here 243.

62. Ludwig Philippson, "Vom Institut zur Förderung israelitischer Literatur: Eine Erklärung," *AZJ* 20 (1869): 387–89; and Heinrich Graetz, "Gegenerklärung gegen die Erklärung des Dr. Philippson," *MGWJ* 18 (1869): 284–86.

63. See his letter to Moses Hess from June 10, 1871, in *Heinrich Graetz: Tagebuch und Briefe*, ed. Reuven Michael (Tübingen: J. C. B. Mohr, 1977), 310; and the review of the eleventh volume in *Literarisches Centralblatt* (1871): 29–31.

5. "Bringing Forth Their Past Glories"

1. Jost, *Geschichte des Judentums und seiner Secten*, 3:285.

2. See Graetz, *Die Konstruktion der jüdischen Geschichte*.

3. Graetz, *Geschichte der Juden*, 11.

4. Nachum Glatzer, "Leopold Zunz and the Revolution of 1848: With the Publication of Four Letters by Zunz," *LBIYB* 5 (1960): 122–39.

5. Compare the correspondence of the 1840s in Glatzer, "Leopold Zunz and the Revolution of 1848," 122–39 with Zunz's correspondence with David Kaufmann from the 1870s on in Markus Brann, "Mittheilungen aus dem Briefwechsel zwischen Zunz und Kaufmann," *JJGL* 5 (1902): 159–209 and 6 (1903): 120–57. See esp. letters 66 and 73.

6. Glatzer, "Leopold Zunz and the Revolution of 1848," 129.

7. Zacharias Frankel, "Einleitendes," *MGWJ* 1 (1852): 1–6, here 1 and 4.

8. Abraham Geiger, "Die Zersetzung," *JZfWL* 9 (1871): 81–84; and "Geist oder Geld," *JZfWL* 10 (1872): 161–65 and 250–54.

9. "Was soll geschehen?" *AZJ* 16 (1852): 437–40, here 437.

10. "Das vorige und das gegenwärtige Jahrhundert," *AZJ* 16 (1853): 367–68, 380–81, 405–6, and 445–47. See also "Die erste und die zweite Hälfte des Jahrhunderts," *AZJ* 43 (1879): 609–10.

11. "Unser Jahrhundert," *AZJ* 34 (1870): 717–21; and "Das neunzehnte Jahrhundert," *AZJ* 63 (1876): 671–73.

12. "Die Zeitlage," *AZJ* 12 (1848): 629–63.

13. Jost, *Geschichte des Judentums und seiner Secten*, 1: viii, 3: iv.

14. Graetz, *Geschichte der Juden*, 11: 549–82.

15. See the introduction by Ludwig Philippson in Ludwig and Phoebus Philippson, *Saron: Novellenbuch*, 2nd ed. (Leipzig: O. Leiner, 1855), iii–v. See also Niza Ben-Ari, *Roman 'im he-'avar: Ha-Roman ha-histori ha-yehudi-ha-germani min ha-me'ah ha-19 we-yezirato shel sifrut le'umit* (Tel Aviv: Devir, 1997), 104–9; and Itta Shedletzky, "Literaturdiskussion und Belletristik in den jüdischen Zeitschriften in Deutschland, 1837–1918," (Ph.D. diss., Hebrew University, 1986), 102–17.

16. Ben-Ari, *Roman 'im he-'avar*, 53–97; and Shedletzky, "Literaturdiskussion und Belletristik," 121–31.

17. Graetz, *Geschichte der Juden*, 11:448–49.

18. Ibid., 11:420. See also Brämer, *Rabbiner Zacharias Frankel*, 262–63.

19. See Luitpold Wallach, *Liberty and Letters: The Thoughts of Leopold Zunz* (London: East and West Library, 1959), 86–87; and Nils Roemer, "Turning Defeat into Victory: *Wissenschaft des Judentums* and the Martyrs of 1096," *Jewish History* 13 (1999): 65–80.

20. Leopold Zunz, *Die synagogale Poesie des Mittelalters* (Berlin: Springer, 1855), 9.

21. Graetz, *Geschichte der Juden*, 4:2.

22. Ibid., 1:xxxiii.

23. See Abraham Geiger's review of *Allgemeine Geschichte*," *WZjT* 2 (1836): 162–71 and 504–18, esp. 171 and 505–6.

24. The eleventh chapter was first published in the third edition. I cite here according to the fourth edition. Heinrich Graetz, *Geschichte der Juden von dem Tode Juda Makkabi's bis zum Untergang des judäischen Staates*, 4th ed. (Leipzig: O. Leiner, 1888), 272–317.

25. Graetz, *Geschichte der Juden*, 7:254 and 11:102.

26. Graetz treated Spinoza, therefore, in the same section of his history as Sabbatai Zevi. For Graetz, allegorical thinking had also led Spinoza astray into atheism. See Graetz, *Geschichte der Juden*, 10:169–258, esp. 171. This was not Graetz's invention but had already a long history that was shared by Abraham Geiger, who equally believed that Spinoza was influenced by the Kabbala. See A. Geiger, *Das Judenthum und seine Geschichte*, 60; and Gershom Scholem, "Die Wachtersche Kontoverse über den Spinozismus und ihre Folgen," Karl Gründer and Wilhelm Schmidt-Biggemann, *Spinoza in der Frühzeit seiner religiösen Wirkung* (Heidelberg: L. Schneider, 1984), 15–25.

27. Heinrich Graetz, *Gnosticismus und Judenthum* (Krotschin: B. L. Monasch, 1846), vi–vii.

28. See Jonathan M. Elukin, "A New Essenism: Heinrich Graetz and Mysticism," *JHI* 59 (1998): 135–48.

29. Graetz, *Geschichte der Juden dem Tode Juda Makkabi's*, 273.

30. Graetz, *Geschichte der Juden*, 1: xxxiv, and 4: 2.

31. Peter Novick, *That Noble Dream the "Objectivity Question" and the American Historical Profession, Ideas in Context* (Cambridge: Cambridge University Press, 1989), 27.

32. Graetz, *Geschichte der Juden*, 11:2. See also his letter to Joseph Perles from October 1876, in the Joseph Perles Collection, Leo Baeck Institute, New York, AR 1351.

33. A. Geiger, *Das Judenthum und seine Geschichte*, viiii–x, and 7.

34. Ibid., 31, and 73–74.

35. Moritz Steinschneider's review of "A. Geiger, *Das Judenthum und seine Geschichte*," *Hebräische Bibliographie* 7 (1864): 123–27.

36. A. Geiger, *Das Judenthum und seine Geschichte*, 1:36 and 131–37; and the appendix "Offenes Sendschreiben an Herrn Professor Holtzmann," 188, and Hans Liebeschütz, *Das Judentum im deutschen Geschichtsbild von Hegel bis Max Weber* (Tübingen: J. C. B. Mohr, 1967), 113–37.

37. Emanuel Hecht, *Israels Geschichte von der Zeit des Bibel-Abschlusses bis zur Gegenwart: Für Schüler jüdischer Lehranstalten, höhere Bürgerschulen und Gymnasien, für Familie und Schulbibliotheken* (Leipzig: Baumgärtner, 1855), 91–93, 189–250, and 287.

38. Ibid., iv, vii, 53, 65, 100, 123, 273–92, and 306.

39. On ghetto novels during this time, see Ritchie Robertson, *The "Jewish Question" in German Literature, 1749–1939: Emancipation and its Discontents* (Oxford: Clarendon, 1999), 411–28.

40. Moritz Steinschneider, "Ueber die Volksliteratur der Juden," *Archiv für Literaturgeschichte* 2 (1872): 1–21, here 2.

41. The reviewer of *Israelitische Wochenschrift* only critically pointed out that the culture Berliner described still existed. See the reviews of Abraham Berliner's *Aus dem inneren Leben der deutschen Juden im Mittelalter*, *Israelitische Wochenschrift* 2 (1871): 352–53 and *AZJ* 35 (1871): 736–37.

42. Abraham Berliner, *Aus dem inneren Leben der deutschen Juden im Mittelalter. Nach den gedruckten und ungedruckten Quellen. Zugleich ein Beitrag zur deutschen Kulturgeschichte* (Berlin: Benzian, 1871), vii, 19, and 49.

43. "Literarische Nachrichten," *AZJ* 15 (1851): 461–63, here 462.

44. "Erinnerungstafeln an die für das Judenthum wichtigen Epochen," *Jahrbuch für Israeliten 5606* (1846), ii–iii. See also Salomon Rapoport, "Über die Chroniken oder Erinnerungstafeln in den israelitischen Kalerndern," *Jahrbuch für Israeliten auf das Jahr 5605* (1844–45): 243–67.

45. Leopold Zunz, *Monatstage des Kalenderjahres: Ein Andenken an Hingeschiedene* (Berlin: Poppelauer, 1872). See also the reviews in *AZJ* 36 (1872): 449–50, 477–78, and 687–88 and *JZfWL* 10 (1872): 184–86; and Schorsch, *From Text to Context,* 334–44.

46. Zunz, *Zur Geschichte und Literatur,* 304–458.

47. Moses Mannheimer, *Die Juden in Worms, ein Beitrag zur Geschichte der Juden in den Rheingegenden* (Frankfurt a. M.: J. S. Adler, 1842).

48. See "Aufruf," *AZJ* 17 (1853): 423–24. Translations of this announcement also appeared in the *Univers Israélite, Archives Israélites* and in the *Jewish Chronicle*. See the introduction to Lewysohn's book, which also mentions Zunz's book *Zur Geschichte und Literatur.* Ludwig Lewysohn, *Nafshot Zadikim: Sechzig Epitaphien von Grabsteinen des israelitischen Friedhofes zu Worms regressiv bis zum Jahr 905 übl. Zeitr. nebst biographischen Skizzen* (Frankfurt a. M.: Baer, 1855), no pagination.

49. Lewysohn falsely attributed these martyrs to 1096. They died in 1349. See Ludwig Lewysohn, *Nafshot Zadikim,* 15–18.

50. Ibid., 18.

51. Ludwig Lewysohn, "Scenen aus dem Jahre 1096," *MGWJ* 5 (1856): 167–77, here 177.

52. *Fest-Predigten zur Säcularfeier der jüdischen Gemeinde in Berlin am 10. September 1871 von den Rabbiner Joseph Aub und Dr. Abr. Geiger* (Berlin: J. Levit, 1871); and Abraham Geiger, "Die jüdische Gemeinde Berlin," *JZWL* 9 (1871): 241–55. The *Israelitische Wochenschrift* and *Der Israelit* critically reviewed the sermons and attacked Geiger for having elaborated on the intolerant treatment Jews had received in the passing centuries in Berlin. See *Israelitische Wochenschrift* 6 (1875): 385; and "Berlin," *Der Israelit* 2 (1871): 301. On the other side, Ludwig Geiger applauded the Prussian State for its tolerance and its ability to absorb Jews, who had gone from strangers to citizens within only one hundred years. See Ludwig Geiger, *Geschichte der Juden in Berlin,* 2 vols. (Berlin: J. Guttentag, 1871), 1: v.

53. Ismar Schorsch, "Moritz Güdemann, Rabbi, Historian and Apologist." *LBIYB* 11 (1966): 42–66, here 46; and C. A. H. Burkhardt and M. Stern, "Aus der Zeitschriftenliteratur zur Geschichte der Juden in Deutschland," *ZGJD* 2 (1888): 1–46 and 109–49.

6. Finding Common Ground in the Creation of a German Jewish Reading Public

1. See the letter from December 26, 1851, to Steinschneider in the Moritz Steinschneider Collection, AR 108 at the Jewish Theological Seminary in New York and the letters from July 19 and July 21, 1864, by Zacharias Frankel to Joseph Perles in the Joseph Perles Collection, Leo Baeck Institute, New York, AR 4884. See also Andreas Brämer,

"Die Anfangsjahre der 'Monatsschrift für die Geschichte und Wissenschaft des Judenthums' (1851–68). Kritische Forschung und jüdische Tradition im Zeitalter der Emanzipation," *Zwischen Selbstbehauptung und Verfolgung. Deutsch-jüdische Zeitungen und Zeitschriften von der Aufklärung bis zum Nationalsozialismus,* ed. Michael Nagel (Hildesheim: Georg Olms Verlag, 2002), 139–57, here 146–52.

2. Ismar Elbogen, "Briefwechsel zwischen Leopold Zunz und Frederick David Mocatta," *Occident and Orient: Being Studies in Semitic Philology and Literature, Jewish History and Philosophy and Folklore in the Widest Sense, in Honor of Haham Dr. M. Gaster's 80th Birthday: Gaster Anniversary Volume,* ed. Bruno Schindler and A. Mamorstein (London: Taylor's Foreign Press, 1936): 144–53, here 145–46.

3. Moritz Steinschneider, "Benjacob's Bibliopolis (Neuhebräische Classiker)," *Hebräische Bibliographie* 5 (1862): 1–2, here 1.

4. Olaf Blaschke, "Das 19. Jahrhundert: Ein Zweites Konfessionelles Zeitalter," *Geschichte und Gesellschaft* 26 (2000): 28–75; and Rudolf Rüppel, "Christliche Leihbibliotheken im 19. Jahrhundert im Gefolge der Erweckungsbewegung," *Die Leihbibliotheken als Institution des literarischen Lebens im 18. und 19. Jahrhundert,* ed. Georg Jäger and Jörg Schönert (Hamburg: E. Hauswedell, 1980), 349–98.

5. For the Breslau Learning and Reading Association, see chapter 3 of this volume, "Recovering Jewish History in the Age of Emancipation and Reform," 38. Other Jewish reading societies were founded, for example, in Buchau, Glückstadt, Krefeld, Bad Homburg, Göppingen, Hannover, Ulm, Laupheim, Jebenhausen, and Munich. See "Breslau," *AZJ* 10 (1846): 52; "Breslau," *AZJ* 25 (1861): 223–24; "Glückstadt," *AZJ* 16 (1852): 505; "Württemberg," *AZJ* 25 (1857): 425; "Reiseskizzen aus Württemberg," *AZJ* 21 (1857): 424–25, 439–40, here 425; "Bad Homburg," *AZJ* 26 (1862): 178–79; "Hannover," *AZJ* 26 (1862): 240; and "Laupheim," *Der israelitische Lehrer* 6 (1866): 89. See also Jacob Toury, *Soziale und politische Geschichte der Juden in Deutschland, 1847–1871: Zwischen Revolution, Reaktion und Emanzipation* (Düsseldorf: Droste, 1977), 225–26.

6. *Katalog der Bibliothek der Synagogen-Gemeinde zu Königsberg in Pr.* (Königsberg: Jacoby, 1893). See also *Hebraische Bibliographie* 4 (1861): 71–72; "Breslau," *AZJ* 25 (1861): 223–23; "Berlin," *AZJ* 20 (1856): 8 and Synagogengemeinde Hagen: Schulbibliothek, 1877, CAHJP, D/Ha6/48.

7. See the statutes in [Moritz Abraham Levy], *Catalog der Bibliothek der Synagogen-Gemeinde zu Breslau (Israelitischer Lehr- und Leseverein)* (Breslau: Sulzbach's Buchdruckerei, 1861) and *Katalog der Bibliothek der Synagogen-Gemeinde zu Königsberg in Pr.*

8. The Association for the Promotion of Jewish Science in Hannover, for example, offered in 1862 lectures by Meir Wiener and Moritz Kayserling, among others, about *midrashim* and psalms. See "Hannover," *AZJ* 26 (1862): 240. Moses Silberstein gave a lecture in 1872 on Moses Mendelssohn at the Munich reading association. See M. Silberstein, *Moses Mendelssohn, ein Lebensbild. Vortrag gehalten in der Lesegesellschaft zu München am 22. Januar 1872. Auf mehrfaches Ersuchen dem Drucke übergeben. Der Reinertrag ist zur Linderung des gräßlichen Elends unter den Israeliten in Persien bestimmt* (Esslingen: R. Voigtländer, 1872).

9. Hans-Ulrich Wehler, *Deutsche Gesellschaftsgeschichte: Von der "Deutschen Doppel-revolution" bis zum Ende des Ersten Weltkrieges, 1848-1914* (München: C. H. Beck, 1987), 433.

10. "Breslau," *AZJ* 10 (1846): 333; and "Laupheim," *Der israelitische Lehrer* 6 (1866): 89.

11. "Lauchheim (Württenberg)," *Gegenwart* 1 (1867): 103; and "Bad Homburg," *AZJ* 26 (1862): 178-79.

12. On the general decline of borrowing libraries during this period, see Albert Martino, "Die 'Leihbibliotheksfrage.' Zur Krise der deutschen Leihbibliothek in der zweiten Hälfte des 19. Jahrhundert," *Die Leihbibliotheken als Institution des literarischen Lebens im 18. und 19. Jahrhundert,* ed. Jäger and Schönert, 89-163 and Georg Jäger and Jörg Schönert, "Die Leihbibliothek als literarische Institution im 18. und 19. Jahrhun-dert—Ein Problemaufriß," *Die Leihbibliotheken als Institution des literarischen Lebens im 18. und 19. Jahrhundert,* ed. Jäger and Schönert, 7-60.

13. "An die jüdischen Buch- und Bücherhandler: An alle Förderer der jüdischen Literatur," *AZJ* 19 (1855): 118-19. Among the subscribers to the publications of the Insti-tute for the Promotion of Jewish Literature were various reading societies, commu-nities, and schools. See *Alphabetische Liste der Förderer der israelitischen Literatur als Abonnenten des Instituts zur Förderung der isralitischen Literatur in seinem achten Jahre vom 1. Mai 1862 bis 1. Mai 1863* (Leipzig: O. Leiner, 1863).

14. See Abraham Geiger's letter to Moritz Steinschneider from February 17, 1851, in the Moritz Steinschneider Collection, Jewish Theological Seminary, AR 108.

15. Hans O. Horch, *Auf der Suche nach der jüdischen Erzählliteratur: Die Literatur-kritik der "Allgemeinen Zeitung des Judentums"* (Frankfurt a. M.: Peter Lang, 1985), 158.

16. Ludwig Philippson, "Aufforderung an alle deutsch-lesenden Israeliten zur Gründung einer israelitischen Literatur-Gesellschaft," *AZJ* 19 (1855): 87-89; "An die jüdischen Buch-und Bücherhändler: An alle Förderer der jüdischen Literatur" *AZJ* 19 (1855): 118-19; A. Jellineck, J. M. Jost, and Ludwig Philippson, "Aufforderung an alle jüdischen Autoren," *AZJ* 19 (1855): 237-38; and "Jahresbericht des Instituts zur Förderung der israelitischen Literatur über das erste Jahr, 1. Mai 1855 bis 1. Mai 1856," *Beilage zur AZJ* 20:10 (1856).

17. See *AZJ* 19 (1855): 277, 317, 342; and "Das Institut zur Förderung israelitischen Literatur," *AZJ* 19 (1855): 251-52 about the progress in finding subscribers. On the increase in the number of book dealers who participated in the Institute's effort, see "Die israelitische Literatur-Gesellschaft" *AZJ* 19 (1855): 118-19, 130-31, 146-47, 156, 169, 183, 198, 213-14, 277, 303, 317, 342, and 403. Further reports about the Institute during the first years continued to appear, as did the announcement that the list of subscribers would be sent to members. See *AZJ* 19 (1855): 547. Finally, Philippson informed his readers about the books they would receive during the first year. See "An alle Theilnehmer des Insti-tuts zur Förderung der israelitischen Literatur," *AZJ* 19 (1855): 571-72.

18. "Vom Institut zur Förderung der israelitischen Literatur," *AZJ* 21 (1857): 624-26, here 624; *Erste Beilage zu der AZJ* 25:13 (1861); and "Das Institut zur Förderung der israelitischen Literatur," *AZJ* 27 (1853): 593-93, here 593.

19. On the Institute in general, see M. Kayserling, Ludwig Philippson: Ein Biographie (Leipzig, 1898), 252–58; and Horch, *Auf der Suche nach der jüdischen Erzählliteratur*, 158.

20. "Das Institut zur Förderung der israel. Literatur," *AZJ* 29 (1865): 101–2; and 31 (1867): 509–11.

21. Guido Kisch, "The Founders of 'Wissenschaft des Judentums' and America," *Essays in American Jewish History: To Commemorate the Tenth Anniversary of the Founding of the American Jewish Archives under the Direction of Jacob Rader Marcus*, ed. Jacob Rader Marcus (New York: Ktav Publishing House, 1975), 147–70; and Michael Meyer, "German-Jewish Identity in Nineteenth-Century America," *Toward Modernity: The European Jewish Model*, ed. Jacob Katz (New Brunswick: Transaction Books, 1987), 247–67.

22. M. Brann, "Verzeichnis von H. Graetzens Schriften und Abhandlungen und Übersetzungen und Bearbeitungen," *MGWJ* 61 (1917): 444–91, and 62 (1918): 266–69, here 481–84; and Feiner, *Haskalah and History*, 266–73.

23. This calculation is based on average of 2,500 subscribers. See also Schorsch, *From Text to Context*, 362–63.

24. Other historical works published by the Institute include Abraham Geiger's *Parschandatha. Die nordfranzösische Exegetenschule: Ein Beitrag zur Geschichte der Bibelexegese und der jüdischen Literatur* (Leipzig: Schnauss, 1855); Meyer Kayserling's *Moses Mendelssohn: Sein Leben und seine Werke* (Leipzig: H. Mendelssohn, 1862), as well as his *Geschichte der Juden in Portugal* (Leipzig: O. Leiner, 1867); Julius Fürst's *Geschichte des Karäerthums. Eine kurze Darstellung seiner Entwicklung, Lehre und Literatur mit den dazugehörigen Quellennachweisen*, 3 vols. (Leipzig: O. Leiner, 1862–69); Levi Herzfeld's *Geschichte des Volkes Israel von der Zerstörung des ersten Tempels bis zur Einsetzung des Mackabäers Schimon zum hohen Priester und Fürsten: Aus seinem dreibändigen Werke des gleichen Titels kürzer dargestellt und überarbeitet* (Leipzig: O. Leiner, 1870); and David Cassel's *Geschichte der jüdischen Literatur*, 2 vols. (Berlin: L. Gerschel, 1872–73).

25. For the initial call to submit manuscripts, see "Aufforderung," *AZJ* 19 (1855): 509. For works subsidized by the Institute see "An alle Abonnenten des Instituts zur Förderung der israelitischen Literatur," *AZJ* 19 (1855): 621; and "Vom Institut zur Förderung der israelitischen Literatur," *AZJ* 21 (1857): 567.

26. "Vom Institut zur Förderung der israelitischen Literatur," *AZJ* 22 (1858): 381; and *AZJ* 23 (1859): 255 and 746.

27. "Das Institut zur Förderung der israelitischen Literatur," *AZJ* 29 (1865): 101–2, here 101.

28. Jost, *Geschichte des Judentums und seiner Secten*, 3: vii.

29. "Vom Institut zur Förderung der israelitischen Literatur," *AZJ* 21 (1857): 624–26, here 624.

30. *Israelitische Wochenschrift* 1 (1870): 155, 163, and 171. *Der Israelit* went to great lengths to warn its readers of Ludwig Philippson's *Neues israelitische Gebetbuch für die Wochentage, Sabbathe und alle Feste zum Gebrauche während des Gottesdienstes und bei der häuslichen Andacht* (Berlin: L. Gerschel, 1864), which was published by the Institute. Yet the review makes quite clear that among the subscribers to the Institute's publications

"are people of all kinds of directions" and explicitly refers to the many subscribers who are of neo-Orthodox background. See "Das Institut zur Förderung der isr. Literatur und das Publikum," *Der Israelit* 4 (1864): 388–89 and the advertisement for Heinrich Graetz's *Geschichte der Juden* in the neo-Orthodox *Die Jüdische Presse* 3 (1872): 16.

31. Moritz Steinschneider, "Schriften des Instituts," *Hebräische Bibliographie* 2 (1859): 98–101; and Steinschneider, "Schriften des Instituts zur Förderung israelit. Lit. V. Jahr," *Hebräische Bibliographie* 3 (1860): 103

32. "Ein Wort über das Institut zur Förderung der israelitischen Literatur," *Der israelitische Volkslehrer* 8 (1858): 309–13. Ludwig Philippson refers to these attacks in "Vom Institut zur Förderung der israelitischen Literatur" *AZJ* 23 (1859): 286; and "Magdeburg," *AZJ* 25 (1861): 529.

33. L. Philippson, "Vom Institut zur Förderung der israelitischen Literatur," *AZJ* 33 (1869): 445–47, 657–58; and Kayserling, *Ludwig Philippson: Ein Biographie,* 254–56.

34. L. Philippson, "Vom Institut zur Förderung israelitischer Literatur: Eine Erklärung," *AZJ* 20 (1869): 387–89, here 388; and Heinrich Graetz, "Gegenerklärung gegen die Erklärung des Dr. Philippson," *MGWJ* 18 (1869): 284–86.

35. "Das Institut zur Förderung der israelitischen Literatur," *AZJ* 19 (1855): 251–52, here 251.

36. "Ein Wort über das Institut zur Förderung der israelitischen Literatur," *Der israelitische Volkslehrer* 8 (1858): 309–13.

37. "Das Institut zur Förderung der israelitischen Literatur," *AZJ* 29 (1865): 101–2, here 101; "Jahresbericht des Instituts zur Förderung der israelitischen Literatur über das erste Jahr, 1. Mai 1855 bis 1. Mai 1856," *Beilage zur AZJ* 20: 10 (1856); "Das Institut zur Förderung der israelitischen Literatur," *AZJ* 27 (1863): 593–93, here 594; "Vom Institut zur Förderung der israelitischen Literatur: Abermals an Alle!" *Beilage der AZJ* 27: 18 (1863); and Horch, *Auf der Suche nach der jüdischen Erzählliteratur,* 158.

38. "Das Institut zur Förderung der israelitischen Literatur," *AZJ* 38 (1874): 467–71; Adolf Frankl-Grün, *Geschichte der Juden in Kremsier mit Rücksicht auf die Nachbargemeinden. Nach Original-Urkunden* (Breslau: S. Schottlaender, 1896), 2:28; and Ludwig Philippson, "Eine Episode aus meinem Leben," *AZJ* 32 (1868): 428–29.

39. "Einladung zum Abonnement auf die Schriften des Israelitischen Literaturvereins," 2 (1876) in Organization: Israelitischer Literatur-Verein, LBI-AR 3238.

40. Organization: Israelitischer Literatur-Verein, LBI-AR 3238; "Der israelitische Literaturverein," *Israelitische Wochenschrift* 6 (1875): 142–43; David Kaufmann, "Schriften des israelitischen Literaturvereins 2. Jahrgang 1876," *Jüdisches Literaturblatt* 6 (1877): 53–55; and Kayserling, *Ludwig Philippson: Ein Biographie,* 258.

41. Leopold Zunz's letter to Bernhard Beer on May 6, 1851, in *Leopold Zunz: Jude-Deutscher-Europäer,* 330. See also "Berlin," *AZJ* 17 (1853): 505–7; and "Liste der Zuhörer des Herrn Dr. Zunz, 15. Mai 1851," Leopold Zunz Collection, JNUL 4° 792/C1. Only Zunz's lecture series endured, whereas Sachs and Graetz gave up since there were not enough attendees.

42. "Vom Niederrhein," *AZJ* 15 (1851): 14; and "Krefeld," *AZJ* 17 (1853): 6.

43. L. Geiger, *Abraham Geiger: Leben und Lebenswerk,* 105.

44. "Breslau," *AZJ* 26 (1862): 127–28, here 128; and *Statuten des Vereins zur Verbreitung der Wissenschaft des Judenthums* (Breslau, 1862), CAHJP, TD/979.

45. "Breslau," *AZJ* 26 (1862): 127–28.

46. See, for example, Berliner, *Aus dem inneren Leben der deutschen Juden im Mittelalter*, v.

47. L. Philippson, "Vom Institut zur Förderung der israelitischen Literatur," *AZJ* 33 (1869): 445–47 and 657–58, here 657.

48. Letter by J. Kaufmann to Leopold Zunz on October 16, 1877, in the Leopold Zunz Collection, JNUL 4° 792/G27.

49. See Graetz's letter to Joseph Perles from March 28, 1877, in the Joseph Perles Collection, LBI-AR 1351.

7. *Wissenschaft* on Trial

1. "Zur Synodalversammlung," *AZJ* 33 (1869): 325–26, 367–68; "Zum deutsch-israelitischen Gemeindebunde," *AZJ* 34 (1870): 41–43; and Robert Liberles, "Emancipation and the Structure of the Jewish Community in the Nineteenth Century," *LBIYB* 31 (1986): 51–67.

2. Ismar Schorsch, *Jewish Reactions to German Anti-Semitism, 1870–1914* (New York: Columbia University Press, 1972), 23–52.

3. S. Gronemann, "Durch Wissenschaft zur Einheit," *Israelitische Wochenschrift* 2 (1871): 162–64, 170–72, and 178.

4. "Unsere Devise," *Israelitische Wochenschrift* 11 (1880): 2–3, here 2.

5. Uriel Tal, *Christians and Jews in Germany: Religion, Politics, and Ideology in the Second Reich, 1870–1914*, translated by Noah Jonathan Jacobs (Ithaca: Cornell University Press, 1975), 100; and Michael A. Meyer, "German Political Pressure and Jewish Religious Response in the Nineteenth Century," *Judaism Within Modernity: Essays on Jewish History and Religion* (Detroit: Wayne State University Press, 2001), 144–67, here 160.

6. Peter Pulzer, *The Rise of Political Anti-Semitism in Germany and Austria*, rev. ed. (London: Halban, 1988), 73–93.

7. Wilhelm Pressel, *Der Thalmud vor dem Schwurgericht am Ende des 19. Jahrhunderts: Ein Zeugnis für die Wahrheit* (Leipzig: Dörffling & Franke, 1893); and Adolph Kohut, *Ritual-Mordprozesse: Bedeutende Fälle aus der Vergangenheit* (Berlin-Wilmersdorf: Basch, 1913).

8. The sources of the trial were published, as well as accounts by Bloch and the defense lawyer. See *Acten und Gutachten in dem Prozesse Rohling contra Bloch* (Vienna: Breitenstein, 1890); Joseph Bloch, *Erinnerungen aus meinen Leben* (Vienna: Löwit, 1922), 59–77 and 99–121; and Joseph Kopp, *Zur Judenfrage nach den Akten des Prozesses Rohling-Bloch*, 2nd ed. (Leipzig: J. Klinkhardt, 1886). See also D. Löwy. *Der Talmudjude von Rohling in der Schwurgerichtsverhandlung vom 28 Oktober 1882* (Wien: Löwy, 1882) and "Die neuste Leistung des Herrn Rohling," *Die Laubhütte* 3 (1886): 123.

9. Otto Boeckel, *Die Juden, die Könige unserer Zeit* (Berlin: Boeckel, 1885); and Alphonse Toussenel, *Les Juifs rois de l'époque, histoire de la féodalité financière* (Paris: Librairie

de l'École Sociètaire, 1845). On Toussenel, see Jacob Katz, *From Prejudice to Destruction: Anti-Semitism, 1700–1933* (Cambridge: Harvard University Press, 1994), 123.

10. "Der Marburger-Prozeß wegen Beschimpfung der jüdischen Religion," *Israelitische Wochenschrift* 19 (1888): 155–57, 163–65, 171–72, and 179–80; "Ein Gutachten über den Talmud," *AZJ* 52 (1888): 355–57; "Nachrichten," *AZJ* 52 (1888): 287–88; "Nachrichten," *AZJ* 52 (1888): 297–98; "Eine Anklage wegen Beschimpfung der jüdischen Religion," *Jüdische Presse* 19 (1888): 161–67; and "Ein Talmud-Prozeß," *Die Laubhütte* 5 (1888): 169–70.

11. Ulrich Sieg, "Die Wissenschaft und dem Leben tut dasselbe not: Ehrfurcht vor der Wahrheit. Hermann Cohens Gutachten im Marburger Antisemitismusprozeß," *Philosophisches Denken — Politisches Wirken: Hermann-Cohen-Kolloquium Marburg 1992,* ed. Reinhart Brandt and Franz Orlik (Hildesheim: Georg Olms Verlag, 1993), 222–49, here 233–34.

12. Cohen's statement was extensively paraphrased in the German-Jewish press. See, for example, "Ein Gutachten über den Talmud," *AZJ* 52 (1888): 355–57; "Der Marburger-Prozeß wegen Beschimpfung der jüdischen Religion," *Israelitische Wochenschrift* 19 (1888): 155–57, 163–65, 171–72, and 179–80, here 171–72, and 179–80; and "Das Gutachten des Herrn Professor Cohen," *Jüdische Presse* 19 (1888): 213–15.

13. Michael Meyer, "Heinrich Graetz and Heinrich von Treitschke: A Comparison of Their Historical Images of the Modern Jew," *Modern Judaism* 6 (1986): 1–12.

14. "Ein Antwortschreiben des Herrn Professor H. von Treitschke," *Israelitische Wochenschrift* 10 (1879): 145; "Rischuß," *Der Israelit* 20 (1879): 242–44; and "Herrn Professor Dr. H. v. Treitschke und die Juden," *Die jüdische Presse* 10 (1879): 206–7.

15. Walter Boehlich, ed., *Der Berliner Antisemitismusstreit,* 2nd ed. (Frankfurt a. M.: Insel-Verlag, 1965), 13. See also the article on a meeting of Stöcker's society, in which he explicitly refers to Treitschke's statements. "Berlin," *AZJ* 43 (1879): 821–23; H. Naudh, *Professoren über Israel von Treitschke und Bresslau* (Berlin: Otto Hentze, 1880); and Wilhelm Endner, "Zur Judenfrage," *Der Berliner Antisemitismusstreit,* ed. Boehlich, 96–124.

16. Michael Meyer, "Great Debate on Antisemitism: Jewish Reaction to New Hostility in Germany, 1879–1881," *LBIYB* 11 (1966): 137–70.

17. M. Joël, *Offener Brief an Herrn Professor Heinrich Treitschke,* 6th ed. (Breslau: Commissions-Verlag der Buchhandlung der Schlesischen Presse, L. Weigert, 1879). The eighth edition also appeared with Weigert in Breslau in 1879. See also "Breslau," *Israelitische Wochenschrift* 11 (1880): 22–23, here 23. On the sermons, see "Wider Herrn von Treitschke," *AZJ* 44 (1880): 19–22 and 100–101, here 19; and Jecheskel Caro, *Worte der Wahrheit und des Friedens. Predigt, gehalten am 15. November 1879. Den Judenfeinden Treitschke, Marr und Stöcker gewidmet* (Erfurt, 1879).

18. Boehlich, *Der Berliner Antisemitismusstreit,* 11. I follow here with only a slight modification the translation in *The Jew in the Modern World,* ed. Mendes-Flohr and Reinharz, 344.

19. See the letter to Moses Hess from March 31, 1868, in *Heinrich Graetz,* ed. Michael, 287.

20. Ludwig Bamberger, "Deutschtum und Judentum," and Hermann Cohen, "Ein Bekenntnis in der Judenfrage," both in *Der Berliner Antisemitismusstreit*, ed. Boehlich, 151–81, here 155, and 126–51, here 141.

21. Ludwig Philippson, "Antwort an Professor Dr. v. Treitschke," *AZJ* 43 (1879): 785–87, here 786; Ludwig Philippson, "Wider Herrn von Treitschke," *AZJ* 44 (1880): 19–22 and 100–101, here 20; the correspondence between Graetz and Philippson in *Beilage to AZJ* 44:6 (1880); and Heinrich Graetz, "Ein kurzes Wort der Erwiderung an Dr. L. Philippson," *Israelitische Wochenschrift* 11 (1880): 77.

22. For the negative reviews of Hermann Cohen's article, see "Schriften über die Judenfrage," *Der Israelit* 21 (1880): 474–76; Steckelmacher "Ein Bekenntnis in der Judenfrage," *Jüdisches Literaturblatt* 9 (1880): 37–39; and "Ein Bekenntnis in der Judenfrage: Von Dr. Herman Cohen," *AZJ* 44 (1880): 148–49 and 161–64. For the reviews of Breslau's pamphlet, see Ludwig Philippson, "Ein Bekenntnis in der Judenfrage," *AZJ* 44 (1880): 148–49 and 161–64; Ehrmann, "Trier," *Der Israelit* 21 (1880): 41–44; and Lewin, "An Herrn Professor Dr. Harry Bresslau," *Jüdisches Literaturblatt* 9 (1880): 18.

23. Moritz Güdemann, "Herr Professor Grätz ausgeliefert," *Israelitische Wochenschrift* 11 (1880): 39–40; "Magdeburg," *Israelitische Wochenschrift* 11 (1880): 96–97; and "Professor Graetz und seine Gegner," *Das Jüdische Literaturblatt* 9 (1880): 17–18.

24. G. Wolf, "In causa Graetz," *Israelitische Wochenschrift* 11 (1880): 76–77.

25. J. Glück, *Ein Wort an den Herrn Professor Heinrich von Treitschke* (Oldenburg: Schmidt, 1880), 13. See also Adolf Radin, *Offener Brief eines polnischen Juden an den Redacteur Herrn Heinrich v. Treitschke* (Löbau: R. Skrzeczek, 1879), 17 and 19.

26. Jecheskel Caro, *Worte der Wahrheit*, 3.

27. [Rahmer], "Die verleugnete Geschichte der Juden," *Der Israelit* 11 (1880): 49–50.

28. [Seligmann Meyer], "Gegen Herrn von Treitschke," *Jüdische Presse* 49 (1879): 547–49, 559–61, 572–74, and 583–85, here 572. These articles also appeared separately as Seligmann Meyer, *Ein Wort an Herren Heinrich von Treitschke* (Berlin: Verlag der Jüdischen Presse, 1880).

29. "Ein offener Brief an Heinrich von Treitschke, ordentlicher Professor an der Universität zu Berlin: Von einem deutschen Israeliten," *Die Laubhütte* 5 (1888): 421–22; "Treitschkes Zahlenblindheit," *Die Laubhütte* 7: 2 (1890) 15–16; [Arnold Kalischer], *Offener Brief an den Königlichen Geheimen Regierungsrath Dr. Heinrich von Treitschke*, 2nd ed. (Berlin: Walther & Appolant, 1888); and "Über den offenen Brief eines preußischen Richters jüdischer Confession an Herrn von Treitschke," *Israelitische Wochenschrift* 19 (1888): 329–30. On Reformers' criticism of Graetz, see, for example, Emanuel Schreiber, *Graetz's Geschichtsbauerei* (Berlin: Ißleib, 1881), who devoted some eighty pages to the eleventh volume.

30. See Heinrich Graetz's letter to Joseph Perles from March 5, 1880, Joseph Perles Collection, Leo Baeck Institute, New York, AR-B414 4884; [G. Valbert] Victor Cherbuliez, "La Question des Juifs en Allemande," *Revue des deux Mondes* 38 (March, 1880): 203–15; and "Das Journal des Débats über die gegenwärtigen Judenverfolgungen in Deutschland," *AZJ* 43 (1879): 737–39.

31. "Eine andere Stimme aus Amerika," *AZJ* 45 (1881): 2–3; and "Eine Stimme aus Amerika," *AZJ* 45 (October 25, 1881): 705–7. See also M. Eisler, *Die Judenfrage in Deutschland* (New York: Verlag des Verfassers, 1880), 73–82.

32. "Eine Amerikanische Stimme," *AZJ* 44 (1880): 824–25. See also "San Francisco," *AZJ* 45 (1881): 312, in which Berthold Grünbaum's lecture "Judenhetze in Deutschland," given in San Francisco, is partly reprinted. After giving an overview on various persecutions in Germany Grünbaum criticizes the events surrounding the *Berliner Antisemitismusstreit*. In his response, the editor, however, distances himself from Grünbaum's description and emphasizes that it is overstated.

33. "Amerika," *AZJ* 45 (1881): 159–60. Among the documents sent from the American ambassador in Berlin to the U.S. was an extensive report on the anti-Semitic movement in Germany. See *Papers Relating to the Foreign Relations of the United States, Transmitted to Congress, with the Annual Message of the President, December 5, 1881* (Washington, 1882, rep. as U.S.-Serial Set vol. 2009), document no. 289, 465–71. The United States, therefore, welcomed also the offer by the Spanish government to invite German and Russian Jews to find refuge in Spain. The offer actually applied only to Russian Jews, but initially, at least, the statement was in a telling fashion misunderstood. Ibid., document no. 649, 1056–57, and 651: 1059.

34. "Aryans and Semites," *Jewish Chronicle* (November 28, 1879): 9; (December 5, 1879): 9; (December 19, 1879): 9–10; "Prof. Lazarus on the Anti-Jewish Agitation," *Jewish Chronicle* (January 16, 1880): 18; "The Judenhetze in Germany," *Jewish Chronicle* (February 27, 1880): 4–5; "The Judenhetze in Germany," *Jewish Chronicle* (March 26, 1880): 5.

35. *The Tenth Annual Report of the Anglo-Jewish Association, in Connection with the Alliance Israélite Universelle,* 1879–80 (London, 1881), 17, 122, 151, and 163, Anglo Jewish Association: Annual Report of the A. J. A., 1872–90, AJ 95/150, Southampton University Archives.

36. Ulrich Langer, *Heinrich von Treitschke: Politische Biographie eines deutschen Nationalisten* (Düsseldorf: Droste, 1998), 305.

37. Theodor Mommsen, *Auch ein Wort über unser Judenthum* (Berlin: Weidmann, 1880), 4–5. See also the defense by Franz Stoepel published in *Merkur, deutsche und internationale Revue* (January, 1880) paraphrased in "Die Streitschriften," *AZJ* 44 (1880): 98–100, 131–32, 164–65 and 177–80, here 98–100 and Hans Liebeschütz, "Treitschke and Mommsen on Jewry and Judaism," *LBIYB* 2 (1962): 153–82.

38. Theodor Mommsen, *Auch ein Wort über unser Judenthum,* 1–16.

39. Reuven Michael, "Graetz contra Treitschke," *BLBI* 4 (1961): 301–22, here 321 and Mordechai Eliav, ed. *Rabbiner Esriel Hildesheimer. Briefe* (Jerusalem: R. Mass, 1965), 177.

40. See Auerbach's letter quoted in Lothar Wickert, "Theodor Mommsen und Jacob Bernays. Ein Beitrag zur Geschichte des deutschen Judentums. Zu Mommsens 150. Geburtstag, 30. 11. 1967," *HZ* 205 (1967): 265–94, here 270, note 9.

41. "Auch ein Wort über unser Judenthum," *AZJ* 44 (1880): 819–21; [Rahmer] "Was

Mommsen den Juden zum Vorwurf macht," *Israelitische Wochenschrift* 12 (1881): 13–14 and 23–24; [Lehmann] "Professor Mommsen gegen die Antisemiten," *Der Israelit* 21 (1880): 1237–38.

42. Moritz Lazarus, "Was heißt national?" *Treu und Frei. Gesammelte Reden und Vorträge über Juden und Judentum* (Leipzig: Winter, 1887), 53–113, here 71–72; and [Julius Stein], *Börne und Treitschke. Offenes Sendschreiben ueber die Juden von Löb Baruch (Dr. Ludwig Börne) an den deutschen Reichstagsabgeordneten und Heidelberger Professor Dr. Heinrich Gotthard von Treitschke* (Berlin: Verlag von Stein'schen Literarischen Büro, 1880).

43. Lazarus, "Was heißt national?" For the positive reviews of Lazarus's pamphlet, see "Lazarus über Nationalität," *AZJ* 44 (188): 36–37; "Was heißt national?" *Jüdische Literaturblatt* 9 (1880): 23–24; and "Was heißt national?" *Der Israelit* 21 (1880): 429–31.

44. See the letter by Paul Heyser to Moritz Lazarus in Franz Kobler, *Jüdische Geschichte in Briefen aus Ost und West. Das Zeitalter der Emanzipation* (Wien: Saturn-Verlag, 1938), 430. Karl Fischer, teacher at a Frankfurt high school, reiterated many of these points. See Karl Fischer, *Heinrich v. Treitschke und sein Wort über unser Judenthum. Ein Wort zur Verständigung* (M. Gladbach: Emil Schellmann, 1880).

45. Reuven Michael, "Graetz contra Treitschke," 317–21; and Michael Meyer, "Great Debate on Antisemitism: Jewish Reaction to New Hostility in Germany, 1879–1881," 158.

46. M. Brann, "Verzeichnis von H. Graetzens Schriften und Abhandlungen und Übersetzungen und Bearbeitungen," 444–91 and 266–69.

47. Emil Lehmann, "Die Aufgaben der Deutschen jüdischer Herkunft," *Emil Lehmann: Gesammelte Schriften* (Berlin: Hermann, 1899), 355–67. This article originally appeared in *Populär-wissenschaftliche Monatsblätter* 3 (1883): 135–43 and 162–66.

48. Moritz Güdemann, *Geschichte des Erziehungswesens und der Cultur der Juden in Frankreich und Deutschland von der Begründung der jüdischen Wissenschaft in diesen Ländern bis zur Vertreibung der Juden aus Frankreich (X.-XIV. Jahrhundert)* (Vienna: Hölder, 1880), 7.

49. Ibid., i–iv. The quote is found in *Das Buch der Frommen nach der Rezension in Cod. de Rossi No. 1133,* ed., Jehuda Wistinetzki (Berlin: Selbstverlag des Vereins Mekize Nirdamim, 1891), 1301. See also Schorsch, "Moritz Güdemann," *LBIYB* 11 (1966): 42–66.

50. Güdemann, *Geschichte des Erziehungswesens und der Cultur der Juden in Frankreich und Deutschland,* 109 and 273–80; and *Geschichte des Erziehungswesens und der Cultur der Juden während des XIV. und XV. Jahrhunderts* (Vienna: Hölder, 1888), 280–97.

51. Schorsch, "Moritz Güdemann," 60–61.

52. Ludwig Geiger, "Zur Kritik der neusten jüdischen Geschichtsschreibung," *ZGJD* 3 (1889): 373–91.

53. Moritz Güdemann, *Ludwig Geiger als Kritiker der neuesten jüdischen Geschichtsschreibung* (Leipzig: Friese, 1889), 30–31.

54. Ibid., 32; and Schorsch, "Moritz Güdemann," 57–58.

55. "Wie Ludwig Geiger Graetz' Sünden an dessen Jüngeren heimsucht," *Israelitische Wochenschrift* 20 (1889): 311–12. See also "Jüdische Geschichtsschreibung," *Jüdische Presse* 20 (1889): 493–94, 505–6, and 521–22.

56. Ludwig Philippson, "Die jüdische Geschichtsschreibung," *AZJ* 53 (1889): 749–52.

57. Ludwig Philippson, "Zu 'Die jüdische Geschichtsschreibung,'" *AZJ* 53 (1889): 800–801.

58. Peter Novick, *That Noble Dream: The "Objective Question" and the American Historical Profession* (Cambridge University Press, 1989), 2; and Calvin Rand, "Two Meanings of Historicism in the Writings of Dilthey, Troeltsch and Meinecke," *Journal of the History of Ideas* 25 (1965): 503–18.

59. Georg G. Iggers, "Nationalism and Historiography, 1789–1996: The German Example in Historical Perspective," *Writing National Histories: Western Europe since 1800*, ed. Stefan Berger, Mark Donovan, and Kevin Passmore (London: Routlege, 1999), 15–29, here 19.

60. Ulrich Muhlack, "Ranke und die politische Schule der deutschen Geschichtswissenschaft im 19. Jahrhundert: Zum Verhältnis von Geschichte und Politik," *Comparativ* 3 (1993): 92–113; and Georg I. Iggers, "The Image of Ranke in American and German Historical Thought," *History and Theory* 2 (1962): 17–40.

61. L. Philippson, "Zu 'Die jüdische Geschichtsschreibung,'" *AZJ* 53 (1889): 800–801.

62. See the review of Güdemann's *Geschichte der Erziehungswesen während des XIV. und XV. Jahrhunderts* in *Jüdische Literaturblatt* 17 (1888): 117–18 and 121–22.

8. History as a Shield of Judaism

1. "Der Liberalismus und das Judenthum," *AZJ* 36 (1872): 441–43, 463–66, 501–4, esp. 442; and "Das Centenarium von 1789," *AZJ* 53 (1889): 49–50. See also "Der neu erwachte Rationalismus," *AZJ* 36 (1872): 199–201; "Der Pseudo-Liberalismus und das Judenthum," *AZJ* 40 (1876): 475–78; Uriel Tal, *Christians and Jews in Germany: Religion, Politics, and Ideology in the Second Reich, 1870–1914*, 96–109; and Uriel Tal, "Liberal Protestantism and the Jews in the Second Reich, 1870–1914," *Jewish Social Studies* 26 (1964): 23–41.

2. "Rückblicke auf die Kämpfe des letzten halben Jahrhunderts," *AZJ* 49 (1885): 35–36, 51–52, 68–70, 86–88, 102–4, 151–54, 168–70, 183–85, 204–6, 332–34, 345–47; and Heinrich Graetz, "Ein Rückblick auf 50 Jahre," *Israelitische Wochenschrift* 22 (1892): 9–10.

3. "Der Liberalismus und das Judenthum," 442.

4. David Blackbourn, *Marpingen: Apparitions of the Virgin Mary in a Nineteenth-Century German Village* (New York: Knopf, 1995): 256–63. See, for example, David Cassel, *Offener Brief eines Juden an Herrn Professor Dr. Virchow* (Berlin: Louis Gerschel, 1869); but also Hermann Cohen, "Virchow und die Juden," *Jüdische Schriften*. 3 vols., ed. Bruno Strauß (Berlin: C. A. Schwetschke, 1924), 2: 457–62. This article was originally published in *Die Zukunft* (August 14, 1868).

5. S. Meyer, *Ein Wort an Herrn Heinrich von Treitschke*, 20.

6. Anton Dohrn, "Darwinismus und Religion," *Israelitische Wochenschrift* 1 (1870): 205–6, 213, 221, 229, 237–39; "Vom Darwinismus," *AZJ* 46 (1882): 508–7; and H. Eisemann and H. N. Kruskal, ed., *Jacob Rosenheim. Erinnerungen, 1870–1920* (Frankfurt am Main: Kramer, 1970), 46.

7. Yaacov Shavit, *Athens in Jerusalem: Classical Antiquity and Hellenism in the Making of Modern Secular Jew*, trans. by Chaya Naor and Niki Werner (Portland: Littman Library of Jewish Civilization, 1997), 176–84.

8. Heinrich Graetz, *The Correspondence of an English Lady on Judaism and Semitism*, Ismar Schorsch, ed., *The Structure of Jewish History and Other Essays* (New York: Jewish Theological Seminary of America, 1975), 191–258, here 197–99 and 213; and Shavit, *Athens in Jerusalem*, 178.

9. "Die öffentliche Meinung und die Juden," *AZJ* 37 (1873): 99–102, esp. 99.

10. See his letter to Cohen from May 1888, in *Rabbiner Esriel Hildesheimer*, ed. Eliav, 232–33 and "Das Gutachten des Herrn Professor Cohen," *Jüdische Presse* 19 (1888): 213–15, esp. 213.

11. "Der sechste Gemeindetag," *AZJ* 56 (1892): 158–59; and Schorsch, *Jewish Reactions to German Anti-Semitism, 1870–1914*, 35.

12. Jehuda Reinharz, *Fatherland and Promised Land: The Dilemma of the German Jew, 1893–1914* (Ann Arbor: University of Michigan Press, 1975), 26–27.

13. Quoted after Schorsch, *Jewish Reactions to German Anti-Semitism, 1870–1914*, 43.

14. L. Philippson, "Die jüdische Geschichtsschreibung," *AZJ* 53 (1889): 749–52, here 749.

15. See David Kaufmann's article written in 1878, but not published until 1891 that makes this point. David Kaufmann, "Die Wissenschaft des Judenthums," *AZJ* 55 (1891): 161–63 and 173–74, here 173–74.

16. "Literarischer Wochenbericht," *AZJ* 41 (1877): 103–4 and "Berlin," *AZJ* 41 (1877): 809. See also the special advertisement in *AZJ* 41 (1877): 31; and Kusznitzki, "Die Juden vor dem Tribunal der Wissenschaft," *Israelitische Wochenschrift* 6 (1876): 479–481 and 9 (1878): 124–26, 159–60.

17. See his letter to Zadoc Kohen from April 26, 1878, in the Zadoc Kohen Collection, JTS, AR. 64, Box 2. See also Schorsch, *Jewish Reactions to German Anti-Semitism, 1870–1914*, 43.

18. "Der Verein für Geschichte der Juden in Deutschland," *AZJ* 49 (1885): 717–18.

19. Schorsch, *Jewish Reactions to German Anti-Semitism, 1870–1914*, 45.

20. See the letter from November 23, 1885, by the Vorstand der jüdischen Gemeinde Berlin in Deutsch-Israelitischer Gemeindebund Historische Commission: Correspondence mit Gemeinden, CAHJP, M1/24.

21. See the letter by Kristeller to Harry Breslau from November 19, 1885, in Deutsch-Israelitischer Gemeindebund Historische Commission: Correspondence mit Gemeinden, CAHJP, M1/24.

22. See, for example, "Die neue Zeitschrift für die Geschichte der Juden," *Die Laubhütte* 3 (1886): 245; and "Jüdische Geschichtsschreibung," *Jüdische Presse* 20 (1889): 493–94, 505–6, and 521–22.

23. See the manuscript by Moritz Steinschneider, "Hebräische Quellen für die Geschichte der Juden Deutschlands im Mittelalter" (1886) in the Moritz Stern Collection, CAHJP, P17/24, which appeared as Moritz Steinschneider, "Zur Quellenkunde für Geschichte der Juden," *ZGJD* 2 (1888): 150–53. See also the "Bericht über die zweite Plenarsammlung der Historischen Commission für Geschichte der Juden in Deutschland," *ZGJD* 1 (1886): 289–92, here 289.

24. The Commission published and sponsored, among others, the following works: Julius Aronius, *Regesten zur Geschichte der Juden im fränkischen und Deutschen Reiche bis zum Jahre 1273* (Berlin: Simion, 1902); Robert Hoeniger, *Das Judenschreinsbuch der Laurenzpfarre zu Köln* (Berlin: Simion, 1888); A. Neubauer and Moritz Stern, *Hebräische Berichte über die Judenverfolgung während der Kreuzzüge* (Berlin: Simion, 1892); and Siegmund Salfeld, *Das Martyrologium des Nürnberger Memorbuches* (Berlin: Simion, 1898).

25. "Der Verein für Geschichte der Juden in Deutschland," *AZJ* 49 (1885): 717–18.

26. See the list of subscribers in DIGB: Historische Commission, 1885–1917, CAHJP M1/23.

27. See the budget for the years 1888–89 and 1891–92 in DIGB: Historische Commission, 1885–1917, CAHJP M1/23; "Bericht über die sechste Plenarsitzung der Historischen Comission für die Geschichte der Juden in Deutschland," *ZGJD* 5 (1892): 408–9.

28. "Breslau," *Orient* 5 (1844): 178; L. Philippson, "Dr. B. Beer," *AZJ* 25 (1861): 411–12, here 412; "Thorn," *AZJ* 30 (1866): 71; and "Mendelssohn Vereine und Stiftungen," *Lessing-Mendelssohn-Gedenkbuch: Zur hundertfünfzigjährigen Geburtstagsfeier von Gotthold Ephraim Lessing und Moses Mendelssohn, sowie zur Säcularfeier von Lessing's "Nathan"* (Leipzig: Baumgärtner, 1879), 394–96.

29. "Leipzig" *AZJ* 43 (1879): 163–64, here 163. See also "Aufruf zur Bildung von Mendelssohn Vereinen," in Deutsch-Israelitischer Gemeindebund, 1874–99: Schriftwechsel Varia in specie 150. Geburtstag Moses Mendelssohn, CAHJP, M 1/33.

30. "Frankfurt a. M.," *AZJ* 43 (1879): 471; "An den Leser," *Populär-wissenschaftliche Monatsblätter* 1 (1881): 1–3, here 1; and *Statuten des Mendelssohnvereins zu Frankfurt am Main* [Frankfurt a. M., 1887].

31. *Verhandlungen und Beschlüsse der Rabbiner-Versammlung zu Berlin am 4. u. 5. Juni 1884* (Berlin: Walther & Upolant, 1885), 31, 94, and 97–99.

32. "Der jüdische Unterricht in der jüdischen Schule," *Der Israelit* 4 (1863): 499–500; and Abraham Levi, "Ideen zur Methodik der jüdischen Geschichte," *Einladungschrift zu der am 26., 27., 28., 29. März d. J. im Schulgebäude, Ecke der Schützen- und Rechneigrabenstraße stattfindenen öffentlichen Prüfung der Unterrichts-Anstalt der Israelitischen Religions-Gesellschaft zu Frankfurt am Main* (Frankfurt a. M., 1860), 3–22.

33. "Sections-Plan in der jüdischen Schule," *Der Israelitischer Lehrer* 7 (1867): 177–79 and Claudia Prestel, *Jüdisches Schul- und Erziehungswesen in Bayern, 1804–1933* (Göttingen: Vandenhoeck & Ruprecht, 1989), 181.

34. David Cassel, *Lehrbuch der jüdischen Geschichte und Literatur* (Leipzig: Brockhaus, 1879). The second edition appeared in 1896. David Cassel, *Leitfaden für die jüdische*

Geschichte und Literatur . . . (Berlin: Louis Gerschel, 1868). See also the review of the *Lehrbuch* in *AZJ* 43 (1879): 5. The *Leitfaden* appeared in 1868, 1869, 1872, 1875, 1878, 1881, 1885, 1890, and 1895.

35. Hecht originally published the textbook in 1855 and 1865. From 1879 on, Moritz Kayserling published the *Handbuch*. It was republished in 1881, 1885, 1888, 1890, 1900, and twice in 1909. Because of its Reform-biased presentation, it was criticized in the *Jüdisches Litteraturblatt*. See the review of *Handbuch* in *Jüdisches Litteraturblatt* 9 (1880): 163–64. It found a more positive evaluation in the pages of the *Allgemeine*. See the review of *Handbuch* in *AZJ* 48 (1884): 559–60. In addition to these works, a few other textbook histories appeared during this period. See Samuel Sharpe, *Geschichte des hebräischen Volkes und seiner Literatur: Berichtigt und ergänzt von H. Jolowicz* (Leipzig: Winter, 1869); and Samuel Bäck, *Die Geschichte des jüdischen Volkes und seiner Literatur vom babylonischen Exile bis auf die Gegenwart: Uebersichtlich dargestellt* (Lissa: Scheibel, 1878), which was republished in Frankfurt a. M. in 1894 and 1906.

36. See the review of *Leitfaden* in *AZJ* 33 (1869): 842; and the review of Bäck's *Die Geschichte des jüdischen Volkes* in *AZJ* 41 (1877): 712.

37. "Correspondenzen," *AZJ* 51 (1887): 199–200; and "Verzeichnis von Thematen zu Vorträgen," *AZJ* 51 (1887): 222–23. On the use of postbiblical history in sermons, see S. Maybaum, *Jüdische Homiletik nebst einer Auswahl von Texten und Themen* (Berlin: Dümmler, 1890), 44–45.

38. Louis Maretzki, *Geschichte des Ordens Bnei Briss in Deutschland, 1882–1907* (Berlin: M. Cohn, 1907), 19.

39. Alfred Goldschmidt, "Der deutsche Distrikt des Ordens Bne Briss" *Zum 50-jährigen Bestehen des Ordens Bne Briss in Deutschland* (Frankfurt a. M.: Kauffmann, 1933), 3–118, here 18. Jacob Katz, *Jews and Freemasons in Europe 1723–1939*, translated from the Hebrew by Leonard Oschry (Cambridge: Harvard University Press, 1970), 164–65.

40. Andreas Reinke, "Eine Sammlung des jüdischen Bürgertums. Der Unabhängige Orden B'nai B'rith in Deutschland." *Juden, Bürger, Deutsche*, ed. Gotzmann, Liedtke and van Rahden, 315–40, esp. 330–32.

41. Maretzki, *Geschichte des Ordens Bnei Briss in Deutschland*, 25 and 157.

42. Maximilian Stein, "Die Existensberechtigung des Ordens Bne Briss. Zum Stiftungsfest der Montefiore-Loge, 1900" *Vorträge und Ansprachen* (Frankfurt a. M.: Kauffmann, 1929), 129–33, esp. 132–33; and Maretzki, *Geschichte des Ordens Bnei Briss in Deutschland,* , 155.

43. Maximilian Stein, "Zur Einführung neuer Brüder," *Vorträge und Ansprachen* (Frankfurt a. M.: Kauffmann, 1929), 138–41, here 139.

44. *Festschrift zum 10. Stiftungsfest des Akademischen Vereins für jüdische Geschichte und Literatur an der Kgl. Friedrich-Wilhelms-Universität zu Berlin* (Berlin, 1893), 78–81.

45. Ibid., 78–81 and 88. For a list of the lectures and lecturers see, ibid, 94; M. Lipschitz, "Der akademische Verein für jüdische Geschichte und Litteratur zu Berlin: Zu seinem 10. Stiftungsfest," *AZJ* 57 (1893): 77–78; and "Rede zur Fahnenweihe des ak. Vereins für jüdische Geschichte und Literatur, Berlin," *Populär-wissenschaftliche Monatsblätter* 18 (1898): 97–99.

46. Keith H. Pickus, *Constructing Modern Identities: Jewish University Students in Germany, 1815–1915* (Detroit: Wayne State University Press, 1999), 81–110.

47. See Hildesheimer's circular from January 23, 1881, in *Rabbiner Esriel Hildesheimer,* ed. Eliav, 177.

48. Breuer, *Modernity within Tradition,* 191.

49. See "Graetz Volkstümliche Geschichte der Juden," *AZJ* 52 (1888): 440–41; E. S. "Volkstümliche Geschichte der Juden," *Die Laubhütte* 4 (1887): 433, 5: 431–32, 46: 441–43, 6: 32:305–7, 33:314–16, 34:322–23, 35:332–33, 36:341–42, 37:351–52; and 16 (1890): 135–36, 17: 146–47, 18:155–56, 20:163–65, 19:172–73, and 20:181–82. On the publication of the third edition of Graetz's *Geschichte der Juden,* see Brann, "Verzeichnis von H. Graetzens Schriften und Abhandlungen und Übersetzungen und Bearbeitungen," 466, and 476–78.

50. Arthur Ruppin, *Erinnerungen: Jugend- und Studienzeit, 1876–1907* (Tel Aviv: Bitaon, 1945), 130–32; and "Berlin," *Israelitische Wochenschrift* 25 (1894): 270.

9. Reconciling the Hearts of the Parents with the Hearts of the Children

1. L. Philippson, "Die jüdische Geschichte," *AZJ* 38 (1874): 49–50, here 50; and R. Ehrenfeld, "Der Unterricht in der jüdischen Geschichte," *Die jüdische Presse* 9 (1878): 105–8, here 105.

2. Olaf Blaschke, "Das 19. Jahrhundert: Ein zweites Konfessionelles Zeitalter," *Geschichte und Gesellschaft* 26 (2000): 28–75; and Chris Clark, "The Fate of Nathan," Helmut Walser Smith, ed. *Protestants, Catholics and Jews in Germany, 1800–1914* (Oxford: Berg, 2001), 3–29.

3. Abraham Geiger, "Man treibt zum Extremen hin," *JZfWL* 9 (1871): 161–64. See also "Die Wissenschaft des Judenthums," *AZJ* 36 (1872): 221–24.

4. Moritz Steinschneider, "Die Zukunft der jüdischen Wissenschaft," *Hebräische Bibliographie* 9 (1869): 76–78.

5. Ludwig Philippson, "Der Fortbestand des Judenthums: An einen Freund in F.," *AZJ* 43 (1879): 625–27, 657–59, 673–75, and 705–7, here 706–7.

6. Joachim Doran, "Rassenbewußtsein und naturwissenschaftliches Denken im deutschen Zionismus während der wilhelminischen Ära," *Tel Aviver Jahrbuch für deutsche Geschichte* 9 (1980): 389–427, here 393–95.

7. L. Philippson, "Die jüdische Geschichtsschreibung," *AZJ* 53 (1889): 749–52, here 749.

8. *Verhandlungen und Beschlüsse der Rabbiner-Versammlung zu Berlin am 4.u. 5. Juni 1884* (Berlin: Walther & Upolant, 1885), 94 and 98; and L. Philippson, "Die jüdische Geschichte," *AZJ* 38 (1874): 49–50. See also R. Ehrenfeld, "Der Unterricht in der jüdischen Geschichte," *Die jüdische Presse* 9 (1878): 105–8, here 105; G. Deutsch, "Hat die Geschichte der Israeliten einen religiösen Werth?" *AZJ* 50 (1886): 805–6; and Goldschmidt, "Lehrplan für den jüdischen Religionsunterricht am Gymnasium zu Colberg," *Israelitische Wochenschrift* 6 (1876): 109–13, here 112.

9. Cassel, *Lehrbuch der jüdischen Geschichte und Literatur,* 521–56; Marcus Brann,

Geschichte der Juden und ihrer Litteratur: Für Schule und Haus, 2 vols. (Breslau: Jacobsohn, 1893–1895), 2: 440–48; and Adolf Kohut, *Geschichte der deutschen Juden: Ein Hausbuch für die jüdische Familie. Illustriert von Th. Kutschmann* (Berlin: Deutscher Verlag, 1898), 705, 721, and 789.

10. Heinrich Graetz, *Volkstümliche Geschichte der Juden,* 3 vols. (Leipzig: O. Leiner, 1888), 3: 749.

11. "Das Grätz-Jubiläum," *Beilage zur Israelitischen Wochenschrift* 10 (1879): 301–2. The address by the *Gemeindebund* is reprinted in "Adresse des Deutsch-Israelitischen Gemeindebundes an Herrn Prof. Graetz," *Beilage zur Israelitischen Wochenschrift* 10 (1879): 304.

12. Benjamin Rippner wrote a biography that was published in several locations. See "Zum 70. Geburtstag von Graetz," *Jüdisches Litteraturblatt* 16 (1887): 151–53, 155–60, and 169–70; and "Zum 70. Geburtstag von Graetz," *Populär-wissenschaftliche Monatsblätter* 7 (1887): 217–24 and 241–48. For the poem, see "Zum 70. Geburtstag von Graetz," *Jüdisches Litteraturblatt* 16 (1887): 169.

13. "Breslau," *Israelitische Wochenschrift* 19 (1888): 351.

14. David Kaufmann, "H. Graetz, der Historiograph des Judenthums," *Jahrbuch zur Belehrung und Unterhaltung* 40 (1892): 3–14, here 14. The same article also appeared as David Kaufmann, "H. Graetz," *AZJ* 55 (1891): 449–51.

15. Wreschner, "Zur Würdigung von Dr. Grätz," *Die Laubhütte* 8 (1891): 344–45; "Professer Dr. H. Grätz," *Die Laubhütte* 8 (1891): 343–44 and "Prof. Dr. H. Graetz," *AZJ* 55 (1891): 433.

16. "Volkstümliche Geschichte der Juden," *AZJ* 52 (1888): 440–41 and "Volkstümliche Geschichte der Juden," *Die Laubhütte* 4 (1887): 433; 5 (1888): 431–32 and 441–43; 6 (1889): 305–7, 314–16, 322–23, 332–33, 341–42, and 351–52; and 7 (1890): 135–36, 146–47, 155–56, 163–65, 172–73, and 181–82.

17. "Zunz-Stiftung für die Wissenschaft des Judenthums," *Hebräische Bibliographie* 7 (1864): 73–74; and "Zunz-Stiftung," *AZJ* 50 (1886): 308–9.

18. See the letter to Philipp and Julie Ehrenberg, August 26, 1864, and Gerson Wolf, September 2, 1864, in *Leopold Zunz,* ed. Glatzer, 432–34. See also "Zunz-Stiftung für die Wissenschaft des Judenthums," *Hebräische Bibliographie* 7 (1864): 73–74; and "Zum Zunz-Jubiläum: Adresse der Szegediner isr. Kultusgemeinde," *Ben Chananja* 7 (1864): 643–44. In his diary entitled "Das Buch Zunz," Zunz kept meticulous records of the newspapers that mentioned him on this occasion as well as the societies, institutions, and individuals who wrote him. He also listed all those who did not write him. See "Das Buch Zunz," Leopold Zunz Collection, JNUL 4° 792/C13, 73r, 73vg .

19. See the circular letter from April 26, 1884, in the Leopold Zunz Collection, JNUL 4° 792/Z 17; and "Das Zunz-Jubliaeum," *Israelitische Wochenschrift* 15 (1884): 259–60 and 266–68, here 268.

20. See the collection of articles in the Leopold Zunz Collection, JNUL 4° 792/Z 17. The collection includes several articles from non-Jewish newspapers on the occasion of Zunz's 90th birthday, including the *Illustrierte Zeitung, Berliner Tageblatt, Nationalzeitung, Frankfurter Zeitung, Berliner Börsen-Curier,* and the *Vossische Zeitung.*

21. D. Selver, "Dr. Leopold Zunz," *Populär-wissenschaftliche Monatsblätter* 4 (1884): 171–79, here 179. See also "Leopold Zunz," *AZJ* 48 (1884): 552–53; and David Kaufmann, "Leopold Zunz," *Oesterreichische Monatschrift für den Orient* 10 (1884): 212.

22. "Berlin," *AZJ* 48 (1884): 537; "Dr. Zunz," *AZJ* 48 (1884): 552–53; and "Berlin," *Vossische Zeitung* (July 30, 1884) in the Leopold Zunz Collection, JNUL 4° 792/Z 17.

23. "Das Zunz-Jubliaeum," *Israelitische Wochenschrift* 15 (1884): 259–60 and 266–68, here 259.

24. "Dem sehr edlen und hochwürdigen Herrn Dr. Leopold Zunz an dessen 90. Geburtstage: Der Deutsch-Israelitische Gemeindebund" in the Leopold Zunz Collection, JNUL 4° 792/Z 17.

25. "Was sich Berlin erzählt," *Börsencurior* (August 10, 1884) and *Nationalzeitung* (August 13, 1884) in the Leopold Zunz Collection, JNUL 4° 792/Z 17. See also "Das Zunz-Jubliaeum," *Israelitische Wochenschrift* 15 (1884): 259–60 and 266–68 that lists at the end the various other societies, institutions and Jewish communities that honored Zunz on this day.

26. "Zum Zunz-Jubilaeum," *Die jüdische Presse* 15 (1884): 331–32.

27. "Das Zunz-Jubliaeum," *Israelitische Wochenschrift* 15 (1884): 259–60 and 266–68, here 259.

28. See, for example, "Leopold Zunz," *AZJ* 50 (1886): 245–47; Heymann Steinthal, "Leopold Zunz: Ein Nachruf," *Über Juden und Judenthum: Vorträge und Aufsätze,* ed. Gustav Karpeles (Berlin: M. Poppelauer, 1906), 226–31; and J. Goldschmidt-Weilburg, "Leopold Zunz," *Israelitische Wochenschrift* 17 (1886): 99.

29. *Die Laubhütte* 2 (1885). The illustrations are on pages 32 and 37, followed by an explanation on pages 37–39. See also Tietz, "Der Nestor der jüdischen Gelehrten-Welt," *Die Laubhütte* 1 (1884): 487–88 and 501–2.

30. "Das Begräbnis des Dr. Zunz," *AZJ* 50 (1886): 280–81.

31. Joel Müller, "Leopold Zunz: Gedenkrede, gehalten bei der Eröffnung des Sommersemesters an der Lehranstalt für die Wissenschaft des Judenthums in Berlin," *AZJ* 50 (1886): 324–27.

32. "Zu Zunz 90. Geburtstag" in the Leopold Zunz Collection, JNUL 4° 792/C18 contains a rich collection of the various articles from the press. See also Gustav Karpeles "Erinnerungen an Leopold Zunz," *AZJ* 58 (1894): 171–73, 199–200, and 234–35; "Aus dem Leben von Leopold Zunz," *Israelitische Wochenschrift* 25 (1894): 113–15; B. Königsberger, "Zum Zunz—Jubliläum," *AZJ* 58 (1894): 114–15; and Marcus Brann, "Leopold Zunz und seine Frankfurter Ahnen," *MGWJ* 38 (1894): 493–500.

33. "Erinnerungen an Leopold Zunz," *Israelitische Wochenschrift* 25 (1894): 265–66.

34. For the memorial service at the *Jüdisch-Theologische Seminar* in Breslau, see "Breslau," *Israelitische Wochenschrift* 17 (1886): 103; S. Neumann, "Leopold Zunz. Ansprache," *AZJ* 58 (1894): 386–87; and "Traurrede, gehalten an der Bahre des Dr. Leopold Zunz," *Israelitische Wochenschrift* 17 (1886): 100–102.

35. Gustav Karpeles, "Leopold Zunz," *AZJ* 58 (1894): 387–90, here 387.

36. Adolf Rosenzweig, *Rede, gehalten am 11.8. in der neuen Synagoge bei der Feier von Leopold Zunz'ens hundertjährigen Geburtstages* (Berlin: B. Weissstock, 1894), 3–6 and 12.

37. "Erinnerungen an Leopold Zunz," *AZJ* 58 (1894): 171–73, 199–200, and 234–35. See, for example, the illustrated feuilleton addition to *Die jüdische Presse* 33 (1884): 131.

38. The crucial passages were reprinted in the German-Jewish press. See "Aus einem Brief der Kaiserin Augusta an Frau von Bonim," *Populär-Wissenschaftliche Monatsblätter* 10 (1890): 224.

39. "Die posthumen Briefe der Kaiserin Augusta und ihre Echtheit," *AZJ* 57 (1893): 110–11; S. Bernfeld, "Serbien," *Die jüdische Presse* 21 (1890): 416; and "Ludwig Marcus: Denkworte (Geschrieben zu Paris den 22. April 1844)," *Heinrich Heine: Gesammelte Schriften*, 8 vols., ed. Klaus Briegleb (München, 1974), 5: 175–91, here 179.

10. Past, Present, and Future of Jewish History: Between Hope and Despair

1. Kohut, *Geschichte der deutschen Juden.*

2. Review of Abraham Berliner's *Aus dem inneren Leben der deutschen Juden im Mittelalter, Israelitische Wochenschrift* 2 (1871): 352–53.

3. Martin Buber, "Juedische Renaissance" *Ost und West* 1 (1901): 7–10; and Asher D. Biemann, "The Problem of Tradition and Reform in Jewish Renaissance and Renaissancism," *Jewish Social Studies* 8 (2001): 58–87.

4. Richard Terdiman, *Present Past: Modernity and the Memory Crisis* (Ithaca: Cornell University Press, 1993), 5; and David Harvey, *The Condition of Postmodernity: An Enquiry into the Origins of Cultural Change* (Cambridge: Blackwell, 1989), 272.

5. David Blackbourn, *The Long Nineteenth Century: A History of Germany, 1780–1918* (Oxford: Oxford University Press, 1998), 397.

6. George L. Mosse, *The Crisis of German Ideology: Intellectual Origins of the Third Reich* (New York: Schocken Books, 1981), 52–66; and Thomas Nipperdey, "War die wilhelminische Gesellschaft eine Untertanen-Gesellschaft?" *Nachdenken über die deutsche Geschichte: Essays* (Munich: C. H. Beck, 1990), 172–85, here 179.

7. Dietrich Scholle, "'Ansichtspostkarte' und 'Gummischuhe': Die Bilanz eines Jahrhunderts," *Geschichtsdidaktik* 11 (1986): 142–53.

8. Rudy Koshar, "'What Ought to be Seen': Tourists' Guidebooks and National Identities in Modern Germany and Europe," *Journal of Contemporary History* 33 (1998): 323–40.

9. Jacob Borut, "Vereine für Jüdische Geschichte und Literatur at the End of the Nineteenth Century," *LBIYB* 41 (1996): 89–114; and his *Ruah hadasha be-kerev 'aheinu be-'ashkenaz: Ha-mifneh be-darkah shel yahadut germaniah be-sof ha-me'ah ha-tesha 'esreh* (Jerusalem: Y.L. Magnes, 1999).

10. Tal, *Christians and Jews in Germany*, 176–91 and 290–305.

11. Nils Roemer "Between Hope and Despair: Conceptions of Time and the German-Jewish Experience in the Nineteenth Century," *Jewish History* 14 (2000): 345–63; and Yaacov Shavit, "'The Glorious Century' and the Cursed Century: Fin-de-Siècle Europe and the Emergence of a Modern Jewish Nationalism," *Journal of Contemporary History* 26 (1991): 553–74.

12. Arnold Paucker, "Zur Problematik einer jüdischen Abwehrstrategie in der deutschen Gemeinschaft," *Juden im Wilhelminischen Deutschland, 1890–1914,* ed. Werner E. Mosse (Tübingen: J. C. B. Mohr, 1976), 479–548, esp. 484–85.

13. Evyatar Friesel, "The Political and Ideological Development of the *Centralverein* before 1914," *LBIYB* 31 (1986): 121–46; and Jacob Borut, "Die jüdischen Abwehrvereine zu Beginn der neunziger Jahre des 19. Jahrhunderts," *Aschkenas* 7 (1997): 467–94.

14. "Das neunzehnte Jahrhundert," *AZJ* 63 (1899): 589–90 and 601–2, here 601.

15. "Rückblicke auf die Kämpfe des letzten halben Jahrhunderts," *AZJ* 49 (1885): 35–36, 51–52, 68–70, 86–88, 102–4, 151–54, 168–70, 183–85, 204–6, 332–34, and 345–47; and Heinrich Graetz, "Ein Rückblick auf 50 Jahre," *Israelitische Wochenschrift* 22 (1892): 9–10. See also Jacob Toury, *Die politische Orientierungen der Juden in Deutschland: Von Jena bis Weimar* (Tübingen: J. C. B. Mohr, 1966), 170–76, who detects the first signs of a crisis as early as 1875 but argues that the real awareness of its existence emerged after 1878.

16. J. Kohn, "Zur Jahrhundertwende," *AZJ* 64 (1900): 76–78, here 77; and Martin Philippson, "Rückblick auf das Jahr 5660," *JJGL* 4 (1901): 1–16.

17. Roemer, "Between Home and Despair," 354.

18. "Unzeitgemäße Betrachtungen zur Jahrhundertwende," *Der Israelit* 42 (1901): 25–27, 41–44, and 219–21, here 27.

19. Ludwig Stein, *An der Wende des Jahrhunderts* (Freiburg: Mohr, 1899), 13.

20. See, for example, Heinrich Graetz, "The Significance of Judaism for the Present and the Future," *JQR* 1 (1889): 4–13 and 2 (1890): 257–69; Hermann Cohen, "Deutschtum und Judentum," *Jüdische Schriften,* 3 vols., ed. Bruno Strauß (Berlin: C. A. Schwetschke, 1924), 2: 237–301; and S. Maybaum, "Die Religion der Zukunft," *AZJ* 55 (1891): 85–87.

21. Jacques Ehrenfreund, *Mémoire juive et nationalité allemande. Les juifs berlinois à la Belle Époque* (Paris: Presses Universitaires de France, 2001), 169–73.

22. M. Lazarus, *Was heißt und zu welchem Ende studiert man jüdische Geschichte und Litteratur? Ein Vortrag* (Leipzig: J. Kaufmann, 1900), 9 and 12.

23. Ibid., 15.

24. Gustav Karpeles, *Sechs Vorträge über die Geschichte der Juden: Gehalten in der Berliner Loge UOBB im Winter 1895–96* (Berlin: Friedlaender, 1896), 4–5; and Abraham Geiger, *Das Judenthum und seine Geschichte von dem Anfange des dreizehnten bis zum Ende des sechzehnten Jahrhunderts: In zehn Vorlesungen* (Breslau: Schletter, 1871), 94.

25. Lazarus, *Was heißt und zu welchem Ende studiert man jüdische Geschichte und Litteratur,* 38.

26. Hans Liebeschütz, *Von Georg Simmel zu Franz Rosenzweig: Studien zum Jüdischen Denken im deutschen Kaiserreich* (Tübingen: J. C. B. Mohr, 1970), 66.

27. Leo Baeck, "Harnacks Vorlesungen über das Wesen des Christenthums," *MGWJ* 45 (1901): 97–120; Leo Baeck, *Das Wesen des Judentums* (Berlin: Nathansen & Lamm, 1905); Moritz Lazarus, *Die Ethik des Judentums,* 2 vols. (Frankfurt a. M.: J. Kauffmann, 1898–1911); Moritz Güdemann, *Jüdische Apologetik* (Glogau: Flemming, 1906); and Liebeschütz, *Von Georg Simmel zu Franz Rosenzweig,* 66.

28. S. Bernfeld, "Das Wesen des Judentums," *Jüdischer Almanach* 5663 (1903): 103–8, here 103, and Elias Jacob Fromer, *Das Wesen des Judentums* (Berlin: Hüpeden & Merzyn 1905), 62.

29. Moritz Steinschneider, "Ueber die Volkslitteratur der Juden," *Archiv für Litteraturgeschichte* 2 (1872): 1–21 and David Kaufmann, *Achtzehn Predigten von David Kaufmann: Aus seinem Nachlasse,* ed. Ludwig Blau and Max Weisz (Budapest: Jabneh 1931), 130–31.

30. "Anzeigen," *MJV* 1 (1898): i–ii; and Christoph Daxelmüller, "Die 'Gesellschaft für jüdische Volkskunde,'" *Die Juden in Hamburg, 1590 bis 1990: Wissenschaftliche Beiträge der Universtität Hamburg zur Ausstellung "Vierhundert Jahre Juden in Hamburg,"* ed. Arno Herzig (Hamburg: Dölling & Galitz, 1991), 361–82.

31. "Verzeichnis der Mitglieder," *MJV* 2 (1899): 84–90.

32. "Vorwort," *MJV* 1 (1898): 1–2.

33. "Zur jüdischen Volkskunde: Ein Wort an unsere Leser," *Ost und West* 5 (1905): 1–6.

34. Max Grünwald, "Zur Volkskunde," *Israelitische Monatschrift* 6, Wissenschaftliche Beilage zur *Jüdischen Presse* 28 (June 16, 1897): 21–22; (July 14, 1897): 25–26; (August 11, 1897): 29–30, here 21–22.

35. Kohut, *Geschichte der deutschen Juden,* 4.

36. S. L., "Kohut, die deutschen Juden," *AZJ* 62 (1898): 552.

37. Kohut, *Geschichte der deutschen Juden,* 7.

38. Ibid., 350.

39. Gustav Karpeles, "Ein allgemeines Archiv der deutschen Juden," *AZJ* (1904): 13–14, here 13.

40. [Gustav Karpeles], "Hundert Literaturvereine," *AZJ* 62 (1898): 553–55, here 553.

41. J. Herzberg, "Ueber jüdische Jugendliteratur," *Israelitisches Familienblatt* 10 (February 2, 1907): 9–10 and (March 7, 1907): 9–10, here (February 2, 1907), 9.

42. Kohut, *Geschichte der deutschen Juden,* 4.

43. J. M. Minty, "*Judengasse* to Christian Quarter: The Phenomena of the Converted Synagogue in the Late Medieval and Early Modern Holy Empire," *Popular Religion in Germany and Central Europe, 1400–1800,* ed. Bob Scribner and Trevor Johnson (New York: St. Martin's Press, 1996), 58–86, 220–39; and Hedwig Röckelein, "'Die grabstein, so vil tausent guldin wert sein': Vom Umgang der Christen mit Synagogen und jüdischen Friedhöfen im Mittelalter und am Beginn der Neuzeit," *Aschkenas* 5 (1995): 11–45.

44. Bernhard Brilling, "Das jüdische Archivwesen in Deutschland," *Der Archivar* 13 (1960): 271–90.

45. E. Zivier, "Eine archivalische Informationsreise," *MGWJ* 49 (1905): 209–54. On Worms, see Samson Rotschild, "Das Archiv der jüdischen Gemeinde von Worms," *Vom Rhein* 1 (1902): 21–22.

46. Karpeles, "Ein allgemeines Archiv der deutschen Juden," 13.

47. "Bericht über die Tätigkeit des Gesamtarchivs der deutschen Juden," *MGDJ* 3 (1911): 55–84 and DIGB Schriftwechsel mit dem D.J.G.B., 1906–1925: Akten des

Gesamtarchivs, CAHJP, M 5/1. For the history of the archives, see Jacques Ehrenfreund, *Mémoire juive et nationalité allemande*, 139–45.

48. Eugen Täubler, "Zur Einführung," *MGDJ* 1 (1909): 1–8, here 2–3; and "Bericht
über die Tätigkeit des Gesamtarchivs der deutschen Juden," 71–72.

49. "Geschäftsbericht," *MGDJ* 1 (1908–9): 45–46; and "Bericht über die Tätigkeit
des Gesamtarchivs der deutschen Juden," 61 and 84. A list of those Jewish communities
that handed over their archives up until 1927 was published in "Geschäftsbericht,"
MGDJ 6 (1926): 114–20. See also "Bericht über die Tätigkeit des Gesamtarchivs der
deutschen Juden," 58, 59, 60, 61, 63, 65, 70, and 84.

50. Jacques Ehrenfreund, *Mémoire juive et nationalité allemande*, 164–66; and Rudy
Koshar, *Germany's Transient Pasts: Preservation and National Memory in the Twentieth
Century* (Chapel Hill: University of North Carolina Press, 1998), 17–73.

51. Heinrich Frauberger, "Zweck und Ziel der Gesellschaft zur Erforschung
jüdischer Kunstmäler," *Mittheilungen der Gesellschaft zur Erforschung jüdischer Kunstmäler*
1 (1900): 3–38 and *Satzungen des Vereins der Gesellschaft zur Erforschung jüdischer Kunst-
Denkmäler. Eingetragener Verein in Frankfurt a. M.*, CAHJP, TD/76.

52. Nils Roemer, "Provincializing the Past: Worms and the Making of a German-
Jewish Cultural Heritage," *JSQ* 12 (2005): 80–100.

53. "Der alte Friedhof der israelitischen Gemeinde zu Frankfurt am Main," *AZJ* 47
(1883): 262–64, here 263.

54. The Baedeker guide to Berlin, for example, lists the grave site of Moses Mendelssohn. Karl Baedeker, *Berlin und Umgebung: Handbuch für Reisende* (Leipzig: Karl
Baedeker, 1894), 143. See Julius Rodenberg, "Im Herzen von Berlin," *Deutsche Rundschau* 49 (1886): 81–101. Julius Rodenberg published a lengthy article in the liberal *Deutsche Rundschau* in 1886, in which he referred to various Jewish sites. Consequently, this
article functioned as a point of reference in the German Jewish press.

55. "Der alte Friedhof der israelitischen Gemeinde zu Frankfurt am Main," *AZJ* 47
(1883): 262–64; Hermann Baerwald, *Der alte Friedhof der israelitischen Gemeinde zu
Frankfurt am Main* (Frankfurt: St. Goar, 1883); and M. Horovitz, *Die Inschriften des
alten Friedhofs der israelitischen Gemeinde zu Frankfurt a. M.* (Frankfurt a. M. Kauffmann, 1901), 5.

56. Paul Arnsberg, *Die Geschichte der Frankfurter Juden seit der Französischen Revo-
lution*, 3 vols. (Darmstadt: Eduard Roether Verlag, 1983), 2:61. This society published
Simon Unna's, *Gedenkbuch der Frankfurter Juden nach Aufzeichnungen der Beerdigungs-
Bruderschaft* (Frankfurt a. M.: Kauffmann, 1914).

57. See, for example, "Aus Frankfurts Vergangenheit," *Frankfurter Familienblätter*
238 (October 10, 1869): 7; Georg Ludwig Kriegk, "Die Judengasse in Frankfurt am Main
und die Familie Rotschild," *Die Gartenlaube* 36 (1865): 564–68 and 583–86; and "Die
Frankfurter Judengasse und die Familie Rothschild," *Die jüdische Presse* 3 (January 26,
1872): 30–31, which was based on Kriegk.

58. "Der letzte Rest der Judengasse in Frankfurt a. M.," *AZJ* 49 (1885): 230; and
"Noch einmal die Judengasse in Frankfurt a. M.," *AZJ* 49 (1885): 726–27.

59. "Wie die Erinnerungen an das Frankfurter Ghetto verschwinden," *AZJ* 49

(1885): 566–67; "Die Judengasse zu Frankfurt," *Die Laubhütte* 1 (1885): 146–47; and "Frankfurt a. M.," *AZJ* 49 (1885): 123.

60. "Der Frankfurter Ghetto," *Frankfurt am Main. Seine Geschichte, Sehens-würdigkeiten und Verkehrsmittel. Den Theilnehmern an der zu Frankfurt vom 11.-15. September 1881 stattfindenen Generalversammlung des Gesamt-Vereins der deutschen Geschichts-und Alterthums-Vereins überreicht* (Frankfurt: Baumbach a. M., 1881), 39–42, here 41.

61. "Das Ende der Frankfurter am Main Judengasse," *AZJ* 48 (1884): 386; and "Die Judengasse in Frankfurt am Main," *Die jüdische Presse* 15 (1884): 103–4, here 104.

62. "Das Ende der Frankfurter am Main Judengasse," *AZJ* 48 (1884): 386. A revived interest in Karl Spindler's *Der Jude* occurred, whose main character Zodick lived in the Judengasse in the 15th century. See "Die Judengasse in Frankfurt a. Main und Spindlers 'Jude,'" *Didaskalia* 130 (1884): 5–19. New historical novels appeared in the German Jew-ish press that took place in the Judengasse, like those by the popular writer Theodore Zedelius. See Th. Justus, "In der Frankfurter Judengasse," *Jüdische Presse* 14 (1883): 479–81, 496–97, 508–9, 524, 536–37, and 550–51.

63. The pictures appeared simply as illustrations and not within the context of an article on Worms. See "Das Aeußere der Synagoge in Worms"; "Der jüdische Fried-hof in Worms"; "Die Synagoge in Worms" and "Das Raschi-Zimmer in Worms," *Il-lustrierte Feuilleton Beilage zur jüdischen Presse* 38–39 (1893): 151, 152, 153, and 155. See also the postcards of Worms in the Postcard Collection at JTS; the Sally Bodenheimer Post-card Collection, LBI AR 7169; and the Synagogue Collection: Worms, LBI. During the late 1860s the first photos of the Frankfurt Judengasse were taken by S. F. Mylius, which were later often reprinted in the German Jewish press or used on illustrated post-cards. See the Rothschild Collection, Department for Frankfurt history, Stadt- und Universitätsbibliothek Frankfurt, Bio 66/500. For illustrations in periodicals see, for example, "Die Judengasse in Frankfurt am Main," *Die jüdische Presse* 15.26 (1884): 103–4, here 103; and "Die ehemalige Judengasse in Frankfurt a. M.," *Illustrierte Feuilleton: Beilage zur Jüdischen Presse* 13 (1893): 53, which was simply placed there without context. On the collection of paintings of the Judengasse, see Georg Heuberger, ed., *Museum Ju-dengasse: Katalog zur Daueraustellung* (Frankfurt a. M.: Jüdisches Museum, 1992), 37, 48–49, and 78–79.

64. *Bücherverzeichnis aus dem Verlag und Lager von J. Kaufmann: Verlags-, Antiquariats- und Sortimentbuchhandlung hebräischer Literatur* (Frankfurt: J. Kaufmann, 1886), 13.

65. Richard I. Cohen, *Jewish Icons: Art and Society in Modern Europe* (Berkeley: University of California Press, 1998), 59–63; and Annette Weber, "Moritz Daniel Op-penheim und die Tradition des Kultgerätes aus der Frankfurter Judengasse," *Jüdische Kultur in Frankfurt am Main von den Anfängen bis zur Gegenwart: Ein internationales Symposium der Johann-Wolfgang-Goethe-Universität Frankfurt am Main und des Franz Rosenzweig Research Center for German-Jewish Literature and Cultural History Jerusalem,* ed. Karl E. Grözinger (Wiesbaden: Harrassowitz, 1997), 321–44.

66. See David Lowenthal, *The Past is a Foreign Country* (Cambridge: Cambridge University Press, 1985), 4–12; Richard Terdiman, *Present Past: Modernity and Memory*

Crisis and Arnold M. Eisen, *Rethinking Modern Judaism: Ritual, Commandment, Community* (Chicago: Chicago University Press, 1998), 156–87.

11. The Jewish Past at the Center of Popular Culture

1. "Köln," *Israelitische Wochenschrift* 23 (1892): 4–5.

2. "Berlin," *Der Gemeindebote. Beilage zur AZJ* 57 (December 1, 1893): 1.

3. In 1903, 180 local associations existed with over 15,000 individual members. By 1914, the number had climbed to 230 associations. See "Hundert Literaturvereine," *AZJ* 62 (1898): 553–55; "Mittheilungen aus dem Verband der Vereine für jüdische Geschichte und Literatur in Deutschland," *JJLG* 2 (1899): 269–300, here 271 and 278.

4. "Mittheilungen aus dem Verband der Vereine für jüdische Geschichte und Literatur in Deutschland," *JJLG* 3 (1900): 281–318, here 282 and Ismar Elbogen, "Aus der Frühzeit der Vereine für jüdische Geschichte und Literatur," *Festschrift: Zum 70. Geburtstage von Moritz Schäfer* (Berlin: Philo Verlag, 1927), 48–54, here 52–53.

5. See *Jahresbricht und Mitgliederverzeichnis, Januar 1899* (Berlin, 1899), 5; "Hundert Literaturvereine," *AZJ* 62 (1898): 553–55, here 555; and M. Hähnlein, *Thätigkeit und Ziele des Vereins für jüdische Litteratur in Bochum: Vortrag gehalten zur Eröffnung der Saison 1896–1897* (Bochum, 1896), 3.

6. There were, however, also exceptions. The Verein in Bochum, for example, failed to generate a strong interest. See M. Hähnlein, *Thätigkeit und Ziele des Vereins für jüdische Litteratur in Bochum,* 1–2 and 4.

7. This apparently was also a source of criticism. See "Berlin," *Israelitische Wochenschrift* 25 (1894): 270; and Jacob Borut, "Vereine für Jüdische Geschichte und Literatur at the End of the Nineteenth Century," 96–102.

8. See the letter by Gustav Karpeles to Felix von Luschan from September 14, 1898, in the Felix v. Luschan Collection, Staatsbibliothek zu Berlin. Preussischer Kulturbesitz Handschriftenabteilung.

9. "Die Literaturvereine," *AZJ* 59 (1895): 25.

10. G. K., "Die jüdische Frauenfrage," *Die jüdische Presse* 3 (1872): 81–82 and G. Schwarz, "Die Frauenfrage im Judentum," *AZJ* 70 (1906): 400–402.

11. J. Lewy-Danzig, "Kulturarbeit im Judentum," *AZJ* 69 (1905): 512–14, 525–26, 538–39, 573–74, and 583–86, here 584.

12. Sabine Knappe, "The Role of Women's Associations in the Jewish Community: The Example of the Israelitisch-humanitärer Frauenverein in Hamburg at the Turn of the Century," *LBIYB* 39 (1993): 153–78.

13. Ella Seligmann, "Ein Wort zur Gründung des deutsch-israelitischen Frauenbundes," *AZJ* 68 (1904): 281; and Marion Kaplan, *The Jewish Feminist Movement in Germany: The Campaigns of the Jüdischer Frauenbund, 1904–1938* (Westport, Conn.: Greenwood Press, 1979).

14. Lazarus Steinthal, Martin Philippson, Ludwig Geiger, Karl Emil Franzos, and Gustav Karpeles sent out a circular in 1895 with the goal of founding a new publication society. See the Harry Breslau Collection, Allgemeiner jüdischer Literarturverein,

Staatsbibliothek zu Berlin. Preussischer Kulturbesitz. Handschriftenabteilung. K. IV, W-Z.

15. See the copies of the invoices from the Rosenfeld company from February 2, 1903 and October 6, 1904 addressed to Benas Levy, as well as the list of book orders in Berlin: Sammlung Benas Levy-Berlin, CAHJP, box 63a, folder 1895d. The Union and the individual associations published, for example, Marcus Brann, *Ein kurzer Gang durch die jüdische Geschichte* (Breslau: Jacobsohn, 1895); Gustav Karpeles, *Die Zionsharfe. Eine Anthologie der neuhebräischen Dichtung in deutschen Uebertragungen* (Leipzig: Rossberg, 1896); and *Samuel David Luzzatto: Ein Gedenkbuch zum hundertsten Geburtstage, 22. August 1900* (Berlin: Katz, 1900). Some of these lectures and monographs published by the he Union were sent to all the members. See "Hundert Literaturvereine," *AZJ* 62 (1898): 553-55, here 554.

16. *Bericht über die Thätigkeit des Vereins für jüdische Geschichte und Litteratur von 1892 bis 1902* (Berlin: A. Lowenthal & Co, 1902), 4.

17. L. A. Rosenthal, "Literaturvereine und gottesdienstliche Fragen," *AZJ* 58 (1894): 64; and "Welche Hindernisse stehen der Gründung von Litteraturvereinen gegenüber?" *AZJ* 59 (1895): 553.

18. Thus, for example, the reading hall in Frankfurt a. M. was founded following the initiative of the local Zionist organization. Once it was established, the Frankfurt a. M. lodge financially supported the library. See *Jahresbericht des Vereins jüdischer Bibliotheken und Lesehalle in Frankfurt am Main 1905* (Frankfurt a. M.: Louis Golde, 1906), 4. The *Lesehalle* in Hamburg was supported by the Israelitische Gemeinschaftsheim, Henry-Jones-Loge U.O.B.B., Israelitischer Frauen-Verein, Israelitische Jugendbund, Verein für jüdische Geschichte und Literatur, Gesellschaft für jüdische Volkskunde, and Hamburgische Zionistische Vereinigung. See Altona-Hamburg-Wandsbek: Bestand jüdische Gemeinde: Jüdische Bibliothek und Lesehalle, CAHJP, HM 9400-01.

19. M. Jung, "Was uns Noth thut," *Der Israelit* 32 (1891): 1907-10.

20. "Frankfurt a. M.," *Der Israelit* 24 (1883): 1685; "Frankfurt a. M.," *Der Israelit* 24 (1883): 1758; and "Frankfurt a. M.," *Der Israelit* 41 (1900): 231-32. See also Breuer, *Modernity within Tradition*, 190-91. Compare the definition of the purpose of the associations in Frankfurt a. M. with the statutes of the Union. See "Frankfurt a. M.," *Der Israelit* 24 (1883): 1758; and "Satzungen des Vereins für jüdische Geschichte und Literatur," JTS Broadside Collection.

21. *Jahres-Bericht des Vereins für jüdische Geschichte u. Literatur in Köln a. Rhein, 1892-1893* (Cologne, 1893); 1-3; Henriette Hannah Bodenheimer, ed., *Im Anfang der zionistischen Bewegung. Eine Dokumentation auf der Grundlage des Briefwechsels zwischen Theodor Herzl und Max Bodenheimer* (Frankfurt a. M.: Europäische Verlags-Anstalt, 1965), 22; and Henriette Hannah Bodenheimer, ed., *The Memoirs of M. I. Bodenheimer: Prelude to Israel* (New York: T. Yoseloff, 1963), 69 and 78-79.

22. "Die Propaganda des Verbandes der Vereine für jüd. Geschichte und Literatur," *AZJ* 58 (1894): 567-68, here 567.

23. "Die Freude an der Thora," *AZJ* 57 (1893): 457-58, here 457. See also "Welche Hindernisse stehen der Gründung von Litteraturvereinen gegenüber?" *AZJ* 59 (1895):

553; "Zum neuen Jahr," *AZJ* 56 (1892): 458; and "Zum weiteren Ausbau der Litteratur-vereine," *AZJ* 59 (1895): 321–22.

24. Ehrmann, "Ein Wort über die Vereine für jüdische Geschichte und Literatur und einige verwandte Bestrebungen," *Der Israelit* 33 (1892): 921–24, 961–64, and 1005–7. See also "Frankfurt a. M," *Der Israelit* 43 (1902): 902–3.

25. Lecture topics included Karaites, Samaritans, Rashi, Jehuda Halevi, Maimonides, Hebrew book printing, Jews in Rome, Friedrich Schiller, and the Bible. Attempts to allow women to attend the lectures failed during the 1880s. See Salomon Goldschmidt, *Geschichte des Vereins Mekor Chajjim: Festschrift zur Fünfzigjährigen Feier* (Hamburg: H. Lessmann, 1912), 14–20. For a concise summary of the history of *Mekor Hayyim*, see Erika Hirsch, *Jüdisches Vereinsleben in Hamburg bis zum Ersten Weltkrieg: Jüdisches Selbstverständnis zwischen Antisemitismus und Assimilation* (Frankfurt a. M.: Peter Lang, 1996), 45–47.

26. "Frankfurt a. M.," *Der Israelit* 39 (1898): 236–37 and Willy Hoffman, "Zum 50-jährigen Jubliäum des Frankfurter *Mekor Hayyim:* Frankfurter jüdische Vereine aus alter Zeit," *Der Israelit* 65 (1924): 14–16. See also M. Breuer, *Modernity within Tradition*, 269–72.

27. *Satzungen des Vereins "Montefiore" Frankfurt a. M.* (Januar 1897); "Vereinsnach-richten," *Der Israelit* 39 (1898): 22; "Frankfurt a. M.," *Der Israelit* 40 (1899): 4–5; and "Berlin," *Jüdische Presse* 15 (1884): 437 and 488. The Society also published a monthly journal and provided summaries of lectures. See *Mitteilungen aus dem Verein "Montefiore": Verein zur Pflege der idealen Interessen jüdischer junger Leute (Gegründet 1896)* 2: 1 (Januar 1903); "Berlin," *Jüdische Presse* 15 (1884): 488; and "Statuten des israelitischen Fortbildungs-Vereins 'Montefiore,'" CAHJP, TD/1061. On the membership, see "Vereinsnachrich-ten," *Der Israelit* 39 (1898): 22; and *Montefiori: Verein zur Pflege der idealen Interesse jüdischer junger Leute. Jahresbericht pro 1907* (Frankfurt a. M.: David Droller, 1908), 3.

28. "Frankfurt a. M.," *Jüdische Presse* 28 (1897): 475–76.

29. See the *Rechenschaftsbericht der Jüdisch-Literarischen Gesellschaft für 1902–1903* (Frankfurt a. M.: J. Wirth'sche Hof-Buchdruckerei, 1904), 9–16; and the open letter from January 1903 by the Jüdisch-Literarische Gesellschaft, JTS Historical Documents, Acc. 85. See also Altona-Hamburg-Wandsbek, Bestand jüdische Gemeinde: Verein für jüdische Geschichte und Literatur, 1901–1907, CAHJP, AHW/ 831–32 and Paul Arns-berg, *Die Geschichte der Frankfurter Juden seit der Französischen Revolution*, 2: 57 and 3: 263.

30. See the *Rechenschaftsbericht der Jüdisch-Literarischen Gesellschaft für 1904–1906* (Frankfurt a. M.: J. Wirth'sche Hof-Buchdruckerei, 1907), 3–5; the letter to Salomon Schechter by the association from October 6, 1905, in Salomon Schechter Collection 101, box 1, JTS; and the introduction to the first yearbook in *Jahrbuch der jüdisch-literarischen Gesellschaft* 1 (1903): iii–v.

31. See *Bericht des Gross-Präsidenten Sanitätsrath Dr. Maretzki über die Ordensbestre-bungen im VIII. Distrikt UOBB* (Berlin, 1897), CAHJP, UOBB Deutschland, M18/2. In 1907, the lodges organized 1,500 public lectures. See Louis Maretzki, *Geschichte des Ordens Bnei Briss in Deutschland, 1882–1907* (Berlin: M. Cohn, 1907), 157 and 167–68, *Festschrift zum 10. Stiftungsfest des Akademischen Vereins für jüdische Geschichte und Litera-tur an der Kgl. Friedrich-Wilhelms-Universität zu Berlin* (Berlin: Baer, 1893), 94; and

Andreas Reinke, "Eine Sammlung des jüdischen Bürgertums'. Der Unabhängige Orden B'nai B'rith in Deutschland." *Juden, Bürger, Deutsche,* ed. Gotzmann, Liedtke, and van Rahden, 315–40, esp. 327.

32. "Mittheilungen aus dem Verband der Vereine für jüdische Geschichte und Literatur in Deutschland, December 1899," *JJLG* 3 (1900): 283.

33. "Redner-Liste für jüdische Literatur-Vereine, 1899–1900" in Berlin: Jüdische Gemeinde. Sammlung Benas Levy, CAHJP, KGc 2/63c; Alexander Margolies, "Der Verein für jüdische Geschichte und Literatur in Berlin, 1892–1927," *JJGL* 28 (1927): 166–85, here 175; and Jacob Borut, "Vereine für jüdische Geschichte und Literatur at the End of the Nineteenth Century," 105–6.

34. Alexander Margolies, "Der Verein für jüdische Geschichte und Literatur in Berlin, 1892–1927," 175; and Abraham Berliner, *Raschi: Vortrag im Verein für jüdische Geschichte und Literatur zu Berlin gehalten* (Berlin: M. Ponnelauer, 1906). Samuel David Luzzatto's one-hundredth anniversary was celebrated with the special commemorative volume *Samuel David Luzzatto: Ein Gedenkbuch zum hundertsten Geburtstage (22. August 1900)* (Berlin: Katz, 1900). See the letters by Gustav Karpeles to Philipp Bloch in the Philipp Bloch Collection, JNUL 4° 1158.

35. See, for example, Marcus Brann, "Leopold Zunz und seine Frankfurter Ahnen," *MGWJ* 38 (1894): 493–500; "Erinnerungen an Leopold Zunz," *AZJ* 58 (1894): 171–73; 199–200, 234–35; "Leopold Zunz: Festreden von Sanitätsrath Dr. Neumann und Dr. Gustav Karpeles," *AZJ* 58 (1894): 386–90; B. Königsberger, "Zum Zunz-Jublіläum," *AZJ* 58 (1894): 114–15; S. Maybaum, "Aus Leopold Zunz Leben," *AZJ* 59 (1895): 54–55; "Erinnerungen an Leopold Zunz," *AZJ* 58 (1894): 171–73, 199–200, and 234–35; and Gustav Jacobsohn, "Zum 100 jährigen Geburtstag von Leopold Zunz," *AZJ* 58 (1894): 385.

36. See, for example, "Was lernen wir aus unserer Geschichte?" *AZJ* 63 (1899): 97–98.

37. "Hundert Literaturvereine," *AZJ* 62 (1898): 553–55, here 554.

38. Gustav Karpeles, *Sechs Vorträge über die Geschichte der Juden,* 3–4, 55, and 64. Karpeles also presented these lectures to the Association of Jewish History and Literature in Berlin in 1898–1899. See *Jahresbricht und Mitgliederverzeichnis, Januar 1899* (Berlin, 1899), 4–5.

39. Karl Emil Franzos, "Denkmäler deutscher Juden," *AZJ* 66 (1902): 463–65.

40. "Moses Mendelssohn: Zum Tage der Enthüllung seines Denkmals in Dessau, am 18. Juni 1890," *Israelitische Wochenschrift* 21 (1890): 189–90; "Professor Lassons Rede zur Enthüllung des Mendelssohn-Denkmals in Dessau am 18. Juni 1890," *Israelitische Wochenschrift* 21 (1890): 197–99; Gustav Karpeles, "Das Mendelssohn-Denkmal in Dessau," *AZJ* 54 (1890): 319–20; and Jacques Ehrenfreund, *Memoire juive et nationalité allemande,* 207–19.

41. In addition, Rabbis Weisse of Dessau, Sahlfeld of Mainz, and Rahmer of Magdeburg endorsed the plan. See Kayserling, "Moses Mendelssohn-Denkmal," *AZJ* 50 (1886): 3–5; and "Das Gutachten Frankels s. A. über Errichtung von Denkmälern und die Fälschung der Orthodoxie," *Israelitische Wochenschrift* 17 (1886): 25–26 and 33–35, here 25 and 34.

42. "Zum Mendelssohn-Gedenktage," *Jüdische Presse* 16 (1885): 519–20; "Moses Mendelssohn," *Der Israelit* 27 (1886): 1–4, here 4; and "Moses Mendelssohn-Denkmal,"

50 *AZJ* (1886): 3–5, here 5. The Conservative press originally endorsed the plan but eventually changed its position in the face of neo-Orthodox criticism. Compare the original support in "Das Mendelssohn-Denkmal und das Judenthum," *Israelitische Wochenschrift* 17 (1886): 5 to the shift in emphasis in "Das Gutachten Frankels s. A. über Errichtung von Denkmälern und die Fälschung der Orthodoxie," *Israelitische Wochenschrift* 17 (1886): 25–26 and 33–35, here 33; and Adolph Jellinek, "Mendelssohn-Denkmal und Mendelssohn-Lessing Vereine," *Israelitsche Wochenschrift* 17 (1886): 41–42.

43. In addition to the speaker Rabbi Weisse, only representatives of the Mendelssohn society in Leipzig and the *Akademische Verein für jüdische Geschichte und Literatur* gratefully accepted the monument on behalf of German Jews. See "Enthüllung des Moses Mendelssohn-Denkmals," *Jüdische Presse* 21 (1890): 297–98.

44. Leopold Zunz, *Deutsche Briefe* (Leipzig: Brockhaus, 1872), 2.

45. "Die jüdische Geschichte in Geschichtsbildern: Ein notwendiger Bestandtheil des Religionsunterrichts," *AZJ* 53 (1889): 752–53; and J. Manefeld, "Jüdische Geschichte, Volks-Familienszenen als Stoffe der bildenden Kunst," *Der Israelit* 30 (1889): 554–56, 580–82, 602–4, and 620–21.

46. Adolph Kohut, *Berühmte israelitische Männer und Frauen in der Kulturgeschichte der Menschheit. Lebens- und Charakterbilder aus Vergangenheit und Gegenwart. Ein Handbuch für Haus und Familie. Mit zahlreichen Porträts und sonstigen Illustrationen* (Leipzig-Reudnitz: Payne, 1900–1901). See, for example, the picture "Sederabend" that was reprinted in *Illustrierte Feuilleton-Beilage der jüdischen Presse* 30 (1899): 49. *Ost und West* in particular used the illustrations from Kohut's history of German Jewry extensively. See, for example, *Ost und West* 1 (1901): 150–52.

47. M. Poppelauer, *Judaica und Hebraica. Katalog 5* (Berlin: M. Poppelauer, 1897), 140. See also *Bücherverzeichnis aus dem Verlag und Lager von J. Kaufmann, Verlags-, Antiquariats-, und Sortimentenbuchhandlung hebräischer Literatur* (Frankfurt a. M.: J. Kaufmann, 1886), 13.

48. Poppelauer, *Judaica und Hebraica. Katalog 5*, 140–41.

49. Ibid., 140.

50. Richard I. Cohen, *Jewish Icons*, 115–53.

51. Börries von Münchhausen, *Juda: Gesänge* (Berlin: Fleischel, 1900), 4; and Theodor Zlocisti, "Juda," *Ost und West* 1 (1901): 63–68, here 66, in which the collage is reprinted. On Lilien, see Michael Stanislawski, *Zionism and the Fin de Siècle: Cosmopolitanism and Nationalism from Nordau to Jabotinsky* (Berkeley: University of California Press, 2001), 98–115.

52. The expression is taken from R. Cohen, *Jewish Icons*, 149.

12. Libraries with and without Walls

1. M. Stern, *Bibliothek der jüdischen Gemeinde zu Berlin. Bericht über die Begründung der Bibliothek und die drei ersten Jahre ihres Bestehens, 3. Februar 1902 bis 31. März 1905. Nebst einer Beilage: Benutzungsordnung* (Berlin: E. Wertheim, 1906), 3.

2. "Berlin," *Der Israelit* 30 (1889): 720; Wilhelm Münz, "Jüdische Schüler-Bibliothek," *AZJ* 53 (1889): 31; "Jüdische Schul-Bibliothek," *AZJ* 53 (1889): 82–84;

"Bibliothek für die jüdische Jugend," *AZJ* 53 (1889): 115–17; "Zur Schul-Bibliotheks-Frage," *AZJ* 53 (1889): 141; "Jugend-Bibliothek," *AZJ* 53 (1889): 209–11; Regina Reisser, "Was sollen unsere Töchter lesen?" *AZJ* 57 (1893): 451–53; "Eine jüdische Vereinsbibliothek," *AZJ* 59 (1895): 88–89 and 103–104; and Adolf Kurrein, "Volks-, Jugend- und Gemeindebibliotheken," *Jüdische Chronik* 4 (1897–98): 36–45.

3. Bernhard Traubenberg, "Gründet Gemeindebibliotheken," *AZJ* 56 (1892): 302; Heinrich Loewe, "Wir sollen Gemeindebibliotheken gründen," *AZJ* 56 (1892): 357; and "Glogau," *AZJ* 53 (1899): 244. See also the article from 1905 in the *Israelitische Familienblatt* reprinted in Ulricke Schmidt, "Jüdische Bibliotheken in Frankfurt am Main: Vom Anfang des 19. Jahrhunderts bis 1938," *Archiv für Geschichte des Buchwesens* 29 (1987): 236–67, here 261–62.

4. *Lesehallen*, for example, were founded in Berlin (1894), Frankfurt a. M. (1905), Hamburg (1909), and Posen (around 1900). See "Breslau," *Jüdische Presse* 30 (1899): 48–49; "Der *Gemeindebote: Beilage zur AZJ* 57 (Februar 24, 1893): 1; "Berlin," *Jüdische Presse* 31 (1900): 55; *Jüdische Lesehalle und Bibliothek. Bericht für das Jahr 1906*, 5 (Berlin, 1906); Berlin: Jüdische Gemeinde. Sammlung Benas Levy, CAHJP, KGc 2/62; and Altona-Hamburg-Wandsbek: Bestand jüdische Gemeinde: Jüdische Bibliothek und Lesehalle, CAHJP, HM 9400–01. See the undated *Katalog der jüdischen Lesehalle zu Posen [1910]* and *Vierter Jahresbricht der jüdischen Lesehalle in Posen* [Posen, 1906].

5. Schmidt, "Jüdische Bibliotheken in Frankfurt am Main: Vom Anfang des 19. Jahrhunderts bis 1938," 261; and "Karlsruhe," *Der Gemeindebote. Beilage zur AZJ* 69 (1905): 4.

6. Schmidt, "Jüdische Bibliotheken in Frankfurt am Main," 236–67; and Christian Wilhelm Berghoffer, *Die Freiherrlich Carl v. Rotschild'sche öffentliche Bibliothek. Ein Grundriß ihrer Organisation. Nebst einen Verzeichnis ihrer Zeitschriften und einem Frankfurter Bibliothekenführer* (Frankfurt a. M.: Baer, 1913).

7. See P. Schwenke and A. Hortzschansky, *Berliner Bibliothekenführer* (Berlin: Weidmann, 1906), 147–48; *Festschrift zum 10. Stiftungsfest des Akademischen Vereins für jüdische Geschichte und Literatur*, 82; and Ludwig Geiger, "Die Bibliothek der jüdischen Gemeinde," *AZJ* 66 (1902): 101–3.

8. The membership fees were rather modest. Membership for the Lesehalle in Berlin, for example, was 6 marks for one year, 150 marks for a lifetime membership, and 300 marks for a family lifetime membership, which could also be named in memory of a deceased person. See "Statuten des Vereins 'Jüdische Lesehalle,'" JTS Broadside Collection.

9. Gershom Scholem, *From Berlin to Jerusalem: Memoirs of My Youth*, trans. Harry Zohn (New York: Schocken Books, 1980), 37.

10. The library of the Jewish community in Königsberg, for example, was only open one day a week. See *Katalog der Bibliothek der Synagogen-Gemeinde zu Königsberg in Pr.* (Königsberg in Pr.: Jacoby, 1893). See also *Jahresbericht des Vereins jüdischer Bibliotheken und Lesehalle in Frankfurt am Main 1905* (Frankfurt: Louis Golde, 1906), 5; *Jahresbericht des Vereins jüdischer Bibliotheken und Lesehalle in Frankfurt am Main 1906* (Frankfurt, 1907), 5; *Jahresbericht und Mitgliederverzeichnis, Januar 1899* (Berlin, 1899), 7; and *Jüdische Lesehalle und Bibliothek: Bericht für das Jahr 1906* (Berlin, 1906).

11. *Jahresbericht und Mitgliederverzeichnis, Januar 1899* (Berlin, 1899), 7.

12. *Jüdische Lesehalle und Bibliothek: Bericht für das Jahr* (Berlin 1907-11). Four hundred and seventy-six users visited the Jewish community library in Berlin between 1902 and 1903. See M. Stern, *Bibliothek der jüdischen Gemeinde zu Berlin,* 9.

13. *Jahresbericht des Vereins jüdischer Bibliotheken und Lesehalle in Frankfurt am Main 1905-1906;* and Schmidt, "Jüdische Bibliotheken in Frankfurt am Main: Vom Anfang des 19. Jahrhunderts bis 1938," 262.

14. See, for example, *Bibliothek der israelitischen Religionsschule zu Frankfurt am Main: Katalog* (Frankfurt a. M., 1909); *Katalog der Bibliothek der Synagogen-Gemeinde zu Königsberg in Pr.,* 9-40; *Bibliothek der Frankfurt-Loge: Systematisches Verzeichnis der Bücher und Zeitschrifte*n (Frankfurt a. M. 1906), 9-17; and "Stuttgart: UOBB Stuttgart-Loge," CAHJP, D/St 3/12. See also *Jahresbericht des Vereins jüdischer Bibliotheken und Lesehalle in Frankfurt am Main 1905,* 6 and *Jahresbericht des Vereins jüdischer Bibliotheken und Lesehalle in Frankfurt am Main 1906,* 6.

15. "Berlin," *Der Israelit* 30 (1889): 720.

16. The library of the Reading and Learning Society in Breslau possessed the collections of Heinrich Herz, S. Guensburg, and M. B. Friedenthal in addition to books they purchased. In Lauchheim, the books came from the book dealer Isaak Heß. In order to maintain the collection, an association was founded. The library of the religious school in Frankfurt a. M. consisted of various donated collections that encompassed the libraries of R. Salmon Geiger, the orientalist Raphael Kircheim, and duplicates from the library of Abraham Berliner as well as the library of Freiherrn Wilhelm Karl von Rotschild. See "Lauchheim (Wüerttenberg)," *Gegenwart* 1 (1867): 103; and *Bibliothek der israelitischen Religionsschule zu Frankfurt am Main: Katalog.*

17. *Jüdische Lesehalle und Bibliothek. Bericht für das Jahr 1910* (Berlin, 1910), 7; and Michael Brenner, *The Renaissance of Jewish Culture in Weimar Germany* (New Haven: Yale University Press, 1996), 225.

18. "Einiges zur Lesebuchfrage," *Israelitisches Familienblatt* 10 (January 3, 1907): 9; Rotschild-Esslingen, "Zur Lesebuchfrage," *Israelitisches Familienblatt* 10 (January, 10, 1907): 9; "Prof. Moritz Steinschneider," *Israelitisches Familienblatt* 10 (January 31, 1907): 5; Julius Spanier-Stolzenau, "Zur Lesebuchfrage," *Israelitisches Familienblatt* 10 (January 31, 1907): 9-10; and "Noch einmal die Lesebuchfrage," *Israelitisches Familienblatt* 10 (February 14, 1907): 10.

19. "Eine judische Vereinsbibliothek," *AZJ* 59 (1895): 88-89.

20. The phrase "library without walls" is taken from Roger Chartier, *The Order of Books: Readers, Authors, and Libraries in Europe Between the Fourteenth and the Eighteenth Centurie*s (Stanford: Stanford University Press, 1994), 61-88. See "Eine jüdische Vereinsbibliothek," *Mitteilungen aus dem Verband der Vereine für jüdische Geschichte und Literatur in Deutschland* (December, 1902): 47-56.

21. The first and second volumes were only published between 1874 and 1876. After the original publication of the eleventh volume in 1870, it was republished once in 1900. See M. Brann, "Verzeichnis von H. Graetzens Schriften und Abhandlungen und Übersetzungen und Bearbeitung," 479.

22. *Stenographisches Protokoll der Verhandlungen des V. Zionisten-Congresses in Basel, 26., 27., 28., 29. and 30. December 1901* (Vienna: Erez Israel, 1901), 389–402 and 418–29.

23. Berthold Feiwel, "Geleitwort," *Juedischer Almanach 5663* (1903): 9–16, here 12.

24. *Stenographisches Protokoll*, 392; and Martin Buber, Berthold Feiwel, and Chaim Weizmann, *Eine jüdische Hochschule* (Berlin: Jüdischer Verlag, 1902).

25. Joseph Chasanowicz, "Die jüdische Nationalbibliothek in Jerusalem," *Die Welt* (December 1, 1899): 5; "Unser Nationalbibliothek," *Die Welt* 8 (May 20, 1904): 2–3; Michael Berkowitz, *Zionist Culture and West European Jewry Before the First World War* (Chapel Hill: University of North Carolina Press, 1993), 82; and Dov Schidorsky, "Jewish Nationalism and the Concept of a Jewish National Library," *Scripta Hierosolymitana* 29 (1989): 45–74.

26. Heinrich Loewe, "Wir sollen Gemeindebibliotheken gründen," *AZJ* 56 (1892): 357.

27. [Heinrich Loewe], "Eine jüdische Nationalbibliothek," *Ost und West* (1902): 101–8; and Heinrich Loewe, *Eine jüdische Nationalbibliothek* (Berlin: Jüdischer Verlag 1905).

28. H. Loewe, *Eine jüdische Nationalbibliothek*, 8–11.

29. "In Sachen der Schullesebibliothek: Liste empfehlenswerter jüdischer Kinder- und Jugendliteratur," *AZJ* 16 (1852): 316 and 386–87; and "Eine jüdische Vereinsbibliothek," *AZJ* 59 (1895): 88–89 and 103–4.

30. Wilhelm Münz, "Jüdische Schüler-Bibliothek," *AZJ* 53 (1889): 31.

31. "Jüdische Schulbibliothek," *AZJ* 53 (1889): 82–84, here 83. Histories of Jewish education no longer provided simply an overview but also offered a bibliography of recommended readings. See, for example, B. Straßburger, *Geschichte der Erziehung und des Unterrichts bei den Israeliten. Von der talmudischen Zeit bis auf die Gegenwart. Mit einem Anhang: Bibliographie der jüdischen Pädagogie* (Breslau: Jacobsohn, 1885), 282–87.

32. Moritz Spanier, "Zur Einführung," *Wegweiser für die Jugendliteratur: Im Auftrage der Grossloge für Deutschland VIII UOBB und der von derselben eingesetzten Kommission zur Schaffung einer jüdischen Jugendliteratur* (April, 1905): 1–2; and Gabrielle von Glasenapp and Michael Nagel, *Das jüdische Jugendbuch: Von der Aufklärung bis zum Dritten Reich* (Stuttgart: Metzler, 1996), 95–99.

33. Verband der jüdischen Jugendvereine Deutschlands, ed., *Katalog für jüdische Jugendvereine (Kurzer literarischer Wegweiser)* (Berlin, 1910).

34. Zohar Shavit and Hans-Heino Ewers, *Deutsch-jüdische Kinder- und Jugendliteratur von der Haskala bis 1945: Die deutsch und hebräischsprachigen Schriften des deutschsprachigen Raumes: Ein bibliographisches Handbuch*, 2 vols. (Stuttgart: Metzler, 1996), 1: 119 and 211.

35. Regina Neisser, "Jugendlektüre. Ein Wort an die Mütter," *Wegweiser für die Jugendliteratur: Im Auftrage der Grossloge für Deutschland VIII U. O. B. B. und der von derselben eingesetzten Kommission zur Schaffung einer jüdischen Jugendliteratur* (December, 1905): 25–26.

36. J. Wiener, "Warum und womit erhalten wir unsere Kinder dem Judenthum," *AZJ* 56 (1892): 221–23 and 231–34, here 233.

37. "Der Geschichtsunterricht," *AZJ* 53 (1889): 642.

38. "Die richtige Auffassung der biblischen Geschichte," *AZJ* 53 (1899): 543–45, here 545.

39. E. Flauter, "Was sollen wir unseren Kindern zu lesen geben?" *AZJ* 56 (1892): 280–81; "Einführung," *Wegweiser für die Jugendliteratur* (April 1905): 1–2; "Durch Geschichte und Kunst zur religiösen Gesinnung," ibid. (June 1905): 9; Hermann Cohen, "Gedanken über Jugendliteratur," *Jüdische Schriften*. 3 vols., ed. Bruno Strauß (Berlin: C. A. Schwetschke, 1924), 2: 126–32.

40. See the introduction to the first edition in Marcus Brann, *Geschichte der Juden und ihrer Litteratur: Für Schule und Haus*, 2 vols. (Breslau: Jacobsohn, 1893–95), 1: iii.

41. See the review in *AZJ* 41 (1877): 712 as well as the review of the second edition in *AZJ* 58 (1894): 106–7.

42. See, for example, the review of David Cassel's *Lehrbuch* in *AZJ* 43 (1879): 5.

43. Markus Lehmann published his historical novels as "Lehmanns jüdische Hausbücherei," while the *Gesellschaft zur Förderung der Wissenschaft des Judentums* advertised their publications as "Bücher für die jüdische Hausbibliothek: Schriften herausgegeben von der Gesellschaft zur Förderung der Wissenschaft des Judentum." See the advertisement in Altona-Hamburg-Wandsbek: Bestand jüdische Gemeinde: Jüdische Bibliothek und Lesehalle, CAHJP, HM 9400-01.

44. Hugo Jacobsohn, *Führer durch die Deutsch-Israel., unterhaltend (schönwissenschaftliche), geschichtlich-belehrende, populär-religiöse Jugendschriftliteratur . . . namentlich für Rabbiner, Lehrer, Gemeindevorsteher und Bibliothekare zusammengestellt* (Breslau, 1890), of which a second edition appeared in 1894.

45. *Bücherverzeichnis aus dem Verlag und Lager von J. Kaufmann, Verlags-, Antiquariats- und Sortimentbuchhandlung hebräischer Literatur*, 62 and 64–65.

46. J. Herzberg, "Barmizwa-bzw. Konfirmationsgeschenke," *Wegweiser für die Jugendliteratur* (November, 1905): 21–22; and "Geschenkliteratur," *Wegweiser für die Jugendliteratur* (December, 1905): 27.

47. Gershom Scholem, *From Berlin to Jerusalem*, 37.

48. *Bücherverzeichnis aus dem Verlag und Lager von J. Kaufmann, Verlags-, Antiquariats- und Sortimentbuchhandlung hebräischer Literatur*, 64–66. See the advertisement in *AZJ* 43 (1879): 207

49. Georg Liebe, *Das Judentum in der deutschen Vergangenheit* (Leipzig: Diederichs, 1903). The book was rightly criticized for its anti-Semitic underpinnings in the *AZJ*. See Heinrich Bloch, "Das Judentum in der deutschen Vergangenheit," *AZJ* 68 (1903): 5–7.

50. L. S. "Kohut, die deutschen Juden," *AZJ* 62 (1898): 552.

51. See the list of occupations in M. Stern, *Bibliothek der jüdischen Gemeinde zu Berlin* (Berlin, 1906), 9–10 and *Jahresbericht des Vereins jüdischer Bibliotheken und Lesehalle in Frankfurt am Main 1906*, 6. See also the membership list of the *Lesehalle* in Berlin that mentions the occupations. See *Jahresbricht und Mitglieder-Verzeichnis, Januar 1899* (Berlin, 1899), 10–24.

52. "Zum zehnten Stiftungstage des Vereins: Jüdische Lesehalle und Bibliothek," *Ost und West* 5 (1905): 137–42.

53. Josef Lin, "Die Berliner jüdische Lesehalle in ihrem neuen Heim," *Ost und West* (November 1908), 683–90, here 683–84.

54. M. Stern, *Bibliothek der jüdischen Gemeinde zu Berlin, 9–10.*

55. *Jahresbericht des Vereins jüdischer Bibliotheken und Lesehalle in Frankfurt am Main 1905,* 10–11.

56. Salomon Goldschmidt, *Geschichte des Vereins Mekor Chajim: Festschrift zur Fünfzigjährigen Feier* (Hamburg: H. Lessmann, 1912) 14–20; and "Breslau," *AZJ* 52 (1888): 104.

Conclusion

1. Michel de Certeau, *The Writing of History,* trans. Tom Conley (New York: Columbia University Press, 1988), 68.

2. See, for example, J. Lewy-Danzig, "Kulturarbeit im Judentum," *AZJ* 69 (1905): 512–14, 525–26, 538–39, 573–74, and 583–86, esp. 514.

3. Evyatar Friesel, "The Political and Ideological Development of the *Centralverein* before 1914," *LBIYB* 31 (1986): 121–46.

4. Arnold Budwig, "Der jüdische Religionsunterricht u. die Kreuz-Zeitung," *AZJ* 19 (1892): 217–18; and "Die Enquete über den jüdischen Religionsunterricht," *AZJ* 57 (1893): 469–70.

5. Jonathan D. Sarna, *JPS: The Americanization of Jewish Culture, 1888–1985: A Centennial History of the Jewish Publication Society* (Philadelphia: Jewish Publication Society of America, 1989), 1–4.

6. Ibid., 1–12; and "Pittsburg," *AZJ* 36 (1872): 44–46.

7. Maurice Halbwachs, *On Collective Memory,* ed. and trans. by Lewis A. Coser (Chicago: University of Chicago Press, 1992), 182–83.

8. Markus Brann, "Aus Graetzens-Lehr-und Wanderjahren," *MGWJ* 62 (1918): 231–65, here 256.

9. Graetz, *Geschichte der Juden,* 11: 448–49.

10. Gustav Karpeles, "Litterarische Jahresrevue," *JJGL* 5 (1902): 19–56, here 21.

11. Theodor Zlocisti, "Juedische Volkslesehallen," *Ost und West* 3 (1903): 277–82, here 280.

12. See, for example, Martin Philippson, *Neuste Geschichte des jüdischen Volkes,* 3 vols. (Leipzig: Buchhandlung Gustav Fock, 1907–11): 2: 148, who regards the popularization of Jewish history as the strongest tie that continued to unite contemporary Jews in Germany; and Gustav Karpeles's letter to Israel Abrahams, "Conference of Jewish Literary Societies: Interesting Discussion. Union of Literary Societies Formed," *Jewish Chronicle* (July 4, 1902): 12–17, here 15.

13. Jacques Ehrenfreund, *Mémoire juive et nationalité allemande.*

14. Hugo Schachtel, "Lesefrüchte," *Ost und West* 4 (1904): 721–23, here 721; and "Was ist eine Nation? Nach Ernst Renan," *AZJ* 51 (1887): 354–55.

15. Schachtel, "Lesefrüchte," 723.

16. Nils Roemer, "Turning Defeat into Victory: *Wissenschaft des Judentums* and the

Martyrs of 1096," 65–80; and David Myers, "Mehabevin et ha-tsarot": Crusade Memories and Modern Jewish Martyrologies," *Jewish History* 13 (1999): 49–64.

17. Hermann Cohen, "Gedanken über Jugendliteratur," *Jüdische Schriften.* 3 vols., ed. Bruno Strauß (Berlin: C. A. Schwetschke, 1924), 2: 126–32. See also Emil Lehmann, "Die Aufgaben der Deutschen jüdischer Herkunft (1891)." *Emil Lehmann: Gesammelte Schriften* (Berlin: Hermann, 1899), 355–67; and in contrast "Achthundertjahre Jahre (1096–1896)," *Die jüdische Presse* 27 (1896), 213–14.

18. Max Nordau, *Der Sinn der Geschichte* (Berlin: C. Duncker, 1909), 5.

19. Stephen M. Poppel, *Zionism in Germany, 1897–1933: The Shaping of a Jewish Identity* (Philadelphia: Jewish Publication Society of America, 1977), 94–101; Shmuel Almog, *Zionism and History: The Rise of a New Jewish Consciousness* (Jerusalem: Magnes Press, 1987), esp. 24–27, 45–51, 67–83 and 130–41; and Michael Berkowitz, *Zionist Culture and West European Jewry Before the First World War* (Chapel Hill: University of North Carolina Press, 1993).

20. S. Samuel, "Jungjüdische Geschichtsauffassung," *AZJ* 68 (1904): 221–22.

21. The declaration by the *Protestrabbiner* is reprinted in Mendes-Flohr and Reinharz, ed. *The Jew in the Modern World,* 538–39. See also Michael Brenner, "Warum München nicht zur Hauptstadt des Zionismus wurde — Jüdische Religion und Politik um die Jahrhundertwende," *Zionistische Utopie — israelische Realität. Religion und Nation in Israel,* ed. Michael Brenner and Yfaat Weiss (Munich: C. H. Beck, 1999), 39–52.

22. "Thesen zur national-jüdischen Vereinigung Köln," *Im Anfang der zionistischen Bewegung,* ed. Bodenheimer, 22–23.

23. "Agitationsplan. Referat des Herrn Rechtsanwalt Dr. Schauer auf dem Delegirtentag in Frankfurt," and the letter by Max Nordau to Max Bodenheimer on May 27, 1914, the Max I. Bodenheimer Archives, http://www.bodenheimer.org/, January 2002.

24. "Thesen zur national-jüdischen Vereinigung Köln," Bodenheimer, ed., *Im Anfang der zionistischen Bewegung,* 23–23.

25. M. Meyer, "Liberal Judaism and Zionism in Germany," *Judaism within Modernity,* 239–55; and Poppel, *Zionism in Germany, 1897–1933,* 45–67.

26. M. J. Bodenheimer, "Rede des Dr. Bodenheimer," *Die Welt* 1 (September 10, 1897): 5–9, here 7.

27. Wilhelm Wachtel, "Gedenktafel," *Jüdischer Almanach* 5663 (1903): 295, 299, 303, and 307.

28. Börries von Münchhausen, *Juda: Gesänge,* 4. See also Martin Buber, "Das Buch 'Juda,'" *Die Welt* 4 (December 12, 1900): 10–11.

29. Jehuda Reinharz, *Fatherland and Promised Land: The Dilemma of the German Jew, 1893–1914* (Ann Arbor: University of Michigan Press, 1975); David A. Brenner, *Marketing Identities: The Invention of Jewish Identities in "Ost und West"* (Detroit: Wayne State University Press, 1998), 21–53; and Gavriel D. Rosenfeld, "Defining 'Jewish Art' in *Ost und West,* 1901–1908: A Study in the Nationalism of Jewish Culture," *LBIYB* 39 (1994): 83–110.

30. "Protokoll des III. Delegirtentages der deutschen Zionisten am 31. Oktober 1897 zu Frankfurt a. M.," The Max I. Bodenheimer Archives, http://www.boden

heimer.org/, January 2002; and "Der dritte Zionistenkongreß," *AZJ* 63 (1898): 398. See also Jacob Borut, who makes a similar observation for the Jewish association of the Weimar Republic. Borut, "'Verjudung des Judentums': Was there a Zionist Subculture in Weimar Germany?,'" 92–114.

31. Bodenheimer, ed., *Im Anfang der zionistischen Bewegung,* 17.

32. See, for example, P. Felix, "Unsere nationale Wissenschaft," *Die Welt* 2 (August 12, 1898): 2–4.

33. N. Sokolov "Jüdische Literatur und Wissenschaft," *Die Welt* 6 (February 21, 1902): 1–5 and (February 28, 1902): 4–6, esp. (February 28, 1902): 5.

34. Eugen Fuchs, "Zur Jahrhundertwende des Emanzipationsedicts (1912)," *Eugen Fuchs: Um Deutschtum und Judentum. Gesammelte Reden und Aufsätze,* ed. Leo Hirschfeld (Frankfurt a. M.: J. Kauffmann, 1919), 120.

35. Maretzki, *Geschichte des Ordens Bnei Briss in Deutschland,* 138.

36. Ibid., 140.

37. Andreas Reinke, "Eine Sammlung des jüdischen Bürgertums. Der Unabhängige Orden B'nai B'rith in Deutschland," 334; and Erika Hirsch, *Jüdisches Vereinsleben in Hamburg bis zum Ersten Weltkrieg,* 57–59 and 63–68.

38. Elenore Lappin, *Der Jude, 1916–1928: Jüdische Moderne zwischen Universalismus und Partikularismus* (Tübingen: J. C. B. Mohr, 2000).

39. D. A. Brenner, *Marketing Identities* and David N. Myers, "'Distant Relatives Happening onto the Same Inn': The Meeting of East and West as Literary Theme and Cultural Ideal," *Jewish Social Studies* 1 (1995): 75–100.

40. M. Brenner, *The Renaissance of Jewish Culture in Weimar Germany.*

41. *Stenographisches Protokoll,* 131–46; and N. Sokolov "Jüdische Literatur und Wissenschaft," *Die Welt* 6 (February 21, 1902): 1–5 and (February 28, 1902): 4–6. See also Martin Buber, "Jüdische Wissenschaft" *Die Welt* 5 (October 11, 1901): 1–2 and (October 25, 1901): 1–2; "Geschichte der Gegenwart," *Die Welt* 3 (October 20, 1899): 4–5; "Achthundert Jahre (1096–1896), *Die jüdische Presse* 27 (1896), 213–14; O. Thon, "Das Problem der juedischen Wissenschaft," *Jüdischer Almanach 5663* (1902): 183–89; and Theodor Zlocisti, "Forderung und Förderung der Wissenschaft des Judentums," *Ost und West* 3 (1903): 73–80.

42. Martin Schreiner, "Was ist uns die Wissenschaft des Judentums?" *AZJ* 62 (1898): 150–52; 14: 164–65, and 175–77; *Stenographisches Protokoll:* 151–69; Buber, "Juedische Wissenschaft," *Die Welt* 5 (October 11, 1901): 1–2 and (October 25, 1901): 1–2; S. Maybaum, "Die Wissenschaft des Judentums," *MGWJ* 51 (1907): 641–54; Gustav Karpeles, "Litterarische Jahresrevue," *JJGL* 2 (1899): 21–25, esp. 23–24; and Ismar Elbogen, "Zum Jubiläum der 'Gesellschaft zur Förderung der Wissenschaft des Judentums,'" *MGWJ* 72 (1928): 1–5, here 3.

43. "Die Woche," *AZJ* 66 (1902): 398. On the Society, see Henri Soussan, "The Gesellschaft zur Förderung der Wissenschaft des Judentums, 1902–1915," *LBIYB* 46 (2001): 175–94.

44. Feiner, *Haskalah and History,* 317–40; Avraham Greenbaum, "The Beginnings of Jewish Historiography in Russia," *Jewish History* 7 (1993): 99–105; and Benjamin

Nathans, "On Russian-Jewish Historiography," *Historiography of Imperial Russia: The Profession and Writing of History in a Multi-National State*, ed. Thomas Sanders (Armonk: M. E. Sharpe, 1999), 397–432.

45. See the excerpt from his autobiography. Simon Dubnow, "Under the Sign of Historicism," *The Golden Tradition: Jewish Life and Thought in Eastern Europe*, ed. Lucy S. Dawidowicz (Syracuse: Syracuse University Press, 1996), 232–42.

46. Robert Liberles, "Postemancipation Historiography and the Jewish Historical Societies of America and England," *Reshaping the Past: Jewish History and the Historians*, ed. Jonathan Frankel (New York: Oxford University Press, 1994), 45–65.

47. "A nos lecteurs" *REJ* 1 (1880): v–viii. On French-Jewish historiography in general, see Jay Berkovitz, "Jewish Scholarship and Identity in Nineteenth-Century France," *Modern Judaism* 18 (1998): 1–33.

48. *Catalogue of the Anglo-Jewish Historical Exhibition, Royal Albert Hall, 1887* (London: William Clowes and Sons, 1887), vii.

49. Heinrich Graetz, "Historical Parallels in Jewish History," Ismar Schorsch, ed. *The Structure of Jewish History and Other Essays* (New York: Jewish Theological Seminary of America, 1975), 259–74.

50. S. Levy, "Anglo-Jewish Historiography," *TJHSE* 6 (1908–10): 1–20, here 14–15.

51. Israel Abrahams, "The Science of Jewish History," *TJHSE* 5 (1902–5): 193–201, here 198.

52. "Literary Societies," *Jewish Chronicle* (September 18, 1903): 23; and "The Literary Societies," *Jewish Chronicle* (October 24, 1902): 18.

53. *American Jewish Historical Society: Report of Organization. Abstract from the Minutes.* (Baltimore: American Jewish Historical Society, 1892), 4.

54. Oscar Straus, "Address of the President, Hon. Oscar Straus, New York," *PAJHS* 1 (1892): 1–4, here 1. See also Ira Robinson, "The Invention of American Jewish History," *AJH* 81 (1994): 309–20; and Nathan M. Kaganoff, "AJHS at 90: Reflections on the History of the Oldest Ethnic Historical Society in America," *AJH* 71 (1982): 466–85.

55. Abrahams, "The Science of Jewish History," 195, 199–200.

56. Heinrich Graetz, *Histoire des Juifs*, trans. by M. Wogue, 5. vols. (Paris: A. Lévy, 1882–97), 5: i–vi, here v.

57. See, for example, "Unsere Literatur-Gesellschaft." *Deborah* 40 (January 3, 1885): 4.

58. Emanuel Schreiber, *Reformed Judaism and its Pioneers: A Contribution to its History* (Spokane: Spokane Printing Company, 1892), x–xv.

59. Jonathan Sarna, *JPS: The Americanization of Jewish Culture, 1888–1985: A Centennial History of the Jewish Publication Society* (Philadelphia: JPSA, 1989), 46.

60. For the translation of Graetz, see M. Brann, "Verzeichnis von H. Graetzens Schriften und Abhandlungen und Übersetzungen und Bearbeitungen," here 481–91. On the translation of German works into Hebrew, see Na'ama Sheffi, *Germanit be'ivrit: Targumim mi-germanit ba-Yishuv ha-'Ivri, 1882–1948* (Jerusalem: Yad Yitshak Ben-Tsevi, 1998).

61. David Cassel and Moritz Steinschneider, *Plan der Real-Encyclopädie des Juden-thums, zunächst für die Mitarbeiter* (Krotoschin: B. L. Monasch & Sohn, 1844).

62. "Die allgemeine Encyclopädie für die Geschichte und Wissenschaft des Juden-thums," *AZJ* 56 (1892): 266.

63. Wilhelm Bacher, "Die Jüdische Enzyklopädie," *AZJ* 70 (1906): 114-16. For the history of the *Jewish Encyclopedia,* see Schuly Rubin Schwartz, *The Emergence of Jewish Scholarship in America: The Publication of the Jewish Encyclopedia* (Cincinnati: Hebrew Union College Press, 1991).

Bibliography

Archival Collections

Central Archives for the History of the Jewish People, Jerusalem. Altona-Hamburg-Wandsbeck: Bestand jüdische Gemeinde: Jüdische Bibliothek und Lesehalle, HM 9400-01.

———. Altona-Hamburg-Wandsbek: Bestand jüdische Gemeinde: Verein für jüdische Geschichte und Literatur, 1901-1907, AHW/ 831-32.

———. U.O.B.B. Deutschland, M18/2.

———. Berlin: Jüdische Gemeinde. Sammlung Benas Levy, Kge 2/62-63.

———. Deutsch-Israelitischer Gemeindebund: Historische Commission. Correspondence mit Gemeinden, M1/24.

———. Deutsch-Israelitischer Gemeindebund: Historische Commission, 1885-1917, M1/23.

———. Deutsch-Israelitischer Gemeindebund, 1874-99: Schriftwechsel Varia in specie 150. Geburtstag Moses Mendelssohn, M 1/33.

———. Deutsch-Israelitischer Gemeindebund. Schriftwechsel mit dem D.J.G.B., 1906-25: Akten des Gesamtarchivs, M 5/1.

———. Moritz Stern Collection, P17/24.

———. Satzungen des Vereins der Gesellschaft zur Erforschung jüdischer Kunst-Denkmäler. Eingetragener Verein in Frankfurt a. M., TD/76.

———. Statuten des israelitischen Fortbildungs-Vereins "Montefiore," TD/1061.

———. Statuten des jüdisch-theologischen Vereins, TD 805.

———. Statuten des Vereins zur Verbreitung der Wissenschaft des Judenthums. Breslau, 1862, TD/979.

———. Stuttgart: UOBB Stuttgart-Loge, D/St 3/12.

———. Synagogengemeinde Hagen: Schulbibliothek, 1877, D/Ha6/48.

Hebrew Union College, Cincinnati, Abraham Geiger Collection.

———. Zacharias Frankel Collection.

———. Ludwig Philippson Collection.

Jewish National and University Library, Jerusalem. Philipp Bloch Collection, 4° 1158.

———. Max Grunwald Collection, 4° 1182.

———. Leopold Zunz Collection, 4° 792.

Jewish Theological Seminary, New York. Jüdisch-Literarische Gesellschaft, Historical Documents, Acc. 85.

———. Satzungen des Vereins für jüdische Geschichte und Literatur, Broadside Collection.

———. Postcard Collection.

———. Rabbiner-Seminar zu Berlin: Studienplan, Broadside Collection.

———. Moritz Steinschneider Collection, AR. 108.

———. Statuten des Vereins "Jüdische Lesehalle," Broadside Collection.

———. Salomon Schechter Collection, AR. 101.

———. Zadoc Kohen Collection, AR. 64.

Leo Baeck Institute, New York. Hermann Baerwald Collection, AR 744.

———. Sally Bodenheimer Postcard Collection, AR 7169.

———. Samuel Echt Collection, AR 7016.

———. Ismar Elbogen "Briefe um Heinrich Heine: Adolf Strodtmanns Anfragen an Leopold Zunz." *ZGJD* 8 (1938): 40–51, Ismar Elbogen Collection, AR 9006.

———. Isaac Jost Collection, AR 4294.

———. Organization: Israelitischer Literatur-Verein, AR 3238.

———. Joseph Perles Collection, AR 1351.

———. Synagogue Collection: Worms.

———. Breslau: Jewish Theological Seminary, AR-2044.

The Max I. Bodenheimer Archives. http://www.bodenheimer.org, January 2002.

Southampton University Archives. Anglo-Jewish Association: Annual Report of the A. J. A., 1872–90, AJ 95/150.

———. *The Tenth Annual Report of the Anglo-Jewish Association, in Connection with the Alliance Israelite Universelle,* 1879–80. London, 1881.

Stadt-und Universitätsbibliothek Frankfurt, Rothschild, Bio 66/500.

Staatsbibliothek zu Berlin: Preussischer Kulturbesitz. Handschriftenabteilung. Harry Breslau Collection. K. IV, W-Z.

———. Felix v. Luschan Collection.

Periodicals

Allgemeine deutsche Bibliothek, 1780.

Allgemeine Zeitung des Judentums, 1837–1910.

Allgemeines Archiv des Judentums, 1839–42.

Ben-Chananja, 1858–67.

Blätter für literarische Unterhaltung, 1865–73.

Deborah, 1885.

Didaskalia, 1884.

Göttingsche gelehrte Anzeigen, 1854–66.

Ha-Me'assef, 1782–1809.

Hebräische Bibliographie, 1858–82.

Der Israelit, 1860–1910.

Israelit des 19. Jahrhunderts, 1839–48.

Israelitische Annalen, 1839–41.

Israelitische Schulbibliothek, 1858–59.

Der israelitische Volkslehrer, 1851–60.

Israelitische Wochenschrift, 1870–94.

Israelitisches Familienblatt, 1898–1910.

Israelitsches Predigt- und Schulmagazin, 1834–36.

Jahrbuch der jüdisch literarischen Gesellschaft, 1903–10.

Jahrbuch für die Geschichte der Juden, 1860–69.

Jahrbuch für Israeliten, Vienna, 1844–45 and 1864–65.

Jahrbuch für Israeliten, Mainz, 1855–67.

Jahrbuch für jüdische Geschichte und Literatur, 1898–1910.

Jahrbuch zur Belehrung und Unterhaltung, 1892.

Jahrbücher für deutsche Theologie, 1865–67.

Jedidja, 1817–31.

Jeschurun, 1854–70.

Jewish Chronicle, 1879–1900.

Jewish Historical Society of England—Transactions, 1893–1910.

Der Jude, 1832–35.

Jüdische Chronik, 1897–98.

Jüdische Zeitschrift für Wissenschaft und Leben, 1862–75.

Jüdischer Almanach, 1902–4.

Jüdisches Literaturblatt, 1872–1910.

Jüdisches Volksblatt, 1854–66.

Kalender und Jahrbuch für Israeliten auf das Jahr der Welt, 1865.

Die Laubhütte, 1884–1910.

Literarisches Centralblatt, 1865–73.

Magazin für Geschichte, Literatur und Wissenschaft des Judentums, 1874–93.

Magazin für die Literatur des Auslandes, 1865–80.

Mitteilungen aus dem Verein "Montefiore." Verein zur Pflege der idealen Interessen jüdischer junger Leute (Gegründet 1896), 1903–9.

Mitteilungen des Gesamtarchivs der deutschen Juden, 1909–26.

Mitteilungen der Gesellschaft für jüdische Volkskunde, 1898–1910.

Monatsblätter zur Belehrung des Judentums, 1881–98.

Monatsschrift für Geschichte und Wissenschaft des Judentums, 1851–1910.

Der Orient, 1840–51.

Orientalische und Exegetische Bibliothek, 1780.

Ost und West, 1901–10.

Populär-wissenschaftliche Monatsblätter, 1881–1908.

Publications of the American-Jewish Historical Society, 1892–1906.

Protestantische Kirchenzeitung für das evangelische Deutschland, 1865–66.

Revue des Études Juives, 1880.

Sulamith, 1806–46.

Der treue Zionswächter, 1845-48.

Wegweiser für die Jugendliteratur, 1905-10.

Die Welt, 1897-1910.

Wissenschaftich Zeitschrift für jüdische Theologie, 1835-47.

Zeitschrift für die Geschichte der Juden in Deutschland, 1882-92.

Zeitschrift für die religiösen Interessen des Judentums, 1844-46.

Zeitschrift für die Wissenschaft des Judentums, 1822-23.

Published Primary Sources

Acten und Gutachten in dem Prozesse Rohling contra Bloch. Vienna: Breitenstein, 1890.

Adams, Hannah. *Die Geschichte der Juden von der Zerstörung Jerusalems an bis auf die gegenwärtigen Zeiten.* Leipzig: Baumgärtner, 1819.

Alphabetische Liste der Förderer der israelitischen Literatur als Abonnenten des Instituts zur Förderung der isralitischen Literatur in seinem achten Jahre vom 1. Mai 1862 bis 1. Mai 1863. Leipzig: O. Leiner, 1863.

American Jewish Historical Society: Report of Organization. Abstract from the Minutes. Baltimore: American Jewish Historical Society, 1892.

Aronius, Julius. *Regesten zur Geschichte der Juden im fränkischen und Deutschen Reiche bis zum Jahre 1273.* Berlin: Simion, 1902.

Auerbach, Berthold. *Briefe an seinen Freund Jacob Auerbach: Ein biographisches Denkmal.* 2 vols. Frankfurt a. M.: Rütten & Loening, 1884.

Bäck, Samuel. *Die Geschichte des jüdischen Volkes und seiner Literatur vom babylonischen Exile bis auf die Gegenwart: Uebersichtlich dargestellt.* Lissa: Scheibel, 1878.

Baeck, Leo. "Harnacks Vorlesungen über das Wesen des Christenthums." *MGWJ* 45 (1901): 97-120.

———. *Das Wesen des Judentums.* Berlin: Nathansen & Lamm, 1905.

Baedeker, Karl. *Berlin und Umgebung: Handbuch für Reisende.* Leipzig: Karl Baedeker, 1894.

Baerwald, Hermann. *Der alte Friedhof der israelitischen Gemeinde zu Frankfurt am Main.* Frankfurt a. M.: St. Goar, 1883.

Bamberger, Fritz, ed. *Das Buch Zunz: Künftigen ehrlichen Leuten gewidmet.* Berlin: Soncino Gesellschaft, 1931.

Baumgarten, Siegmund Jacob. *Uebersetzung der Algemeinen Welthistorie die in England durch eine Geselschaft von Gelehrten ausgefertigt worden.* Halle: Gebauer, 1744.

Bendavid, Lazarus. *Etwas zur Charackteristick der Juden.* Leipzig: Stabel, 1793.

Berghoffer, Christian Wilhelm. *Die Freiherrlich Carl v. Rotschild'sche öffentliche Bibliothek. Ein Grundriß ihrer Organisation. Nebst einen Verzeichnis ihrer Zeitschriften und einem Frankfurter Bibliothekenführer.* Frankfurt a. M.: Baer, 1913.

Bericht über die Thätigkeit des Vereins für jüdische Geschichte und Litteratur von 1892 bis 1902. Berlin: A. Lowenthal & Co., 1902.

Berliner, Abraham. *Aus dem inneren Leben der deutschen Juden im Mittelalter. Nach den gedruckten und ungedruckten Quellen. Zugleich ein Beitrag zur deutschen Kulturgeschichte.* Berlin: Benzian, 1871.

———. *Geschichte der Juden in Rom von der ältesten Zeit bis zur Gegenwart (2050 Jahre)*. Frankfurt a. M.: Kauffmann, 1893.

———. *Die persönlichen Beziehungen der Juden und Christen im Mittelalter*. Halberstadt: H. Meyer, 1882.

———. *Raschi: Vortrag im Verein für jüdische Geschichte und Literatur zu Berlin gehalten*. Berlin: M. Poppelauer, 1906.

Bibliothek der Frankfurt-Loge: Systematisches Verzeichnis der Bücher und Zeitschriften. Frankfurt a. M., 1906.

Bibliothek der israelitischen Religionsschule zu Frankfurt am Main. Katalog. Frankfurt a. M.: M. Slobotzky, 1909.

Blanke, Horst Walter, and Dirk Fischer, ed. *Theoretiker der deutschen Aufklärungshistorie*. 2 vols. Stuttgart-Bad Cannstatt: Frommann-Holzboog, 1990.

Bloch, Joseph. *Erinnerungen aus meinen Leben*. Vienna: Löwit, 1922.

Bodenheimer, Henriette Hannah, ed. *Im Anfang der zionistischen Bewegung. Eine Dokumentation auf der Grundlage des Briefwechsels zwischen Theodor Herzl und Max Bodenheimer von 1896 bis 1905*. Frankfurt a. M.: Europäische Verlags-Anstalt, 1965.

———, ed. *The Memoirs of M. I. Bodenheimer: Prelude to Israel*. New York: T. Yoseloff, 1963.

Bodenschatz, Johann Christoph G. *Kirchliche Verfassung der heutigen Juden sonderlich derer in Deutschland in IV. Haupt=Theile abgefasset aus ihren eigenen und anderen Schriften umständlich dargethan und mit 30 sauberen Kupfern erläutert*. Frankfurt a. M.: Becker, 1748-49.

Boeckel, Otto. *Die Juden, die Könige unserer Zeit*. Berlin: Boeckel, 1885.

Boehlich, Walter, ed. *Der Berliner Antisemitismusstreit*. 2nd ed. Frankfurt a. M.: Insel-Verlag, 1965.

Brann, Marcus. *Ein kurzer Gang durch die jüdische Geschichte*. Breslau: Jacobsohn, 1895.

———. *Geschichte der Juden und ihrer Litteratur: Für Schule und Haus*. 2 vols. Breslau: Jacobsohn, 1893-1895.

Brück, Moses. *Rabbinische Ceremonialgebräuche in ihrer Entstehung und geschichtlichen Entwicklung*. Breslau: A. Schulz, 1837.

Buber, Martin, Berthold Feiwel, and Chaim Weizmann, *Eine jüdische Hochschule*. Berlin: Jüdischer Verlag, 1902.

Bücherverzeichnis aus dem Verlag und Lager von J. Kaufmann, Verlags-, Antiquariats- und Sortimentbuchhandlung hebräischer Literatur. Frankfurt a. M.: J. Kaufmann 1886.

Büsching, Anton Friedrich. *Geschichte der jüdischen Religion*. Berlin: J. C. F. Eisfeld, 1779.

Canstatt, Oscar. *Drangsale der Stadt Worms und deren Zerstörung durch die Franzosen am 31. Mai 1689: Zum 200jährigen Gedenktage*. Worms: Kranzbühler, 1889.

Caro, Jecheskel. *Worte der Wahrheit und des Friedens. Predigt, gehalten am 15. November 1879. Den Judenfeinden Treitschke, Marr und Stöcker gewidmet*. Erfurt, 1879.

Cassel, David. *Geschichte der jüdischen Literatur*, 2 vols. Berlin: L. Gerschel, 1872-73.

———. *Lehrbuch der jüdischen Geschichte und Literatur*. Leipzig: Brockhaus, 1879.

———. *Leitfaden für die jüdische Geschichte und Literatur: Nebst einer kurzen Darstellung der biblischen Geschichte und einer Uebersicht der Geographie Palestinas*. Berlin: Louis Gerschel, 1868.

———. *Offener Brief eines Juden an Herrn Professor Dr. Virchow*. Berlin: Louis Gerschel, 1869.

Cassel, David, and Moritz Steinschneider, *Plan der Real-Encyclopädie des Judenthums, zunächst für die Mitarbeiter*. Krotoschin: B. L. Monasch & Sohn, 1844.

Catalogue of the Anglo-Jewish Historical Exhibition, Royal Albert Hall, 1887. London: William Clowes and Sons, 1887.

Chiarini, Luigi. *Théorie du Judaisme appliquée à la forme des Israélites de tous les Pays de l'Europe et servant en même temps d'ouvrage préparatoire à la version du Talmud de Babylone*. 2 vols. Paris: J. Barbezat, 1830.

Cohen, Hermann. *Jüdische Schriften*. 3 vols. Edited by Bruno Strauß. Berlin: C. A. Schwetschke, 1924, 237-301.

———. *H. Cohen: Briefe. Ausgewählte*. Edited by Bruno Strauss. Berlin: Schocken Verlag, 1939.

Cohen, Shalom Jacob. *Morgenländische Pflanzen auf nördlichem Boden: Eine Sammlung neuer hebräischer Poesien, nebst Deutschen Uebersetzungen*. Rödelheim: Varrentrapp und Wenner, 1807.

———. *Seder Ha-avodah. Historisch-kritische Darstellung des jüdischen Gottesdienstes und dessen Modifikationen, von den ältesten Zeiten an, bis auf unsere Tage*. Leipzig: Rein'sche Buchhandlung, 1819.

Dawidowicz, Lucy S., ed. *The Golden Tradition: Jewish Life and Thought in Eastern Europe*. Syracuse: Syracuse University Press, 1996.

Delitzsch, Franz. *Zur Geschichte der jüdischen Poesie vom Abschluss der heiligen Schriften des Alten Bundes bis auf die neueste Zeit*. Leipzig: Tauchnitz, 1836.

Dessauer, Julius Heinrich. *Geschichte der Israeliten mit besonderer Berücksichtigung der Kulturgeschichte derselben. Von Alexander dem Großen bis auf gegenwärtige Zeit. Nach den besten vorhandenen Quellen bearbeitet*. Erlangen: Palm, 1846.

Dohm, Christian Wilhelm. *Ueber die bürgerliche Verbesserung der Juden*. 2 vols. Berlin: Nicolai, 1781-83.

Eisemann, H., and H. N. Kruskal, ed., *Jacob Rosenheim. Erinnerungen, 1870-1920*. Frankfurt a. M.: Kramer, 1970.

Eisenmenger, Johann Andreas. *Entdecktes Judenthum*. 2 vols. Königsberg, 1700.

Eisler, M. *Die Judenfrage in Deutschland*. New York: Verlag des Verfassers, 1880.

Elbogen, Ismar. "Briefwechsel zwischen Leopold Zunz und Frederick David Mocatta." *Occident and Orient: Being Studies in Semitic Philology and Literature, Jewish History and Philosophy and Folklore in the Widest Sense, in Honor of Haham Dr. M. Gaster's 80th Birthday: Gaster Anniversary Volume*. Edited by Bruno Schindler and A. Mamorstein. London: Taylor's Foreign Press, 1936, 144-53.

Elbogen, Ismar, and I. Höniger. *Lehranstalt für die Wissenschaft des Judentums: Festschrift zur Einweihung des eigenen Heims*. Berlin: H. S. Hermann, 1907.

Eliav, Mordechai, ed. *Rabbiner Esriel Hildesheimer: Briefe*. Jerusalem: R. Mass, 1965.

Elkan, Moses. *Leitfaden beim Unterricht in der Geschichte der Israeliten, nebst einem kurzen Abriß der Geographie Palaestinas für israelitische Schulen*. Minden: F. Essmann, 1839.

Emden, Jacob. *Sefer Mor u-kezy'ah*. Altona, 1761-1768.

Erster Bericht der Hochschule für die Wissenschaft des Judenthums in Berlin (die ersten zwei Jahre ihres Bestehens 1872 und 1873 umfassend). Berlin: G. Bernstein, 1874.

Fest-Predigten zur Säcularfeier der jüdischen Gemeinde in Berlin am 10. September 1871 von den Rabbiner Joseph Aub und Dr. Abr. Geiger. Berlin: J. Levit, 1871.

Festschrift zum 10. Stiftungsfest des Akademischen Vereins für jüdische Geschichte und Literatur an der Kgl. Friedrich-Wilhelms-Universtität zu Berlin. Berlin, 1893.

Fischer, Karl. *Heinrich v. Treitschke und sein Wort über unser Judenthum. Ein Wort zur Verständigung.* M. Gladbach: Emil Schellmann, 1880.

Formstecher, S. *Die Religion des Geistes: Eine wissenschaftliche Darstellung des Judentums nach seinem Charakter, Entwicklungsgängen und Berufen in der Menschheit.* Frankfurt a. M.: Joh. Chr. Hermann'sche Buchhandlung, 1841.

Frankel, Zacharias. *Darkhe ha-Mishnah ve-darkhe ha-sefarim ha-nilvim 'elehah Tosefta, Mekhilta, Sifra ve-Sifrey.* Leipzig: H. Hunger, 1859.

———. *Die Eidesleistung der Juden in theologischer und historischer Beziehung.* Dresden: Arnold, 1840.

———. *Der gerichtliche Beweis nach mosaisch-talmudischen Rechte. Ein Beitrag zur Kenntniss des mosaisch-talmudischen Criminal-und Civilrechts. Nebst Untersuchungen über die Preussischen Gesetzgebung hinsichtlich der Zeugnisse der Juden.* Berlin: Veit, 1846.

Frankfurt am Main. Seine Geschichte, Sehenswürdigkeiten und Verkehrsmittel. Den Theilnehmern an der zu Frankfurt vom 11.-15. September 1881 stattfindenden Generalversammlung des Gesamt-Vereins der deutschen Geschichts- und Alterthums-Vereins überreicht. Frankfurt a. M.: Baumbach, 1881.

Frauberger, Heinrich. "Zweck und Ziel der Gesellschaft zur Erforschung jüdischer Kunstmäler." *Mittheilungen der Gesellschaft zur Erforschung jüdischer Kunstmäler* 1 (1900): 3-38.

Friedländer, David. *Ueber die durch die neue Organisation der Judenschaften in den Preußischen Staaten notwendig gewordene Umbildung 1. ihres Gottesdienstes in den Synagogen 2. ihrer Unterrichts-Anstalten und deren Lehrgegenstand und 3. ihres Erziehungswesens überhaupt, ein Wort zu seiner Zeit* [1812]. Edited by Moritz Stern. Berlin: Verlag Hausfreund, 1934.

———. *Worte der Wahrheit und des Friedens an die ganze jüdische Nation.* Breslau, 1788.

Fries, J. F. *Ueber die Gefährdung des Wohlstandes und Charakters der Deutschen durch die Juden.* Heidelberg: Mohr, 1816.

Fromer, Elias Jacob. *Das Wesen des Judentums.* Berlin: Hüpeden & Merzyn, 1905.

Fuchs, Eugen. *Um Deutschtum und Judentum. Gesammelte Reden und Aufsätze.* Edited by Leo Hirschfeld. Frankfurt a. M.: J. Kauffmann, 1919.

Fürst, Julius. *Geschichte des Karäerthums. Eine kurze Darstellung seiner Entwicklung, Lehre und Literatur mit den dazugehörigen Quellennachweisen,* 3 vols. (Leipzig, 1862-69).

Geiger, Abraham. *Das Judenthum und seine Geschichte von dem Anfange des dreizehnten bis zum Ende des sechzehnten Jahrhunderts: In zehn Vorlesungen.* Breslau: Schletter, 1871.

———. *Das Judenthum und seine Geschichte von der Zerstörung des zweiten Tempels bis zum zwölften Jahrhundert: In zwölf Vorlesungen.* 2nd ed. Breslau: Schletter, 1865.

————. *Lehr-und Lesebuch zur Sprache der Mischna.* Breslau: Leuckart, 1845.

————. *Parschandatha. Die nordfranzösiche Exegetenschule: Ein Beitrag zur Geschichte der Bibelexegese und der jüdischen Literatur.* Leipzig: Schnauss, 1855.

————. *Über die Errichtung einer jüdisch-theologischen Facultät.* Wiesbaden: L. Riedel, 1838.

————. *Urschrift und Uebersetzung der Bibel in ihrer Abhängigkeit von der inneren Entwicklung des Judentums.* Breslau: Hainauer, 1857.

————. *Was hat Mohammed aus dem Judentume aufgenommen? Königl. Preussische Rheinuniversität gekrönte Preisschrift.* Bonn: F. Baaden, 1833.

Geiger, Ludwig, ed. *Abraham Geiger's nachgelassene Schriften.* 5 vols. Berlin: L. Gerschel, 1875–78.

————. "Geist der Rabbiner: Ein geplantes Werk von Leopold Zunz." *AZJ* 80 (1916): 413–14.

————. *Geschichte der Juden in Berlin.* 2 vols. Berlin: J. Guttentag, 1871.

————. "Leopold Zunz und Abraham Geiger." *Liberales Judentum* 8 (1916): 131–39.

————, ed. *Michael Sachs und Moritz Veit: Briefwechsel.* Frankfurt a. M.: Kauffmann, 1897.

————. "Zunz im Verkehr mit Behörden und Hochgestellten." *MGWJ* 60 (1916): 245–62 and 321–47.

————. "Zur Kritik der neusten jüdischen Geschichtsschreibung." *ZGJD* 3 (1889): 373–91.

Glatzer, Nahum N. "Aus unveröffentlichten Briefen von I. M. Jost." *In zwei Welten: Siegfried Moses zum fünfundsiebzigsten Geburtstag.* Edited by Hans Tramer, Tel Aviv: Verlag Bitaon, 1962, 400–413.

————, ed. *Leopold and Adelheid Zunz: An Account in Letters 1815–1885.* London: East and West Library, 1958.

————, ed. *Leopold Zunz: Jude-Deutscher-Europäer.* Tübingen: J. C. B. Mohr, 1964.

Glück, J. *Ein Wort an den Herrn Professor Heinrich von Treitschke.* Oldenburg: Schmidt, 1880.

Goldschmidt, Salomon. *Geschichte des Vereins Mekor Chajim: Festschrift zur Fünfzigjährigen Feier.* Hamburg: H. Lessmann, 1912.

Graetz, Heinrich. "Die Entwicklungsstadien des Messiasglaubens." *Jahrbuch für Israeliten 5625* 9 (1864–65): 1–30.

————. *Geschichte der Juden von den ältesten Zeiten bis auf die Gegenwart: Aus den Quellen neu bearbeitet.* 11 vols. Leipzig: O. Leiner, 1853–74.

————. *Geschichte der Juden von dem Tode Juda Makkabi's bis zum Untergang des judäischen Staates.* 4th ed. Leipzig: O. Leiner, 1888.

————. *Gnosticismus und Judenthum.* Krotschin: B. L. Monasch, 1846.

————. *Histoire des Juifs,* trans. by M. Wogue, 5. vols. Paris: A. Lévy, 1882–97.

————. *Die Konstruktion der jüdischen Geschichte.* Edited by Ludwig Feuchtwanger. Berlin: Schocken Verlag, 1936.

————. "The Significance of Judaism for the Present and the Future." *JQR* 1 (1889): 4–13 (1890): 257–69.

————. *Sinai et Golgotha ou les Origines du Judaisme et de Christianisme.* Translated by Moses Hess. Paris: M. Lévy, 1867.

————. *The Structure of Jewish History and Other Essays.* Translated and edited by Ismar Schorsch. New York: The Jewish Theological Seminary of America, 1975.

————. "Die Verjüngung des jüdischen Stammes." *Jahrbuch für Israeliten* 10 (1864): 1–13.

————. "Die Verjüngung des jüdischen Stammes." *Volks-Kalender und Jahrbuch für Israeliten auf das Jahr der Welt 5625.* 2 (1865): 16–27.

————. *Volkstümliche Geschichte der Juden.* 3 vols. Leipzig: O. Leiner, 1888.

Güdemann, Moritz. *Geiger als Kritiker der neuesten jüdischen Geschichtsschreibung.* Leipzig: Friese, 1889.

————. *Geschichte des Erziehungswesens und der Cultur der Juden in Frankreich und Deutschland von der Begründung der jüdischen Wissenschaft in diesen Ländern bis zur Vertreibung der Juden aus Frankreich (X.-XIV. Jahrhundert).* Vienna: Hölder, 1880.

————. *Geschichte des Erziehungswesens und der Cultur der Juden während des XIV. und XV Jahrhunderts.* Vienna: Hölder, 1888.

————. *Jüdische Apologetik.* Glogau: Flemming, 1906.

Hähnlein, M. *Thätigkeit und Ziele des Vereins für jüdische Litteratur in Bochum: Vortrag gehalten zur Eröffnung der Saison 1896–1897.* Bochum, 1896.

Hecht, Emanuel. *Israels Geschichte von der Zeit des Bibel-Abschlusses bis zur Gegenwart: Für Schüler jüdischer Lehranstalten, höhere Bürgerschulen und Gymnasien, für Familie und Schulbibliotheken.* Leipzig: Baumgärtner, 1855.

Hegel, Georg Wilhelm Friedrich. *Vorlesungen über die Philosophie der Geschichte.* Edited by Eva Modenhauer and Karl Markus. Frankfurt a. M.: Suhrkamp, 1992.

Heine, Heinrich. *Heinrich Heine. Säkularausgabe. Werke. Briefwechsel. Lebenszeugnisse.* Edited by Fritz H Eisner. 20 vol. Berlin: Akademie-Verlag, 1970.

————. *Heinrich Heine: Sämtliche Schriften.* Edited by Klaus Briegleb. 7 vols. Munich: Deutscher Taschenbuch Verlag, 1997.

————. *The Poetry and Prose of Heinrich Heine.* Edited and translated by Frederic Ewen. New York: Citadel Press, 1948.

Heinemann, J. *Moses Mendelssohn. Sammlung theils noch ungedruckter, theils in andern Schriften zerstreuter Aufsätze und Briefe von ihm, an und über ihn.* Leipzig: Wolbrecht, 1831.

Herder, Johann Gottfried. *Herders Sämtliche Werke.* Edited by Bernhard Suphan. 33 vols. Berlin: Weidmann, 1877–1913.

Herzfeld, Levi. *Geschichte des Volkes Israel von der Zerstörung des ersten Tempels bis zur Einsetzung des Makkabäers Schimon zum Hohen Priester und Fürsten.* 3 vols. Braunschweig-Nordhausen: Westermann, 1847–57.

————. *Geschichte des Volkes Israel von der Zerstörung des ersten Tempels bis zur Einsetzung des Mackabäers Schimon zum hohen Priester und Fürsten: Aus seinem dreibändigen Werke des gleichen Titels kürzer dargestellt und überarbeitet.* Leipzig: O. Leiner, 1870.

————. *Handelsgeschichte der Juden des Alterthums.* Braunschweig: Meyer, 1879.

Hess, M. *Freymüthige Prüfung der Schrift des Herrn Prof. Rühs über die Ansprüche der Juden an das deutsche Bürgerrecht.* Frankfurt a. M.: Hermann, 1816.

Hess, Moses. *The Revival of Israel: Rome and Jerusalem, the Last Nationalist Question.* Trans. by Meyer Waxman. Lincoln: University of Nebraska Press, 1995.

Hildesheimer, Esriel. *She'elot u-tshuvot.* Tel Aviv: H. Gitler, 1976.

Hirsch, Samson Raphael. *Gesammelte Schriften.* 6 vols. Edited by Naphtali Hirsch. Frankfurt a. M.: J. Kauffmann, 1902–12.

Hirsch, Samuel. *Die Religionsphilosophie der Juden oder das Prinzip der jüdischen Religionsanschauung und sein Verhältnis zum Heidenthum, Christenthum und zur absoluten Philosophie.* Leipzig: Hunger, 1842.

Hoeniger, Robert. *Das Judenschreinsbuch der Laurenzpfarre zu Köln.* Berlin: Simion, 1888.

Holberg, Ludvig. *Jüdische Geschichte von Erschaffung der Welt bis auf gegenwärtige Zeiten.* Translated by Georg August Detharding. Altona: Korte, 1747.

Horovitz, M. *Die Inschriften des alten Friedhofs der israelitischen Gemeinde zu Frankfurt a. M.* Frankfurt a. M.: J. Kauffmann, 1901.

Humboldt, Wilhelm von. "On the Historians's Task." *History and Theory* 6 (1967): 57–71.

Ibn Verga, Salomon. *Shevet Yehuda.* Edited by A. Shohat with an introduction by Y. Beer. Jerusalem: Mosad Bialik, 1947.

Jacobsohn, Hugo. *Führer durch die Deutsch-Israel., unterhaltend (schönwissenschaftliche), geschichtlich-belehrende, populär-religiöse Jugendschriftliteratur vom Beginn des 18. Jahrhunderts bis heute.....* Breslau, 1890.

Jahresbericht des Rabbiner-Seminars für das orthodoxe Judentum pro 5634 (1873–1874). Berlin: M. Driesner, [1874].

Jahresbericht des Vereins jüdischer Bibliotheken und Lesehalle in Frankfurt am Main 1905–1906. Frankfurt a. M.: Louis Golde, 1906–07.

Jahresbricht und Mitglieder-Verzeichnis, Januar 1899. Berlin, 1899.

Joel, Manuel. *Offener Brief an Herrn Professor Heinrich Treitschke,* 6th ed. Breslau: Commissions-Verlag der Buchhandlung der Schlesischen Presse, L. Weigert, 1879.

Jost, I. M. *Allgemeine Geschichte des israelitischen Volkes, sowohl seines zweimaligen Staatslebens als auch der zerstreuten Gemeinden und Sekten, bis in die neueste Zeit in gedrängter Übersicht, zunächst für Staatsmänner, Rechtsgelehrte, Geistliche und wissenschaftlich gebildete Leser, aus den Quellen bearbeitet.* 2 vols. Berlin: Amelang, 1832.

———. *Geschichte der Israeliten seit der Zeit der Maccabäer bis auf unsre Tage nach den Quellen bearbeitet.* 9 vols. Berlin: Schlesinger, 1820–28.

———. *Geschichte des Judenthums und seiner Secten.* 3 vols. Leipzig: Dörfling und Franke, 1857–1859.

———. *Neuere Geschichte der Israeliten von 1815 bis 1845,* 3 vols. Breslau: Jacobsohn, 1846–1847.

———. *Offenes Sendschreiben an Herrn Geh. Ober-Regierungs-Rath K. Streckfuss zur Verständigung über einige Punkte in den Verhältnissen der Juden.* Berlin: Lückritz, 1833.

———. *Was hat Herr Chiarini in Angelegenheiten der europäischen Juden geleistet? Eine freimüthige und unparteiische Beleuchtung des Werkes théorie du Judaïsme.* Berlin: A. W. Hayn, 1830.

Jüdische Lesehalle und Bibliothek: Bericht für das Jahr. Berlin, 1907–11.

[Kalischer, Arnold]. *Offener Brief an den Königlichen Geheimen Regierungsrath Dr. Heinrich von Treitschke,* 2nd ed. Berlin: Walther & Appolant, 1888.

Kant, Immanuel. *Immanuel Kant: Werkausgabe.* Edited by Wilhelm Weischedel. 12 vols. Frankfurt: Suhrkamp, 1977.

Karpeles, Gustav. *Sechs Vorträge über die Geschichte der Juden: Gehalten in der Berliner Loge UOBB im Winter 1895-96.* Berlin: Friedlaender, 1896.

———. *Die Zionsharfe. Eine Anthologie der neuhebräischen Dichtung in deutschen Uebertragungen.* Leipzig: Rossberg, 1896.

Katalog der Bibliothek der Synagogen-Gemeinde zu Königsberg in Pr. Königsberg: Jacoby, 1893.

Katalog für jüdische Jugendvereine (Kurzer literarischer Wegweiser). Edited by Verband der jüdischen Jugendvereine Deutschlands. Berlin, 1910.

Katalog der jüdischen Lesehalle zu Posen [Posen, 1910].

Katalog des antiquarischen Bücher-Lagers von J. Kauffmann: Verlags-, Antiquariats-und Sortimentbuchhandlung hebräischer Literatur. Frankfurt: J. Kaufmann 1895.

Kaufmann, David. *Achtzehn Predigten von David Kaufmann: Aus seinem Nachlasse.* Edited by Ludwig Blau and Max Weisz. Budapest: Jabneh, 1931.

Kayserling, Moritz. *Geschichte der Juden in Portugal.* Leipzig: O. Leiner, 1867.

———. *Ludwig Philippson. Eine Biographie.* Leipzig: H. Mendelssohn, 1898.

Kirschbaum, Eliezer. *Hilkhot yemot ha-mashiah.* Berlin, 1822.

Kobler, Franz. *Jüdische Geschichte in Briefen aus Ost und West. Das Zeitalter der Emanzipation.* Vienna: Saturn-Verlag, 1938.

Kohut, Adolph. *Berühmte israelitische Männer und Frauen in der Kulturgeschichte der Menschheit. Lebens- und Charakterbilder aus Vergangenheit und Gegenwart. Ein Handbuch für Haus und Familie. Mit zahlreichen Porträts und sonstigen Illustrationen.* Leipzig-Reudnitz: Payne, 1900-1901.

———. *Geschichte der deutschen Juden: Ein Hausbuch für die jüdische Familie. Illustriert von Th. Kutschmann.* Berlin: Deutscher Verlag, 1898.

———. *Memoiren eines jüdischen Seminaristen. Zur Würdigung des Breslauer jüdisch-theologischen Seminars Fränkelscher Stiftung.* Prag: Senders & Brandeis, 1870.

Kopp, Joseph. *Zur Judenfrage nach den Akten des Prozesses Rohling-Bloch.* 2nd ed. Leipzig: J. Klinkhardt, 1886.

Kriegk, Georg Ludwig. "Die Judengasse in Frankfurt am Main und die Familie Rotschild." *Die Gartenlaube* 36 (1865): 564-68, 583-86.

Lazarus, Moritz. *Die Ethik des Judentums.* 2 vols. Frankfurt a. M.: J. Kauffmann, 1898-1911.

———. *Treu und Frei: Gesammelte Reden und Vorträge über Juden und Judenthum.* Leipzig: Winter, 1887.

———. *Was heißt und zu welchem Ende studiert man jüdische Geschichte und Litteratur? Ein Vortrag.* Leipzig: J. Kaufmann, 1900.

Lehmann, Emil. *Gesammelte Schriften.* Berlin: Hermann, 1899.

Lessing, Gotthold Ephraim. *Gotthold Ephraim Lessing: Werke.* Edited by Herbert G. Göpfert. 8 vols. Darmstadt: Wissenschaftliche Buchgesellschaft, 1996.

Lessing-Mendelssohn-Gedenkbuch: Zur hundertfünfzigjährigen Geburtstagsfeier von Gotthold Ephraim Lessing und Moses Mendelssohn, sowie zur Säcularfeier von Lessing's "Nathan." Leipzig: Baumgärtner, 1879.

Levi, Abraham. "Ideen zur Methodik der jüdischen Geschichte." *Einladungsschrift zu der am 26., 27., 28., 29. März d. J. im Schulgebäude, Ecke der Schützen-und Rechneigrabenstraße stattfindenen öffentlichen Prüfung der Unterrichts-Anstalt der Israelitischen Religions-Gesellschaft zu Frankfurt am Main*. Frankfurt a. M., 1860.

[Levy, Moritz Abraham]. *Catalog der Bibliothek der Synagogen-Gemeinde zu Breslau (Israelitischer Lehr-und Leseverein)*. Breslau: Sulzbach's Buchdruckerei, 1861.

Lewysohn, Ludwig. *Nafshot Zadikim: Sechzig Epitaphien von Grabsteinen des israelitischen Friedhofes zu Worms regressiv bis zum Jahr 905 übl. Zeitr. nebst biographischen Skizzen*. Frankfurt a. M.: Baer, 1855.

Liebe, Georg. *Das Judentum in der deutschen Vergangenheit*. Leipzig: Diederichs, 1903.

Löw, Leopold. *Gesammelte Schriften*. 5 vols. Edited by Immanuel Löw. Szegedin: Baba, 1889-1900.

Loewe, Heinrich. *Eine jüdische Nationalbibliothek*. Berlin: Jüdischer Verlag, 1905.

Löwy, D. *Der Talmudjude von Rohling in der Schwurgerichtsverhandlung vom 28. Oktober 1882*. Vienna: Löwy, 1882.

Mannheimer, Moses. *Die Juden in Worms, ein Beitrag zur Geschichte der Juden in den Rheingegenden*. Frankfurt a. M.: J. S. Adler, 1842.

Maimon, Salomon. *Lebensgeschichte: Von ihm selbst geschrieben*. Edited by Karl Philipp Moritz. 2 vols. Berlin: Vieweg, 1792.

Marx, Alexander. "Steinschneideriana II." *Jewish Studies in Memory of George A. Kohut, 1874-1933*. Edited by Salo Baron and Alexander Marx. New York: The Alexander Kohut Memorial Foundation, 1935, 492-527.

Marx, Alexander. "Zunz's Letters to Steinschneider." *PAAJR* 5 (1933-34): 95-153.

Maybaum, S. *Jüdische Homiletik nebst einer Auswahl von Texten und Themen*. Berlin: Dümmler, 1890.

Mendelssohn, Moses *Moses Mendelssohn. Gesammelte Schriften. Jubiläumsausgabe*. Edited by Alexander Altmann et al. Stuttgart-Bad Canstatt: Frommann-Holzboog, 1971- .

Mendes-Flohr, Paul and Jehuda Reinharz, ed. *The Jew in the Modern World: A Documentary History*. New York: Oxford University Press, 1995.

Meyer, S. *Ein Wort an Herrn Heinrich von Treitschke*. Berlin: Verlag der Jüdischen Presse, 1880.

Michael, Reuven, ed. *Heinrich Graetz: Tagebuch und Briefe*. Tübingen: J. C. B. Mohr, 1977.

Michaelis, Johann David. *Mosaische Recht*, 6 vols., 2nd edition. Reutlingen: J. Grözinger, 1793.

Mommsen, Theodor. *Auch ein Wort ueber unser Judentum*. Berlin: Weidmann, 1880.

Montefiore: Verein zur Pflege der idealen Interessen jüdischer junger Leute. Jahresbericht pro 1907. Frankfurt: David Droller, 1908.

Münchhausen, Börries von. *Juda: Gesänge*. Illustrated by E. M. Lilien. Berlin: Fleischel, 1900.

Naudh, H. *Professoren über Israel von Treitschke und Bresslau*. Berlin: Otto Hentze, 1880.

Neubauer, Adolf, and Moritz Stern, ed. *Hebräische Berichte über die Judenverfolgung während der Kreuzzüge*. Berlin: Simion, 1892.

Nordau, Max. *Der Sinn der Geschichte.* Berlin: C. Duncker, 1909.

Ottensosser, David. *Geschichte der Jehudim: Von ihrer Rückkehr aus der babylonischen Gefangenschaft an bis auf unsere Zeiten.* Fürth: I. Zirndorff, 1821.

Papers Relating to the Foreign Relations of the United States, Transmitted to Congress, with the Annual Message of the President, December 5, 1881. Washington, 1882 (rep. as U.S.-Serial Set vol. 2009).

Philippson, Ludwig. *Entwicklung der religioesen Idee im Judenthume, Christenthum und Islam.* Leipzig: Baumgärtner, 1847.

———. *Neues israelitisches Gebetbuch für die Wochentage, Sabbathe und alle Feste zum Gebrauche während des Gottesdienstes und bei der häuslichen Andacht.* Berlin: L. Gerschel, 1864.

Philippson, Ludwig and Phoebus. *Saron: Novellenbuch.* 2nd ed. Leipzig: O. Leiner, 1855.

Philippson, Martin. *Neueste Geschichte des jüdischen Volkes.* 3 vols. Leipzig: Buchhandlung Gustav Fock, 1907-11.

Poppelauer, M. *Judaica und Hebraica. Katalog 5.* Berlin: M. Poppelauer, 1897.

Protokolle der ersten Rabbiner-Versammlung, abgehalten zu Braunschweig. Brunswick: Vieweg, 1844.

Protokolle und Aktenstücke der zweiten Rabbiner-Versammlung, abgehalten zu Frankfurt am Main. Frankfurt a. M.: E. Ullmann, 1845.

Radin, Adolf. *Offener Brief eines polnischen Juden an den Redacteur Herrn Heinrich v. Treitschke.* Loebau, R. Skrzeczek, 1879.

Rapoport, Solomon. *Divre shalom ve-'emet, 'odot ha-sefer ha-mehulal Darkhe ha-Mishnah ve-divre plugot 'alav.* Prague: D. Ehrmann, 1861.

Rechenschaftsbericht der Jüdisch-Literarischen Gesellschaft für 1902-1903. Frankfurt a. M.: J. Wirth'sche Hof-Buchdruckerei, 1904.

Rechenschaftsbericht der Jüdisch-Literarischen Gesellschaft für 1904-1906. Frankfurt a. M.: J. Wirth'sche Hof-Buchdruckerei, 1907.

Reinharz, Jehuda, ed. *Dokumente zur Geschichte des deutschen Zionismus.* Tübingen: J. C. B. Mohr, 1981.

Rodenberg, Julius. "Im Herzen von Berlin." *Deutsche Rundschau* 49 (1886): 81-101.

Rosenzweig, Adolf. *Rede, gehalten am 11.8. in der neuen Synagoge bei der Feier von Leopold Zunz'ens hundertjährigen Geburtstages.* Berlin: B. Weissstock, 1894.

Rosenzweig, Franz. *Der Stern der Erlösung.* 3rd ed. Frankfurt a. M.: Suhrkamp, 1990.

Rossi, Azariah de. *Me'or 'Enayim.* Berlin, 1794.

Rubaschoff, Salman. "Erstlinge der Entjudung: Drei Reden von Eduard Gans im Kulturverein." *Der jüdische Wille* 1 (1918): 30-35, 108-21, 193-203.

Rühs, Friedrich. *Über die Ansprüche der Juden an das deutsche Bürgerrecht: Mit einem Anhange über die Geschichte der Juden in Spanien.* 2nd ed. Berlin: Realschulbuchhandlung, 1816.

Ruppin, Arthur. *Erinnerungen: Jugend- und Studienzeit, 1876-1907.* Tel Aviv: Bitaon, 1945.

Sachs, Michael. *Die religioese Poesie der Juden in Spanien.* Berlin: Veit und Camp, 1845.

Salfeld, Siegmund. *Das Martyrologium des Nürnberger Memorbuches.* Berlin: Simion, 1898.

Samuel David Luzzatto: Ein Gedenkbuch zum hundertsten Geburtstage, 22. August 1900. Berlin: Katz, 1900.

Satzungen des Vereins "Montefiore" Frankfurt a. M. (Januar 1897). [Frankfurt a. M. 1897].

Schleiermacher, Friedrich. *On Religion: Speeches to Its Cultured Despisers.* Translated by John Oman. New York: Harper & Row, 1958.

Scholem, Gerschom. *From Berlin to Jerusalem: Memoirs of My Youth.* Translated by Harry Zohn. New York: Schocken Books, 1980.

Schreiber, Emanuel. *Graetz's Geschichtsbauerei.* Berlin: Ißleib, 1881.

———. *Reformed Judaism and its Pioneers: A Contribution to its History.* Spokane: Spokane Printing Company, 1892.

Schudt, Johann Jacob. *Jüdische Merkwürdigkeiten.* 4 vols. Frankfurt: S. T. Hocker, 1714-18.

Schwenke, P., and A. Hortzschansky, *Berliner Bibliothekenführer.* Berlin: Weidmann, 1906.

Semler, Johann Jacob. *Uebersetzung der Algemeinen Welthistorie der Neuen Zeiten die in England durch eine Gesellschaft von Gelehrten ausgefertigt worden.* Halle: Gebauer, 1765.

Sharpe, Samuel. *Geschichte des hebräischen Volkes und seiner Literatur: Berichtigt und ergänzt von H. Jolowicz.* Leipzig: Winter, 1869.

Silberstein, M. *Moses Mendelssohn, ein Lebensbild: Vortrag gehalten in der Lesegesellschaft zu München am 22. Januar 1872.* Esslingen: R. Voigtländer, 1872.

Spinoza, Baruch. *Theological-Political Treatise.* Translated by Samuel Shirley. Indianapolis: Hackett Publishing Company, 1998.

Statut für das jüdisch-theologische Seminar Fraenkel'scher Stiftung zu Breslau. Breslau, [1854].

Statuten des Mendelssohnvereins zu Frankfurt am Main. [Frankfurt a. M., 1887].

[Stein, Julius]. *Börne und Treitschke. Offenes Sendschreiben ueber die Juden von Löb Baruch (Dr. Ludwig Börne) an den deutschen Reichstagsabgeordneten und Heidelberger Professor Dr. Heinrich Gotthard von Treitschke.* Berlin: Verlag von Stein'schen Literarischen Büro, 1880.

Stein, Ludwig. *An der Wende des Jahrhunderts.* Freiburg: Mohr, 1899.

Stein, Maximilian. *Vorträge und Ansprachen.* Frankfurt a. M.: Kauffmann, 1929.

Steinheim, S. L. *Die Offenbarung nach dem Lehrbegriffe der Synagoge.* 4. vols. Frankfurt a. M.: 1835-65.

Steinschneider, Moritz. "Ueber die Volkslitteratur der Juden." *Archiv für Litteraturgeschichte* 2 (1872): 1-21.

Steinthal, Heymann. *Über Juden und Judenthum: Vorträge und Aufsätze.* Edited by Gustav Karpeles. Berlin: M. Poppelauer, 1906.

Stenographisches Protokoll der Verhandlungen des V. Zionisten-Congresses in Basel, 26., 27., 28., 29. und 30. December 1901. Vienna: Erez Israel, 1901.

Stern, M. *Bibliothek der jüdischen Gemeinde zu Berlin: Bericht über die Begründung der Bibliothek und die drei ersten Jahre ihres Bestehens, 3. Februar 1902 bis 31. März 1905. Nebst einer Beilage: Benutzungsordnung.* Berlin: E. Wertheim, 1906.

Straßburger, B. *Geschichte der Erziehung und des Unterrichts bei den Israeliten. Von der talmudischen Zeit bis auf die Gegenwart. Mit einem Anhang: Bibliographie der jüdischen Pädagogie.* Breslau: Jacobsohn, 1885.

Tendlau, Abraham M. *Das Buch der Sagen und Legenden jüdischer Vorzeit: Nach den Quellen bearbeitet nebst Anmerkungen und Erläuterungen.* 3rd ed. Frankfurt a. M.: J. Kauffmann, 1873.

Toussenel, Alphonse. *Les Juifs rois de l'époque, histoire de la féodalité financière.* Paris: Librairie de l'École Socìètaire, 1845.

Unna, Simon. *Gedenkbuch der Frankfurter Juden nach Aufzeichnungen der Beerdigungs-Bruderschaft.* Frankfurt a. M.: Kauffmann, 1914.

Usque, Samuel. *Consolation for the Tribulation of Israel.* Translated and edited by Martin A. Cohen. Philadelphia: Jewish Publication Society of America, 1965.

Verhandlungen und Beschlüsse der Rabbiner-Versammlung zu Berlin am 4. u. 5. Juni 1884. Berlin: Walther & Upolant, 1885.

Vierter Jahresbericht der jüdischen Lesehalle in Posen. [Posen, 1906].

Wessely, Naphtali Herz. *Divre shalom ve-'emet le-kahal 'adat yisra'el ha-garim be-'arazot memshelet ha-kaisar ha-gadol ha-'ohev 'et ha-'adam u-mesameah ha-briyot.* Berlin, 1782-1785.

Wistinetzki, Jehuda, ed. *Das Buch der Frommen nach der Rezension in Cod. de Rossi No. 1133.* Berlin: Selbstverlag des Vereins Mekize Nirdamim, 1891.

Willstätter, Ephraim. *Allgemeine Geschichte des Israelitischen Volkes. Von der Entstehung desselben bis auf unsere Zeit. Ein kurzer Abriß nach den vorliegenden Quellen und größern Werken der Geschichte für die ersten Klassen israelitischer Elementarschulen und zum Selbststudium bearbeitet.* Karlsruhe: Marx, 1836.

Wolf, Friedrich A. "Darstellung der Altertums-Wissenschaft nach Begriff, Umfang, Zweck und Werth." *Museum der Alterthums-Wissenschaft* 1 (1807): 10-145.

Wolf, Immanuel. "Ueber den Begriff einer Wissenschaft des Judenthums." *ZWJ* 1 (1823): 1-24, reprinted in Immanuel Wolf, "On the Concept of a Science of Judaism (1822)." Translated by Lionel Kochan. *LBIYB* 2 (1957): 194-204.

Wolf, J. and G. Salomon. *Der Charakter des Judenthums nebst einer Beleuchtung der unlängst gegen die Juden von Prof. Rühs und Fries erschienenen Schriften.* Leipzig: C. G. Schmidt, 1817.

Zirndorf, Heinrich. *Isaak Markus Jost und seine Freunde: Ein Beitrag zur Kulturgeschichte der Gegenwart.* Cincinnati: The Bloch Publishing and Printing Company, 1886.

Zum 50 jährigen Bestehen des Ordens Bne Briss in Deutschland. Frankfurt a. M.: Kauffmann, 1933.

Zunz, Leopold. *Deutsche Briefe.* Leipzig: Brockhaus, 1872.

———. *Gesammelte Schriften.* 3 vols. Berlin: Gerschel, 1875-1876.

———. *Die gottesdienstlichen Vorträge der Juden, historisch entwickelt: Ein Beitrag zur Altertumskunde und biblischen Kritik, zur Literatur- und Religionswissenschaft.* Berlin: Asher, 1832.

———. "Mein erster Unterricht in Wolfenbüttel." *JJGL* 30 (1936): 131-40.

———. *Monatstage des Kalenderjahres: Ein Andenken an Hingeschiedene.* Berlin: Poppelauer, 1872.

Zunz, Leopold and L. L. Hellwitz, *Die Organisation der Israeliten in Deutschland: Ein Versuch.* Magdeburg: Kommission bei Fred. Rubach, 1819.

———. *Die synagogale Poesie des Mittelalters.* Berlin: Springer, 1855.

——, et al. "Zeittafel über die gesammte heilige Schrift." *Die vier-und-zwanzig Bücher der Heiligen Schrift. Nach dem masoretischen Texte.* Berlin: Veit, 1838.
——. *Zur Geschichte und Literatur.* Berlin: Veit, 1845.

Secondary Literature

Almog, Shmuel. *Zionism and History: The Rise of a New Jewish Consciousness.* Jerusalem: Magnes Press, 1987.

Altmann, Alexander. "Moses Mendelssohn as the Archetypal German Jew." *The Jewish Response to German Culture. From the Enlightenment to the Second World War.* Edited by Jehuda Reinharz and Walter Schatzberg. Hanover: University Press of New England, 1985, 17-31.

——. "Zur Frühgeschichte der jüdischen Predigt in Deutschland." *LBIYB* 6 (1961): 3-59.

Anderson, Benedict. *Imagined Communities: Reflections on the Origin and Spread of Nationalism.* London: Verso, 1995.

Arnsberg, Paul. *Die Geschichte der Frankfurter Juden seit der Französischen Revolution.* 3 vols. Darmstadt: Eduard Roether Verlag, 1983.

Aschheim, Steven E. "German History and German Jewry: Boundaries, Junctions and Interdependence." *LBIYB* 43 (1998): 315-22.

Awerbuch, Marianne. "Die Hochschule für die Wissenschaft des Judentums." *Geschichtswissenschaft in Berlin im 19. und 20. Jahrhundert: Persönlichkeiten und Institutionen.* Edited by Reimer Hansen and Wolfgang Ribbe. Berlin: Gruyter, 1992, 517-52.

——. *Zwischen Hoffnung und Vernunft: Geschichtsdeutung der Juden in Spanien vor der Vertreibung am Beispiel Abravanels und Ibn Vergas.* Berlin: Institut Kirche und Judentum, 1985.

Bamberger, Benhard J. "Formstecher's History of Judaism." *HUCA* 23 (1950-1951): 1-35.

Barkai, Avraham. "The German Jews at the Start of the Industrialization: Structural Change and Mobility, 1835-1860." *Revolution and Evolution: 1848 in German-Jewish History.* Edited by Werner E. Mosse, Arnold Paucker, and Reinhard Rürup. Tübingen: J. C. B. Mohr, 1981, 123-49.

Baron, Salo Wittmayer, "Ghetto and Emancipation: Shall We Revise the Traditional View?" *The Menorah Journal* 14 (June 1928): 515-26.

——. "The Impact of the Revolution of 1848 on Jewish Emancipation," *Jewish Social Studies* 11 (1949): 195-248.

——. "The Jewish Communal Crisis in 1848," *Jewish Social Studies* 14 (1952): 99-144.

——. "Jewish Studies at Universities: An Early Project." *HUCA* 46 (1975): 357-76.

——. "Newer Approaches to Jewish Emancipation." *Diogenes* 29 (1960): 56-81.

——. *A Social and Religious History of the Jews.* 18 vols. New York: Columbia University Press, 1952-83.

Barzilay, Isaac. *Shlomo Yehuda Rapoport [Shir] (1790-1887) and his Contemporaries: Some Aspects of Jewish Scholarship of the Nineteenth Century.* Ramat-Gan: Massada Press, 1969.

Ben-Ari, Niza. *Roman 'im he-'avar: Ha-Roman ha-histori ha-yehudi-ha-germani min ha-me'ah ha-19 we-yezirato shel sifrut le'umit.* Tel Aviv: Devir, 1997.

Berkovitz, Jay. "Jewish Scholarship and Identity in Ninteenth-Century France." *Modern Judaism* 18 (1998): 1–33.

Berkowitz, Michael. *Zionist Culture and West European Jewry Before the First World War.* Chapel Hill: University of North Carolina Press, 1996.

Biemann, Asher D. "The Problem of Tradition and Reform in Jewish Renaissance and Renaissancism." *Jewish Social Studies* 8 (2001): 58–87.

Blackbourn, David. *The Long Nineteenth Century: A History of Germany, 1780–1918.* New York: Oxford University Press, 1998.

———. *Marpingen: Apparitions of the Virgin Mary in a Nineteenth-Century German Village.* New York: Knopf, 1995.

Blanke, Horst Walter. *Historiographiegeschichte als Historik.* Stuttgart-Bad Cannstatt: Frommann-Holzboog, 1991.

Blaschke, Olaf. "Bürgertum und Bürglichkeit im Spannungsfeld des neuen Konfessionalismus von den 1830er bis zu den 1930er Jahren," *Juden, Bürger, Deutsche: Zur Geschichte von Vielfalt und Differenz, 1800–1933.* Edited by Andreas Gotzmann, Rainer Liedtke, and Till van Rahden. Tübingen: J. C. B. Mohr, 2001, 33–66.

———. "Das 19. Jahrhundert: Ein Zweites Konfessionelles Zeitalter." *Geschichte und Gesellschaft* 26 (2000): 28–75.

Bonfil, Robert. "How Golden was the Age of the Renaissance in Jewish Historiography?" *History and Theory: Beiheft* 27 (1988): 78–102.

———. "Jewish Attitudes Towards History and Historical Writing in Pre-Modern Times." *Jewish History* 11 (1997): 7–40.

Borut, Jacob. "Die jüdischen Abwehrvereine zu Beginn der neunziger Jahre des 19. Jahrhunderts." *Aschkenas* 7 (1997): 467–94.

———. *Ruah hadasha be-kerev 'aheinu be-'ashkenaz: Ha-mifneh be-darkah shel yahadut germaniah be-sof ha-me'ah ha-tesha 'esreh.* Jerusalem: Y. L. Magnes, 1999.

———. "Vereine für Jüdische Geschichte und Literatur at the End of the Nineteenth Century." *LBIYB* 41 (1996): 89–114.

———. "'Verjudung des Judentums': Was there a Zionist Subculture in Weimar Germany?" *In Search of Jewish Community: Jewish Identities in Germany and Austria, 1918–1933.* Edited by Michael Brenner and Derek J. Penslar. Bloomington: Indiana University Press, 1998, 92–114.

Bourel, Dominique. "Bendavids Trinkspruch auf Moses Mendelssohn, Berlin 1829." *Mendelssohn Studien* 6 (1986): 41–47.

Brämer, Andreas. "Die Anfangsjahre der 'Monatsschrift für die Geschichte und Wissenschaft des Judenthums' (1851–1868). Kritische Forschung und jüdische Tradition im Zeitalter der Emanzipation," *Zwischen Selbstbehauptung und Verfolgung. Deutsch-jüdische Zeitungen und Zeitschriften von der Aufklärung bis zum Nationalsozialismus.* Edited by Michael Nagel. Hildesheim: Georg Olms Verlag, 2002, 139–57.

———. *Rabbiner Zacharias Frankel: Wissenschaft des Judentums und konservative Reform im 19. Jahrhundert.* Hildesheim: Georg Olms Verlag, 2000.

———. "Revelation and Tradition: Zacharias Frankel on the Controversy Concerning the 'Hodgetica in Mischnam' from his Letters to Bernhard Beer." *JQS* 5 (1998): 171-86.

Brann, M. "Verzeichnis von H. Graetzens Schriften und Abhandlungen und Übersetzungen und Bearbeitungen." *MGWJ* 61 (1917): 444-91, and 62 (1918): 266-69.

Brenner, David A. *Marketing Identities: The Invention of Jewish Identities in Ost und West*. Detroit: Wayne State University Press, 1998.

Brenner, Michael. "Between Haskalah and Kabbalah: Peter Beer's History of Jewish Sects." *Jewish History and Jewish Memory: Essays in Honor of Yosef Hayim Yerushalmi*. Edited by Elisheva Carlebach, John M. Efron, and David N. Myers. Hanover: University Press of New England, 1998, 389-404.

———. *The Renaissance of Jewish Culture in Weimar Germany*. New Haven: Yale University Press, 1996.

———. "Warum München nicht zur Hauptstadt des Zionismus wurde—Jüdische Religion und Politik um die Jahrhundertwende." Edited by Michael Brenner and Yfaat Weiss, *Zionistische Utopie—israelische Realität. Religion und Nation in Israel*. Munich: C. H. Beck, 1999, 39-52.

Breuer, Edward. *The Limits of Enlightenment: Jews, Germans, and the Eighteenth-Century Study of Scripture*. Cambridge: Harvard University Press, 1996.

———. "Politics, Tradition, History: Rabbinic Judaism and the Eighteenth-Century Struggle for Civil Equality." *HTR* 85 (1992): 357-83.

———. "(Re) Creating Traditions of Language and Texts: The Haskalah and Cultural Continuity." *Modern Judaism* 16 (1996): 161-83.

Breuer, Mordechai. "Modernism and Traditionalism in Sixteenth Century Jewish Historiography." *Jewish Thought in the Sixteenth Century*. Edited by Dov Coopermann. Cambridge: Harvard University Press, 1983, 49-88.

———. *Modernity within Tradition: The Social History of Orthodox Jewry in Imperial Germany*. Translated by Elizabeth Petuchowski. New York: Columbia University Press, 1992.

Brilling, Bernhard. "Das jüdische Archivwesen in Deutschland." *Der Archivar* 13 (1960): 271-90.

Brummack, Jürgen, ed. *Heinrich Heine: Epoche—Werke—Wirkung*. Munich: C. H. Beck, 1980.

Burnett, Stephen. "Distorted Mirrors: Antonious Margaritha, Johann Buxtorf and Christian Ethnographies of Judaism." *Sixteenth Century Journal* 25 (1994): 275-87.

Cerny, Gerald. *Theology, Politics and Letters at the Crossroad of European Civilization: Jacques Basnage and the Baylean Huguenot Refugees in the Dutch Republic*. Hague: M. Nijhoff, 1987.

Certeau, Michel de. *The Practice of Everyday Life*. Berkeley: University of California Press, 1984.

———. *The Writing of History*. Translated by Tom Conley. New York: Columbia University Press, 1988.

Chartier, Roger. *The Order of Books: Readers, Authors, and Libraries in Europe Between the Fourteenth and the Eighteenth Centuries*. Stanford: Stanford University Press, 1994.

Cohen, Gerson D. "German Jewry as a Mirror to Modernity." *LBIYB* 20 (1975): ix–xxi.

Cohen, Mark R. *Under Crescent and Cross: The Jews in the Middle Ages*. Princeton: Princeton University Press, 1994.

Cohen, Richard I. *Jewish Icons: Art and Society in Modern Europe*. Berkeley: University of California Press, 1998.

Confino, Alon. "Collective Memory and Cultural History: Problems and Methods." *AHR* 102 (1997): 1386–1403.

Dann, Otto. "Voltaire und die Geschichtsschreibung in Deutschland." *Voltaire und Deutschland: Quellen und Untersuchungen zur Rezeption der Französischen Aufklärung*. Edited by Peter Brockmeier et al. Stuttgart: Metzler, 1979, 463–67.

Daxelmüller, Christoph. "Die 'Gesellschaft für jüdische Volkskunde.'" *Die Juden in Hamburg, 1590 bis 1990: Wissenschaftliche Beiträge der Universität Hamburg zur Ausstellung "Vierhundert Jahre Juden in Hamburg."* Edited by Arno Herzig. Hamburg: Dölling & Galitz, 1991, 361–82.

———. "Jüdische Volkskunde in Deutschland vor 1933." *Volkskunde als akademische Diziplin*. Edited by Wolfgang Brückner. Vienna: Verlag der Österreichischen Akademie der Wissenschaften, 1983, 117–42.

Degani, Ben-Zion. "Ha-mivneh shel historiah ha-'olamut we-ge'ulat yisra'el be-Zemah David le-R. David Gans." *Zion* 45 (1980): 173–200.

Doran, Joachim. "Rassenbewußtsein und naturwissenschaftliches Denken im deutschen Zionismus während der wilhelminischen Ära." *Tel Aviver Jahrbuch für deutsche Geschichte* 9 (1980): 389–427.

Ehrenfreund, Jacques. *Mémoire juive et nationalité allemande. Les juifs berlinois à la Belle Époque*. Paris: Presses Universitaires de France, 2001.

Eisen, Arnold M. *Rethinking Modern Judaism: Ritual, Commandment, Community*. Chicago: University of Chicago Press, 1998.

Elbogen, Ismar. "Aus der Frühzeit der Vereine für jüdische Geschichte und Literatur." *Festschrift: Zum 70. Geburtstage von Moritz Schäfer*. Berlin: Philo Verlag, 1927, 48–54.

———. "Zum Jubiläum der 'Gesellschaft zur Förderung der Wissenschaft des Judentums.'" *MGWJ* 72 (1928): 1–5.

Ellenson, David. "Rabbi Esriel Hildesheimer and the Quest for Religious Authority: The Earlier Years." *Modern Judaism* 1 (1981): 279–97.

———. "Scholarship and Faith: David Hoffman and his Relationship to 'Wissenschaft des Judentums.'" *Modern Judaism* 8 (1988): 27–40.

———. "Traditional Reactions to Modern Jewish Reform: The Paradigm of German Orthodoxy." *History of Jewish Philosophy*. Edited by Daniel H. Frank and Oliver Leaman. London: Routledge, 1997, 732–58.

Elukin, Jonathan M. "Jacques Basnage and the 'History of the Jews': Anti-Catholic Polemic and Historical Allegory in the Republic of Letters." *Journal of the History of Ideas* 53 (1992): 603–30.

———. "A New Essenism: Heinrich Graetz and Mysticism." *JHI* 59 (1998): 135–48.

Erlin, Matt. "Reluctant Modernism: Moses Mendelssohn's Philosophy of History." *Journal of the History of Ideas* 63 (2002): 83–104.

Feiner, Shmuel. *Haskalah and History: The Emergence of a Modern Jewish Historical Consciousness.* Translated by Chaya Naor and Sondra Silverston. Oxford: Littman Library of Jewish Civilization, 2002.

Frankel, Jonathan. "Assimilation and the Jews in Nineteenth-Century Europe: Toward a New Historiography?" *Assimilation and Community: The Jews in Nineteenth-Century Europe.* Edited by Jonathan Frankel and Steven J. Zipperstein. Cambridge: Cambridge University Press, 1992, 1–37.

———. *The Damascus Affair: "Ritual Murder," Politics, and the Jews in 1840.* Cambridge: Cambridge University Press, 1997.

Frankl-Grün, Adolf. *Geschichte der Juden in Kremsier mit Rücksicht auf die Nachbargemeinden: Nach Original-Urkunden.* Breslau: S. Schottlaender, 1896.

Friedländer, Albert. "The Wohlwill-Moser Correspondence." *LBIYB* 11 (1966): 262–99.

Friesel, Evyatar. "The Political and Ideological Development of the *Centralverein* before 1914." *LBIYB* 31 (1986): 121–46.

Fuks, Leo and Rena. "Jewish Historiography in the Netherlands." *Salo Wittmayer Baron Jubilee Volume on the Occasion of His Eightieth Birthday.* 3 vols. New York: Columbia University Press, 1975, 1: 432–66.

Funkenstein, Amos. "The Dialectics of Assimilation." *JSS* (1995): 1–15.

———. *Perceptions of Jewish History.* Berkeley: University of California Press, 1993.

Geiger, Ludwig. *Abraham Geiger: Leben und Lebenswerk.* Berlin: G. Reimer, 1910.

Glasenapp, Gabrielle von, and Michael Nagel. *Das jüdische Jugendbuch. Von der Aufklärung bis zum Dritten Reich.* Stuttgart: Metzler, 1996.

Gotzmann, Andreas. *Eigenheit und Einheit. Modernisierungsdiskurse des deutschen Judentums der Emanzipationszeit.* Leiden: Brill, 2002.

———. *Jüdisches Recht im kulturellen Prozeß: Die Wahrnehmung der Halacha im Deutschland des 19. Jahrhunderts.* Tübingen: J. C. B. Mohr, 1997.

———. "Zwischen Nation und Religion: Die deutschen Juden auf der Suche nach einer bürgerlichen Konfessionalität." *Juden, Bürger, Deutsche: Zur Geschichte von Vielfalt und Differenz, 1800–1933.* Edited by Andreas Gotzmann, Rainer Liedtke, and Till van Rahden. Tübingen: J. C. B. Mohr, 2001, 241–61.

Greenbaum, Avraham. "The Beginnings of Jewish Historiography in Russia." *Jewish History* 7 (1993): 99–105.

Halbwachs, Maurice. *On Collective Memory.* Edited and translated by Lewis A. Coser. Chicago: University of Chicago Press, 1992.

———. "The Question of Cultural Identity." *Modernity and Its Futures.* Edited by Stuart Hall, David Held, and Tony McGrew. Cambridge: Open University, 1992, 273–16.

Harvey, David. *The Condition of Postmodernity: An Enquiry into the Origins of Cultural Change.* Cambridge: Blackwell, 1989.

Heimpel, Hermann. "Geschichtsverein einst und jetzt." *Geschichtswissenschaft und Vereinswesen im 19. Jahrhundert.* Göttingen: Vandenhoeck & Ruprecht, 1972, 45–73.

Herzig, Arnold. "Die Anfänge der deutsch-jüdischen Geschichtsschreibung in der Spätaufklärung." *Tel Aviver Jahrbuch für Deutsche Geschichte* 20 (1991): 59–75.

Herzog, Dagmar. *Intimacy and Exclusion: Religious Politics in Pre-Revolutionary Baden.* Princeton: Princeton University Press, 1996.

Heschel, Susannah. *Abraham Geiger and the Jewish Jesus.* Chicago: University of Chicago Press, 1998.

———. "Jewish Studies as Counterhistory." *Insider/Outsider: American Jews and Multiculturalism.* Edited by David Biale, Michael Galchinsky, and Susannah Heschel. Berkeley: University of California Press, 1998, 101-15.

Hess, Jonathan M. "Johann David Michaelis and the Colonial Imaginary: Orientalism and the Emergence of Racial Antisemitism in Eighteenth-Century Germany." *Jewish Social Studies* 6 (2000): 56-101.

Heuberger, Georg, ed. *Museum Judengasse: Katalog zur Dauerausstellung.* Frankfurt a. M.: Jüdisches Museum, 1992.

Hirsch, Erika. *Jüdisches Vereinsleben in Hamburg bis zum Ersten Weltkrieg: Jüdisches Selbstverständnis zwischen Antisemitismus und Assimilation.* Frankfurt a. M.: Peter Lang, 1996.

Hobsbawn, Eric J., and Terence Ranger, ed. *The Invention of Tradition.* Cambridge: Cambridge University Press, 1992.

Hoffmann, Christhard. *Juden und Judentum im Werk deutscher Althistoriker des 19. Jahrhunderts und 20. Jahrhunderts.* Leiden: E. J. Brill, 1988.

Hoffmann, Stefan-Ludwig. "Bürger zweier Welten? Juden und Freimaurer im 19. Jahrhundert," *Juden, Bürger, Deutsche: Zur Geschichte von Vielfalt und Differenz, 1800-1933.* Edited by Andreas Gotzmann, Rainer Liedtke, and Till van Rahden. Tübingen: J. C. B. Mohr, 2001, 97-119.

Holub, Robert C. *Reception Theory: A Critical Introduction.* London: Routledge, 1989.

Horch, Hans O. *Auf der Suche nach der jüdischen Erzählliteratur. Die Literaturkritik der "Allgemeinen Zeitung des Judentums."* Frankfurt a. M.: Peter Lang, 1985.

Iggers, Georg G. "The Image of Ranke in American and German Historical Thought." *History and Theory* 2 (1962): 17-40.

———. "Nationalism and Historiography, 1789-1996: The German Example in Historical Perspective." *Writing National Histories: Western Europe since 1800.* Edited by Stefan Berger, Mark Donovan, and Kevin Passmore. London: Routledge, 1999, 15-29.

Jäger, Georg and Jörg Schönert. "Die Leihbibliothek als literarische Institution im 18. und 19. Jahrhundert—Ein Problemaufriß." *Die Leihbibliotheken als Institution des literarischen Lebens im 18. und 19. Jahrhundert.* Edited by Georg Jäger and Jörg Schönert. Hamburg: E. Hauswedell, 1980, 7-60.

Johanning, Klaus. *Der Bibel-Babel-Streit: Eine forschungsgeschichtliche Studie.* Frankfurt a. M.: Lang, 1988.

Jospe, Alfred. "The Study of Judaism in German Universities before 1933." *LBIYB* 27 (1982): 295-313.

Kaganoff, Nathan M. "AJHS at 90: Reflections on the History of the Oldest Ethnic Historical Society in America." *AJH* 71 (1982): 466-85.

Kaplan, Marion. *The Jewish Feminist Movement in Germany: The Campaigns of the Jüdischer Frauenbund, 1904-1938.* Westport: Greenwood Press, 1979.

———. *The Making of the Jewish Middle Class: Women, Family, and Identity in Imperial Germany*. New York: Oxford University Press, 1991.

———. "Women and the Shaping of Modern-Jewish Identities in Imperial Germany." *Deutsche Juden und die Moderne*. Edited by Shulamit Volkov and Elisabeth Müller-Luckner. Munich: Oldenbourg, 1994, 57–74.

Katz, Jacob. *Exclusiveness and Tolerance: Studies in Jewish-Gentile Relations in Medieval and Modern Times*. New York: Behrman House, 1961.

———. *Jews and Freemasons in Europe 1723–1939*. Translated from the Hebrew by Leonard Oschry. Cambridge: Harvard University Press, 1970.

———. *From Prejudice to Destruction: Anti-Semitism, 1700–1933*. Cambridge: Harvard University Press, 1994.

Kern, Stephen. *The Culture of Time and Space, 1880–1918*. Cambridge: Harvard University Press, 1983.

Kirchner, Joachim. *Das deutsche Zeitschriftenwesen, seine Geschichte und seine Probleme*. 2 vols. Wiesbaden: Harrassowitz, 1962.

Kirshenblatt-Gimblett, Barbara. *Destination Culture: Tourism, Museums, and Heritage*. Berkeley: University of California Press, 1998.

Kisch, Guido. "The Founders of 'Wissenschaft des Judentums' and America." *Essays in American Jewish History: To Commemorate the Tenth Anniversary of the Founding of the American Jewish Archives under the Direction of Jacob Rader Marcus*. Edited by Jacob Rader Marcus. New York: Ktav Publishing House, 1975, 147–70.

Knappe, Sabine. "The Role of Women's Associations in the Jewish Community: The Example of the Israelitisch-humanitärer Frauenverein in Hamburg at the Turn of the Century," *LBIYB* 39 (1993): 153–78.

Kober, Adolf. "Aspects of the Influence of Jews from Germany on American Jewish Spiritual Life of the Nineteenth Century. *Jews from Germany in the United States*. Edited by Eric E. Hirschler. New York: Farrar, Straus and Cudahy, 1955, 129–46.

Kohut, Adolph. *Ritual-Mordprozesse. Bedeutende Fälle aus der Vergangenheit*. Berlin-Wilmerdorf: Basch, 1913.

Koltun-Fromm, Kenneth. "Public Religion in Samson Raphael Hirsch and Samuel Hirsch's Interpretation of Religious Symbolism," *Journal of Jewish Thought and Philosophy* 9 (1999): 69–105.

Korn, Bertram W. "German-Jewish Intellectual Influences on American Jewish Life, 1824–1972," *Tradition and Change in Jewish Experience*. Edited by A. Leland Jamison. Syracuse: Syracuse University Press, 1978, 106–40.

Koselleck, Reinhart. "Einleitung." *Geschichtliche Grundbegriffe: Historisches Lexikon der politisch-sozialen Sprache in Deutschland*. Edited by Otto Brunner et al. Stuttgart: E. Klett, 1972–1997), xiii–xviii.

———. "'Space of Experience' and 'Horizon of Expectation': Two Historical Categories." *Futures Past: On the Semantics of Historical Time*. Translated by Keith Tribe. Cambridge: MIT Press, 1985, 267–88.

Koshar, Rudy. *From Monuments to Traces: Artifacts of German Memory, 1870–1990*. Berkeley: University of California Press, 2000.

———. *Germany's Transient Pasts: Preservation and National Memory in the Twentieth Century*. Chapel Hill: University of North Carolina Press, 1998.

———. "'What Ought to be Seen': Tourists' Guidebooks and National Identities in Modern Germany and Europe." *Journal of Contemporary History* 33 (1998): 323-40.

Langer, Ulrich, *Heinrich von Treitschke: Politische Biographie eines deutschen Nationalisten*. Düsseldorf: Droste, 1998.

Lappin, Elenore. *Der Jude, 1916-1928: Jüdische Moderne zwischen Universalismus und Partikularismus*. Tübingen: J. C. B. Mohr, 2000.

Lehmann, James A. "Maimonides, Mendelssohn and the Me'asfim: Philosophy and the Biographical Imagination in the Early Haskalah." *LBIYB* 20 (1975): 87-108.

Liberles, Robert. "Champion of Orthodoxy: The Emergence of Samson Raphael Hirsch as Religious Leader." *AJS Review* 6 (1981): 43-60.

———. "Emancipation and the Structure of the Jewish Community in the Nineteenth Century." *YLBI* 31 (1986): 51-67.

———. "Postemancipation Historiography and the Jewish Historical Societies of America and England." *Reshaping the Past: Jewish History and the Historians*. Edited by Jonathan Frankel. New York: Oxford University Press, 1994, 45-65.

Liebeschütz, Hans. *Das Judentum im deutschen Geschichtsbild von Hegel bis Max Weber*. Tübingen: J. C. B. Mohr, 1967.

———. "Treitschke and Mommsen on Jewry and Judaism." *LBIYB* 2 (1962): 153-82.

———. *Von Georg Simmel zu Franz Rosenzweig: Studien zum Jüdischen Denken im deutschen Kaiserreich*. Tübingen: J. C. B. Mohr, 1970.

Livneh-Freudenthal, Rachel. "Ha-'igud le-tarbut u-mada shel yehudim (1819-1824) behipus 'aher musag hadash shel yehudim." Ph.D. diss., Tel Aviv University, 1996.

Löwenbrueck, Anna-Ruth. *Judenfeindschaft im Zeitalter der Aufklärung: Eine Studie zur Vorgeschichte des modernen Antisemitismus am Beispiel des Göttinger Theologen und Orientalisten Johann David Michaelis (1717-1791)*. Frankfurt a. M: Peter Lang, 1995.

Lowenstein, Steven M. "The 1840s and the Creation of the German-Jewish Religious Reform Movement." *Revolution and Evolution: 1848 in German-Jewish History*. Edited by Werner E. Mosse, Arnold Paucker, and Reinhard Rürup. Tübingen: J. C. B. Mohr, 1981, 255-97.

———. "The Rural Community and the Urbanization of German Jewry." *Central European History* 8 (1980): 218-36.

Lowenthal, David. *The Past is a Foreign Country*. Cambridge: Cambridge University Press, 1985.

Lutz, Edith. *Der "Verein für Cultur und Wissenschaft der Juden" und sein Mitglied H. Heine*. Stuttgart: Metzler, 1997.

Maretzki, Louis. *Geschichte des Ordens Bnei Briss in Deutschland, 1882-1907*. Berlin: M. Cohn, 1907.

Margolies, Alexander. "Der Verein für jüdische Geschichte und Literatur in Berlin, 1892-1927." *JJGL* 28 (1927): 166-85.

Martino, Albert. "Die 'Leihbibliotheksfrage'. Zur Krise der deutschen Leihbibliothek in der zweiten Hälfte des 19. Jahrhundert." *Die Leihbibliotheken als Institution des literarischen Lebens im 18. und 19. Jahrhundert.* Edited by Georg Jäger and Jörg Schönert. Hamburg: E. Hauswedell, 1980, 89-163.

Meisl, Josef. *Heinrich Graetz: Eine Würdigung des Historikers und Juden zu seinem 100. Geburtstag 31. Oktober 1917 (21. Cheschwan).* Berlin: L. Lamm, 1917.

———. "Ha-va'adah ha-historit le-toldot ha-yehudim be-germaniah." *Zion* 19 (1954): 171-72.

Mevorah, B. "Ikvoteha shel 'alilat Damesek be-hitpathuta shel ha'itnonut ha-yehudit ba-shanim 1840-1846." *Zion* 28 (1958): 46-65.

Meyer, Michael. "Abrahams Geiger's Historical Judaism." *New Perspective on Abraham Geiger: An HUC-JIR Symposium.* Edited by Jacob J. Petuchowski. New York: Ktav Pub. House, 1975, 3-16.

———. "The Emergence of Jewish Historiography: Motives and Motifs." *History and Theory* 27 (1988): 160-75.

———. "German-Jewish Identity in Nineteenth-Century America," *Toward Modernity: The European Jewish Model.* Edited by Jacob Katz. New Brunswick: Transaction Books, 1987, 247-67.

———. "Great Debate on Antisemitism: Jewish Reaction to New Hostility in Germany, 1879-1881." *LBIYB* 11 (1966): 137-70.

———. "Heinrich Graetz and Heinrich von Treitschke: A Comparison of Their Historical Images of the Modern Jew." *Modern Judaism* 6 (1986): 1-12.

———. "Jewish Religious Reform and Wissenschaft des Judentums: The Positions of Zunz, Geiger and Frankel." *LBIYB* 16 (1971): 19-41.

———. "Jewish Scholarship and Jewish Identity: Their Historical Relationship in Modern Germany." *Studies in Contemporary Jewry* 8 (1992): 181-93.

———. *Judaism Within Modernity: Essays on Jewish History and Religion.* Detroit: Wayne State University Press, 2001.

———. *The Origins of the Modern Jew: Jewish Identity and European Culture in Germany, 1749-1824.* Detroit: Wayne State University Press, 1967.

———. *Response to Modernity: A History of the Reform Movement in Judaism.* New York: Oxford University Press, 1988.

———. "Universalism and Jewish Unity in the Thought of Abraham Geiger." *The Role of Religion in Modern Jewish History: Proceedings of Regional Conferences of the Association for Jewish Studies Held at the University of Pennsylvania and the University of Toronto in March-April 1974.* Edited by Jacob Katz. Cambridge: Association for Jewish Studies, 1975.

Meyer, Michael, and Michael Brenner, ed. *German-Jewish History in Modern Times.* 4 vols. New York: Columbia University Press, 1996-98.

Michael, Reuven. "Graetz contra Treitschke." *BLBI* 4 (1961): 301-22.

———. *Ha-ketiva ha-historit ha-yehudit: meha-renesans 'ad ha-'et ha-hadasha.* Jerusalem: Mosad Bialik, 1993.

Minty, J. M. "*Judengasse* to Christian Quarter: The Phenomena of the Converted Synagogue in the Late Medieval and Early Modern Holy Empire." *Popular Religion in Germany and Central Europe, 1400-1800.* Edited by Bob Scribner and Trevor Johnson. New York: St. Martin's Press, 1996, 58-86 and 220-39.

Möller, Horst. "Aufklärung, Judenemanzipation und Staat: Ursprung und Wirkung von Dohms Schrift *Über die bürgerliche Verbesserung der Juden.*" *Tel Aviver Jahrbuch des Instituts für deutsche Geschichte:* Beiheft 3: Deutsche Aufklärung und Judenemanzipation (1980): 119-49.

Mosse, George L. *The Crisis of German Ideology: Intellectual Origins of the Third Reich.* New York: Schocken Books, 1981.

———. *German Jews Beyond Judaism.* Bloomington: Indiana University Press, 1985.

———. *The Jews and the German War Experience, 1914-1918.* New York: Leo Baeck Institute, 1977.

Moyn, Samuel. "German Jewry and the Question of Identity: Historiography and Theory." *LBIYB* 41 (1996): 291-308.

Muhlack, Ulrich. "Ranke und die politische Schule der deutschen Geschichtswissenschaft im 19. Jahrhundert: Zum Verhältnis von Geschichte und Politik." *Comparativ* 3 (1993): 92-113.

Myers, David. "'Distant Relatives Happening onto the Same Inn': The Meeting of East and West as Literary Theme and Cultural Ideal," *Jewish Social Studies* 1 (1995): 75-100.

———. "Eugen Täubler, the Personification of 'Judaism as Tragic Existence.'" *LBIYB* 39 (1994): 131-50.

———. "The Fall and Rise of Jewish Historicism: The Evolution of the Akademie für die Wissenschaft des Judentums (1919-1934)." *HUCA* 63 (1992): 107-44.

———. "'Mehabevin et ha-tsarot'": Crusade Memories and Modern Jewish Martyrologies." *Jewish History* 13 (1999): 49-64.

———. *Re-Inventing the Jewish Past: European Jewish Intellectuals and the Zionist Return to History.* New York: Oxford University Press, 1995.

———. "Selbstreflexionen im modernen Erinnerungsdiskurs." *Jüdische Geschichtsschreibung heute: Themen, Positionen, Kontroversen.* Edited by Michael Brenner and David N. Myers. Munich: C. H. Beck, 2002, 55-74 and 268-74.

Nathans, Benjamin. "On Russian-Jewish Historiography." *Historiography of Imperial Russia: The Profession and Writing of History in a Multi-National State.* Edited by Thomas Sanders. Armonk: M. E. Sharpe, 1999, 397-432.

Niehoff, Maren R. "Zunz's Concept of Haggadah as an Expression of Jewish Spirituality." *LBIYB* 43 (1998): 3-24.

Nipperdey, Thomas. "War die wilhelminische Gesellschaft eine Untertanen-Gesellschaft?" *Nachdenken über die deutsche Geschichte: Essays.* Munich: C. H. Beck, 1990, 172-85.

Novick, Peter. *That Noble Dream: The "Objectivity Question" and the American Historical Profession.* Cambridge: Cambridge University Press, 1989.

Paucker, Arnold. "Zur Problematik einer jüdischen Abwehrstrategie in der deutschen Gemeinschaft." *Juden im Wilhelminischen Deutschland, 1890-1914.* Edited by Werner E. Mosse. Tübingen: J. C. B. Mohr, 1976, 479-548.

Pickus, Keith H., *Constructing Modern Identities: Jewish University Students in Germany, 1815-1915.* Detroit: Wayne State University Press, 1999.

Popkin, Richard H. "Jacques Basnage's *Histoire des Juifs* and the Bibliotheca Sarraziana." *Studia Rosenthaliana* 21 (1987): 154-62.

Poppel, Stephen M. *Zionism in Germany, 1897–1933: The Shaping of a Jewish Identity.* Philadelphia: Jewish Publication Society of America, 1977.

Pressel, Wilhelm. *Der Thalmud vor dem Schwurgericht am Ende des 19. Jahrhunderts: Ein Zeugnis für die Wahrheit.* Leipzig: Dörffling & Franke, 1893.

Prestel, Claudia. *Jüdisches Schul- und Erziehungswesen in Bayern, 1804–1933.* Göttingen: Vandenhoeck & Ruprecht, 1989.

Pulzer, Peter. *The Rise of Political Anti-Semitism in Germany and Austria.* 2nd ed. London: Halban, 1988.

Rahden, Till van. "Mingling, Marrying, and Distancing Jewish Integration in Wilhelminian Breslau and its Erosion in Early Weimar Germany," *Jüdisches Leben in der Weimarer Republik.* Edited by Wolfgang Benz, Arnold Paucker, and Peter Pulzer. Tübingen: J. C. B. Mohr, 1998, 197–222.

Rand, Calvin. "Two Meanings of Historicism in the Writings of Dilthey, Troeltsch and Meinecke," *Journal of the History of Ideas* 25 (1965): 503–18.

Reill, Peter. *The German Enlightenment and the Rise of Historicism.* Berkeley: University of California Press, 1975.

Reinharz, Jehuda. *Fatherland and Promised Land: The Dilemma of the German Jew, 1893–1914.* Ann Arbor: University of Michigan Press, 1975.

Reinke, Andreas. "Eine Sammlung des jüdischen Bürgertums. Der Unabhängige Orden B'nai B'rith in Deutschland." *Juden, Bürger, Deutsche: Zur Geschichte von Vielfalt und Differenz, 1800–1933.* Edited by Andreas Gotzmann, Rainer Liedtke and Till van Rahden. Tübingen: J. C. B. Mohr, 2001, 315–40.

Reissner, Hans G. *Eduard Gans: Ein Leben im Vormärz.* Tübingen: J. C. B. Mohr, 1965.

Reuter, Fritz. "Vom Erwachen des historischen Interesses am jüdischen Worms bis zum Museum des Isidor Kiefers," *Aschkenaz* 12 (2002): 13–44.

———. *Warmaisa: 1000 Jahre Juden in Worms.* Frankfurt a. M.: Jüdischer Verlag bei Athenäum, 1987.

Richarz, Monika. *Der Eintritt der Juden in die akademischen Berufe. Jüdische Studenten und Akademiker in Deutschland, 1678–1848.* Tübingen: J. C. B. Mohr, 1974.

Robertson, Ritchie. "Enlightened and Romantic Views of the Ghetto: David Friedländer versus Heine." *Ghetto Writing: Traditional and Eastern Jewry in German-Jewish Literature from Heine to Hilsenrath.* Edited by Anne Fuchs and Florian Krobb. Columbia, S.C.: Camden House, 1999, 25–40.

———. *The "Jewish Question" in German Literature, 1749–1939: Emancipation and its Discontents.* Oxford: Clarendon, 1999.

Robinson, Ira. "The Invention of American Jewish History." *AJH* 81 (1994): 309–20.

Röckelein, Hedwig. "'Die grabstein, so vil tausent guldin wert sein': Vom Umgang der Christen mit Synagogen und jüdischen Friedhöfen im Mittelalter und am Beginn der Neuzeit." *Aschkenas* 5 (1995): 11–45.

Roemer, Nils. "Between Hope and Despair: Conceptions of Time and the German-Jewish Experience in the Nineteenth Century." *Jewish History* 14 (2000): 345–63.

———. "Breaching the 'Walls of Captivity': Gershom Scholem's Studies of Jewish Mysticism." *Germanic Review* 72 (1997): 23–41.

————. "Colliding Visions: Jewish Messianism and German Scholarship in the Eighteenth Century," *Hebraica Veritas? Christian Hebraists and the Study of Judaism in Early Modern Europe.* Edited by Allison Coudert and Jeffrey Shoulson. Philadelphia: University of Pennsylvania Press, 2004, 266–85.

————. "Provincializing the Past: Worms and the Making of a German-Jewish Cultural Heritage," *JSQ* 12 (2005): 80–100.

————. "Turning Defeat into Victory: *Wissenschaft des Judentums* and the Martyrs of 1096." *Jewish History* 13 (1999): 65–80.

Rosenfeld, Gavriel D. "Defining 'Jewish Art' in *Ost und West,* 1901–1908: A Study in the Nationalism of Jewish Culture." *LBIYB* 39 (1994): 83–110.

Rotschild, Samson. "Das Archiv der jüdischen Gemeinde von Worms." *Vom Rhein* 1 (1902): 21–22.

Rüppel, Rudolf. "Christliche Leihbibliotheken im 19. Jahrhundert im Gefolge der Erweckungsbewegung." *Die Leihbibliotheken als Institution des litrarischen Lebens im 18. und 19. Jahrhundert.* Edited by Georg Jäger and Jörg Schönert. Hamburg: E. Hauswedell, 1980, 349–98.

Rürup, Reinhard. "The European Revolution of 1848 and Jewish Emancipation," *Revolution and Evolution: 1848 in German-Jewish History.* Edited by Werner E. Mosse, Arnold Paucker, and Reinhard Rürup. Tübingen: J. C. B. Mohr, 1981, 1–53.

————. "Jewish Emancipation and Bourgeois Society." *LBIYB* 14 (1969): 67–91.

————. "The Tortuous and Thorny Path to Legal Equality: 'Jew Law' and Emancipatory Legislation in Germany from the Late Eighteenth Century." *LBIYB* 31 (1986): 3–33.

Rüsen, Jörn. *Zeit und Sinn: Strategien historischen Denkens.* Frankfurt a. M.: Fischer Taschenbuch Verlag, 1990.

Sarna, Jonathan D. *JPS: The Americanization of Jewish Culture, 1888–1985: A Centennial History of the Jewish Publication Society.* Philadelphia: Jewish Publication Society of America, 1989.

Schidorsky, Dov. "Jewish Nationalism and the Concept of a Jewish National Library." *Scripta Hierosolymitana* 29 (1989): 45–74.

Schmidt, Ulricke. "Jüdische Bibliotheken in Frankfurt am Main: Vom Anfang des 19. Jahrhunderts bis 1938." *Archiv für Geschichte des Buchwesens* 29 (1987): 236–67.

Scholem, Gershom. "Mi-tokh hirhurim 'al hokhmat yisra'el." [1944] *Devarim be-go: Pirke morashah u-tehiyah.* 2 vols. Tel Aviv: 'Am 'oved, 1982, 385–403.

————. "Toward an Understanding of the Messianic Idea in Judaism." *The Messianic Idea in Judaism and Other Essays on Jewish Spirituality.* New York: Schocken, 1995, 1–36.

————. "Die Wachtersche Kontroverse über den Spinozismus und ihre Folgen." *Spinoza in der Frühzeit seiner religiösen Wirkung.* Edited by Karl Gründer and Wilhelm Schmidt-Biggemann. Heidelberg: L. Schneider, 1984, 15–25.

————. "Wissenschaft vom Judentum einst und jetzt." *Judaica.* Frankfurt a. M.: Suhrkamp, 1963, 1: 147–64.

Scholle, Dietrich. "'Ansichtspostkarte' und 'Gummischuhe': Die Bilanz eines Jahrhunderts." *Geschichtsdidaktik* 11 (1986): 142–53.

Schorsch, Ismar. *From Text to Context: The Turn to History in Modern Judaism.* Hanover: University Press of New England, 1994.

———. *Jewish Reactions to German Anti-Semitism, 1870-1914.* New York: Columbia University Press, 1972.

———. "Moritz Güdemann, Rabbi, Historian and Apologist." *LBIYB* 11 (1966): 42-66.

Schwartz, Barry. "The Social Context of Commemoration: A Study in Collective Memory." *Social Forces* 61 (1982): 374-97.

Schwartz, Schuly Rubin. *The Emergence of Jewish Scholarship in America: The Publication of the Jewish Encyclopedia.* Cincinnati: Hebrew Union College Press, 1991.

Segal, Lester A. *Historical Consiousness and Religious Tradition in Azariah de' Rossi's Me'or 'Einayim.* Philadelphia: Jewish Publication Society of America, 1989.

Shavit, Yaacov. *Athens in Jerusalem: Classical Antiquity and Hellenism in the Making of Modern Secular Jew.* Translated by Chaya Naor and Niki Werner. Portland: Littman Library of Jewish Civilization, 1997.

———. "The 'Glorious Century' and the Cursed Century: Fin-de-Siècle Europe and the Emergence of a Modern Jewish Nationalism," *Journal of Contemporary History* 26 (1991): 553-74.

Shavit, Zohar, und Hans-Heino Ewers. *Deutsch-jüdische Kinder- und Jugendliteratur von der Haskala bis 1945: Die deutsch und hebräischsprachigen Schriften des deutsch- sprachigen Raumes: Ein bibliographisches Handbuch.* 2 vols. Stuttgart: Metzler, 1996.

Shear-Yashuv, Aharon. *The Theology of Salmon Ludwig Steinheim.* Leiden: E. J. Brill, 1986.

Shedletzky, Itta. "Literaturdiskussion und Belletristik in den jüdischen Zeitschriften in Deutschland, 1837-1918." Ph.D. diss., Hebrew University, 1986.

Sheffi, Na'ama. *Germanit be-'Ivrit: Targumim mi-germanit ba-Yishuv ha-'Ivri, 1882- 1948.* Jerusalem: Yad Yitshak Ben-Tsevi, 1998.

Sieg, Ulrich. "Die Wissenschaft und dem Leben tut dasselbe not: Ehrfurcht vor der Wahrheit. Hermann Cohens Gutachten im Marburger Antisemitismusprozeß." *Philosophisches Denken—Politisches Wirken. Hermann-Cohen-Kolloquium Marburg 1992.* Edited by Reinhart Brandt and Franz Orlik. Hildesheim: Georg Olms Ver- lag, 1993, 222-49.

Sinasohn, Max, ed. *Adass Jisroel Berlin: Entstehung, Entfaltung, Entwurzelung, 1869- 1939.* Jerusalem: M. Sinasohn, 1969.

Smith, Helmut Walser, ed. *Protestants, Catholics and Jews in Germany, 1800-1914.* Ox- ford: Berg, 2001.

Smith, Woodruff D. *Politics and the Science of Culture in Germany, 1840-1920.* New York: Oxford University Press, 1991.

Soussan, Henri. "The *Gesellschaft zur Förderung der Wissenschaft des Judentums,* 1902- 1915." *LBIYB* 46 (2001): 175-94.

Sorkin, David. "Die zwei Gesichter des Moses Mendelssohns." *Menora* 4 (1993): 275-89.

———. "The Impact of Emancipation on German Jewry. A Reconsideration," *Assimila- tion and Community: The Jews in Nineteenth-Century Europe.* Ed. Jonathan Fraenkel and Steven J. Zipperstein. Cambridge: Cambridge University Press, 1992, 177-98.

―――. *The Transformation of German Jewry, 1780–1840.* Oxford: Oxford University Press, 1987.

Stanislawski, Michael. "The Yiddish Shevet Yehudah: A Study in the 'Ashkenization' of a Spanish-Jewish Classic." *Jewish History and Jewish Memory: Essays in Honor of Yosef Hayim Yerushalmi.* Edited by Elisheva Carlebach, John M. Efron, and David N. Myers. Hanover: University Press of New England, 1998, 135–49.

―――. *Zionism and the Fin de Siècle: Cosmopolitism and Nationalism from Nordau to Jabotinsky.* Berkeley: University of California Press, 2001.

Steinschneider, Moritz. *Die Geschichtsliteratur der Juden.* Frankfurt a. M.: J. Kaufmann, 1905.

Stern, Fritz. *Gold and Iron: Bismarck, Bleichröder, and the Building of the German Empire.* New York: Knopf, 1977.

Tal, Uriel. *Christians and Jews in Germany: Religion, Politics, and Ideology in the Second Reich, 1870–1914.* Translated by Noah Jonathan Jacobs. Ithaca: Cornell University Press, 1975.

―――. "Liberal Protestantism and the Jews in the Second Reich, 1870–1914." *Jewish Social Studies* 26 (1964): 23–41.

Tänzer, Aron. *Die Geschichte der Juden in Jebenhausen und Göppingen. Mit erweiternden Beiträgen über Schicksal und Ende der Göppinger Judengemeinde 1927–1945.* Edited by Karl-Heinz Rueß. Weissenhorn: Konrad, 1988.

Terdiman, Richard. *Present Past: Modernity and Memory Crisis.* Ithaca: Cornell University Press, 1993.

Thompson, Martyn P. "Reception History and the Interpretation of Historical Meaning." *History and Theory* 32 (1993): 248–72.

Toury, Jacob. "Ein Dokument zur bürgerlichen Einordnung der Juden (Hamm/Westfalen, 1818)." *Michael* 7 (1967): 77–91.

―――. *Die politische Orientierungen der Juden in Deutschland: Von Jena bis Weimar.* Tübingen: J. C. B. Mohr, 1966.

―――. "Die Revolution von 1848 als innerjüdischer Wendepunkt," *Das Judentum in der Deutschen Umwelt, 1800–1850.* Edited by Hans Liebeschütz and Arnold Paucker. Tübingen: J. C. B. Mohr, 1977, 359–76.

―――. *Soziale und politische Geschichte der Juden in Deutschland, 1847–1871: Zwischen Revolution, Reaktion und Emanzipation.* Düsseldorf: Droste, 1977.

Trautmann-Waller, Celine. *Philologie Allemande et Tradition Juive: Le Parcours Intellectual de Leopold Zunz.* Paris: Cerf, 1998.

Ucko, Siegfried. "Geistesgeschichtliche Grundlagen für die Wissenschaft des Judentums (Motive des Kulturvereins vom Jahre 1819)." *ZGJD* 5 (1935): 1–34.

Volkov, Shulamit. "Die Erfindung einer Tradition: Zur Entstehung des modernen Judentums in Deutschland." *HZ* 253 (1991): 603–28.

Wallach, Luitpold. *Liberty and Letters: The Thoughts of Leopold Zunz.* London: East and West Library, 1959.

Weber, Annette. "Moritz Daniel Oppenheim und die Tradition des Kultgerätes aus der Frankfurter Judengasse." *Jüdische Kultur in Frankfurt am Main von den Anfängen bis zur Gegenwart. Ein internationales Symposium der Johann-Wolfgang-Goethe-Universität Frankfurt am Main und des Franz Rosenzweig Research Center for German-Jewish Literature and Cultural History Jerusalem.* Edited by Karl E. Grözinger. Wiesbaden: Harrassowitz, 1997, 321–44.

Weczerka, Hugo. "Die Herkunft der Studierenden des Jüdisch-Theologischen Seminars zu Breslau, 1854–1938." *Zeitschrift für Ostforschung* 35 (1986): 88–138.

Wehler, Hans-Ulrich. *Deutsche Gesellschaftsgeschichte: Von der "Deutschen Doppelrevolution" bis zum Ende des Ersten Weltkrieges, 1848–1914.* Munich: C. H. Beck, 1987.

Werses, Shmuel, "Ha-mahapekha ha-tsorfatit be-'aspeklariah shel safrut ha-'ivrit." *Tarbiz* 58 (1989): 483–521.

Wickert, Lothar. "Theodor Mommsen und Jacob Bernays. Ein Beitrag zur Geschichte des deutschen Judentums. Zu Mommsens 150. Geburtstag, 30. 11. 1967," *HZ* 205 (1967): 265–94.

Wiese, Christian. *Wissenschaft des Judentums und Protestantische Theologie im Wilhelminischen Deutschland: Ein Schrei ins Leere?* Tübingen: J. C. B. Mohr, 1999.

Wieseltier, Leon. "Etwas über die jüdische Historik: Leopold Zunz and the Inception of Modern Jewish Historiography." *History and Theory* 20 (1981): 135–49.

Wilhelm, Kurt. "The Jewish Community in the Post-Emancipation Period," *LBIYB* 2 (1957): 47–75.

Yerushalmi, Yosef Hayim. "Clio and the Jews: Reflections on Jewish Historiography in the Sixteenth Century." *Essential Papers on Jewish Culture in Renaissance and Baroque Italy.* Edited by David Ruderman. New York: New York University Press, 1992, 191–218.

———. "Exile and Expulsion in Jewish History." *Crisis and Creativity in the Sephardic World, 1391–1648.* Edited by Benjamin R. Gampel. New York: Columbia University Press, 1997, 3–22.

———. "Jüdische Historiographie und Postmodernismus: Eine abweichende Meinung." *Jüdische Geschichtsschreibung heute: Themen, Positionen, Kontroversen.* Edited by Michael Brenner and David N. Myers. Munich: C. H. Beck, 2002, 75–94 and 275–79.

———. *The Lisbon Massacre of 1506 and the Royal Image in the "Shebet Yehuda."* Cincinnati: Hebrew Union College, 1976.

———. "Messianic Impulses in Joseph ha-Kohen." *Jewish Thought in the Sixteenth Century.* Edited by Bernard Dov Cooperman. Cambridge: Harvard University Press, 1983, 460–87.

———. *Zakhor: Jewish History and Jewish Memory.* New York: Schocken, 1989.

Index

Studies in German Jewish Cultural History and Literature

PAUL MENDES-FLOHR, SERIES EDITOR

Spinoza's Modernity: Mendelssohn, Lessing, and Heine
Willi Goetschel

Jewish Scholarship and Culture in Nineteenth-Century Germany: Between History and Faith
Nils H. Roemer